HAT TRICK

HARLEY HOTCHKISS

To our family, the centre of our lives,
and the reason for this book

And to the memory of our dear friend,
Daryl Kenneth (Doc) Seaman
(1922—2009)

A LIFE IN THE **HOCKEY RINK,** **OIL PATCH** AND **COMMUNITY**

HARLEY HOTCHKISS

with *Paul Grescoe*

Library and Archives Canada Cataloguing in Publication

Hotchkiss, Harley, 1927-
    Hat trick : a life in the hockey rink, oil patch, and community / by Harley Hotchkiss, Paul Grescoe.

ISBN 978-1-55488-427-8

    1. Hotchkiss, Harley, 1927-. 2. Calgary Flames (Hockey team)--Biography. 3. Businessmen--Canada--Biography. 4. National Hockey League--Biography. 5. Philanthropists--Alberta--Calgary--Biography. 6. Calgary (Alta.)--Biography. I. Grescoe, Paul, 1939- II. Title.
HC112.5.H68A3 2009   338.092   C2009-900002-4

1 2 3 4 5   13 12 11 10 09

This book was produced for Dundurn Press by:

Tribute Books Inc.
Box I-33
1424 Eaglecliff Road
Bowen Island, British Columbia
V0N 1G0
www.tributebooks.ca

Editor: Audrey Grescoe
Designer: Janine Vangool, Vangool Design & Typography, Calgary

 Canada Council   Conseil des Arts
for the Arts   du Canada

 Canadä   ONTARIO ARTS COUNCIL
CONSEIL DES ARTS DE L'ONTARIO

We acknowledge the support of the **Canada Council for the Arts** and the **Ontario Arts Council** for our publishing program. We also acknowledge the financial support of the **Government of Canada** through the **Book Publishing Industry Development Program** and **The Association for the Export of Canadian Books**, and the **Government of Ontario** through the **Ontario Book Publishers Tax Credit** program, and the **Ontario Media Development Corporation**.

Printed in Canada by Friesens, Altona, MB

www.dundurn.com

Dundurn Press   Gazelle Book Services Limited   Dundurn Press
3 Church Street, Suite 500   White Cross Mills   2250 Military Road
Toronto, Ontario, Canada   High Town, Lancaster, England   Tonawanda, NY
M5E 1M2   LA1 4XS   U.S.A. 14150

CONTENTS

INTRODUCTION

FACEOFF

I T WAS A BITTER PROSPECT FOR ALL THE FANS AND players, the teams' managers and owners: the season without the National Hockey League, without the Stanley Cup. The first time any professional sport faced the possibility of cancelling a whole year of competition. All the NHL battles were off the ice. The season-to-be had been stillborn and, as the months passed through Christmastime, there were no signs of some miraculous revival. Maybe even a second season would be abandoned.

On January 19, 2005, as we gathered at Chicago's O'Hare Airport, the game I'd loved since boyhood was on life-support, its vital juices draining away amid anger, suspicion, and fear. Fear that pro hockey in North America had reached a tipping point. The league's lockout of players was going into its fourth month with little hope that the season could be saved and, more important, that the sport itself could be restored to the vibrant health it once had. Unless we fixed things.

But Trevor Linden, the Vancouver Canucks captain and the president of the NHL Players' Association, had asked for a meeting in the United Airlines lounge that day with me, the chairman of the NHL board of governors. Not Bob Goodenow, the association's executive director, not Gary Bettman, the league commissioner. Instead, their seconds-in-command and two lawyers discussed the issues face to face with Trevor and me. I hoped that at some point he and I could meet alone.

Afterwards, the chance came when Trevor invited me to talk on our own in the lounge. As a co-founder of the Calgary Flames, I'd watched the six-foot-four, thirty-three-year-old centre with interest since his professional debut with Vancouver in 1998-99. That season his stickhandling was so good he'd come close to derailing the Flames during our playoff series on our way to the Cup. All these years later, he was still popular, nicknamed Captain Vancouver, not just for his record but also for his charitable works off the ice, which had recently earned him the Order of British Columbia.

We talked, we listened to one another. He recognized that the Flames had reached the Cup final again in 2004. But our club was typical of too many franchises that were confronted with crippling financial losses. On the other hand, he was still suspicious that some owners didn't report their figures to the players accurately. Despite our differences, he seemed to return the respect I felt for him. Speaking to the media after the get-together, Trevor said, "We engaged in good dialogue today and will continue our discussions in the near future."

Nothing was solved at O'Hare. Commissioner Bettman and the league had a well-conceived plan that we the team owners supported. The NHL and the union would meet over long months to come. And that private encounter between a couple of guys, lovers of the game, decades apart in age, offered me hope.

MY STORY IS ABOUT MORE THAN THE NHL. BUT WHILE hockey has been only part of my life and business career and involvements in the community, it's shown me many measures of success—the talent and the determination of athletes and the beauty of being on a team in tune, pushing each other to reach personal aspirations. I find one phrase that neatly records excellence in this sport: the hat trick, the scoring of three goals in one game.

In life, as in hockey, there's the goal you aim for, and—if you're hopeful and hard-working, accomplished and sometimes just plain lucky—there's the one you achieve. It was luck that landed me in an ownership position with an NHL franchise in my adopted hometown. I trust it was some basic skill set and hard work that led me to a gratifying career in the Oil Patch in Alberta. And it was certainly a hope of improving things around me, combined with some purposeful effort, that involved me so rewardingly in my community.

There's another goal, of course, which is so obvious and important that it may not have to be spelled out. But let me define it: the desire to create your own universe of family and friends, filled with mutual respect and unselfish caring for one another. If you're fortunate, you learn to shoot for that goal in your youth. As I did long ago, living on a small farm in southern Ontario—surrounded by loving parents and siblings and dreaming of being as swift and strong and smart as my hockey heroes.

CHAPTER 1

THE FARM TEAM

Growing Up In Tobacco Country

S YL APPS WAS A GENTLE BUT BATTLE-READY KNIGHT on the ice. Even I knew that as a kid, the youngest of six siblings on a hardscrabble Depression farm. My father, kind but tough, had me pitching hay while my mother led me to the likes of Longfellow and Wordsworth. Dad started planting tobacco as a cash crop in 1936, the same year that Bayham Township in southwestern Ontario got hydro power and the Hotchkisses got our first radio. Now we could hear the Saturday-evening hockey matches from Maple Leaf Gardens in Toronto, as the forerunner of Imperial Oil's Hockey Night in Canada began airing coast to coast on November 7, 1936. In that game, Toronto—our team—lost to the New York Americans by a heartbreaking 3-2. ("Hockey fans throughout Ontario were asking the question, 'What's wrong with the Maple Leafs?'" *The Globe and Mail* reported.) We came to love listening to the riveting voice of Foster Hewitt while a newcomer named Syl Apps and his fellow Leafs scored enough goals to take them to the Stanley Cup finals three times during the rest of the decade.

Syl was my hero, right from the season when he won the first Calder Trophy as the best rookie in the NHL. It wasn't just that he was a local boy, raised in Paris, Ontario, only fifty miles from our farm near a speck on the map called Guysborough. I figured we had a lot in common. He didn't drink or swear and neither of my folks really did either. He was smart, graduating from McMaster University with a major in economics, and in my house,

Playing shinny on the ice of a frozen pond in southwestern Ontario, my ten-year-old self is all suited up in a Toronto Maple Leafs' blue-and-white uniform bearing the number of my boyhood hero, Syl Apps.

with my mother a retired schoolteacher, brains were highly valued. As a kid, I was probably more impressed that he was a terrific third baseman with the Paris baseball team—I once saw him perform in an exhibition game—and I liked baseball too, eventually playing the infield like Syl. He was more an all-round athlete than I was: a star halfback in intercollegiate football, a superb natural golfer, and the winner of the British Empire pole-vaulting championship, competing for Canada in the 1936 Berlin Olympics.

But hockey proved to be his great love, as it did mine. Growing up, he'd practised his skills by firing a puck against a barn door, just the way I did against our woodshed. And when as a nine-year-old I went with my dad to see number 10 play centre on a line with Gordie Drillon for the Maple Leafs in Toronto, I found that he was not only fast and strong but clean and fair. So it was a shock that season when an opponent knocked out a couple of his teeth with a high stick and Syl attacked the defenceman—in one of only three fights he'd have in his long career. Both he and Drillon would win the Lady Byng Trophy for gentlemanly play. He went on to become Ontario's athletic commissioner, a member of the provincial legislature, and minister of correctional services. Decades later, meeting him at a Hockey Hall of Fame induction ceremony, I recognized I couldn't have picked a better role model than Syl Apps—someone who would come to colour my view of hockey, and the world at large.

I CAME INTO THIS WORLD IN TILLSONBURG, ONTARIO, on July 10, 1927: Harley Norman, the only one of the four Hotchkiss brothers and two sisters born in a hospital, delivered by our faithful family doctor, Roy Rankin. "Harley," an unusual first name today, ranked in every decade since 1880 as one of the thousand most popular boy's monickers in North America (and not just because it formed half the name of the famous motorcycle first produced in 1903).

My parents were Morley and Carrie, who were then growing grain and corn and raising some livestock and poultry on the poor sandy soil of a mixed farm in Elgin County. It sat atop an ancestral Lake Erie glacial delta that gave us good and plentiful water at shallow, fifteen-foot depths. Five generations of the family would live on the farm, amid the mild southwest of the province, close to the church and public school of Guysborough in next-door Norfolk County.

The countryside I grew up in, just north of the lake, is dramatically different from the Alberta landscape where I would later spend most of my life. No mountains rearing like giants on the western horizon, no vast vistas of prairie ranches just outside the cities, no mountain goats and grizzlies and the ghosts of buffalo, no great Douglas firs and looming spruce. As a boy, I knew gently lilting hills, tidy, compact farms, rabbits and squirrels, American chestnut trees of the temperate Carolinian forest and Canadian sugar maples that we tapped for the sweet surprise of their sap to make syrup.

My parents didn't own the farm. It was still in the name of my grandfather John Hotchkiss, who lived with us after the death of his wife, Mary. His father had left half of his hundred acres to him and twenty-five to each of sons Edwin and Fred. The fact that for so many years—until grandpa died—my folks were farming land that wasn't truly theirs became a lesson to me in later life: don't wait till you're dead to pass on some of your good fortune to your family.

Morley Hotchkiss, who had an elementary-school education and voted Conservative, was my firm but caring dad. Quiet, standing nearly six feet, he was the family's fourth generation to farm the land in Elgin County near Lake Erie.

Carrie Hotchkiss, my petite mother who taught in a one-room school, is typically holding a book in her hand. Independent of mind, she loved the classics and history that inspired me to love language and be interested in current events.

My dad, who grew up on that farm, was the second of John and Mary's five children, descendants of seventeenth-century English immigrants to North America (see *Shaking the Family Tree*, page 339). Morley Roy Hotchkiss had only an elementary-school education, but he was a strong, determined worker, clearing the stumps and levelling the land on a spread that eventually expanded to about 110 acres. In winter, it was a huge job to cut trees with a crosscut saw, split them, and haul the wood into a shed. He got up at 4:30 a.m. to build the two wood-stove fires in winter, milk the cows and clean the stables before breakfast, and then in summer spend the long day ploughing or harvesting behind a team of horses. He was a gentle man, mostly quiet but often laughing and talking openly, who expressed his caring for us kids by deed rather than by being demonstrative. My nephew Ross reminds me that my father had that proverbial twinkle in his eye and once, after moving to town, told him a joke that was a bit off-colour—"and I just about fell over." But his overwhelming memory of his grandfather is of a man "who was very good at giving you a feeling of your self-worth." While Dad was well liked by his farm neighbours, the height of his social life was probably getting dressed up to attend Masonic meetings in Vienna, a hamlet about five miles southwest.

He was nearly six feet and solid; my mother, Carrie, was a slip of a woman, never weighing over a hundred pounds. She was the opposite of him in many ways, though she wasn't one to fuss over and hug us either. She expressed her love through her intellect—my niece Roma, Ross's sister, insists Mom was a true intellectual—she'd honed her mind at a so-called model school, or teachers' college, and then in the one-room rural school where she taught. It wasn't far from dad's farm and they likely met at a community social. While he voted Conservative by rote, she may have often cancelled his ballot by being such an independent thinker, with a streak of the skepticism of her Scottish ancestors. They were the one branch of the Todd family that had the gumption to brave a voyage across the sea, in the mid-nineteenth century. ("Their circumstances in Scotland is not known," she once wrote. "They came to Canada in a sailing vessel which took three months to cross the Atlantic.") While my folks attended the United Church in Guysborough, neither of them wore their faith on their sleeves and my mother was even less religious than my father. I came to feel more as she did about organized religion.

Dad read the *Tillsonburg News* and the *London Free Press*. Mom devoured the classic English writers, Dickens and Shakespeare among them. By the light of a coal-oil lamp, she read to me regularly from a small bookcase of literature, starting with children's books such as the Peter Cottontail

PLANK ROAD LOOKING SOUTH
STRAFFORDVILLE ONT

Straffordville was the hub of Bayham County, where two of my brothers had businesses and my folks moved in later years. Here I played hockey and baseball in the town and befriended the grandsons of the owner of Walsh's general store on the left.

stories of Thornton W. Burgess and moving on to the poems of Alfred Lord Tennyson. Eventually I was reading and re-reading the books in our home library all on my own (when I wasn't devouring colour comics like Mutt and Jeff and the Katzenjammer Kids in the *Free Press*). I can still remember the lines of Longfellow's "Evangeline:" "This is the forest primeval. The murmuring pines and the hemlocks, / Bearded with moss, and in garments green, indistinct in the twilight, / Stand like Druids of eld, with voices sad and prophetic…" Roma recalls visiting my mother years later when she and my dad had moved into the town of Straffordville, less than five miles from the farm, and seeing her so excited: a Shakespeare festival was opening under a tent in the southwestern Ontario city of Stratford.

"We're going, and I'm taking you," her grandmother told Roma, "but you have to learn the line of kings up to Richard III"—which was the title of the play they would see with Alec Guinness as the king.

When I visited Mom as an adult and underwent her routine quizzing about current events, English history, and literature, I realized she was still better read than I was. Her Morley had died in 1960, aged seventy-two, unsuited for town life. Even when living alone and with her eyesight failing, she listened to books on tape, often till 2:00 a.m. Roma's brother Ross, who visited my mother into her eighties and early nineties, also saw her as an intellectual, "hidden on the farm, then in a small town. And because of that, she ended up being a very private person." She would endure until ninety-five, in 1982, after spending only three days in hospital—once when I was born and the last two days of her life.

Despite her size, this refined woman had been as tough physically as mentally (which I knew first-hand from the occasional spanking she meted out). She had to be during the Great Depression when stock markets plummeted and half of Canada's workers went on relief. These were the days before the township got electricity, when a washboard and a hand wringer substituted for a powered washing machine, and the bathroom was a wooden outhouse, which in winter was colder than Siberia. The outhouse was my first exposure to the legendary Eaton's mail-order catalogues: old ones wound up as toilet paper and I got to look at the pictures of ladies in their underwear.

My mother had left teaching to focus on her family and the farm, raising a brood of six and having to feed harvest workers with roast chicken and red raspberry pies. Only the most basic staples came from the general store (sugar, salt, tea) and from the Raleigh and Watkins travelling salesmen (cough medicine, ointments, spices). She canned our apples and sour cherries, the peas and beans and everything else we grew in a widespread garden. I had to hoe it, reluctantly, but being among the bounty of vegetables led me to pursue gardening with a quiet zeal throughout my life. In Mom's hands, cabbage became sauerkraut. We had carrots winter-long, stored in a box in sand-rich soil, and turnips and potatoes stayed cold in a cement pit in the ground. When Dad butchered our pigs and cows, Mom cured pork and beef for man-pleasing meals. In December, she sold our turkeys to the doctors and lawyers in Tillsonburg to raise money for Christmas. I hated plucking the birds' pinfeathers but liked going on great spy hunts in the spring to find the secretive hens' hidden nests and rescue their eggs from the skunks and other varmints so they could hatch in an incubator.

Our two-storey, board-and-batten farmhouse had been built with square nails in 1878, ten years before my dad was born. All the traffic went over the back *stoep* (the Dutch word for a little covered platform), which led to either stairs to the cellar where the fruit and the hams were kept or to the spacious kitchen. This was the centre of our universe with its dining table, big wall clock, and a considerable wood stove to heat food and water (it made the kitchen hot as hell in the summer). A wash room held a wood box and a sink with two pumps, one with hard well water for cooking and drinking and the other with soft rainwater for washing up—and, for Dad, shaving with a straight razor. And we bathed in a big tub in the kitchen. Another small space on the ground floor was my grandfather's bedroom, a third was my sister Marion's. The rest of us slept upstairs in uninsulated quarters under goose-feather ticks and, as a treat on the coldest nights, with hot irons from the kitchen stove wrapped in newspapers to keep our feet toasty. The downstairs living room had its own small round stove, a chesterfield, the bookcase, and always a piano that my brother Ralph played.

Roma knew all my siblings as the observant daughter of the first-born Hotchkiss kid, John William. Big brother Jack, despite our seventeen-year age difference, would play an important role in my life, employing me until I made up my mind what I wanted to do with my teenaged self. He'd worked in Straffordville for City Dairy, which made powdered milk and other products, before starting his own trucking business. By then he had met a warm-hearted, generous woman named Treva Chute and made her his wife. A close friend of hers was Margaret Brown, married to Bob Grant, who worked for Jack. She remembers Treva as a petite, easygoing woman: "She worked hard. She was involved in the United Church, in quilting and bake sales. Treva was friends with everybody." She and Jack had four kids: Roma, Ross, and two others who died: Doreen, a young mother with a hidden heart defect at age thirty, and Paul, a heart-attack victim at forty-eight.

Verna, the next-oldest in my family, was married young to a barber in Vienna named Earl Smyth, who opened a poolroom and sold men's clothing, fitting me out in my first suit at age twelve. In Margaret's excellent ninety-year-old memory, "Verna was a lady, more like her mother. Kind of trim, fine-featured. Maybe my height, and I'm a shrinking five-one." Roma remarks, "Verna was attractive and neat—fastidious—and kind, but she kept to herself." Among her problems were severe migraines she suffered in later years. After her untimely death, her husband married Roma's widowed mother, Treva.

Ralph was the third-born, eleven years older than me. A lifelong bachelor who trained as a school teacher like our mother, he taught locally and became a principal in Brantford, Ontario, until retiring to help look after her in Straffordville. A wonderful brother, a good athlete, and he may have been the smartest of us all. Ross saw him as "fairly reserved but he had a really good chuckle." Roma recalls that he was sensitive and shy—"but not with me. I was quite close to Ralph; he was very encouraging. And he was quite handsome, a head-turner."

Blake arrived five years after Ralph. Unlike his three brothers, he was never interested in sports. With a boyhood skill for fixing radios, Blake turned a workers' changing shed on the farm into a shop after our township got hydro power. Then he studied at Ryerson Technical College in Toronto and opened his own electronics and appliance business in Straffordville. Never married either, he lived in an apartment above his store. Margaret and Bob Grant bought their first appliances from what they knew only as Blake's, up on Plank Road. "He wasn't a hard man to do business with," she says. "Of course, we never bought unless we had the money to pay for it."

And then there was Marion, just three years older than I was and the closest to me in other ways too. She was clever, getting an education degree and teaching high school later in life. Marion wed a tobacco grower named George Grant and they raised four children. Margaret, who was George's sister-in-law, describes her as "very talented. She taught school and made quilts and knit—there wasn't anything in that line that she couldn't do. And she had a very good memory." Roma says, "Marion was bubbly, always laughing, a very nice personality."

A DEPRESSION KID, I NEVER FELT THE EFFECTS OF THE hard times playing economic hell with North America. The only signs I saw of them were the itinerant, hopeful men who came down our long, maple-lined lane during the Thirties, desperate for work. Between our garden and crops, we had plenty of food and by selling milk, eggs, and turkeys earned just enough cash to survive despite the size of our family. It may seem like an old guy gazing through roseate glasses at a distant past, but I look back on my growing-up years as a kind of classic rural Canadian childhood. My only bad memory from earliest childhood is a nightmare at about age six in which I was at a neighbour's house and the sky blackened with thunderstorm clouds that sent chunks of burning coal down on me as I fled home. Home was always a safe haven. I never heard my folks exchange harsh words. I had kind older brothers and sisters to look up to. And surrounding me were the playground of an adventure-filled farm and the warmth of a welcoming community.

The farm was hills and gulleys to rollick through; streams to float sticks and paper boats down and to fish in for tiny trout; luscious morel mushrooms to hunt in the woods and develop a lifelong passion for; raspberries and blackberries to pick for pies; rabbits to catch with ferrets and, later, plump squirrels to shoot with my .22 rifle (and to have for dinner); willows to carve whistles from; and flint arrowheads and pieces of clay pipes to collect in my little red wagon. They were artifacts from the long-gone Neutral tribe of native people, sometimes called the Tobacco Indians because they smoked the plant in their pipes well before the white man started cultivating it.

More than my siblings, I was inclined to the fine details of nature. I knew where all the wildflowers were. The white trilliums, the floral emblem of Ontario, were beautiful but the red trilliums stank like rotten meat. Adder's tongue (or dogtooth violets); what we called mayflowers (which were really the delicate, sweet-scented hepaticas of the buttercup family); and early white bloomers called bloodroot (they ran with red sap if you broke the stem). As much as I loved the new growth of the warm, gentle springs, I enjoyed fiery-coloured autumns and hazy, smoky Indian summers.

I found the nests of birds, from common robins and starlings to the more exotic killdeers and doves, red-crested cardinals and the black-headed, orange-breasted Baltimore orioles whose big pouch nests swing from maple, elm, and poplar trees. The best kind of tree for a small boy was the maple with its yield of syrup and taffy. My folks drilled holes in the trunk and hammered in spiles, little spouts with a hook to hang buckets that caught the slowly dripping sap. (Not long ago, the people who'd bought our old house tore it down and saved some spiles and square nails for me.) Then the sap was boiled in a wide pan above a wood fire on a grate over cement blocks, strained through three layers of cotton, and the syrup stored in four-gallon milk cans. There was a more immediately gratifying process of boiling the syrup till it was thicker and then pouring it on the snow to congeal and make instant maple taffy. As a teenager, I would try all this myself one season when I was at home from high school quarantined for six weeks with mumps. I dug out all the old equipment and tapped the trees for sap.

In summer, I could run free, barefoot all season (decades later, a writer for *National Geographic* would record an inaccurate report from one of my friends that "Harley went through all the grades of a one-room country school without owning a pair of shoes"). For sheer fun, there was always a dog named Buster or Carlo or Whiskers sleeping under the *stoep* and cats in the barn to pester. And I can't believe now the hundreds of miles I must have travelled propelling a barrel hoop down the lane and onto the road with a stick, trying to keep it upright in the sandy soil. Not that I always played alone as a little kid. My dad's only brother, Uncle George, lived in a big, many-gabled square house on a nearby farm. That's where my first cousin once removed, Jack Claus, moved with his widowed mother—Audrey, George's daughter—and became my good friend.

Our friendship started off badly. Jack, about my size but six months younger, was an aggressive kid from a Toronto suburb and early on tried to bully me. When he put his dukes up, I hauled off and socked him smack dab in the nose. We never fought again. From then on, the only time we squared off against one another was on the ice.

BY AGE FIVE, I HAD DISCOVERED HOCKEY. FIRST CAME A gift of skates—double-bladed *baby* skates. I wore them through freshly fallen snow to a frozen pond in the woods a half-mile from home. With a broom to steady me, I tried to keep standing, only to fall and smack the back of my head and see stars. But I learned, and within a year or two had a fifteen-cent puck and a forty-cent stick from the hardware store to practise shots on an icy puddle against the woodshed wall—left- and right-handed, then backhanded, endlessly. It was more fun to play one-on-one pond hockey with Jack for hours at a time. We could spend what seemed like half the day just shovelling the snow from the ice. Sometimes it would simply be a keep-away match, other times we'd see who could score twenty goals first, using our boots as goal posts. I'd even play with big sister Marion, who liked hockey too.

It was a winter sport of speed and skill and physicality—this was no pantywaist game. I loved it so much that one Christmas I asked for, and got, a blue-and-white uniform of what had become my favourite NHL team, Toronto. It was just a pair of striped pants and a sweater with the maple leaf and Syl Apps' number 10 on the back—the whole outfit probably cost no more than $10 from the Eaton's catalogue. Out on the pond, I was a Leaf on the loose. But it wasn't until 1936 that all of my passion for the game came together for me.

That was the year the Hydro-Electric Power Commission finally brought electricity to our area, a quarter-century after it had come to much of southwestern Ontario. Before the hydro hookup, Jack had bought us a radio ("Here's a world of entertainment you can command at a touch," the Eaton's catalogue promised) and strung an aerial across our lawn in anticipation (Eaton's aerial outfit, complete, for $1.25). And sitting outside one warm August evening, we began to hear music. *Whoa!* we thought, *the aerial's playing! It's a miracle!* In fact, there was a more down-to-earth explanation: a Jehovah's Witness truck on a concession road was blaring hymns from a loudspeaker.

When hydro did arrive in our living room, so did professional hockey. That November, on the national network of the just-created Canadian Broadcasting Corporation, Imperial Oil became sponsor of what evolved into Hockey Night in Canada. It was known then as the Imperial Esso Hockey Broadcast, featuring Foster Hewitt and his "Hello, Canada—and hockey fans in the United States and Newfoundland" (which wasn't then a province). He announced the games live from a gondola five storeys above the Maple Leaf Gardens rink in his high-pitched, high-energy voice and trademark staccato style: "Leafs are turning it on. Jackson dashes up the far boards into the corner, passes puck back to Thoms, Thoms to Conacher, Conacher goes around Johnston, he shoots, Thoms grabs the rebound, he shoots, HE SCORES!"

On Saturday nights, Marion and I perched in front of the radio, often joined by Dad, whom I'd never even seen on skates. I don't think I ever missed a game in following the fate of Toronto, especially Syl Apps, with his hawk eyes and shock of thick, dark hair. Aside from seeing him that once in person on the ice during the Thirties, I knew what he looked like from the hockey cards I got free by collecting labels of Bee Hive Golden Corn Syrup and sending them in to the St. Lawrence Starch Company in Port Credit, Ontario. Because we made our own maple syrup and my mom wouldn't buy the store-bought corn variety, I had to convince Jack and Treva in Straffordville to save labels or box tops of Bee Hive and other St. Lawrence products and then get into town myself to find more in the dump. I painstakingly wrote business-like letters to the company: "Enclosed please find two (2) Bee Hive Corn Syrup labels for which please send me the following picture: Syl Apps from Toronto Maple Leafs. ..." My handwriting was so terrible that sometimes the return envelope would be addressed to Harily Hitchcock.

The portraits were about the size of a letter page, usually bordered with what looked like wood frames. I still recall most of the players from that era who captivated me: left-wingers Gordie Drillon and Bob Davidson, goalie Turk Broda and other guys with colourful nicknames like Bucko Mc-Donald, Bingo Kampman, and Red Horner.

RADIO HELPED FILL THOSE LONG WINTER NIGHTS AND so did board games, including crokinole, developed in rural Canada in the 1860s, which had us flicking discs with our fingers across a wooden board into scoring circles—sort of like curling in miniature. But the biggest event to brighten up the season was always Christmas.

We cut our own Christmas tree. Blake, Marion, and I journeyed into the well-stocked woods with a sled to find the finest specimen to set up in the living room and decorate with tinsel and candles, popcorn strings and other homemade ornaments. We opened the presents Christmas morning. They came from the catalogue of the T. Eaton department store in Toronto and were mailed to Tillsonburg for pickup. One of my earliest gifts was a wind-up engine with a roller in front, but frustratingly, because it was winter, I couldn't play with the toy outdoors. At age eleven, I got every boy's favourite present, a bicycle to roam the township roads on. Our family rotated Christmas dinner with my father's three sisters—Ella, Phenia, and Clara—with the

The one-room school in Guysborough dated back to the late 1800s and a single teacher handled the many grades of pupils. I'm at the far right, third row from front.

common denominator of turkey and dressing and often a dessert of Jell-O, which I loved then but can't stand now.

Christmas was exciting at our one-room school too, when our parents were invited to the annual concert. The teacher rigged up a backdrop of white sheets hiding the blackboards at the front of the room, and every kid had a role on the makeshift stage as we nervously sang, recited verse, and performed seasonal plays with a Jesus in the manger. We all got the same present, a little paper sack with an orange, nuts, and hard candy. Jean Brayley was a tremendous teacher, patient and caring with a class of thirty to forty children from grades one through eight, warmed in winter with a large sheet-metal stove. There were separate entrances for boys and girls to a classroom that was one large open space, where I could listen in on the lessons the older pupils were learning. The public school, along with the church, comprised all of what was left of the hamlet of Guysborough. It had been there since the late nineteenth century, as the *Tillsonburg News* from that era pointed out in an article titled "Guysborough School Pupils of 1882 appear in rhyme":

There's Mary Bates and William Culp.
With Annie Wharton, too,
We've Harry Garnham, George Marshall,
Will French and Travis Lew…
Hannah, George and Sarah French,
Maggie and Fred Hotchkiss,
Orpha Stratton, Louise House,
Berton and Frank Travis…

Fred Hotchkiss in that rhyme was my grandfather's youngest brother and Maggie an older sister. What's interesting is that many of those family names were still around when I went to the school. And all these years later, a photograph hanging on my office wall shows my class, including Blake and Marion and my cousin Marie Hotchkiss, and I can name every one of the thirty kids. We were lucky to have Miss Brayley give us such a swell kick-start to our lives. If we were good, she read to us, which encouraged my interest in the English language, and held spelling bees, which helped make me the respectable speller I am today. And if an airplane was flying overhead, a rarity in those days, she let us out to see it. Under her direction, I skipped two grades. Unfortunately, she was followed by two teachers, one of them undisciplined and the other, Vera Bartlett, a martinet hired as a disciplinarian who once swatted me on the side of my ten-year-old head when I'd forgotten a fact over the summer. Replacing her was Helen Hedges, a good teacher for my last year in elementary.

Getting to school, SS #8 Houghton (the township in Norfolk County), was a three-and-a-half-mile walk there and back. In the mild months, I went shoeless with Marie and the other neighbour kids, Billy and Helen Howey and the Clarks' two adopted sons, Andy and Gordon. In autumn, we found wild apples along the way, stuck them on willow sticks, and flicked them at one another. Sometimes, as a childish joke, we boys disguised a cow flap on the road with sand so an unwary barefoot walker would step in it. On the way home, my job was herding our Ayrshire cattle in a single file a half-mile from the thirty-acre summer pasture to the farm for milking and overnighting. Other times, I raced home, cutting through the woods so I wouldn't miss my favourite radio program. That was "Renfrew of the Mounted," a daily American serial set in Canada about the intrepid Inspector Douglas Renfrew of the RCMP. It always began with a howling gale, a haunting wolf call, and the cry "Rennnnfrewwww—of the Mounted!" The stories were full of vivid sound effects, such as horses stampeding through rivers, to spark a kid's imagination.

At ten, I'm on our family farm astride our horse Maude as the driver of a boat (behind us in the picture), which pulled a contraption made of a box on skids with canvas sides that went down rows of tobacco to hold the leaves. I had other, more risky encounters with our work horses.

There were also Sunday school and church service. Because we had to drive to Guysborough United, I had to stay for both events, which was a double whammy of religion I disliked. Despite my boyish cynicism, I did get a Bible for perfect attendance at Sunday school and still have that volume from 1936. The most fun at the white-pine, pioneer-built church was proudly putting a nickel in the collection plate. The least was fidgeting through the circuit preacher's sermon. After leaving home, I would get out of the habit of attending church. And I gather my parents did too. As my niece Roma, who often visited them, says now, "I don't recall them being church people at all."

My Granddad Hotchkiss was the one who sat at the head of the table at mealtime and said grace: "Bless the food to our use and we ask it in Christ's name, amen." During her stays at the farm as a little girl, Roma remembers, he sat by the wood stove in the kitchen, gazing out the window. She snuggled up on his lap and he said, "The first one asleep, whistle." I have an image of him carefully peeling an orange, a treat to be savoured. Some of my memories of him are sadder. Living with us on his own farm, he tried to help, milking cows and unloading tobacco when Dad got into that crop. But cataracts blinded him so badly that he sometimes got lost coming in from the barn. He had an operation in 1935, returning with fat bandages on his eyes, and had to wear thick glasses to read the newspaper up close. One of his great joys was walking our lengthy stretch of laneway to get the mail. Mischievously, I tormented him from time to time by running ahead and grabbing the letters from the box. He would die in 1950, at ninety-two, and despite my pranks leave me his round, golden pocket watch in his will. My great regret is that I didn't spend more time with him, learn more about this man who sired my father.

I felt sad as well about my mother's father, William Todd, during his final years. We visited him on his farm about twenty miles away in North Oxford county (between London and Woodstock). A self-reliant guy with a big moustache, he didn't want anyone feeling sorry for him, but we did anyway because he had to make his own meals and look after the house himself. He and his son Archie, a retired railroad telegrapher, lived together there after Grandpa Todd's wife died the year I was born. Two rail lines passed by, carrying fast trains that thrilled me. The farm lay up a hill behind the Niagara escarpment, the lengthy forested ridge that runs from near Niagara Falls to the tip of the Bruce Peninsula. We kids sledded down the long hill; one winter my brother Jack and I rode so swiftly on nice crusty snow that he fell off and ripped all the buttons from his overcoat.

FARM LIFE COULD BE FUN, BUT RISKY TOO. MY DAD CUT the cornstalks in our fields with a triangular hoe that had to be razor-sharp. One day when I was five or six and he was honing the blade, I acted silly and leapt over the wooden platform of our well—and fell bum-first onto the corn hoe. I still have a scar on my behind from that deep cut. When I got older, our farm became less a playfield and more a workplace. Because Dad never owned a tractor, it was all horses, hard manual labour, and we kids as unhired hands. Beside herding the cattle home and hoeing the darn garden, I brought the hardwood in for the stoves. When I was about nine and told my mother I wasn't going to do that chore, she chased me around the house with a little switch from a bush.

As a youngster, I was in more danger one February after helping Dad haul the carcass of a freshly killed cow up a tree where he could gut it. I had some blood on my mittens when my friend Jack Claus and I went into the barn to see a gentle Percheron horse named Prince. He was in a stall, tied to the manger where we kept his hay. The smell of the blood must have scared him because he was soon snorting and acting strange. As I ducked under his head, he went crazy, with a high-pitched whinny and his forelegs raised like an avenging angel. I was scrambling over the heavy manger when Prince reared back and pulled it down, me with it, and his hooves struck the inside of my knee. I still have that scar too.

That wasn't the only close encounter I had with work horses. The springtime I was seven, Dad was breaking a field with a team pulling a single-furrow walking plough. Meanwhile, I was nearby sitting on the seat of a roller, a set of large steel drums hauled by another team to pack down the furrows. We were turning at the end of a row beside a steep gully when the lines to the horses got caught up in the drums and began to tighten so

My dad stands in a sea of Virginia tobacco, which he started growing in 1936, a crop that flourished in the sandy soil on fields spread over twenty-five acres.

hard that the animals reared up, backing closer and closer to the gully. I didn't have enough sense to jump off. Seeing what was happening, my father began racing to save me—just as one of the lines broke and released the pressure on the frightened horses.

Before becoming a teenager (a term unknown in those times), I was already helping with the haying. Come July, our teams pulled a mower with wheels that turned toothed blades back and forth to cut hay in eight-foot swaths and leave it behind in rows. Once the hay was dry, the horses pulled a hay rake with taller wheels and metal tines in back that raked it into windrows. Then with a three-tined fork, we pitched the hay into small mounds we called haycocks. Finally, when it was dry enough, my dad loaded the hay on a horse-drawn wagon, brought it to an earthen bridge that led to the upper half of the two-storey, tin-roofed barn, and unloaded it with a hayfork connected to a series of horse-powered ropes and pulleys that could dump the hay in precisely chosen spots in what's called the mow. As kids, we often dug tunnels into the hay mow, dangerous if it ever collapsed on us. All this time later, I still remember the smell of new hay.

There was just as much hard labour in harvesting our grain—wheat, oats, rye—cut with a horse-drawn binder that tied it with twine in sheaves kicked out with a canvas conveyer belt, after which we had to gather ten or twelve sheaves into a stook. At harvest time, all the neighbours would get together with teams of horses to haul the sheaves to a noisy wood-fired, steam-engine threshing machine—*Whof! Whof! Whof!*—that separated the grain from the husks and straw. It was stored in bins in a granary.

One harvest when I was all of eleven, Dad asked my brother Jack to bring one of his Fargo trucks to help out. I got to drive it while Jack was in back loading grain. Barely able to see over the top of the steering wheel, I had trouble working the heavy clutch. My jerky driving rattled Jack and after he yelled at me a couple of times, I hopped out of the cab, slammed the door, and told him, "Drive your own damn truck!" The story became a family legend.

The same steam engine that separated the grain also ran a cutting box during our corn harvest, which all happened in a single day. Dad and the gang of neighbours cut the twelve-foot-high stalks with corn hoes and gathered them into corn shocks, and on silo-filling day collected the shocks in wagons. They took them to the cutting box fitted with whirling knives that chopped the corn into bits that a blower propelled into a forty-foot-tall silo with a conical roof. The corn fermented and became silage to feed the cattle. One of my jobs over the winter was to pitch the silage through small windows down from the silo and into each cow's manger.

The economy of our modest farm, which had poor crops grown on sandy soil, changed dramatically in 1936 when we started growing a small crop of Virginia tobacco (see *Stompin' Tom's Territory*, page 32). The relatively light earth in our area, lying quite far south for Canada and with a lot of rainfall, was ideal for a plant more commonly grown in places like Kentucky and North Carolina. It produced a more lucrative yield for us, except in '40 when a late-August frost killed up to two-thirds of the plants in what was known as the New Ontario Tobacco Belt, where our farm lay. We were one of the few local farmers to grow tobacco. Belgian, Dutch, and other European immigrants replaced many of the original families.

While my mother didn't smoke, my father liked his pipe. In those days, people didn't really understand the ills of the cigarette. In some Sunday schools, kids did chant "Tobacco is a nasty weed, and from the devil it doth proceed. It robs your pockets, stinks your clothes, and makes a smokestack out of your nose." But a not-untypical 1930s magazine ad for Lucky Strikes showed a stylish woman smoking while delivering the reassuring message: "20,679 Physicians say Luckies are less irritating…Toasting removes dangerous irritants that cause throat irritation and coughing." Not a mention of lung cancer. Heck, Jack Claus and I first started making our own tobacco blends before we'd turned ten. We rolled the leaves tight, shaved them with a razor blade, and had our homemade cigarettes with a chaser of a honeycomb we pinched from my mother. Smoking secretly in a gully, I got so sick, I had to crawl partway home. Not until I'd finished high school and joined the Merchant Marine did I take up cigarettes seriously.

But I wound up working in tobacco from age nine. Sometimes in the spring, along with the hands we hired, I popped greenhouse plants into the soil from a horse-drawn machine, which was essentially a barrel on two wheels and an apparatus in back with two seats on either side for a couple of planters with boxes of tobacco plants on their laps. In the growing season, as well as weeding with a hoeing attachment on a cultivator, we often had to hoe by hand to get close enough to the plants. During the harvest, I helped a gang of primers who, in those late-Depression years, might make $2 a day and room and board—which meant good farm food prepared by my mom. These bent-over primers, with the toughest job of all, picked the leaves from the bottom up. A single horse lugged a boat (a box on skids with canvas sides) down the rows to hold the leaves. Then a team of horses brought the laden boat to one of five tall wooden kilns for flue-curing, the use of heat to dry the leaves. Leaf handlers passed the leaves in bundles of three to tyers, who strung about thirty bunches of leaves on a stick to be hung in the kilns and cured. Like everything else on our farm, this was labour-intensive work.

At various times, my sister Marion handled the leaves, my brothers Ralph and Blake tied them. Margaret Grant once tried the job with her mother-in-law at our farm: "I worked one whole day and handed leaves to her. I took my daughter Elizabeth, when she was just a baby. But I'm not an outside worker. And it is hard work." To start with, we had an American curer drying the tobacco with wood and coal fires, but it didn't take long for Canadians to get the knack of doing it, later using fuel oil.

Tobacco-company graders visited our farm periodically during harvest to evaluate our crop and and then showed up on opening market day to offer a price. It could be a nerve-wracking, cat-and-mouse game of bargaining. Dad could take a bid or leave it, but by turning the figure down he ran the risk of not being able to sell at all—except as processed tobacco for what was nicknamed the black market. Post-harvest, we steamed the tobacco to soften it, stripped the leaves off the stick, sorted them into grades, baled them, and hired a truck to take the tobacco to the company that bought it. My dad, honest and not very hard-nosed about bargaining, usually would sell first time around to Imperial Tobacco. While we never had a crop bigger than twenty-five acres, about half the size of a large grower, my folks kept growing the nasty weed until they sold the farm and moved into town in 1950.

WE HAD BEEN IN TOBACCO FOR THREE YEARS WHEN I entered high school in 1939, a little young at age twelve after skipping two elementary grades. My first year, grade nine, I went to the same plain, boxy, two-room school Marion was attending in nearby Vienna (in a fit of nostalgia, Ontario burghers had named many of their towns for Old World cities, like London and Paris and even Berlin, now Kitchener-Waterloo). But wanting more of a sports program and the relative excitement of a bigger centre, I switched the following year to the high school in Tillsonburg for my remaining four grades.

Thirteen miles from home, the town of about four thousand was beginning to burgeon as a focus of the tobacco industry. It had one of the widest main streets in the province (roomy enough to turn around a team of oxen in the old days). There was a department store, two movie theatres, a Greek restaurant and a Chinese café, the Astoria, where you could get a full-course meal with a thick soup, hamburger steak, and dessert of mediocre pie for thirty-five cents. But while Ontario came out of the Depression, the world became engulfed in war. Now the radio where I'd heard hockey broadcasts and Renfrew of the Mounted, and the newspapers where I read the sports stories, were brimming with Winston Churchill's speeches and sobering accounts of the battles between Germany and France, Britain, and the Commonwealth countries—including Canada. By June 1940, French, Dutch, and Belgian troops had surrendered; their defeats had a direct impact on all the Belgian immigrants who had settled in our area as tobacco farmers.

Aside from the scary news reports and the rationing of gas   and the lack of chocolate bars and chewing gum—I was insulated from all this; none of my immediate family was in the service. I was in the security of Tillsonburg High, a three-storey, nineteenth-century school full of angles and gables and topped by a tall bell tower. We rode to town in cars driven alternately by my dad, Alva Brinn of Guysborough with three daughters, and Charlie Walsh, the owner of a Straffordville general store. I became friends with Charlie's grandsons Al and Gene. We pals played baseball and hockey together and competed in track and field.

Once, when I was old enough to drive my brother Jack's car, some friends and I urged Gene, two years younger than me, to hitch his homemade wagon to the back bumper. Promising not to drive fast, I of course took off down the road at high speed, with him holding on for sweet life, until the wheels of the wagon fell off. Telling the story today, Gene says, "I was scraping on the gravel, Harley, and you were all in the car, laughing." I was obviously developing my lifelong taste for practical jokes. Despite such shenanigans, we were buddies who wrestled shoeless in a vacant lot in Straffordville and boxed with gloves on after hours above Walsh's store.

I spent so much time in the town that Jack and Treva's place became my welcoming second home during my high-school years; I slept in the same bed as my cousin Paul. His brother Ross recalls that while I saw Treva as a surrogate mom, she treated me like one of her own sons and both she and Jack continued to take pride in my later accomplishments.

We took our lunches to school and sometimes I'd eat in the boiler room in the basement, chatting up the old janitor, Walter Wright. Surrounded by older teens, I was soon aware of being a little out of my depth socially. In later years, I'd also feel embarrassed that I was maybe a bit backward compared to the city kids with their nicer-looking homes and modern conveniences. But until my last year, I was always in the top half-dozen in my classes of thirty to forty students. Some of the girls got higher marks than me, bookworms like Carol Teeter and the more outgoing Grace Backus, who became a teacher. I shone in English literature, being particularly fond of Shakespeare and poetry (Wordsworth's long "Michael, A Pastoral Poem" still resonates with me as a story about the love of a father for his son, Luke: "There is a comfort in the strength of love;/'Twill make a thing endurable, which else/Would overset the brain, or break the heart.")

Throughout those years, sports were my abiding preoccupation. Untalented in basketball, a game Tillsonburg took seriously (it sent a team to the Olympics a few years later), I also didn't play on the school football team because I just wasn't big enough and as a farm kid usually couldn't hang around after classes to practise. Later on, when I did stay occasionally for sports, I'd have to hitchhike home or often bunk in with Jack and Treva in Straffordville.

Track and field was my best school sport. Despite my short legs, I was good in the running broad jump and hop, step and jump and was a strong runner, competing in the 100, 220 and 440. In third-year high school, I was still hovering around 100 pounds, the cutoff point between juvenile, where I'd cleaned the competition, and junior—the division I had to run in this time because I now weighed 102. To my lifetime regret, Harry Buchner beat me in a tight battle of a race. My phys-ed teacher convinced me to fast a little to lose some weight for the fall inter-high track meet. This time I was beaten because my old, unsuitable baseball cleats clogged up on the muddy field of a rainy day. It's funny how you can remember the little high-school humiliations years later.

I was reasonably good in baseball, which was much easier to play than hockey in southwestern Ontario, with its brief winter season and shortage of outdoor ice. Every town had ball teams; I started in Tillsonburg at the juvenile and junior levels. The team was run by Gerry Livingston, the owner of a wood-products factory who in 1952 sponsored the town's Olympics-bound basketball club. He hauled us around the various towns in a large old De Soto sedan. An infielder, I could hit and run but had an erratic throwing arm. Straffordville had a better, intermediate team (it had won the Ontario championship in 1937) and eventually I wound up playing shortstop for it with old friends. Among them was Gene Walsh—who likes to pull out an old news clipping about a game we had against a team in Aylmer, a neighbouring town: "Aylmer got a run in the second as Langton singled and advanced to second on Hugh Howey's error and scored on Hotchkiss's error. . . .Gene Walsh hammered a triple to left field with the bases loaded to bring in three of the Straffordville runs."

He and I also played hockey in Straffordville on weekends. They were unorganized pickup games on a small pond down in the Howey Flats. Mr. Howey himself, nearing sixty, played goal wearing a baseball cap and shin guards in place of goalie pads. Bill, Bob, and Hugh Howey were on that team, along with Bill and Vic Baldwin, John Howlett, and Max Stewart, who went on to be a township councillor. Just as Jack Claus and I had as little kids, we scraped the ice with brooms and shovels and went at it, uncoached and raw, but still feeling all the excitement and exhilaration—feeling *alive*. Stephen Leacock, the British-born humorist raised on a farm near Toronto, said, "Hockey captures the essence of Canadian experience in the New World. In a land so inescapably and inhospitably cold, hockey is the chance of life, and an affirmation that despite the deathly chill of winter we are alive." That's a fancy description. In my teens, I would have agreed with the anonymous joker who remarked, "When hell freezes over, I'll play hockey there too."

By my last year of high school, when I was sixteen, my social life had improved even though I was two years junior to my peers. I'd grown taller, almost six feet, was shaving with my dad's straight razor, and had picked up a couple of nicknames, Hotch and Hod. I was in the school's Army cadet corps. And I had certainly discovered girls. Georgina Ottewell was the youngest of three sisters living in Springford, north of Tillsonburg. An older sister, Margaret, was going with a friend of mine, Richard Neale, and on Sundays he and I would hitchhike to their house, have lunch and stroll around their town with them. One June night just after school was out for the year, Richard and I missed the bus back and had to walk the half-dozen miles to Tillsonburg on a cold evening. Richard was home, but I had to go on to Straffordville to help out Jack's trucking business. Only two cars passed me that night and neither stopped. In all, it took me nearly five hours to trudge those fifteen miles, wearing out the soles of my shoes. Not long after I snuck into bed, Jack woke me at 6 a.m. I think Georgina wound up marrying a doctor.

MY FINAL YEAR, GRADE THIRTEEN, WAS A WICKED ONE. The principal, Mr. Wightman, thought I should qualify for a university scholarship, and so I loaded up on eleven subjects (two more than normal): English literature and composition, French authors and composition, algebra, geometry, trigonometry, physics, chemistry, ancient and medieval history, and civics. Meanwhile, I was more preoccupied with girls and sports. And the almighty fact of war was finally getting to me, with endless reports in the newspapers of Canadian soldiers dying overseas as they marched up the boot of Italy. Hauling books home but never looking at them, I just screwed up. In some subjects, English among them, I continued to get good marks. Writing the final departmental exam in chemistry, though, I sat frustrated in the rickety old school auditorium, realizing I'd made a hash of it, and finally went up to the teacher to ask, "How long do I have to stay here?"

She looked at me, surprised, and said, "What's wrong with you?"

"I just got to get out of here." And stupidly I did, as soon as I could.

Knowing I'd done poorly in courses required to go on to university, I was embarrassed; maybe I had to get right out of town. But except for trips to Maple Leaf Gardens in Toronto, I had never travelled further than Tillsonburg. It was the early summer of 1944. Not quite seventeen, I was about to embark on a voyage of discovery that would transport me to a world of adults and take me through dangerous waters to another continent—where I knew no one, where people spoke languages I'd never heard, where comforting Canadian icons like Syl Apps and hockey itself were completely unknown. Lines from Wordsworth's poem "Michael" would seem highly appropriate:

> *...ignominy and shame*
>
> *Fell on him, so that he was driven at last*
>
> *To seek a hiding-place beyond the seas.*

In the uniform of Tillsonburg High School's #240 corps of the Royal Canadian Army Cadets in 1943. I was learning about rifles and bren guns and champing at the bit to serve somehow during the Second World War raging overseas.

STOMPIN' TOM'S TERRITORY

Now there's one thing you can always bet
If I never smoke another cigarette,
I might get taken in a lot of deals,
But I won't go work in them tobacco fields.
Tillsonburg, Tillsonburg,
My back still aches when I hear that word.
(Copyright 1971 Crown-Vetch Music)

Stompin' Tom Connors, the legendary country singer with an Order of Canada, memorialized Tillsonburg in his hit song about the back-busting labour of picking tobacco.

Since the pine-swathed townsite in Oxford County had first been settled in 1825 by a New England iron-maker, George Tillson, it had been a centre for lumbering, then oil exploration, and eventually milling of various kinds. In the 1920s, the incorporated town was transformed after the first commercial tobacco crop was grown in the sand plains of the adjoining county of Norfolk. The year I was born, 1927, a pioneering Belgian tobacco farmer named Constant Vuylsteke established business ties to Tillsonburg.

Early on, there was a mix of American tenant farmers from Virginia and the two Carolinas and Belgian, Dutch, Polish, and Hungarian immigrants who owned their land. "Harvest time in August and September brought hordes of transient workers," reports *Tillsonburg: A History*. "They trailed into Tillsonburg, turning the streets into scenes recalling John Steinbeck's *Grapes of Wrath*. During the Depression years of the 1930s, hope of 'work in tobacco' was the magnet that brought men, women, and children from all over Ontario and Quebec."

We saw many of these hopeful people coming to our farm for temporary jobs. One task my folks needed help with was transplanting seedlings that they'd raised until they were no more than five inches tall. Sown under greenhouse glass in muck—black soil from low, swampy areas—the seedlings were irrigated with water electrically pumped from a stream. The seed for our twenty-five acres was so fine, you could hold it all in two hands. About May 20, hired women lifted the plants with their tiny leaves and boxed them for our planters.

Over the decades, technology changed tobacco farming from horses and hand-picking to tractors and automatic harvesters. The other big change has been the North American decline in smoking. My boyhood friend Gene

Posing proudly with fellow workers and my dog Buster in 1937, I almost reach the shoulders of the hired tobacco harvesters and those of my father and our neighbouring farmer Frank Howey (second and third from left).

Walsh was a buyer for Canadian Leaf Tobacco Company, which evolved into Japan Tobacco Incorporated. In his thirty-eight years with the company, he became a vice-president and witnessed the effects that competition from Africa, South America, and China and especially health concerns have had on the business.

"The medical profession was condemning cigarettes for years and it just gradually snowballed and people would quit smoking," he recalls. "When I started, there were as many as sixty-two hundred growers around here, from Brantford to St. Thomas and down the lake east to Simcoe. Now there's less than a thousand. The farmers have tried everything: sweet potatoes, lima and white beans, ginseng. When the decline started, they went into orchard apples, then the apple market was glutted. Now corn might be the right thing—for making ethanol."

My brother-in-law Don Boyd has been successfully growing tobacco in the area on their original homestead for half a century. Now that his grandson Gregory has joined him after graduating in agriculture from the University of Guelph, they're replacing tobacco with other crops, including perhaps corn and sweet potatoes for ethanol.

Eighty years after Constant Vuylsteke started farming tobacco in southwestern Ontario, Gene says, "I don't think there's any future in it."

PARTICULARS OF NATIONAL REGISTRA-
TION, NAME AND ADDRESS OF HOLDER

ELECTORAL DISTRICT	No.135	Oxford
		(NAME)
POLLING DIVISION	No.P.	O. Tillsonburg
		(NAME, IF ANY)

NAME OF HOLDER (PRINT IN BLOCK LETTERS)
HARLEY NORMAN HOTCHKISS,

FULL POSTAL ADDRESS OF HOLDER (BLOCK LETTERS)
R.R.#1, STRAFFORDVILLE, ONTAR

SIGNATURE OF HOLDER

Harley D Hotchkiss

PHOT

AUG 21
TORONTO, ONT.

No 34608

IDENTITY
CERTIFICATE

MERCHANT MARINE
CANADA

IF THIS CERTIFICATE IS LOST THE FINDER IS AT
ONCE TO PLACE IT IN THE NEAREST MAIL BOX
WHEN IT WILL BE FORWARDED TO—

THE CENTRAL REGISTER OF SEAMEN

DEPARTMENT OF TRANSPORT
HUNTER BUILDING, OTTAWA

4500
9-43

THUMB

THUMB

PARTICULARS OF NATIONAL REG
TION, NAME AND ADDRESS OF H

ELECTORAL DISTRICT	No.35	Oxford
		(NAME)
POLLING DIVISION	No.P.	O. Tillsonbu
		(NAME, IF AN

NAME OF HOLDER (PRINT IN BLOCK LETT
HARLEY NORMAN HOTCHKISS

CHAPTER 2

SHIPPING OUT

Me and the Merchant Marine

New York, N.Y.
Oct. 1, 1944

Dear Mother,

Here it is Sunday and 3 weeks since I last wrote you from Barranquilla. . . .

We didn't have a very big convoy coming up—only about 40 ships counting the escort vessels. I guess they figure the submarines are pretty well licked although we heard over the ship's news that a U.S. vessel was damaged by a sub off Cape Hatteras a few days before we passed there. Nothing exciting happened on the way up except the first day out of Cartagena. We caught the tail end of that hurricane and was it ever rough. I walked out on the boat deck to get some air and when I looked up all I could see was water. I grabbed the rail and hung on but did I ever get wet. . .

HOW A JUST-TURNED SEVENTEEN-YEAR-OLD kid from a tobacco farm in southwestern Ontario, fresh out of high school, ended up on a Norwegian merchant ship steaming out of New York down to South America in the tail-end years of the Second World War is a story.

It may have had its start in school when I joined Tillsonburg High's #240 corps of the Royal Canadian Army Cadets. Being a cadet during those war years had more meaning than it would have had in peacetime. Our

The Canadian Merchant Marine first rejected me because of my tender age—sixteen—but I persisted and finally got photographed and fingerprinted for an identity card that would let me join a Norwegian ship needing crew.

bigger brothers and older friends were fighting, and getting killed, over the seas—and it seemed to be our patriotic duty to don a uniform and train on the home front. There was more to it than that, of course: it was fun to take apart and put together rifles and even get instruction on bren guns, those .303-calibre machine guns that could pump out five hundred rounds a minute.

I was a decent shot, practising on rabbits with my dad's Canadian-made Cooey shotgun—which was the only way you could bag those rapid runners—and on squirrels with a small .22-calibre rifle. (The town kids had those sissy BB guns to shoot at us visiting farm boys.) Our high school had a rifle range in the attic to further hone my skill. R.J. Sinclair, our chemistry teacher, also taught cadets and often gave me the keys to the range for extra time with the targets and supervising other shooters. In my final year, I won the Lord Strathcona Medal as Top Gun.

For about ten days in each of two summers, I went to cadet camp for two weeks at the Thames Valley Golf Course on the outskirts of London, Ontario, which the government had transformed into a training ground for militiamen and cadets. There, amid the narrow, tree-edged fairways and undulating terrain, we pitched our tents, woke up to the bugle's reveille, marched around in formation, ate army food in mess tents, fired real military arms, and took a one-day side trip to a Canadian army base at Ipperwash on Lake Huron. And played practical jokes. One of them took advantage of the long troughs of water that ran under the wooden seats of the latrines. The water flushed through every once in a while to carry away the waste. We would wait for a weary cadet to doze off sitting on a latrine, then light a fat bunch of toilet paper, set it afire, and howl with laughter as the blaze scorched his bum. Another silly gag was to tie together the boot laces of a cadet sleeping on his stomach as he listened to a lecture on the grass—and wait for him to stand up and fall flat on his nose. Some evenings, when we got into London and strutted around in our uniforms, we told curious townsfolk the damndest stories about how we were Russian soldiers on loan to the Canadian army.

Despite such hijinks, I became a sixteen-year-old platoon leader with the rank of captain in my second summer there. That meant I got to bark orders to my mates as we drilled on the parade ground. Being boss, and determined to win the ten-mile cross-country race on our annual sports day, I told my platoon members, "Listen, every one of you suckers is going in the run." While a lot didn't enter, I had stacked the odds enough that we took eight of the ten top places—which gave us enough points to cinch our winning of the whole day's sports trophy.

All this was *Boy's Own Annual* playing at war while the real one was happening far away. I had felt for the Americans after the Japanese destroyed Pearl Harbor in December 1941 and brought our southern neighbours finally, firmly into the war. I knew about the disaster of the badly planned Dieppe raid in 1942, when nearly thirty-five hundred Allied troops—most of them Canadian—were left behind on that coastal beach in France, killed, wounded, or captured. One of the regiments decimated was the Essex Scottish, based along the north shore of Lake Erie, not that far from my home. There was page after page of pictures of these lost young men in the *London Free Press*, a memorial that made a huge impression on me. The following year, British Prime Minister Winston Churchill met in Quebec City with American President Franklin Delano Roosevelt and, in a broadcast to the world, said, "Here at the gateway of Canada, in mighty lands which have never known the totalitarian tyrannies of Hitler and Mussolini, the spirit of freedom has found a safe and abiding home." And just a month ago, on June 6, brave Canadians had fought their way up Juno Beach on the coast of Normandy, flanked by American and British troops, in the successful Allied invasion of France called Operation Overlord—D-Day. (Even to this day, I well up seeing the words of the plaque in front of an old house on Normandy's Juno Beach: "Here on the morning of June 6, 1944, men of the Royal Regiment of Canada died striving to reach the heights beyond. You on this beach remember that these men died here far from home in order that others here and everywhere might freely enjoy life in God's mercy."

Back then, my budding Canadian nationalism had reared up. It was time to do my part to help save the world. Many of the guys I knew in the same grade at school, two years older than me, had already signed up and were serving in the forces. My brothers Ralph, exempt from regular service as a schoolteacher, and Blake, with a slight heart problem, were in the militia (the size of Jack's family and his trucking business kept him out of the war). At sixteen going on seventeen, I was too young to serve as a regular soldier, sailor, or airman. So as soon as cadet camp finished in early July 1944, I hitchhiked to Montreal with a pal named Bud Pettman, whose sisters I knew at high school. Bud, about four years older than me, had been discharged from the Canadian Navy with a foot problem. Despite my age and his medical condition, we reckoned that the Canadian Merchant Marine might be inclined to accept both of us, whatever our drawbacks.

During the Second World War, this so-called "fourth arm" of the Canadian services carried troops, fuel, food, and munitions across the seas to support the Allied cause. The 12,000 civilian volunteers who ran these 180 supply ships under Navy commanders were at no less risk than their military counterparts. One in seven died in the doing, more per capita than those in the three armed forces. Being a merchant mariner, I decided, would be no pantywaist job. If my parents had any serious objection to my headstrong teenaged determination, they kept it to themselves.

Leaving from Tillsonburg for the Merchant Marine headquarters in Montreal, Bud and I hitchhiked our way through the summer landscape, car by car. We reached Cornwall near Quebec in a single day, arriving at 6 a.m. I promptly sent my mother a suitably nautical postcard of a steamboat running the local rapids, assuring her that I was "feeling fine and everything is O.K....Hope to get to Montreal this morning with good luck." Our luck didn't hold; the hitching got tough. Stranded along the highway in a town just across the Quebec border, we eventually gave up in frustration and took a train back to Cornwall and another on to Montreal. And there, the merchant-marine recruiter essentially told me, "Go on home. We've got no place for anybody your age."

Bud was rejected too. We had just enough cash to take a train back to Ingersoll, Ontario, about twenty miles from my home; at that point, I had five cents left in my pockets. But during that trip, we finally got lucky by meeting a fellow in the Canadian Air Force and telling him our sad story.

"I'll tell you how to solve your problem," he said. "I was in the Canadian Merchant Marine and I sailed on *Norwegian* ships. The reason Norway will take inexperienced guys like you is they're an occupied country—and they can't get any replacements. They lose people and there's nowhere to get any others. So you should stop in Toronto and join the Canadian Seamen's Union."

The CSU, formed in 1936, contributed strongly

Certificate of Membership

Name HARLEY N. HOTCHKISS.   No. 10576

THIS CERTIFICATE, when signed by the Secretary, is evidence of the fact that the bearer, when in Good Standing, is a member of the

CANADIAN SEAMEN'S UNION

entitled to all rights and benefits of membership; and due faith, confidence, credit and assistance from all members, and all or any of the organized seamen of the world.

In witness whereof,

PAT SULLIVAN,   D. FERGUSON,   C. E. LENTON,
Nat'l President   Acting President   Nat'l Sec'y Treas.

Issued by *Fred L. Hackett*   Port Delegate

Canadian Seamen's Union

Signature of Member   Harley Hotchkiss

Address   Straffordville, Ontario

Rating   Mess.

When Joined   Aug 9 1944

"EVERY C. S. U. MAN AN ORGANIZER"

Membership in the Canadian Seamen's Union was my first step in going to sea by making a landlubber a sudden sailor who could be accepted by the Merchant Marine.

to the war effort, but our motive for joining it was to become union members in hope that the Norwegian merchant marine would recognize us as sailors worthy of hire. We paid the initial dues and on August 21 got Canadian Merchant Marine identity certificates declaring that we had somehow satisfied the authorities that we were "seamen" (though I was a landlocked farmboy who'd never even seen salt water). I still have my card; it says my height was five-eleven, my weight 143, and my eyes were hazel.

The Norwegian vessels that would accept us as crew were based in New York City. No merchant ship was currently available to have us serve aboard, so we had to bide our time in Toronto. In the big city, the only place I knew my way around was Maple Leaf Gardens—which was empty of all my hockey heroes in the off-season. In a letter home August 13, I reported that I had seen *The Story of Dr. Wassell*, a Cecil B. DeMille movie starring Gary Cooper as the real Navy doctor who'd saved nearly a dozen wounded American sailors during the Japanese invasion of Java. "It certainly is good. If it comes to Tillsonburg don't miss it . . . Bud and I have gone to one or two shows and that's about all the excitement we have. Cities certainly are dull places."

Bunking in a men's hostel called Trinity Square Lodge, we'd managed to land jobs immediately in the labour-short capital. A construction company had us helping excavate the basement of a downtown jewellery store on Yonge Street called Proctor's. It was a dirty, hard-shovel dig, but I was pretty strong from the farm. Though we earned seventy cents an hour, a reasonably handsome sum for the times, digging dirt instead of serving at sea was frustrating: "The way the war looks," I wrote Mom, "it may all be over before we sail." But after about two weeks, we got our call: it appeared that an oil tanker out of Mobile, Alabama, named the *Nordal Grieg*—Grieg for the Norwegian composer—could use Canadian volunteers.

Before leaving, I went back home to say goodbye and collect my things. At five in the morning of a Sunday in August, daylight barely on the horizon, my mother and brother Ralph drove me to Tillsonburg to catch the bus back to Toronto. Mom being Mom, a strong woman caring for a large family on a challenging farm, there was no flowery emotional farewell to her son who had just turned seventeen.

She simply said, "Harley, you take good care of yourself and write me and I'll write you—and if you need anything, let me know." That was it, along with a hug.

I was pleased to get a letter from my sister Marion, living in Quebec:

I hope this reaches you before you leave on Saturday.

I think you'll like it in the Navy and I've heard that the Norwegian Navy is one of the highest paid.

Write when you know your address and I'll see that you have some mail when you reach port and from experience I know how nice letters from home are when you're away.

I know you can take care of yourself and I'm proud of you Harley.

Good luck and Bon Voyage.

Love

Marion

I was among five young Canadians, officially designated seamen, who travelled together in a sleeping car on a train to New York at Norwegian-government expense. Getting off in Grand Central Station on August 22, we walked into a city of 7.5 million, the most populous in the world at the time. A city that exceeded all my rural expectations: in our first days there, we took the elevator to the top of the 102-storey Empire State Building, gazing down on the other Manhattan skyscrapers that dwarfed anything I'd ever seen in my life. We visited Rockefeller Center, with fourteen buildings sprawling over seventeen acres and its famous outdoor rink, which later helped me keep my skating legs limber on rented skates during the odd winter shore leave. We went to Radio City Music Hall, where a brand-new movie, *Dragon Seed*, had Katharine Hepburn and Walter Huston as Chinese villagers battling Japanese invaders. And we got to Coney Island and gulped at the Bobsled and Tornado roller coasters, the Wonder Wheel ("the highest ferris wheel in the world"), and two-seater parachute drops. We also ogled bathing beauties being blanket-tossed on the wide, teeming beaches.

But the centre of my universe, where I picked up my mail from home, became the Maritime Exchange at 80 Broad Street in the Wall Street area, the U.S. headquarters of the Norwegian Shipping and Trade Mission (Nortraship). The thirty-six-storey office tower is still there today, a few blocks from the New York Stock Exchange: a 1930 classic Art Deco building with an elegant entrance of metalwork that extends into the lobby with a mural of ships at sea on its high ceiling.

The mission, which also had an office in London, was created in 1940 to run the 85 per cent of Norway's merchant fleet outside German-controlled regions. Germany had just invaded the nation of 2.9 million

46:—BOBSLED, CONEY ISLAND, N. Y.

48442

The trackless toboggan of the Bobsled was one of the many thrills for a farm kid at New York's Coney Island, where servicemen and merchant mariners could relax during the war—and watch the girls on the beach.

and ordered all those ships to neutral ports where it could take command of them. Their captains refused. (Jan Furst, a naval architect who lived in Norway at the time, was recently translating some Norwegian documents about my ship for me and recalled that one of those captains radioed German authorities with the succinct message: "Kiss my ass.")

The Norwegian government-in-exile was now determined to support the Allied cause through Nortraship. The new, for-profit company was soon operating more than a thousand of these "free ships" with about thirty thousand crew—the world's biggest shipping fleet. Even before the first year ended, Nortaship had lost ninety-six vessels and hundreds of seamen in the North Atlantic, prompting many Norwegian sailors to leave their ships. As a result, the remaining ones got two wage increases by December 1942. I would make $110 a month to start, half of which I'd mail home.

Neither Bud nor I ever served on the tanker in Alabama, which had to leave before we could get there. Though I was really counting on having my older friend aboard the same vessel, he was the first of our group to ship out, on another tanker bound for Murmansk. It was a tough, dangerous run to the extreme northwest of Russia—which he would survive, but come back home with a bad case of nerves. Three others went off on tankers and I was the last one left, boarding at a small, comfortable rooming house in Brooklyn for sailors in transit. "It is sure smart," I told my folks. "We each have a

The *Ørnefjell*, seen here during its Great Lakes service at dock in Milwaukee in 1942, was my home afloat on the Atlantic to South America.

private room and we can have anything we want to eat. It doesn't cost us a cent. Everyone we have talked to says the Norwegians have the best boats in the world."

Not long after, I got my own boat: the diesel-powered, single-funnel cargo steamer SS *Ørnefjell* —Eagle Mountain—launched in 1937 at the Nyland shipyard in Oslo (where, in an amazing coincidence, my naval-architect translator, Jan Furst, was then working as a very young marine draughtsman). She was only 250 feet long with a gross tonnage of 1,334, or 2,500 deadweight, the maximum weight of the cargo, crew, stores, and bunkers. On her side was the name "Great Lakes." Jan says she was the fourth of six of the same size built for Norway's Olsen & Ugelstad shipping company, specifically designed to be small enough to pass through the locks of the Welland Canal—which just happens to link lakes Ontario and Erie in my southern half of the province. In 1940 she began sailing out of Halifax and Sydney, Nova Scotia, in armed Allied convoys across the Atlantic and out of the United Kingdom and Gibraltar to ports in Nigeria and Freetown in Sierra Leone. Her cargo ranged from lumber and army stores to oranges and other produce. She could travel more than ten knots, fast enough while I was aboard to allow her to sail independent of convoys on some voyages.

The *Ørnefjell* was docked in the Brooklyn naval yard and when I showed up, duffel bag on my shoulder, she looked a mess as workers were doing a minor refit, cleaning her hull and welding parts in place. This was wartime and there was a guard on the gangplank who inspected my papers before sending me up to the ship's purser. Settled in my shared cabin, a tiny room with a single porthole that was blacked out at night, I was taken to meet the master.

He proved to be a wonderful middle-aged man, Captain Sigurd Andreas Andresen, decked out in a smart blue uniform with stripes. From a small town in southern Norway, he became a sailor at fourteen. Round-faced with a high brow and a strong nose, he had a kindly and generous disposition. As I would learn, he'd been separated from his wife since Germany invaded Norway and had no communication with her except the occasional skimpy letter sent through the Red Cross. I wrote home once that "he received a letter this time smuggled through Sweden (the first in 2 years) saying that the Germans had taken his house and that there was very little to eat."

The skipper spoke fluent English, which was a good thing because I was going to be captain's boy. That meant I made his bed, served his meals, which he usually ate alone in his suite of rooms, cleaned his dishes and replaced them in a pantry, and then tidied his usually neat quarters. He never uttered a harsh word to me; it was a pretty soft job. A little bonus was his modest personal library, from which he let me borrow books. As a member of the steward's department, I also looked after the chief mate and chief engineer. We often had American naval escorts from Norfolk, Virginia, generally destroyers, and occasionally one of the commanders would stay aboard the *Ørnefjell* and I'd help look after his needs. Sending half my pay home to Mom, I wrote her, "Don't be alarmed if it tells you on the draft that I work in the saloon. That's just the Norwegian way of saying the captain's quarters and the mess room. There are no drinks of any kind on these ships."

Used to acres of familiar, solid land where I could range freely on foot, suddenly I was constrained in the confines of an elaborate tin can riding the limitless ocean surrounding me. But I was always curious about the nautical nuts and bolts—learning how to splice ropes, signal with flags, and communicate with Morse Code. Before long, I was bumped up to the role of ordinary seaman and, along with chipping rust and swabbing decks, got to steer the ship, two hours in each of my four-hour watches, morning and night.

Most of the officers and some of the crew spoke English, though they routinely lapsed into Norwegian around me. If it had been today, when Norwegians like Patrick Thoresen and Anders Myrvold play in the NHL, we at least would have had the common language of hockey to share. (I didn't know then that in Norway, people had been playing a hockey-like game on ice as early as the seventeenth century.) I did learn to count (*en, to, tre*) and say a few words (*venliggst* for "please" and *takk* for "thanks") in this earthy, Germanic-sounding language. Later I'd discover that having an English-speaking teenager on board wasn't such a novelty: a fifteen-year-old from Liverpool had joined the *Ørnefjell* as a messboy in 1942. And while I was aboard, an Englishman served briefly as an assistant cook.

We had about three dozen crew members, including three mates, four engineers, a wireless operator, a bosun in charge of the six seamen, a purser handling stores and pay, a donkey man running the engineering gang of six oilers and stokers, and a cook and mess attendants for the officers. Because this was a so-called Defensively Equipped Merchant Ship, two Norwegian navy gunners were on board to operate five-pound guns fore and aft—no bigger than the artillery that the British fleet had used during the American Revolutionary War—and two rapid-fire, 50-calibre Oerlikon machine guns that were more suited to a little torpedo boat than a ship. Unfortunately, unlike some Norwegian tankers, we didn't carry any Hotchkiss machine guns (named for a French arms and car company established by American engineer Benjamin B. Hotchkiss in the late nineteenth century).

I shared a cabin mid-decks with a gunner for a while after bunking with an Icelandic guy whose name I still recall: Rickard Asgierrson, whom everyone called Ricky. In our off-hours, munching apples and oranges, peaches and plums, or over dinners of pork chops or chicken on Sunday, the mariners might tell me fascinating tales. Some were about of life in Scandinavia, like the bosun's story of growing up on an island and having to row a boat to school. Others were more sobering, like those from a seaman who'd endured forty-eight days on a raft when his ship went down in the North Atlantic and then another eleven days on a raft when a Japanese raider sank his next ship in the Indian Ocean. I would spend Christmas aboard with these mates in a South America of heat and mosquitos, settling for little gifts of candy and neckties from charities in New York. There I was, a green landlubber on an ocean-going ship, an untested farm lad among seasoned men—in Shakespeare's words, "Not yet old enough for a man, nor young enough for a boy."

My first voyage, to the ports of Cartagena and Barranquilla in Colombia, was memorable. Though the South American country had a sizable German-immigrant population, it had allowed the U.S. to build and run air and naval bases there in 1940. After the attack on Pearl Harbor, it broke off diplomatic relations with the Axis powers of Germany, Italy, and Japan and then started supplying the Allies with petroleum products. In 1943, after German U-boats sunk a Colombian schooner and cargo ships, it formally declared war against the Axis.

On this trip, the *Ørnefjell* was carrying munitions and general cargo when we left New York the evening of August 28, as I recounted in a seven-page letter to my folks from Barranquilla:

. . . we joined the convoy at two that [Monday] night. When I woke up (at 5:30 every morning) we were at sea and land was just a faint blur on the horizon. I must admit I felt sort of blue watching America and New York fade away. We were at sea 11 days sighting land on Thursday nite and docking at Cartagena on Friday. On the way down we passed through the West Indies where we broke convoy and came on 3 days alone at full speed. We passed between Cuba and Haiti and came quite close to Jamaica. The water on the way down was a brilliant blue and you could see thousands of flying fish. During the nite the moon was always up and you could see the other ships in the convoy shining white in the moonlight. We had good weather except for the last day at sea when it grew sort of rough. I guess I was lucky to get this trip. The fellows all say that it's the best there is. The only sign of danger was when a corvette came by our ship and dropped 4 depth charges. Everybody laughed and said it must have been a fish.

Down here at Barranquilla we are on the Magdalena river about 2 miles inland and is it ever hot—about 130° in the shade. I can look out the port-holes and see natives paddling down a stream in dugouts and old paddle wheel steamers chugging along. It looks like a scene from the Mississippi in the olden days. There are big black birds of some kind circling around all the time. I sure wouldn't want to live here. They have all kinds of fruit though. One peso—about 75¢ will buy 300 bananas. I bought a bunch for 1 packet of cigarettes. Cigarettes (Camels, Luckies etc.) cost us only 5¢ a pack on ship so I bought a couple of cartons for trading purposes. [I later did take up smoking on the ship.]

I was certainly sea sick on the way down. I didn't care if they threw me overboard. The sailors couldn't understand it because the sea was quite calm. I hope I get over it because it is an awful feeling. . . .

I get pretty homesick at times, especially out to sea, but so does everyone else. All you hear about the boys being tough is so much eyewash. They are as good a bunch of fellows as you would meet anywhere. . . .

I wish I had worked harder last year and gone to college this year but maybe I can do that later. I need some experience in the world first I guess. . . .

Love to All,

Harley

The sixteenth-century Santa Domingo cathedral in Cartagena, an exotic port in Colombia where our ship stopped in a wartime service operated by the Norwegian government-in-exile.

Barranquilla was actually as many as fifteen miles from the Caribbean Sea, on a silt-choked river thick with the steady traffic of dugout canoes and paddlewheelers laden with firewood, animals, and people. It was the first major port developed in Colombia, its second-biggest city at that time, and supposedly among the most modern centres in the Caribbean. When the trade winds weren't blowing, it was a steamy tropical hothouse of about 150,000 Spanish-speaking people, which shipped coffee and bananas around the globe. Fascinating, but not as pretty as Cartagena, another port on the northern coast, which looked picturesque even while I was seasick. Before we docked in the harbour, I could smell the blessed land and see the leaves of the trees floating in the water and the shorebirds dancing, and looked up in wonder at the seventeenth-century Santa Cruz convent five hundred feet atop La Popa hill. Firmly on my first South American soil, I got to wander around the old Spanish colonial town, which would later become a UNESCO World Heritage Site, famed for the beauty of its coralstone forts and walled city. Heading back to New York, I was seasick again but when we arrived the captain sent me to a doctor who gave me pills, which were probably placebos.

My first foreign port had been Guantanamo Bay, the naval base the Americans had leased from Cuba in 1903 (and still holds more than a century later to imprison al-Qaeda and Taliban operatives in the wake of 9/11). We laid anchor out in the huge, well-sheltered harbour, a dispersal point for our convoys. Once, we passed close to a enormous American warship where two thousand sailors were lined up for morning exercises, and sometimes I used binoculars to watch movies being shown at night on the decks of surrounding ships. Only once did I get onto dry land there, in the nearby town of Boqueron, where we were loading 325-pound sacks of raw, dark-brown sugar for the Jack Frost refineries in New York. Most often during our time ashore, I hung around with the older sailors, especially in tough ports like Cristobal, on Limon Bay at the eastern end of the Panama Canal. It was a seedy town brimming with prostitutes, whose wares I never sampled, and bars where I hesitantly tried the great-tasting beer and wicked rum. I never knew enough to be afraid.

I was a bit more nervous out at sea, always making sure I knew where my lifejacket and the lifeboats were. Ships were sometimes strung out in long convoys, way over the horizon, and in April 1945, after hearing that a couple in our convoy were hit, we saw depth charges being dropped from a distance. Our route down to South America took us past Cape Hatteras, on the North Carolina coast, which could be whipped by whing-dingers of hurricanes—and if that wasn't scary enough, I'd worried my mother in that letter of October 1944 that "a U.S. vessel was damaged by a sub off Cape Hatteras a few days before we passed there." Two years earlier, a U-boat had torpedoed and sunk a London-based freighter off the cape. The submarine captain, Jochen Mohr, later radioed German Command with a verse celebrating his success in American waters:

The new moon night is black as ink,
Off Hatteras the Tankers sink.
While sadly Roosevelt counts score —
Some fifty thousand tons—by MOHR!

President Roosevelt died in April 1945. "The war looks good now," I wrote my brother Ralph, "but it was too bad about Roosevelt. He was a good man, I think." The night of his death, Toronto was facing Detroit in the Stanley Cup playoffs at the Gardens and there was some doubt that the game would go ahead. It did, and my Maple Leafs (minus Syl Apps, who was in the Canadian Army) shut out the Red Wings for the third straight time in the series. "Toronto is really hot in the play-offs," I remarked. "I saw the score in to-day's paper. Three shutouts is pretty good." (The Leafs won the Cup four games to three.)

We made one trip up north, through weather-battered Canadian waters to take supplies to St. John's, Newfoundland. After war broke out, Ottawa had built a naval base there on behalf of the British Admiralty, with the Royal Canadian Navy running it as a vital forward port that let escort vessels extend their coverage of Allied convoys more than six hundred miles further into the Atlantic. It's the only time I've been to what would become our tenth province.

In April, with hostilities winding down, I wrote Mom from New York about my cousin Quentin, who'd joined the U.S. Marines, and said, "I've thought of enlisting here when I'm 18. What do you think of that?" I soon thought better of it. Early the following month, the war in Europe ended. I was in Cartagena, Colombia, and when Colombian warships blew their horns and waved their flags in the harbour, I wondered where the hell they'd been throughout all the hostilities—I hadn't even known the nation had a navy.

I had been to sea for weeks at a time, braved hurricanes and the potential threat of U-boat attacks, learned to steer a ship, and seen a whole new continent and countries where everyone spoke a language I didn't understand. I'd come to know one of the most exciting cities in the world, New York, walked Times Square and Central Park, watched the Ringling Brothers and Barnum & Bailey Circus at Madison Square Garden, got to figure out the subway system, and eventually made my way around town without having to ask directions. I visited servicemen's canteens and ate at church suppers and the Automats. Meanwhile, some of my letters to Ontario had expressed my longing for home and my concern for my mother's ailing dad, Grandpa Todd. When he died in January 1945, I'd written her, "I sincerely believe that what small amount of fortitude our family possesses came from him."

The war with Germany was over. It was time to go home.

Near the end of May, after nine months' service and nine trips to South America, I took my leave of the ship. Duffel bag on my shoulder for the last time, I strode down the gangplank and waved to my captain as he stood watching me from the bridge. My parting gift from Sigurd Andresen, master of the SS *Ørnefjell*, was a typewritten letter of commendation that read:

Harley Hotchkiss has served aboard the Norwegian ship Ørnefjell in the capacity of Ordinary Seaman from August 24th 1944 to May 24th 1945.

During his service on this ship his conduct has been excellent and he has given entire satisfaction in the discharge of his duties, on the strength of which I give him my best recommendation.

New York, May 24th 1945.

After the war, Captain Andresen would be decorated by the King of Norway for his forty-four years of merchant-marine service, nearly five of them commanding a ship through the perilous waters of wartime. Decades later in Calgary, a visiting Norwegian captain of an offshore drilling vessel on the Canadian east coast found me a book that mentioned Andresen as the longest-serving captain in the Fjell line. To my regret, I learned through the Norwegian consulate in Montreal that he'd died at home just two years before I had a chance to look him up and thank him again.

Under his leadership, in the company of men, I had grown to the cusp of manhood—old enough to know what a bit of the world was about, but still too young to find my place in it. That would require a few years' seasoning.

CHAPTER 3

THE LEARNING CURVE

Hockey Sticks and Ancient Stones

F OR ALL MY LOVE OF HOCKEY, IT WAS AT A BASE-ball game on Labour Day in 1945 where I made the first of three dramatic decisions that would transform my life in those hopeful post-war years.

That May, I had taken the train from Grand Central Station to Tillsonburg, my duffel bag stuffed with about thirty cartons of dirt-cheap Sea Store cigarettes and rum and cigars from my Cuban shore leave. A kind Canadian customs man, turning a blind eye, let me through without declaring them or paying duty. Trying to surprise my family, I hadn't even told them I was coming home. The European war was over, but the battles in the Pacific were still raging and I'd written my folks about rumours that our ship might be heading there. In Tillsonburg I took a taxi the thirteen miles to our farm and got out at the head of the lengthy, maple-rimmed lane. It was (in T.S. Eliot's words) "the violet hour, the evening hour that strives / Homeward, and brings the sailor home from sea." Dad was outside, washing up for supper, and when I reached the house, this quiet, undemonstrative man gave me a hug and brought me inside for another from my startled and (I now know) greatly relieved Mom.

The whole country would be relieved when the Japanese surrendered that August after the U.S. dropped atomic bombs on Hiroshima and Nagasaki. Canadians were proud of the role we'd played during the Second World War. As Robert Collins, a writer of my generation, observed in his book *You*

At twenty-one, I'm a hapless Canadian experienced only in rural hockey on outdoor rinks, now playing on artificial ice with a hapless American college team—the Spartans—in a sport just newly revived at Michigan State.

Had To Be There: "We had entered the war as a producer of grain and ore, and came out a manufacturer and trader. A nation of only 11.5 million people had become the world's fourth-largest supplier of wartime munitions and machines *and* had given $3.4 billion worth of aid to its allies."

There were some changes on our own personal homefront. Grandpa Todd, a widower living on his farm with his son Archie, had died recently without my being able to say goodbye. On my first evening back, I learned that our dog Whiskers had been run over by a neighbour. Yet aside from those passages, life was pretty much the same here, the farm the familiar haven I'd known as a boy. Too familiar. That summer I soon slipped into the pattern of my school days, helping with the haying and tobacco harvest and even hiring myself out to nearby farmers (including one sharecropper who had me picking the tips of ripe tobacco plants till eleven at night and then moved on without paying me). My father, in his late fifties, probably would have wanted his youngest son to take over his operation some day—he never pushed me—but I just wasn't interested in farming. Jack had his trucking business, Ralph was a schoolteacher, Blake was into radios and other appliances. I'm sure they all wondered what in hell I was going to do with my life.

So did I. "Maybe I can scrape up my Senior Matric yet," I'd written Ralph from aboard ship. "I have felt rather guilty and ashamed at missing it when I could have had it so easily. I couldn't seem to concentrate at all but when you're away from school you sure miss it." That summer I did complete my high-school courses, applied to the University of Western Ontario, and was accepted. I fully intended to go to London in September and board with four friends who'd been behind me in school but had caught up while I was in the Merchant Marine.

Then on the day before I was to leave home, there was a call from the university that I'd now have to wait till January to attend: an influx of war veterans had clogged the system. I wasn't considered a military vet myself; merchant mariners were not included in federal programs designed to speed other sailors' adjustment to civilian life. (In fact, it wasn't until a few years ago that I received $10,000 in tax-free compensation from Ottawa for my service during the war.) My nose was out of joint. Feeling rejected by the university and the federal government, I just said to hell with it and decided to forget college. It was a dumb decision. All my good intentions about higher learning seemed to evaporate as I drifted for nearly the next three years, working in tobacco and eventually accepting Jack's generous offer to drive a truck for him again.

My eldest brother was a hero of mine, short but sturdy and as strong as Paul Bunyan's Babe the Blue Ox—a fun guy to be with. He ran his first two

All swagger, just back from the Merchant Marine in 1945, I am ready to take on the world in peacetime—If only I can figure out what to do with my life.

Fargo trucks ("Built by Chrysler... in Canada"), with their distinctive globe symbols on the dash and chrome headlights and large hubcaps. I'd driven one during the summer after my last year of high school. Jack's business had been growing since he began hauling milk from Straffordville to a dairy in nearby Simcoe. Now he was bringing fertilizer from Ingersoll and Hamilton to tobacco farms in spring, carrying coal from barges on Lake Erie in summer, taking tobacco from the farms to the factories in the surrounding towns in autumn, and delivering Christmas trees to Buffalo and Detroit in winter.

Driving truck seemed at first like an easy way to evade the future. My real interest during those aimless days was playing hockey and baseball in Straffordville and going to the dance halls dotted along the north shore of Lake Erie. It was during my first summer home, having just turned eighteen, that I went dancing in the fishing village of Port Burwell and first saw Becky Boyd.

Nellie Ball was in my arms on the dance floor that August evening. Glancing over her shoulder, I spotted this younger-looking girl with long, reddish-blonde hair that framed fine features and shining hazel eyes. She was all of about five-foot-five, and more than cute; maybe this was what Byron meant when he wrote, "She walks in beauty . . .". Except she was dancing—with another guy. I started flirting from afar, winking at her, to no real response. That was the sum of our silent encounter.

I had no idea who she was; she sure hadn't gone to my high school or I'd have noticed her before. It didn't take me long to learn her name. On Labour Day, the first Monday in September, our Straffordville Red Caps ball team was playing in Langton, a village twenty minutes away in Norfolk

Suddenly I knew what I'd like to do with my young life: to woo sixteen-year-old Becky, the beautiful Norma Rebecca Boyd, whom I'd first seen at a dance and then at a baseball game where I was playing against a team coached by her dad. Whatever the score of the game was, I won her.

County. Our game was the star attraction at the Langton fair that fall. Pitching for the home team was a blond-haired guy named Earl Boyd, whom I'd played with on the Tillsonburg junior team. I knew he had some pretty attractive sisters because my brother Ralph had taught school just up the road from the Boyd farm in the Langton area.

And there once again, in the bleachers around the ball diamond on the fairgrounds, was the girl I'd made eyes at in Port Burwell. Her name, I found out, was Becky.

She was watching her brother Earl play while her father, Gordon Boyd, coached the Langton Lions. He was a fine coach who took many teams of local farm boys to Ontario junior championships over the years. I spent most of the afternoon trying to impress Becky from a distance. Our side might have lost this game, but personally I hit a home run: screwing up my courage afterwards, I approached her and asked to call on her the next afternoon at her family farm three miles southeast of Langton on the tenth concession of North Walsingham Township.

She accepted. As Becky has told friends in the years that followed, "It was love at first sight. I'd had crushes and flirtations with boys before Harley. But he was the first man I ever loved and wanted to be with my whole life." The feeling was wonderfully mutual. That weekend, the film playing at the Odeon in Tillsonburg, the nearest town with a movie theatre, featured Katharine Hepburn and Spencer Tracy in *Without Love*. Before I'd gone to the game, that title had sure described me. Now, it no longer applied.

When I showed up at Becky's home in my father's 1941 Ford the following day, Gord Boyd answered the kitchen door out back. He'd been a crack senior ball player himself, even with only a stub of his right arm after a brother had accidentally shot him at age twelve. I'd seen him pitch, play second base, and hit the ball by cradling the bat over his stump. Never letting the missing arm be a handicap, he drove a car, a tractor, and teams of horses, even tied his own tie. So meeting him formally that first day, I was too much in awe to get right to the point of my visit. We wound up talking baseball for what seemed a terribly long time—he was probably sizing me up—and all the while, Becky and her sisters were in the next room giggling their heads off at my frustration.

Finally, after about fifteen minutes, Becky came to my rescue. That very moment was the beginning of our lifetime romance. As the big-band vocalists, inspired by Fred Astaire, used to sing at our dances, I was "putting all my eggs in one basket, betting everything I've got on you."

I found that Norma Rebecca (named for her grandmother) was two and a half years younger than me, the middle of seven children, between her older sisters Helen and Thelma and brother Earl and her younger brothers Don and Jim and sister Eileen. The ancestors on their father's side were Northern Irish Protestant and on their mother's side, the Boughners were Pennsylvania Dutch stock, from Germany, who became United Empire Loyalists in Canada. Her paternal great-grandfather, William Samuel Boyd, had settled briefly in Montreal before bringing his family of nine kids by horseback to southwestern Ontario. There they farmed, married, and had their own offspring, Gordon among them.

A hard worker with a nice sense of humour, he could be a stubborn debater when it came to the politics he kept current with in well-read newspapers and weekly magazines. He'd studied education at Normal School in North Bay and returned to the Langton area to take over the family farm while teaching nearby. He knew an eighteen-year-old local girl named Marion, whom he'd grown up with and would marry and bring to the productive two-hundred-acre farm, where they raised dairy cattle and poultry and grew grain and eventually tobacco. Their daughter recalls, "Dad would lean on the fence and look at his cattle and say, 'This is the best place to be.'"

She describes her less-educated mom as "a truly good person—selfless—who never complained" despite raising seven children and having her husband's parents living with her in the early years. "A rather large woman, but she was very stylish and liked nice things"—much like her petite daughter, who also inherited her mom's great organizing skills. Becky had attended a two-room elementary school close to the farm and was now busing to classes fifteen miles away in Simcoe, where she was a good student and was voted High School Queen in Grade 12. Her father's daughter, lithe and athletic, she skated to music on Langton's little outdoor rink and competed on the girls' village baseball and school basketball teams. She had a musical bent too, singing in a choir and playing the organ at Carholme United Church (which I attended reluctantly just to be near her; she recalls that Earl and I sat in a back pew and told jokes). She never smoked and there was never any liquor in her house. "My mom and dad were so prim—my mother still called women she'd known all her life 'Mrs.'"

Becky and I would be a courting couple for the next six years. She was closest to her oldest sister, Helen, despite the eight-year difference in ages, and Helen and her husband, Bob, invited us for Sunday dinners in Aylmer. Sometimes we double-dated with Thelma and her boyfriend Frank, went dancing in Long Point and Port Dover (where the Summer Garden featured greats like Count Basie and Gene Krupa), and took little trips up to Muskoka cottage country—where, trying to impress her with my motor-boat skills, I wound up in the rocks instead of the water. We went to watch her brother

Earl play hockey and once witnessed her usually staid mom
lean over the boards and with her
purse swat a player who'd given
him a bad hit.

Becky grew to love my
parents, enjoying the warmth
of my father but even venturing
to kiss my sedate mother, who
would tell her, "We don't show
our emotions much" (in contrast
to Becky's own mom: "I remember sitting on her lap even when
I was twenty-one"). She met
my siblings and took to Jack and
his wife, Treva; their daughter
Roma remembers, "When you
brought Becky to our home and
introduced her to us, we probably just sat around with our eyes
wide open because she was so
beautiful."

Courting Becky over the next six years becomes my most pleasurable task.

BY THE TIME WE MET, BECKY HAD MADE UP HER MIND
to study nursing after high school. And, in the first of my major post-war
decisions I had decided to marry her someday. Yet during our first two and
a half years together, I seemed to have no other real ambitions. Working for
Jack Hotchkiss General Trucking turned out to be a waste of my time, not
to mention a damn hard job. Humping furniture for people moving house
and hauling cordwood for farmers' tobacco kilns were bad enough, but
shovelling eight tons of coal in ninety-five-degree heat and spirit-sapping
humidity was a killer (I stopped at Frogget's service station and downed six
straight bottles of Coke). The work could prove embarrassing too. Once
in December, hauling local Christmas trees to Detroit and passing through
St. Thomas, Ontario, in the middle of the night, I drove down a main street
decorated with garlands of Christmas lights—and, on reaching Detroit,
discovered several strings of bulbs on the truck that my load had torn from
their moorings.

It was the frantic springtime fertilizer runs that finally convinced
me to question my increasingly dim future. Fertilizer for tobacco came in

100- and 125-pound burlap bags from the CIL chemical plant in Hamilton—
eighteen tons in one haul that you usually had to unload yourself. In the
spring of 1947, while working around the clock, cat-napping in the truck, I
was driving a load at three in the morning from the factory.

On the dark Highway 6 out of Hamilton, weary and alone, wielding
my body but not my mind, I got to thinking, *What am I doing here? What am
I going to do?* I was as adrift as a lifeboat in the North Atlantic.

Becky, meanwhile, was determined to start nurse's training at Victoria
Hospital in London in the fall of '48. Maybe it was darn well time to get an
advanced education, after all. Sure, I could re-apply to Western and we'd be
in the same city the following year, but I was still stupidly mad at the university for turning me down to accommodate the military vets. *If I won't study
there, then where?*

Well, two of my mother's sisters, Annie and Georgia, had moved to
the northern U.S., Annie becoming a nurse and marrying a doctor in Michigan. After I got home from that life-deciding drive through the night and
announced the second big decision of my young adulthood—the renewed
resolve to get a degree—Dr. McFarland suggested I apply to Michigan State
College (now University). Though I knew nothing about the place, the idea
had a suitably exotic ring to it: studying in a foreign country, even if it was
less than a four-hour drive from home. It wasn't the University of Michigan,
its more prominent arch rival, but the college had been around since 1855,
first as an agricultural school and since 1925 as an applied-sciences institution as well.

Okay, I'll try it. But what exactly do I study? Growing up amid the trees
and rocks of a farm, I was reasonably interested in the possibilities of both
forestry and geology—something that would take me outdoors. Apparently
MSC had a good geological-sciences department, and that decided me. Now
I just had to announce my decision to Becky. That was hard. She was upset
at the thought of us being apart for much of the year but in the end generously supported my plan, probably reassured that the guy she'd committed
her heart to might just make something of himself. In later years, she would
muse, "I wonder what would have happened if you'd stayed driving a truck?
You'd probably have owned a whole fleet of trucks now."

In January 1948, Becky came to see me off in a heavy-hearted farewell
at the train station in Ingersoll. We'd been inseparable for more than two
years. I promised her lots of letters and long-distance phone calls, and as
many visits home as I could manage.

The Red Cedar River coursing through the Michigan State campus in the 1950s was a perfect place to canoe with your girl—unless she was back home.

DESPITE MY MONTHS ABOARD SHIP, I WASN'T THAT worldly. My mother had even packed my clothes for college and labelled my trunks for me. Now I was on my own again. The Grand Trunk Railway took me through the wintry landscape to Michigan State College of Agriculture and Applied Sciences in the small residential city of East Lansing, across Lake Huron in the south-central part of the state. The campus was reputed to be one of the most beautiful in the country, with the Red Cedar River (dyed very red for the annual water carnival) winding through it thirty-six hundred rolling acres rich with trees—spruce and ash, pine and oak—as a backdrop to the red-brick buildings. There were thousands of species and varieties of woody plantings, a number that would do an arboretum proud.

This was among the earliest land-grant educational institutions in the U.S., given federally controlled land to teach agriculture, mechanical arts, and military tactics as well as classical studies. A botanical garden established in 1873 was the oldest continuously operated one of its kind in North America. Strolling the snow-streaked grounds, I came across two landmarks: the Beaumont Tower, with a carillon that chimed every fifteen minutes, and

Sparty, the college symbol, named the Spartans hockey team and one day my own business.

a statue called the Spartan (nicknamed "Sparty"), supposedly the world's largest free-standing ceramic figure. Its formal title, from ancient Greece, was also the name of the college's sports teams, a name I'd one day borrow for my own company.

I was among 16.450 students, the girls in long skirts, bobbysocks and two-tone saddle shoes, the boys with Brylcreem'd hair and sporting plaid work jackets and full-cut pants. This was the year the long-playing phonograph record and the Polaroid camera would be introduced, McDonald's hamburger stands were first franchised, and Ed Sullivan's *Toast of the Town* made its debut on the one million TV sets in the U.S. Outside the confines of the campus, the Cold War was slowly heating up, Israel was about to become an independent state, and across the Pacific the Republic of Korea in the south and the People's Democratic Republic in the north came into being—to launch a confrontation that would explode two years later and affect the lives of many of my fellow students.

None of this mattered to me at the beginning of 1948. I was more concerned with my course load. Michigan State's innovative president, John Hannah, was transforming the college from a good regional undergraduate institution to a comprehensive national research university. His philosophy had led to the pioneering Basic College curriculum, from which freshmen and sophomores had to take five of the seven core subjects before specializing. I chose written and spoken English, physical science, history of civilization, effective living (life goals and human relationships), and another topic that I quickly forgot. MSC was on a term system: all courses were one-year long, taken over three terms, fall, winter, and spring. But if students felt confident enough, they could write a comprehensive exam on a subject after even one term. I decided early on to attempt to "comp out" and abbreviate my four-year college program so I could get back into the wide world sooner.

Meanwhile, money was a problem because as a Canadian, I couldn't work in the U.S. while attending college, and the devalued Canadian dollar was soon worth ten cents less than the American greenback. Fortunately, my parents had offered to help out and when I was identified as an above-average student, Michigan State funded my tuition and out of state fees.

I lived in residence on the third floor of Snyder Hall—three-tier bunk beds, a desk, and a closet to a room. My roommates that first year were a couple of big Americans, Jim Caird and Don King, who'd met in the Navy where Jim had been drafted after taking two years at the college. I slept on the bottom bunk, Jim on the top. With a little more money than I had, they went partying on Saturday nights and often woke me up on their return and read me the newspaper comics; they were the only ones laughing. One night, after they'd come back from a night of drinking and went to sleep, Jim fell out of his bunk with a horrible crash and then left the room. Worried that he was hurt, I started to follow him. Suddenly there was a mighty commotion and a student cried out, "There's somebody in my room and he's pissing all over everything!" Of course, it was Jim, who'd turned left instead of right into the washroom.

The three of us became pals, playing intramural fastball together and going to taverns in East Lansing for the odd beer and on special occasions to Frankenmuth ("Michigan's Little Bavaria"), just northeast, to devour the all-you-can-eat chicken dinners for a dollar at Zehnder's famous Prohibition-era restaurant. The whole gang on our floor at Snyder Hall had lunch and dinner together in the cafeteria, where we snuck extra pats of butter by dropping our plates on them so they'd stick to the bottom, and in the dining room, where we had to wear a jacket and tie—as Jim says, "They were trying to teach us table manners." We had to butt out our cigarettes before dinner and some student paupers collected slightly used tobacco from the ashtrays to roll their own.

My first summer off, after just a few months of college, I went home to earn some money, working for a tobacco farmer sharecropping on Gordon Boyd's land—but mostly to be with Becky, newly graduated from high school. I slept in her brother Earl's room, being a good boy with Becky nearby all night. We had a few sweet months together before she started nurse's training in London and my classes resumed in September. That August, I asked her dad, in the formal way of the time, if I could marry his daughter. With her folks' approval, I became engaged to Becky after three years' courting, buying her a small diamond ring for not much money from a Birks jewellery store.

Back at MSC, with about $600 in my bank account, I was soon in the deep-water swim of things. Between the onslaught of tough new courses and my lovesickness in being away from Becky, I was one unhappy college student. One of my first letters to her that month said it all:

Darling,

I got two letters to-day and it made me feel warm inside to know that you love me and were thinking of me. They really helped and I love you Becky for being so wonderful.

I have piles of homework to do and believe me I really have some hard courses. Physics has got me snowed under already. I guess it means work every night from 8 'till two or I won't pass. I'm afraid I've bitten off more than I can handle. At least I have more to work for than anyone else. Keep loving me dearest and I'll get by somehow. It's a good feeling to have someone to work for that loves and believes in you. . . .

I love you darling and I miss you terribly. I only hope the time flies by until we are really one. Then at last I will be happy.

> *'night Becky,*
> *Yours always,*
> *Harley*

While I later pledged to a fraternity, that environment proved foreign to me, an impoverished farm kid-turned-merchant-mariner. My frat brothers at Sigma Gamma Epsilon were soon telling me, "Harley, you can't afford the time and you can't afford the money—it's not your lifestyle. Get the hell out of here." So I went. Where I did find close friends was by indulging in my lifetime sporting love: hockey.

MICHIGAN STATE HAD NO STERLING HISTORY OF The Game. A team called the Aggies started playing without a coach in 1922 and continued fitfully for the next eight years, with the first matches on the iced-over Red Cedar and later on flooded tennis courts. In a country that had no NHL team until the Boston Bruins formed in 1924, hockey had little public profile and the college didn't recognize it as even a minor athletic endeavour.

After poor weather cancelled the season in 1931, the sport didn't resurface until 1948 when Harold Paulsen was hired as Michigan State's first hockey coach. A short, blond, bespectacled twenty-nine-year-old, he had been a triple All-American player and a member of the University of Minnesota's Golden Gophers, winners of the 1939-40 Amateur Athletic Union championship. His task now was daunting: "You just couldn't get hockey

In 1950, I'm number 9 with the Spartans, made up mostly of raw Michigan players now playing colleges with established hockey programs. Highlights of our road trips will be an invitation from the Montreal Canadiens to their club car on a train—and a visit to London, Ontario, where Becky is becoming a nurse.

players to come here," he later reminisced. "It was pretty sad because we just didn't have the talent."

Among the talentless students he was stuck with was a Canadian named Harley N. Hotchkiss. Paulsen probably thought I was a natural coming from hockey's home and native land. He didn't realize my experience was limited to playing shinny on ponds and rural hockey on outdoor rinks around Straffordville. I'd never even been coached. In skill, I was pretty typical of most of a team that was now known as the Spartans.

A couple of Bills on our squad, who lived in my residence and became my lasting buddies, had played in organized leagues in larger centres. Bill McCormick—who'd grown up in Hagersville, Ontario, an hour from our farm, before moving to Iowa—was our Gordie Howe, if anyone was. A fine skater, stronger and bigger than me, he went on to teach and coach hockey for thirty-six years at Williams, an excellent small college in Williamstown, Massachusetts. Bill Calvert, a smart guy who whipped through the daily crossword puzzles, had played a lot in midget leagues and at his high school in Montreal. His debut hockey game at MSC was a scrimmage on the briefly frozen Red Cedar just before Paulsen put out a first call for players. As Bill describes our fledgling team, "We had pretty good spirit, were pretty close, and played as far as our talent could take us—but we didn't win many games."

The first season, in early 1949, we played only a half-dozen or so exhibitions, to no great effect, The next year, there were eighteen of us, mostly from Michigan, competing in our first regularly scheduled games against colleges with established hockey programs: Michigan Tech and the universities of Michigan, Minnesota, North Dakota, and Western Ontario. "We'll be lucky to win a single game," Paulsen predicted, accurately; we were 0-14 for the season. Playing at centre in the eleven games, I had two goals and two assists and two penalties (I take a little comfort in multiplying my record by the number of games in the team's contemporary schedule, which would make me about a fifteen-goal scorer). If anything, I was merely a middle-of-the-road journeyman on the ice.

Our cause wasn't helped by the fact that Coach Paulsen had to salvage old equipment from the 1920s team, including gloves that were stiff with age. The college did manage to give us uniforms in the MSC colours, green pants and green-and-white sweaters. We provided our own skates and, of course, no one wore helmets in those days. On the other hand, we had a terrific NHL-sized sheet of artificial ice, the first I'd ever played on, created with a dozen miles of piping in the renovated Demonstration Hall. And our own primitive Zamboni: a couple of carts on car tires squirting hot water through towels sweeping the surface. So good was the rink that we had to squeeze in practice time between ice shows, figure skaters working out, and the public hogging the ice. Another drawback was that Dem Hall didn't have either players' washrooms or locker rooms (we had to go across the street to suit up). It did have four thousand seats, often filled for our games by students paying seventy-five cents, even though there were only a few seats with unrestricted views.

One of our road trips took us to play Western in London, where Becky was studying at Victoria Hospital, and she lined up dates with student nurses for the other players after the game. "And then afterwards," she recalls, "we had to use our secret way of sneaking into residence through the basement windows." There was great camaraderie among us Spartans, which may have reached its peak one late night near season's end in Minneapolis. Between games with Minnesota, a group of us were rooming far away from the others in the twin-towered Curtis Hotel and decided the coach wouldn't hear us having a party. We got soused enough to draw up an oath on a piece of paper—"signed in beer and blood," and mostly illegible—that we would all meet again for a reunion in ten years. Which never did happen.

We travelled to out-of-town games by train. Once, on a trip back from Michigan Tech in the north of the state, the Montreal Canadiens were aboard returning from Chicago and invited us to come to their special car. There were the Flying Frenchmen, among then Butch Bouchard, the giant of a defenceman who'd just become captain, replacing coach-to-be Toe Blake, and the legendary Rocket—Maurice Richard, the heart and soul of the Habs, puffing on a fat cigar. (When he died in 2000, I took a red-eye to Montreal for a funeral service I just had to attend, along with 115,000 other people.) Other, more intimate brushes with the greats were shinny practices we had with the Detroit Red Wings when they were displaced by the Ice Capades from their home rink, the Olympia. We traded goalies and other players, among them a new defenceman named Red Kelly, just my age and raised on a tobacco farm near Simcoe, who went on to become a star centre for the Leafs and a member of Parliament (and whom I last saw, half a century later, at my induction to the Hockey Hall of Fame.)

The 1949-50 season was my last with the Spartans. To play in '50-'51 would have affected my course load and delayed my graduation by at least one term. As a kid, I might have dreamed about being a Syl Apps or a Gordie Drillon. The reality is that, while I was a decent enough athlete in young adulthood, I wasn't good enough to go anywhere in hockey. Decades later, when Michigan State generously gave me a Distinguished Hockey Alumnus Award, I know it was because of my later monetary and other contributions to what became a full-fledged university—and not because of any sporting prowess.

I was an onlooker during the 1950-51 season, which was a better one for a team that now included Richard Lord of Montreal, an engineering student who was the first black to play American college hockey. Their 6-11 record still wasn't enough to save Paulsen's job. He was replaced by Amo Bessone, a minor-league pro hockey and baseball player, who would coach for twenty-eight years. It took him the first seven to achieve a winning season and in 1966 the team captured its first national championship. His successor was Ron Mason, who over his twenty-three-year stint made the Spartans one of the most successful hockey clubs in the National Collegiate Athletic Association and earned himself honours as national coach of the year in 1992.

It's interesting to think that I was there on the ice just when the sport got its second wind at Michigan State, in 1949, and slowly began flexing its muscles to become what it is today under current coach Rick Comley: one of the leading hockey programs in the U.S., winning the NCAA championship in 2007, when the college sent me a team championship ring.

I HAD LEFT THE SPARTANS TO PURSUE MY STUDIES, which were increasingly onerous as I tried to cram four years into three and a bit. Among my friends and some professors, I had the reputation of being brainy—perhaps in part simply more well-informed with my solid Ontario high-school education than my American college mates. Jim Caird tells a story about being with me in a little tavern just outside East Lansing that had a machine dispensing trivia quizzes: "I never beat you at answering the questions, Harley; it was very frustrating." Yet he also recalls that he never saw me study, suspecting I must have cracked the books while he and Don were having their nights out. In fact, it felt as if I was studying tough courses like calculus around the clock. The atmosphere on campus was changing too, becoming more serious as American students realized they could be drafted for the Korean War when it flared up in 1950 and the U.S. and countries within the newly created United Nations, including Canada, came to the aid of South Korea.

As I delved deeper into my major, the courses grew more complex and the textbooks—*Principles of Petroleum Geology, A Descriptive Petrography of the Igneous Rocks*—more challenging. I was loaded up with math, physics, and lab work. The most difficult class was micropaleontology, where we studied hundreds of tiny fossils under a microscope and had to memorize their makeup—how many whorls on the septum and other minutiae. The complexity of this field of science can be read in the specialties pursued by my professors. Dr. Gustaf Bergquist was head of the geology department and specialized in glacial geology and geomorphology (the nature and history of the landforms on the surface), Dr. William Kelly taught paleontology (fossilized forms of life existing in prehistoric or geologic times) and structural, sedimentary, and petroleum geology. We had a female professor, Jane E. Smith, teaching introductory and historical geology courses; Justin Zinn and Bennett Sandefur on petrography, petrology, and crystallography (study of crystal structure by x-ray diffraction techniques), and Jim Trow, fresh out of university, focusing on structural geology (the processes that deform the earth's crust and create mountains). More than half a century later, you can still find their names on scientific papers on the Internet.

At the time, I found the whole field interesting because it had more uncertainty about it, left more room for the imagination, than a cut-and-dried technical discipline like engineering. As a geologist, you hope to get a three-dimensional picture of what happened and is happening underground and try to grasp the challenging notion of the eons of time that constitute the planet's history.

But, in truth, I was not particularly passionate about geology. Nor sure of what I wanted to do with my degree. Going into the infant Canadian oil and gas industry—just a couple of years after the seminal gusher at Leduc, Alberta—wasn't particularly alluring. My textbooks told me that Canada had only 0.22 per cent of the world petroleum reserves while the U.S. had 31 per cent. Mining seemed more attractive, partly because of the encouragement of Professor William Alton Kelly. He was a demanding paleontologist from Edmonton who took an interest in me, a fellow Canadian, and wrote a nice letter of recommendation when I applied for work with the Ontario Department of Mines during my second college summer.

I went with field parties into the rugged bushland of northern Ontario on the Canadian Shield. Seven of us students led by a University of Toronto professor did geological mapping where uranium had been found at Theano Point on Lake Superior. Carrying Geiger counters to measure radiation and the famous Brunton compasses to make accurate degree and angle measurements, we paced out certain distances and then took rock samples. After a month there, I joined a tough-as-nails geologist in his sixties, Bill Harding, and a quiet Cambridge University grad doing his PhD in geochemistry, Denis Shaw (later chair of the geology department and dean of graduate studies at McMaster University). We had to map the area around a new road being cut from Thessalon on the north shore of Lake Huron to Chapleau. Though tourists came to fish and swim in the wilderness lakes, this was lonely country. We were amid the Peshu Lake area in the Algoma district, where over three months in the spring and summer before, a forest fire had destroyed 323,000 acres, with its smoke seen as far away as Chicago. We cooked our own meals and washed our own clothes—as I did one day in the lake and left soapy water that Bill Harding scooped out to drink. He was as angry as a southern Ontario tornado.

About halfway to Chapleau, I developed a bad pain in a wisdom tooth and drove seventy rough miles to find a dentist in the town. A local said there was a "boy" looking after the regular dentist's office. He turned out to be Roy Rasmussen from Standard, Alberta, just graduated in dentistry from the University of Toronto. Two years later when I came to Calgary, I was in the company doctor's office for a medical, looked in another room, and saw a familiar face. When I asked a nurse if this dentist had ever practised in Chapleau, she said No—but he overheard me and said, "Hey, I pulled your tooth!" I went to Dr. Roy Rasmussen for more than forty years until he retired.

I wrote Becky July 18 to explain the mapping work I was doing in that blackened landscape:

We have a new jeep truck and we loaded it up and left Thessalon about 11 o'clock Thursday morning. There are three of us—Dr. Harding, Denis Shaw (who came with me from the other party) & myself. We came up the Mississaga road & it was a deuce of a mess. We came up about 70 miles & it took us 6 hours. We are camped now near a forestry station & it isn't nearly as nice as our old camp. We have no cabin & it's in the area burned out last year so looks rather bleak. It is hot too with no forest and dirty with all the ashes around. We have to map an area from Chapleau to Thessalon (about 160 miles). We are about halfway now & will be around here for a couple weeks & then go back to Thessalon for more supplies...

In the afternoon we started out to map the shore geology of this lake we are near. It turned out to be bigger than we expected; we were in a canoe & it was about 10 miles around so we didn't get back until after 6. By the time we made supper & got the dishes done it was late & I crawled into bed pretty tired. We neglected to bring any lamps or candles so when it gets dark we just have to go to bed.

Being away from Becky over the summer as well as most of the college year was a test of our relationship. I thought nothing of leaving from East Lansing after my last course on a Friday afternoon, getting out to the highway, and sticking out my thumb to hitch a ride to London. I always carried a little suitcase bearing a big Michigan State sticker. One farmer who

Becky and I at lakeside one sweet summer when I'm not at college or in the bush earning money for my tuition. Being on a see-saw is a pretty good symbol of my emotions,
going up and down, as I write letters of longing, hoping that she still cares for me.

stopped told me to put my case in his trunk, which held a crateful of chickens. When he let me off, I opened the trunk and half the hens flew out; I spent an hour helping corral them again. Another farmer dumped me along a cold, lonely, unlit road outside of Sarnia, Ontario. When none of the rare passing cars even saw me in the night, I stepped out into the middle of the road and waved the next vehicle down. When it stopped, I ran and jumped in the back seat, saying, "Boy, thanks a lot!"

Then I realized it was an Ontario Provincial Police car. "What are you doing here?" one of the two constables demanded.

I quickly explained: just a student, travelling all the way from Michigan, trying to get home to see his girl.

They laughed and drove me twenty miles to the end of their patrol area, where they pulled off and doused their headlights. We waited fifteen minutes before a car came speeding in my direction, and they turned their flashers on. The rattled driver stopped and, when the police told him a student needed a ride to London, he delivered me right to Becky's doorstep.

The many weekends I couldn't get back to her prompted plaintive letters: "You never said what you did Saturday night Becky. I get so jealous at times—not as much as I used to but I love you and I guess I just want to know everything you do. . . . Don't forget all your promises darling and please do tell me everything. I hate to get that feeling that you are keeping something from me."

These were just the romantic jitters of a young man, too far away from home and the girl he loved. Becky, meanwhile, was having her own concerns—not about our commitment to one another but about the sheer drudgery of her nursing studies. In another letter, I reflected her worries: "You sounded pretty sick of it all and I guess it is monotonous and a lot of hard work. I'm sorry things aren't going so well but I'm sure it's all over by now. I feel pretty miserable at times too & I know it's because I'm so far from you."

Like her, I was being weighed down by my course load and—as the months passed—my desire to complete college as soon as I could. Part of me had wanted to get a graduate degree. In the fall of 1949, I was on the Dean's Honour Roll with an A in every subject and went for a celebratory dinner with the progressive college president, John Hannah.

The summer of 1950 before my last year at college, I was in the bush again for the Ontario Department of Mines in an area of the Eastern Counties so noted for its fascinating and varied mineral occurrences that it was like nature's textbook on mineralization. A half-dozen of us were led by Don Hewitt, a department geologist who later wrote important papers and books on Ontario rocks and minerals. We were mapping Lyndoch Township in Renfrew county northeast of Bancroft. An intriguing igneous rock called pegmatite presented a whole suite of minerals, including beryl of which emeralds and aquamarines are composed. It was a good summer: we stayed in an old wood camp building and went for meat-and-potatoes dinners made by a nice old woman, Mrs. Quade, in a nearby village called Quadeville. Black bear abounded in some areas, but never bothered us. One day, I did come face to face with a moose that charged me.

My brief stint in the Merchant Marine had given me my fill of the sea. Here, tramping the woods and paddling the lakes, I was out in the open, amid nature, where I belonged. While learning some on-the-ground basics about geology, I wasn't working too hard or too long. We ate well—often steaks—and I could catch a dozen speckled trout in one outing. As I reported in a letter to my family, "They sure use us well."

Coming back to college, I was being urged by some professors to apply for a fellowship to get my master's in geology. Encouraged, I applied to several universities and among those that replied favourably were Columbia, Louisiana State, and Michigan, which had a prominent hard-rock geologist, Dr. Abe Heinrich, a specialist in pegmatite. Maybe I could attend U of M, only an hour away in Ann Arbor, and do my thesis on this mineral assembly that interested both of us. In the end, I was offered a fellowship there as well as getting the promise of a job for the following summer with the Department of Mines in the same Lyndoch Township area I'd been mapping. My path was all set: I would earn my advanced degree starting in 1951 and later go to work in the mining industry.

Yet, assured as my future seemed, I was torn: Becky would be finished nursing in the fall of '51 and I'd still be in college. And I was frankly sick and tired of scrimping along through school on a summer's wages. That's when I wrote the letter that changed my life irrevocably.

Much as mining attracted me, my fellow students were more interested in the petroleum industry, which was burgeoning in the U.S. While I'd read about the 1947 Leduc discovery in Alberta, the jobs being posted in MSC's geology department were all with American companies. Classmates in my final year were going down the alphabetical list and firing off letters of application. One Sunday evening in January 1951, I sat there thinking, *Well, why don't I try too?* It was almost a whim. Using a borrowed typewriter, I hunted-and-pecked out two letters detailing my good marks and the summer experience that loomed very large on a resumé. I addressed them to Shell Oil, which had a service station back in Straffordville, and Superior Oil of California, which sounded kind of romantic. I took the mail to a campus postbox that same night.

Three evenings later, I had what purported to be a phone call from Western Union in Lansing. The fellow calling read the telegram to me: "Mr. Feldmeyer or Mr. Jones from Calgary will contact you regarding possible job. Signed John T. Isberg, Chief Geologist, Superior Oil Company."

In my last term, I had another roommate, a geology student named Tim Monaghan, an Irish liquor-salesman's son who'd served in the U.S. Navy's aviation branch before entering college in 1947. When I introduced him to the world of hockey, he became a fervent fan and we became as close as brothers. He was a very funny guy, fond of practical jokes. Well, given the speed with which Superior had seemed to reply, I was now sure this was just another one of Tim's pranks. He was pulling my leg and I wasn't going to give him the satisfaction of even mentioning the call. But—*wait a minute*—he could never keep a straight face after playing a joke and this time he was as silent about the wire as I was. A day or two later, I thought, *Maybe it was real, after all*. I called Western Union and asked if they could trace the telegram and see where it came from. They could: it had originated in Los Angeles, which was Superior's headquarters.

On Saturday, the follow-up phone call came—from Art Feldmeyer, president of *Canadian* Superior Oil of California, based in Calgary, a 100-percent subsidiary of the American parent. He said Jack Isberg had forwarded my application. "Are you still interested in a job?"

"Well, you know, Mr. Feldmeyer, I am, but I've sort of set another course."

My little whim had suddenly turned concrete. After we talked a little, and I didn't give him a definite No, he decided: "I'll come down and interview you."

When he showed up at my residence, it was one of those miserable Michigan January days, raw cold and snowy, and the airline had lost his luggage. Art, a geologist from California who'd worked around the world for Superior, was a small man in his late thirties, prematurely bald, methodical and slow-talking—he's been described in print as taciturn. Yet he was quietly positive in the two or three hours of our interview in the cafeteria of Snyder Hall, asking me lots of questions about my courses and summer work and showing me a map of the company's holdings in Manitoba, Saskatchewan, and Alberta, where Superior had offices in Edmonton and Calgary.

"We're an active company, just nicely getting started in Canada," he said after a couple of hours, "and we'd like you to join us as a geologist working out of our Calgary office."

"That's exciting and I'm interested, but I need some time because I have these other commitments and have to reflect on this—it's a total change in direction. Can you give me a week?"

The first thing I did after he left was phone Becky in London. She didn't know I'd made those job applications out of the blue. "You're not going to believe this," I told her, "it's $325 a month"—which was a nice starting salary at the time. The more we talked, and she gave me her blessing, the more I was definite: "I'm going to do it."

I called Calgary the next morning: "Mr. Feldmeyer, I'm coming to work for you." After committing myself to Becky and going back to school, this was the third momentous decision I made since coming home from the sea.

On March 30, 1951, I graduated from Michigan State College with a bachelor of science degree in geology and high honours, which made me a member of Kappa Sigma Phi, a national honorary fraternity for students "of high scholarship, fine character, and good fellowship."

The next day, I got on a plane and flew back to Canada, to pick up my clothes at home—and a day later to Calgary, a city I'd never seen.

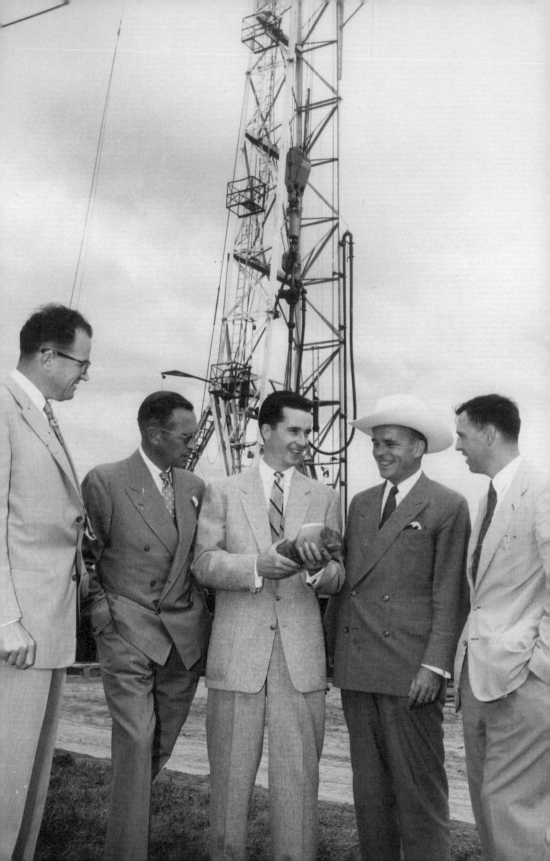

CHAPTER 4

INTO THE OIL PATCH

*Canadian Superior and
the Canadian Bank of Commerce*

ALGARY, ALBERTA, APRIL FOOL'S DAY—AND WAS
I the fool? Away from Becky and my Ontario roots yet again, I
was in a city ringed by unfamiliar cattle ranches and wheat fields,
the home of the thirty-nine-year-old Calgary Stampede. I had
explored the teeming streets of New York and Toronto, visited places like
Barranquilla and Montreal, where people might as well have been speaking
in tongues. This city had a population of 120,000 and its most exotic offer-
ings were the shops and restaurants of a compact Chinatown. Until 1950,
the Stampede parade had always honoured "the first white woman in the
West"—not till late in the decade would a Chinese-Canadian girl be chosen
as Miss Stampede. The most dominant group of immigrants in 1951 were
Americans, like the ones I'd come to know at college, lured here by the rich
promise of the Leduc gusher four years earlier. Calgary was a feisty little city,
feeling its oats, but it was still raw around the edges, still living with its well-
earned label of Cowtown—epitomized by the Calgarian who rode horseback
through Toronto's Royal York Hotel during the '48 Grey Cup celebrations.

The day after I arrived, a north wind was blowing along 8th Avenue
West. No Calgary Tower or any oil-company headquarters loomed (the first
skyscraper, the Elveden Centre, would go up in 1960). The street was lined
with low-rise buildings, some of them sandstone beauties dating back to the
nineteenth century. But as I walked from the Palliser Hotel, the gravel dust

Resettling in Calgary, I was into my second job there in 1955, this time as a geologist
in the Canadian Bank of Commerce's oil and gas department. I'm surrounded here by
regional superintendent Keith Smith, senior vice-president Page Wadsworth, president Neil McKinnon, and director Don Harvie.

on the springtime sidewalks whipped my face. It felt like the North Pole, like the end of the world.

I'd arrived on a Sunday, after flying from London to Toronto aboard a Trans-Canada Air Lines DC-3 (my first commercial-aircraft flight) and then on to Calgary on a DC-4M. The four-propellor North Star seemed to stop everywhere in between and I fell asleep, only to wake in the dark over the prairies and gaze out the window—to see what looked like a red-hot flame streaming from the wing. *Migod, my first long flight and we're on fire!* Stifling my urge to summon the stewardess, I sat there worried until finally realizing that it was simply exhaust from the engines glowing in the night. We landed uneventfully beside Calgary's old Quonset-hut terminal, where an office boy from Canadian Superior picked me up and drove me to the hotel.

Monday morning, I walked 8th Avenue through the blustery morning to the Rio Building, christened for my new employer's original company name in Canada, Rio Bravo. The offices were in a third-floor walkup. I met Art Feldmeyer again and he introduced me to Burnett Jones, the chief geologist, an Australian in his mid-thirties with a craggy, weather-beaten face and, as I'd discover, a heart of beaten gold. Burnie showed me around the place and had me meet the other geologists, all of them a little older than me, most of them westerners, many of whom would become my long-term friends. Wilf Loucks and Keith Laatsch, both from Saskatchewan, Gordon Hargreaves and Mac Love from Alberta. George Lamont was a fellow Ontarian of Irish stock, a wiry older guy who'd been in the mining business before returning to petroleum geology. Bill MacDonald (who I still bump into on the streets of Calgary) was the senior geologist, studying drill cuttings to determine the type and age of rock samples. In the first couple of weeks, I spent a lot of time with him peeking through a microscope.

I'd learn that our parent, Superior Oil, was on its way to becoming one of the largest petroleum producers in the U.S. Controlled by the William Keck family in California, it and another independent had built the first offshore oil platform off the Gulf Coast of Louisiana, in 1938. Superior had started as a drilling company in the Twenties, and that side of the business was always important—Barney Barnett, who oversaw the Canadian drilling, reported directly to the Kecks. Otherwise, Art Feldmeyer could run his own domestic show, deciding which wells to drill and which to farm out, though he kept in constant communication with his American counterparts.

Compared to giants like Imperial Oil and Mobil Oil, Canadian Superior—operating in Canada since the mid-1940s—was relatively modest. It had four western offices, with headquarters in Calgary, which along with geologists and the top brass had such support staff as accountants. The head of drilling and the chief engineer and landman, as well as legal people, were based in a drilling and production office in Edmonton. And there were branches in Regina and Virden, Manitoba, where the company had considerable freehold lease properties (controlled by private parties, not the Crown). In Alberta, it was enjoying some early success northwest of Calgary in the Crossfield area and northeast of Edmonton in the Excelsior field.

On my second day, I got out into the dramatically different countryside, past cattle ruminating along the Bow River (named not for its meandering course from Banff National Park but for the bow reeds that grow on its banks). Burnie Jones was taking me to see my first well, near Didsbury, a forty-minute drive northwest of Calgary. It was just a stone's throw from the foothills of the Rocky Mountains I'd seen from the city looming on the horizon, those massive sedimentary layers that had made up the old sea bottom, some of them more than four hundred million years ago.

George Lamont was the geologist on this wellsite just being drilled. He and Burnie introduced me to a rig, that complicated-looking mass of machinery ranging from a derrick and a big string of drill pipe to all the pumps and paraphernalia used to sink a wellbore. On the rig floor, I looked at the samples of the rock that the drill bit was chewing through and went into George's trailer as he peered through a microscope to determine how porous the rocks were and whether there were any oil and gas shows. It was one of the first wells in the area and though it didn't amount to anything, hundreds more have been successfully drilled in that area since.

Interesting as all this was, back in town I was concerned about finding a room to bunk in. The day before, I'd picked up my first copy of the *Calgary Herald*. The front page said 6,000 Canadian troops would soon be going into battle in the Korean War, while Canadian-American relations were at low ebb after External Affairs Minister Lester Pearson criticized American generals for suggesting the use of an atomic bomb against Chinese Communist troops. The main story was about the Canadian Air Force's bombing of an ice jam on the South Saskatchewan River near Medicine Hat. And on the sports page, I noted my team, the Maple Leafs, and the Boston Bruins were even with one win each and one game tied in their Stanley Cup semi-finals (the Leafs went on to take the Cup from the Montreal Canadiens four games to one).

I checked out local department-store ads—men's sport shirts $2.99, all-wool blankets $3.99—and the features playing at the fifteen movie theatres (the Hitchin' Post on 8th Avenue East had *Kangaroo Kid*, a cowboy film set in Australia). But I was most interested in combing the classified section to find somewhere to stay before bringing Becky to join me in a few months as my bride. I could get a furnished basement bedsitting room and kitchen

Downtown Calgary, early 1950s: the Bank of Montreal and Hudson's Bay at opposite corners of 8ᵗʰ Avenue and Iˢᵗ Street Southwest.

and share a bath for $30 a month or a nicer-sounding three-room suite with toilet and shower—but no, that was for "abstainers only". In the end, after a couple of weeks in the Palliser, I took a room in a boarding house in the Sunalta area south of downtown. Sitting there at night, I wondered what I'd got myself into here. *Is this where I really want to be? Is this the work I want to do? Should I go back to school and become a doctor or something?* All the insecurities of being in a new place away from friends and family. And Becky.

Not long after, I ran into a Tillsonburg high-school friend on the street, the son of a doctor from Langton, who had delivered Becky. Bruce Nicholson had a room in a house in the Hillhurst area (just north of the Bow River cutting through the downtown)—why didn't I share it with him and we'd both save some money? He also had a girlfriend's car we could use. The only problem with Bruce, who didn't have steady work, was his habit of waiting until I went to work and then borrowing my clothes to wear.

On the job, I was soon sharing an office with another newcomer about my age, George McLeod, a real pick-and-shovel geologist trained at the University of Saskatchewan. He was a city boy from Saskatoon freshly married to Betty, a farm girl, and they would become close friends with Becky and me. In those early days, he and I trained under Bill MacDonald, who was a dozen years older. George still says Bill is "one of the best sedimentary geologists—sample examiners and interpreters—that I've ever known. He has a mind like a steel trap." (Now in his early nineties, Bill goes out to work every day as an independent consultant.) George had worked two summers during college for the revered Jack Porter in the company's Regina office. Reminiscing, he says, "If the world was full of Jack Porters, it would be a marvellous place to be. And he was an absolute mine of geological knowledge of the western Canada Basin." I came to know Jack as a thoughtful and intelligent chief geologist and later, when he moved to Calgary, as a friend.

In July, I got to sit on my first well as a geologist, helping log its drilling progress at a site near Clive in central Alberta. This was a British American (BA)/Cities Service play, in which Canadian Superior had a small interest. It turned out to be the discovery well that then led to a significant pool of oil, the Clive D-2 field. Meanwhile, our company had found its own discovery well at New Norway, about forty miles northeast, where the wellsite geologist was Lloyd Bebensee, another Ontario guy. Working out of the Edmon-

Lloyd Bebensee

ton office, he was senior to me in the company by a year and so had the use of a sleep-and-work trailer that I had to share. We soon learned that our girlfriends—his was Elaine, whom he'd marry—were both in nurse's training at Victoria Hospital in London and had found out by sheer chance that their men were working for the same company in the same neck of the woods across the country.

The area around Clive is parkland, well-treed and with good soil for farming. Because this was the first well drilled locally, farmers would drive over on a Sunday to talk about prospects. Being a young guy, I felt pretty important answering their questions. My colleagues and I sometimes drove into Clive, a typical one-horse prairie village, to have a beer in the hotel where I occasionally stayed overnight to avoid driving to the trailer. Lloyd and I had to report every morning to our office by phone from there. Driving like hell from opposite directions in our company Chevrolets, we sometimes met coming up over a hill—it's a wonder we didn't kill ourselves. Reports done, we might have breakfast and sneak off for a game of pool.

That was the beginning of a beautiful friendship. He was a quiet, reserved guy from a big, fatherless family so poor that he and his brothers pinched diesel fuel from road graders to light their coal-oil lamps. Eventually he moved to the Calgary office and we became best friends, buying recreational land to share and even working together in two of the companies I'd one day launch. He was a much better geologist than me, and stubborn as a goat, but that didn't stop me from arguing with him about anything in our business.

During those early days, I was mightily impressed by the fact that both of us had sat on discovery wells and witnessed oil flowing time after time after time. I thought, *Man, there's nothing to this business*. That's how naive I was. Over the next few months, Art made me geologist-in-charge of the company's Peace River region in northwest Alberta. I kept track of who was drilling where, studied the drilling logs, and mapped the area for oil and gas prospects. There were only a few wells drilled there and no production of significance.

AUTUMN COULDN'T COME SOON ENOUGH. BECKY AND I had planned our wedding for October 3 in Simcoe. We hadn't seen one another in six months, communicating by phone and letter as she graduated from nursing and I was busy launching my career. On the night I was to fly home, my fellow geologists decided to throw a bachelor party in Calgary. Burnie Jones advised me, "Hotch, they're going to try to get you really drunk. Why don't you come over to our house for dinner first?"

Well, he was part of the conspiracy. Everybody was there, determined to liquor me up and send me off in grand stag-party style. They were so successful that Burnie had to get on the Trans-Canada plane (in that era of relaxed security) and tell the pilot: " You've got a young guy here who works for me. He's important, and I want you to make damned sure you get him home all right—he's getting married."

It was a long haul with many pit stops, and I was badly hung over. Transferring in Toronto to a rough, low-level flight to London worsened my natural motion sickness. When Becky met me at the airport in a new Chevy my folks had bought for us, I hardly said hello before crawling into the back seat. Reflecting today, she says ironically, "I thought this was a real nice homecoming after all those months away." But she adds, "The wedding was fabulous." It was a sparkling fall day, with the leaves turning

Becky, the graduate nurse

Becky, my bride in her long, flowing wedding gown, with her parents, Gordon and Marion Boyd (at left), and my folks, Carrie and Morley Hotchkiss.

hues, as we were wed in the handsome old St. James United Church. Becky's school-teacher sister, Eileen, and a nursing-student friend were bridesmaids and Gene Walsh's sister-in-law, Pat Gracey, was the maid of honour. My nephew Paul Hotchkiss was my best man. My new bride's family gave us $1,000 her grandfather had left in his will. We spent a bit on a couple of nights' honeymoon in—where else but that classic Canadian destination?—Niagara Falls. ("I don't remember much about that," Becky says now.)

We returned to her parents' place and became the victims of a shivaree, an Ontario tradition to wake up a newlywed couple with a hullabaloo of noise and joking. My orangutan friends from Straffordville arrived in the middle of the night banging on washtubs and firing shotguns into the sky till we got up and handed out cigars to the celebrants.

A couple of days later, Becky and I drove off to Calgary. "That was a very difficult time, leaving my parents," she remembers. "I'd never been anywhere but London, Ontario. Calgary was a big city to me. Being with all these strangers was difficult to adapt to, but everybody at Canadian Superior was in the same situation." My boss's wife, Jean Feldmeyer, befriended Becky, even showing her how to make pies. We'd settled into a pleasant little basement suite rented from a single mom with twin daughters in the Rosedale neighbourhood on the city's North Hill.

We stayed there for our first couple of years, through two of Becky's pregnancies—which meant that she never did have a chance to practise nursing. Our eldest, Paul Gordon, arrived in June 1952, nearly nine months to the day of our honeymoon. The Canadian philosopher Thomas Haliburton talks about "the smile that lights on the firstborn babe, and assures it of a mother's love." Becky says more simply, "your firstborn is always special." I saw Paul in Holy Cross Hospital a couple of times, marvelling at his littleness and fuzz of red hair, before bringing Burnie Jones to view our son. When a nurse brought a swaddled infant out from the nursery and we stared at him for a few minutes, I was thinking to myself, *Whoa! What's happened to Paul? This baby has long, straight black hair!* It turned out she'd picked up a native child with a similar last name on its wrist tag.

Paul proved to be a good babe in arms—at least, that's what his mother tells me. A month after his birth, I was sent on a six-week field trip into the mountains around Jasper. As Becky reminded me, "That was one of the most difficult times. That's when our friends came into play; they remain our closest friends today." Most of them were my workmates and their wives.

IT WAS FORTUNATE THAT CANADIAN SUPERIOR PEOPLE filled in for me while the company dispatched the new dad into the mountains. Earlier that summer of 1952, I'd still been the site geologist as we drilled on our own land near the Clive discovery well that BA / Cities Service had found. We'd seen the same oil at the D-2 level, named for Devonian-age carbonates (from 360 to 415 million years ago)—limestone and dolomite, the calcium and magnesium carbonate sedimentary rocks where petroleum often shows up in porous reefs. Drilling superintendent Barney Barnett said we should go down to the next level, the D-3 pool.

"Oh, Barney, I think we're wasting our money," I said.

"Well," he replied, "it's only a few feet; let's do it."

"Fine, but I don't think it's going to do any good."

When we cut a core in the well and took some rock samples, the D-3 was porous with what we called "vugs" (cavities in a rock) and was bleeding some oil, but there was also saltwater, which confused things. We decided to test for the presence of hydrocarbons and ran a flare line from the rig to a flare pit with a bucket of burning diesel-soaked rags to ignite if any petroleum showed up. A group of us were sitting around this pit, chatting and waiting for results. All of a sudden a gusher of sludge erupted and then exploded with a big cloud of black smoke, knocking us all over backwards—ass over teakettle, as they say. It proved to be an even more important discovery well, the Clive D-3 pool.

Again, I thought, *this is pretty easy stuff.* And even at this early stage, I started to wonder, *What does all this mean? What rate will the well produce at? How much will it cost to operate it? And what kind of money will it make?* My mind was already moving me from pure geologist to the business side of the petroleum game.

Meanwhile, I was learning plenty about the technical side of things, mostly from a minor mechanical genius named Bill Brown. He later became a topnotch drilling superintendent for the company, even patenting an innovation to reduce the amount of mud used while drilling a well (the mix of water or oil distillate and heavy minerals circulates down a drill pipe to cool and lubricate the bit and control the well pressure and bring up the drill cuttings—samples of the rock). A Texan who'd fought in the Second World War, Brownie was a toolpush, the rig manager, who invited me—the young newlywed—to barbecues with his wife and kids and played fastball with me using gloves I brought to the wellsite. During a slow patch of drilling, he and I hunted ducks on the sloughs around the rig and drove into the countryside, where he sometimes shot pheasants and partridge right out of his driver's-side window while I grabbed the steering wheel.

This relaxed state of affairs ended after Paul's birth when I was sent to train in field geology. The idea was to sample and measure rocks exposed up in the mountains and try to correlate them with geologically equivalent rocks drilled into on the prairies. I met up with Gord Hargreaves in Jasper, where his father was an outfitter, supplying equipment for hunting and fishing expeditions. The four in our party had twenty-two horses to ride and to tote our food and gear for six weeks; mine was the steady and reliable Jack, the same name as Gord's dad. A big horse named Dumbo carried the sheet-metal cook stove. Russ Cooper was the horse wrangler and his sister, Lillian, the cook. Our pack train travelled northwest through Jasper National Park's high, ragged ranges, starting at the Snake Indian River and crossing the Smoky River into British Columbia, past spots along the trail that white men had christened Little Heaven and Twin Tree Lake.

Setting up our tents, Gord and I worked in both directions from the camp, climbing peaks all morning like mountain goats, lunching on the heights, and then descending while we measured rocks and collected samples. It was summer, but in August we suffered a few snow squalls and in September even more. I nearly froze to death. An Ontario dude, I'd asked Jack Hargreaves if I should pack along a heavy Mackinaw. "Laddie," he'd said, "you don't need that coat." As it turned out, I had to walk behind my horse, holding his tail, just to keep warm, and pile horse blankets on my sleeping bag in the tent at night. Every few days, I braved the icy mountain streams to bathe.

There were wild animals around, including grizzlies that spooked our horses, but the only group of people we saw was an Alberta-based field party from California Standard coming out with bad news. One of their group, a wrangler on a horse fording the big Smoky near a whirlpool, had been swept away to his death. We carefully crossed at that same place in an old rowboat. That's when we met the only other person during our six-week expedition, a trapper in a rough cabin bearing a sign with a skull and crossbones, "Beware All Men." He was warning intruders to stay clear of his trapline. When we invited him over for some whiskey, he complained that his last season's trapping had been okay, but he had too much company. It seemed that another trapper forty miles away had visited him for Christmas and they'd quarrelled.

Working so closely together over those weeks, Gord and I got a little testy with one another. At one point we were running out of fresh food, eating pancakes for breakfast and pancake sandwiches for lunch while he was holding on to a canned ham to take back to his mother.

"Gordon," I said, "we've *got* to eat that."

He walked angrily out of the tent, purposely bumping me, and then strode ahead, trying to out-march me up the mountain. Both mad as hell, we moved so fast that we walked out our exasperation. On that trip, we did manage to shoot deer, caribou, and mountain goat for their meat—even though Gord had annoyed me by bringing along only a .30-.30 open-sight rifle and seventeen short-range bullets.

Being so deep into that high country was an adventure I would experience only once more, at the end of the decade, when I went hunting there with Russ Cooper. The ruggedness of its ridges and peaks, the wild glory of its valleys, its sheer majesty stay vivid in my memory to this day.

Back home again, I continued to oversee the Peace River area for the company. As the winter passed into spring, I was faced with the prospect of another mouth to feed. Becky was expecting our second child and we had to find a bigger place to live. Wanting to buy this time, we committed to a 920-square-foot, three-bedroom, single-bathroom wood-frame bungalow for $9,200 in Altadore, a new residential subdivision of stuccoed one-storeys ris-

Doing field geology through the peaks of Jasper National Park and into British Columbia, I bagged a mountain goat for meat on our expedition.

ing in southwest Calgary, bordered on the east by the Elbow River. It wasn't ready to move into yet, so we had to rent two temporary quarters during the summer of 1953, once camping in the house of a soldier who was away for a few weeks. It was a worrisome time because a polio epidemic had broken out across Canada and a woman on the next street over had died of the disease—and here was Becky pregnant. She delivered our first and only daughter on September 13, three weeks prematurely. Brenda Elizabeth was all of five pounds, but very soon this lovable small being was flashing us a big smile that her mom still says is just like mine.

When we did move to Altadore at month's end, there was a big fancy stove in the kitchen but no furniture for the living room, and the streets and sidewalks weren't in yet. I had to walk through a couple of blocks of mud to reach our house, which had no eavestroughs or fencing. George and Betty McLeod, who lived a couple of blocks from us, nearly lost their three-year-old daughter when she sank into the mire up to her thighs. Luckily, we were surrounded by Canadian Superior people and other (small-"s") superior neighbours who collaborated to pour cement, build fences, and help create a tight-knit community over the next four years. The old saying about good fences making good neighbours should be changed to "good neighbours make good fences—together."

A beaming Paul was our first-born, here at two years old in the arms of a pleased mom in the yard of our basement suite in Rosedale.

TO BUY OUR FIRST HOME, WE HAD TO BORROW PART of the $2,700 down payment.

The only financial institution I'd known was the Canadian Bank of Commerce, in the hamlet of Straffordville, where my father and brother dealt. In Calgary, I opened an account at a branch across the street from Canadian Superior's office and got to know the manager, Jack Williamson. He became a wonderful friend, one of those guys who didn't bank by the book; if he liked and believed in you, he'd go to bat on your behalf. I was only twenty-six, working for a still-modest monthly salary of $400, with a wife and a kid and another one in the hopper.

One day, in the course of our dealings, Jack surprised me by asking, out of the blue, "Would you ever be interested in working in the oil department of the Commerce?" The bank had one of the first dedicated oil and gas departments to serve the fledgling Canadian industry.

"Well, Jack, I hadn't thought of it. I don't think so. Although I'm always kind of interested in the business side."

"At least go down and talk to Keith Smith," he urged. K.B. Smith, the bank's regional superintendent.

I went for an interview with him—and he offered me a job as the geologist in the Petroleum and Natural Gas Department.

Harley Norman really had to debate with himself. I was happy at Canadian Superior, a fine organization with a good spirit—and there was a future for me there. Yet I *was* one of the last hires in its four offices; a lot of capable people loomed ahead of me in the pecking order. And I was forever pondering the economics of petroleum. *If you have a 100-barrel-a-day well, and the price of oil is $2.50 a barrel, labour costs you so many dollars, and the provincial royalties are ten per cent, what do you end up with?* That sort of thinking about the financial implications intrigued me, perhaps more than the fundamentals of geology. And there was an element of the proposed job being a bit more high-profile, even glamorous.

Canadian Superior proved to be a good home and launching pad for talented people. Some of them stayed for many years or their whole careers. Fair-minded Art Feldmeyer would remain president until his retirement in the late 1970s. Mobil Canada's respected Arne Nielsen succeeded him and then rejoined his former company—while retaining his presidency of Canadian Superior—when Mobil Oil in the U.S. bought Superior Oil of California in 1984. Ten years later, Nielsen retired.

In 1953, my great friend George McLeod left to work for an Alberta drilling contractor and eventually a private, Oklahoma-based company called Samedan Oil. He became president and later headed its parent, Noble Affiliates, a mighty successful petroleum exploration and drilling enterprise that was one of the first independent producers to explore in the Gulf of Mexico.

I left Canadian Superior just a couple of months after George. My timing was good. By mid-decade, Alberta—led by the solid, business-oriented Social Credit government of Premier Ernest Manning—would celebrate its fiftieth anniversary on a wave of optimism fuelled by the petroleum boom. (Reflecting the premier's Prophetic Bible Institute background, an Alberta farm woman told *Time* magazine, "God knew that Mr. Manning would use the oil wisely, so He let it be discovered.")

The Canadian industry had exploded since 1947, when only 331 oil wells were being explored and developed; by 1955 there were 2,935, and crude oil had supplanted coal as Canada's prime source of energy. While natural gas was found in Alberta as early as 1904, large new fields like Crossfield and Carstairs were being discovered and TransCanada was building a pipeline to transport gas to eastern Canada. About the same time, the Syncrude Canada consortium of four majors received their first oil sands leases at Fort McMurray and the Geological Survey of Canada issued a study that suggested Canada's Arctic Islands were a possible site of petroleum reserves.

And twenty-six-year-old Harley Hotchkiss was working in the throbbing heart of the Canadian oil boom's capital—Centre Street and 8th Avenue—for a major national bank. My immediate boss in the oil and gas department was C.H. Munro—Cec, a career banker from small-town Manitoba who'd joined the Commerce right out of high school and had become manager of the new department shortly before I came on. The Canadian banks, the Royal in particular, were just realizing the potential of the industry, and the Commerce wanted to portray itself as a progressive institution to attract newly flush clients.

Cec Munro (middle), the head of the Commerce's oil and gas department, is on a well-site with me (at left) and a workmate in 1955.

Even though I had only a few years in the business, I could talk its language. My role was to evaluate the quality of assets, the anticipated petroleum production, that clients offered as collateral for loans. If a client was defaulting, the bank could theoretically seize his operating properties. It was probably a job more suited to a reservoir engineer than a geologist, but I had my science degree and a fairly good background in the kinds of things an engineer would study—the reading of logs and cores and samples, which was my strong suit. In fact, I was simply overseeing the evaluations done by the companies' own engineers and independent consultants.

Of course, I was also evaluating the clients themselves, the people behind the properties. Calculating the value of petroleum assets is still not an exact science. In the early days of a well, you don't have any specific history to rely on and in the early years of the industry especially, it was particularly vital to know who you were dealing with—were they people of ability and integrity? One of the most valuable lessons I learned at the bank was to sort those qualities out.

Among my perks was membership in the six-year-old Petroleum Club, housed then on the second floor of the Motor Car Supply Building on 6th Avenue West. It was a welcome watering hole in an era when Calgary had no bars and no mixed drinking, only beer parlours with separate entrances for men and women. Some clients were more interested in taking me to the club and buying me a lunch and a drink rather than telling how they ran their business. Others would offer me minimal data about their properties in an effort to snow the bank into giving them the loan. One burly guy who had a sports background came in with a fancy story about how good his wells were and how he'd even bought an airplane to fly up to see them—an extravagant purchase that helped scare me into recommending against a loan for him.

In 1955, the Commerce put up a new bank building above a branch office at 309 8th Avenue (the site of Bankers Hall today). Our oil and gas department moved there into an office with a large map of western Canada on the wall where we used coloured push-pins to keep track of every single well being drilled across the provinces (black for a dry hole, red for a producer). We dressed things up with a mural portraying geologists and geophysicists at work and had a collection of core and crude-oil samples, even a can of the Athabaska tar sands being newly explored.

Becoming more comfortable in my banking skin, I was able to hire an engineer for the department, a fellow from Texas who'd worked in the Venezuelan oil business. And I started travelling—a lot. The Commerce, like other Canadian banks, had so-called correspondent relationships with

American banks. If customers of a bank in the U.S. wanted to do business in western Canada, the bank would steer their funds our way. One major reason we'd make those trips south was to renew and promote these commercial alliances. A second was to learn about the evaluation and lending practices of banks more experienced in the petroleum game. And another was to call on potential customers, such as drilling companies, that the banks might identify for us.

I tag-teamed down there with my boss, Cec Munro, once chiding him with youthful righteousness about his drinking too much. One trip had me on the road for six weeks in the spring of 1956. I was travelling with an enjoyable business-development officer named Jay Moreton, a Second World War vet who had a steel plate in his head after being wounded during a tank battle in Caen, France. He handled our trip expense accounts, some of which were of concern to the bank's regional superintendent. Among other petroleum hotspots, we visited Carlsbad in New Mexico, Dallas, Houston and Midland in Texas, and Tulsa, Oklahoma, and met with Commerce people in Chicago (with a weekend side trip to see my folks in Ontario). The days were interesting—"spent all Saturday down a potash mine," I told Becky in one letter—but the nights were lonely. Reporting home from the Statler Hilton in Dallas, I wrote her, "I'm so tired of this trip and so lonesome for you and the kids. I never thought I could miss you more than I did the first week but every day is worse." Jay and I, both family men, were young and energetic but the trip was much too long. Only occasionally did we find time to relax—in New Orleans I went to the French Quarter and had my portrait sketched by a street artist.

On my own I visited two oil companies in El Dorado, Arkansas, the state's optimistically named petroleum capital. I flew from Dallas in an old DC-3 operated by Trans Texas Airways (which its rivals nicknamed Tree Top Airlines and Tinker Toy Airlines). It hopscotched from one town to another, including Shreveport, Louisiana, where I stepped off the plane for a coffee. Reboarding, I was warned about ground fog that might divert the flight. In fact, when the weather did sock in El Dorado, the aircraft detoured to Little Rock, Arkansas, and the next morning headed back to El Dorado. I awoke early to a wind-and-rain storm. On this leg I was the sole passenger, served by a stewardess who looked all of fourteen. There were two stops before my destination and when we landed at the second one, I was a mere fifteen miles from El Dorado.

"Maybe I should just take a bus or a car there," I told the pilots.

"Hell, we'll get you there," they assured me.

Instead, we slammed into one of those ferocious fronts that sweep down the Mississippi Valley. As the winds batted us this way and that, I was never so scared in my life. My mood wasn't helped by the flight attendant saying, "Oh, I'm really frightened!" We were up in the air for a couple of hours—or an eternity—and never did land in the promised El Dorado. The plane returned to Shreveport, at which point a pilot said, "We're sorry, Mr. Hotchkiss, but we'll have another flight going back in about an hour."

"Not with me," I said, and rented a car.

FROM MY STRATEGIC PERCH IN THE BANK, I GOT TO know many of the players in Alberta's burgeoning Oil Patch. Three very different men—one a Canadian, the others American—would become so close to me that we wound up as business partners and as friends for life.

All these years later, I don't recall exactly when or where Doc Seaman and I met, and neither did he. Born in 1922, Daryl Kenneth Seaman was the eldest son of a road contractor in tiny Rouleau, Saskatchewan (which is still such a classic prairie town that the TV comedy series *Corner Gas* is filmed there). He and the other kids—brothers Byron Jr and Donald and their big sister, Dorothy—were baseball and hockey fanatics, like most people in that agricultural heartland. Daryl was reputed to be the best on skates. While I played keep-away with a puck on a frozen country pond, he learned to shoot frozen horse droppings in the tradition of other small-town boys. In his office boardroom at Dox Investments today, there's a painting of a game on Rouleau's icy streets, with a poem by the artist, an amateur versifier, which reads in part:

> *Road apples in abundance*
> *Ideal for our shinny game.*
> *Those little brown gems*
> *were lots of fun*
> *No matter from where they came.*

As a teenager, Daryl played for the celebrated Hounds organized by Father Athol Murray at Notre Dame College next door in the town of Wilcox. While many Hounds graduated to professional teams, his talent took him to the Moose Jaw Canucks, a leading Canadian junior club. And he signed a "protection card" that would have him play for the NHL's New York Americans if he ever turned professional. The Second World War intruded, in September 1939. Bright as a brand-new penny, he'd finished high school a year ahead of time and reluctantly followed Dorothy to the University of Saskatchewan. But he left his engineering course after the first term to sign up as an eighteen-year-old with the Royal Canadian Air Force. With a silk stocking in his helmet as a lucky charm, he flew bombing missions in Lockheed Hudsons to Algeria, Tunisia, and Italy, sometimes barely surviving the raids on submarines, ships, and harbours. On one mission, "I got bullets in both legs. I had to fly back with two dead guys lying in the plane." He spent six weeks in hospital and within a month was flying again.

Reminiscing about the basic life lessons he brought back from his five years' service, he said, "I learned that once we crewed up in our own squadron, we could compete with anybody. We ended up being one of the best crews. There were Brits and New Zealanders and Australians and a few Americans, and as captain of the crew, I had to organize and get guys to work with me because it's really a team effort. Any organization is all about people so you have to learn to get along, get them to co-operate and work together."

Coming back to Saskatoon in late 1944, he decided to return to university and pursue his mechanical-engineering degree, financing himself as a player for the city's championship senior baseball team. That's where Doc got his nickname by toting his gear in a black bag like a doctor's satchel. By the time we met somewhere around the early Fifties, Doc and a partner had built a promising petroleum-services company called Seaman Engineering and Drilling (*see page 95*).

The details of where we first came across one another have since been withdrawn from our memory banks. Was it on a baseball field? I'd played fastball for the Sun Oil team's Super Suns in the Petroleum League (Superior didn't have enough people for its own team), and then Doc and I did occasionally play ball together. Or did we meet at the Earl Grey club where we both golfed? It wasn't while curling, a game he loved but I didn't indulge in much. And we never played hockey together (he would still be on the ice in pickup games into his seventies). Our first encounter might have been at the Commerce, where Doc had an account, though he wasn't borrowing on his petroleum assets at the time and wouldn't have done business with me. Wherever it was, we clicked as compatriots in the same business and as pals. We eventually went upland bird hunting and salmon fishing together and, with brothers B.J. and Don and their colleagues and friends, took a memorable train trip to the 1957 Grey Cup in Vancouver. During that hard-drinking party, somebody pulled a stop cord and broke a coupling, forcing the train to turn around.

Fun aside, Doc was a true visionary as an entrepreneur, a quiet leader who brought his brothers into an expanding company and created a family business that would one day go international.

IN 1954, JUST A YEAR AFTER I JOINED THE BANK, HARRY Van Rensselaer arrived in Calgary. Christened Henry Camman Van Rensselaer, he came from establishment stock: his father had been an investment banker who was wiped out in the 1929 Crash. Dutch-American ancestors were distinguished military men who led regiments in the American Revolutionary War and the War of 1812 against Canada. Harry was a decade older and a lot slighter than me, a lean, wiry, intense guy who's been described as emotional, even mercurial. Within three years he'd be ranked eighteenth among American tennis players, the first over age thirty-five ever to break into the top twenty. As a golfer, he sometimes played seventy-two holes a day. As a skier, he was so skilful that he won his international instructor's certificate at fifty-three. His athletic ability had helped get him into Princeton, but he left college in 1942 to serve overseas with the U.S. Air Force for five years. After a fling in the pioneering radar and television industries, he joined the Bank of New York as an investment analyst, with an interest in petroleum.

That specialty brought him to Alberta, initially to check out the newly discovered Pembina oil field, about sixty miles southwest of Edmonton, which evolved into the most significant reservoir in the West—in fact, at the time, the most expansive oil field on the continent. He convinced the bank to invest in three companies with good holdings in the area. In the course of his casing the local industry, he showed up at my office. Harry and I were instant pals. At one point, he had me clandestinely scouting a key well for him in the sizable Innisfail field between Calgary and Red Deer. I drove up there in the middle of the night and peered through binoculars to scout the activities.

Harry and his wife, Sue, and their two daughters, Jacqueline and Roseanne, became smitten with the province. Rosie Doenz, who lives in Calgary, remembers my visits to their home in Connecticut when their neighbours exclaimed that I was Canadian—"They play hockey in Canada!"—and were tickled as I skated at the local rink. In the summers, they came to Alberta to holiday at Num-Ti-Jah Lodge, which the legendary outfitter and mountain man Jimmy Simpson built in the late 1930s on Bow Lake, north of Lake Louise, near the peaks of the Great Continental Divide. It was there in the rustic log lodge one night that I, ever the practical joker, borrowed the bear rug in front of the river-rock fireplace, hid in the bushes as Sue walked from their cabin to dinner, and leaped out at her growling. It's a wonder she ever spoke to me again—but that was the relaxed nature of the relationship Becky and I had with the Van Rensselaers. It would become even tighter near the end of the Fifties as Harry and I began talking partnership.

My partner and friend Boone Pickens (seated) with his colleague Lawton Clark.

Meanwhile, in 1957, I'd met the other American who came to loom so large in my world: T. Boone Pickens Jr. Boone has always been bigger than life. Critics have labelled the founder of Mesa Petroleum, the natural-gas giant in Amarillo, Texas, as a corporate raider and greenmailer. His admirers call him a dazzling deal-maker and the shareholders' champion. I call him a close friend, as I have for the past fifty years. When I met him, the oilman's son from Holdenville, Oklahoma, had grown into a budding entrepreneur just about my age. Only five-foot-eight, Boone was a star guard on the basketball team in Amarillo, where the family had moved, and after graduating in geology from Oklahoma State University got a job where his father worked as a lease broker—at Phillips Petroleum. But the son soon bristled at big-company bureaucracy and in 1956 founded his own drilling venture, Petroleum Exploration Inc., with $2,500 cash, a $100,000 line of credit (half of it from his wife Lynn's uncle), and a heap of nerve.

Not surprisingly, he came calling in Calgary, lured by all the action bubbling here only a decade after Leduc. I might have been the first Canadian that Boone really talked to. He showed up in my office with a couple of colleagues, including Lawton Clark, who would eventually move to Calgary to run their operation here. Boone immediately struck me as a straight-shooter with a wonderfully folksy wit. Summing up what he was looking for north of the border, he might say, "That's the blood, guts, and feathers of it." Speaking about an unsuccessful oilman: "He couldn't find oil if he was standing ankle-deep in it." And explaining the philosophy that would someday make him such a huge success: "If you're on the right side of the issue, just keep driving until you hear glass breaking. Don't quit."

By 1959, he'd cobbled together $35,000 to invest in Canadian drilling sites. And his first foray would be with me, Harry Van Rensselaer, and Doc Seaman.

THE BROTHERS SEAMAN

In a chapter about Calgary in *Titans: How the New Canadian Establishment Seized Power,* Peter C. Newman—the chronicler of eastern Old Boys and western Mavericks—wrote:

The Establishment's grand old man—Daryl "Doc" Seaman—is also the capo of its most important network: the Saskatchewan mafia of farm and small-town boys who swarmed over the Alberta border like a marauding guerrilla force to take charge of the promised land. Doc is more than a businessman: he is the Totem of the Titans, a symbol of the long siege during which Canadians wrested dominion over the Oil Patch away from the multinationals.

With their mechanical-engineering degrees in hand after the war, Doc and his next-oldest brother, B.J., began working on a seismic crew for a geophysical company in Edmonton. It drilled shot-holes—shallow holes to hold dynamite that creates sound waves, which are recorded in layers of underground rock to help geologists map potential petroleum-bearing structures. The shot-holes were drilled from small rigs mounted on trucks.

Doc decided to buy his own rigged truck with a partner, a fledgling driller named Bill Warnke, and with $15,000—half their own money, half a loan—they got a new vehicle that Doc drove up from Dallas. It soon became a family business when B.J. joined Warnke in operating a second truck-mounted rig financed by the Seamans' father. In 1950, brother Don borrowed money from their dad and an uncle to buy a third rig. Soon Don was back home in Saskatchewan running a more diversified seismic-services company in which the Seamans were partners with a college friend. Doc then got a minority partner to open a machine-shop service for the oil industry and, going even further afield, approached another friend to start a road-construction venture.

B.J. and Don oversaw the operations side of the business while Doc focused on growth and diversification. Eventually they moved into big drills to bore actual oil wells. At one point, Doc reminded me, he'd approached Al Johnson, the manager of the main branch of the Commerce in Calgary, for a loan to buy new drilling equipment. "You're growing too fast," Al said. "I don't think we can do it." He'd grant the loan only with a mortgage on Doc's home as collateral. Doc, disgruntled, went away empty-handed and was outside the bank when Al came running after him, saying, "Seaman, I think we can

Doc Seaman (standing) and his two brothers, B.J. and Don, in 1985. They became my partners a quarter-century earlier when we went into a business called Alcon Petroleums with Harry Van Rensselaer.

do the deal for you." Instead, the brothers got a much more substantial loan from Charterhouse Canada, a subsidiary of a small British merchant bank, which became a one-quarter partner in their company.

To outbid rivals for drilling contracts, the Seamans took pieces of the action instead of cash from companies exploring for oil. This was only one of their innovative approaches that made them successful—another was to offer all the other services involved in drilling a well for a fixed package price. So successful were they that Charterhouse and the brothers—who used borrowed money—bought a cash-rich public company, about double the size, called Hi-Tower Drilling. (It was founded by a Colorado geologist, driller and oil entrepreneur named Ralph Will, who was also the first president of Alberta Gas Trunk Line, which the Manning government had created to feed natural gas to export pipelines.)

Hi-Tower had more than $1 million in assets, including $300,000 in cash. Within a year, Hi-Tower under its new owners bought out all the shares of Seaman Engineering and Drilling. Essentially, the Seamans had used the bigger company's own money to finance their purchase. Doc became president, B.J. vice-president, and Don vice-president, geophysical operations.

The Hi-Tower acquisition happened in 1959—the very year the Seamans and I went into business together.

CHAPTER 5

GOING SOLO

Alcon Petroleums and Sabre Petroleums

I
N THE FINAL YEAR OF THE FIFTIES, CALGARY'S population, at 218,418, had more than doubled since Leduc. Becky and I had contributed to that growth with the births of our second son, John Stephen, in February 1955, and James Richard two years later. John was an average-sized tyke—and "easy-going and outgoing," in his mom's words—while Richard (as he came to be called) was a *big* baby who was soon displaying his sense of humour and an ambition that Becky insists is much like mine. Having four kids in such a short time, and not necessarily stopping there, we were following the pattern of our own prolific families.

All of us Hotchkisses were leading a good life in our adopted city. I was able to relax a little with sports, particularly pickup hockey in my early years there. I played with friends and colleagues in informal leagues and that's when, at age twenty-five after one tough Sunday-night game, I stopped smoking cold-turkey to regain some of the wind of my youth. I loved fastball too during my Canadian Superior days. (When I asked frugal Art Feldmeyer to pay for the equipment of his employees who played for the Sun Oil team in the Petroleum League, he replied, "Hotch, we pay you enough money to buy your own bats and balls.") In 1955, my last year on the diamond, I won trophies for leading the league in batting average, runs batted in, and home runs. I always followed the NHL on radio and watched the Stanley Cup on TV, still cheering on Toronto, and during the World Series

Partners and friends over the years: Alcon Petroleums' Harry Van Rensselaer (top), here in 1968, and again during a visit in my backyard with me, Baron Carlo von Maffei—my colleague in my later company, Sabre Petroleums—and Paul Jackson, a boyhood friend from Straffordville.

went to the Palliser Hotel with colleagues from other companies who made watching the ballgames a real social event. Becky and I skated on outdoor rinks and not surprisingly, we followed the former and future NHLers of the Calgary Stampeders in the senior Western Hockey League at the old Corral, which would one day briefly house a new NHL team. Living in Altadore, we were close to recreational areas such as River Park/Sandy Beach for picnics and swimming and the Elbow River, where folks went tubing in the summer. I golfed at the nearby Earl Grey club and Becky and I curled occasionally at community rinks.

In late 1957, we moved from Altadore to a roomier house in Glendale Meadows. It was a two-year-old neighbourhood of nice middle-class, single-family homes in southwest Calgary, less than three miles from downtown, with curving streets and views of the Rockies. "There were a hundred kids on our block on Glenview Drive," Becky recalls. "Everybody had four, five kids. And to this day, there isn't one of those families where the parents divorced." In a typical communal action, our neighbours managed to get the heavy rink boards from the old Victoria Arena when it was torn down near the site of the present Calgary Stampede. We put up an outdoor rink using those boards and I still have the blisters from digging the damn post holes.

So there I was, as the decade of the Sixties was about to dawn, with a large mortgage, not much spare cash, and a wife and four kids to support—and what was a pretty decent job with a national bank. It was still the Commerce at that time; only a couple of years later it merged with the Imperial (in the largest such alliance in Canadian history) to become the Canadian Imperial Bank of Commerce, with more resources and more branches than any other bank in the country. By now I was an assistant manager and my immediate future in that pre-CIBC era was to get into the mainstream of banking and possibly have to leave Calgary for other postings—which would mean I'd have to leave the petroleum department.

But I had fallen for the oil and gas game and simply didn't want to abandon it.

HARRY VAN RENSSELAER CAME TO MY RESCUE. WE AND our wives had developed a close relationship; Becky and I visited them to fly-fish and hike the mountain trails at the Num-Ti-Jah Lodge when they holidayed there. Harry and I went further afield later, once with Doc and B.J. on a lake in the B.C. Interior. We weren't having any luck so I jerked Harry's line from the stern where I was steering our boat. He yelled at me to cut the engine— "I've got a strike!"—and when he came up empty, I did it a couple of more times before he caught on to my gag. We were all travelling back by train on that same trip when he met a couple of lovely young women on board who were interested in the geology of the Rockies (or so he told me). He suggested I describe the rock formation and, just before getting off at Lake Louise, asked us to disembark before him. His wife, Sue, was waiting on the station platform. "Where's Har?" she wondered. And then saw him strolling off the train arm in arm with these two beauties. He was always doing this sort of thing to tease her. As intense as he was, Harry was a lot of fun to be with.

During our times together, we inevitably fell to talking about business prospects. He'd left the Bank of New York for Henderson, Harrison & Struthers, a New York brokerage firm. Some of his wealthy friends on the U.S. eastern seaboard, he said, were looking for places to invest their money. In *From Rigs to Riches*, which recounts the story of the Seaman brothers until the mid-Eighties, Peter Foster described how it all happened:

It was a combination of his business speciality and sports talent which led [Harry] to become much more involved in the Canadian oil business. One day, his doubles partner, Alastair Martin, who was related to the enormously wealthy Phipps family [Henry Phipps was a partner in Andrew Carnegie's steel company as well as a real-estate tycoon], said that his family holding company, Bessemer Securities, would like to invest some money in Canada. Did Harry know of likely prospects? Van Rensselaer suggested that they go and have a look for themselves, so they set off with their wives for Calgary. There, Van Rensselaer intended to introduce Martin to Harley Hotchkiss. . . .

When asked about potential investment properties, Hotchkiss gave the two men some names, but afterwards he took Van Rensselaer aside and said he was interested in running the sort of company of which they were thinking. Why didn't he and Van Rensselaer put something together?

That's about right. What it doesn't mention is that my decision to go out on my own was mixed with some trepidation befitting a husband and father who'd always worked for a large, stable company, surrounded by colleagues to confer with and counting on the safety net of a steady pay cheque. It was the fabulously successful oilman J. Paul Getty who said, "There are one hundred men seeking security to one able man who is willing to risk his fortune." Just how able was I? Becky, as always, was generously supportive of my desire to stay in petroleum and, besides, she didn't want to leave Calgary either. If I wanted to risk whatever modest resources we had, she supported me.

As I told Harry, why not have me set up a company, with him on the board, to find potential oil and gas plays in Alberta and have his rich friends invest with us?

It seemed like a plan. The only problem was that we needed seed capital to launch our business. We travelled to New York to present our concept to Bessemer Securities—Martin's family company—and to the massive Scudder, Stevens and Clark, founded in 1919 as one of the first American investment firms. Despite some interest, neither of them bit.

That's when I introduced Harry to Doc. He, B.J., and Don liked the high-energy Harry and the feeling was mutual. Doc got to calling him the Hawk—"he was always swooping around." The idea was to lure U.S. investors by beefing up a new company with an infusion of the Seamans' petroleum-producing acreage in southeast Saskatchewan and the earnings it was generating. The arrangement worked for them because they were still primarily a drilling operation and didn't want to be seen blatantly competing as producers with the oil companies who were their clients. The brothers transferred their assets into the stock of what Harry and I christened Alcon, a combination of Alberta and Connecticut, where he lived. We were directors along with Bill Howard, the Seamans' lawyer.

So in 1959, after six years with the bank, I left the support group of big business and became a lone entrepreneur—with a salary of $1,000 a month (about $250 more than the bank paid me), a company car, and an option to buy equity over five years. Doc gave me lots of room, never looking over my shoulder. Being partners with the Seamans proved to be rewarding and stress-free. In *From Rigs to Riches*, Peter Foster pointed out one of the key qualities of the eldest brother: "Doc believed that an essential element of any new venture was the management expertise either installed in or that came with the acquired company. In order to retain and motivate that expertise, Doc believed managers should be left with equity or with some profit incentive scheme. There were no greater motivators than pride of ownership and the prospect of a share in success."

As a director, Harry acted mainly as my pipeline to the Americans we hoped to attract as financial backers. Unfortunately, there was a big slump in the stock market just as we got going and some of them lost their appetite for investment. In my first year, I had about $150,000 in production cash from the Seamans and only $100,00 from Harry's contacts down south. Among them were Alastair Martin (one of the finest amateur court tennis players in the U.S. during the 1950s) and his brother, Townsend; Eckley B. (Buzzy) Coxe IV, Harry's friend and a senior partner of Scudder; Francis (Frank) Pemberton, a senior employee with the Rockefeller dynasty; and Frederick (Ted) Remsen, a Connecticut investor with family money who became a friend of Doc's.

Of them all, only a few really became significant in Alcon Petroleums' history. Financiers Landon Clay and Harris, his younger brother who spent a lot of time in Alberta, came from a family with a cotton and textile-mill fortune. (Landon much later chaired the huge Boston mutual-fund management firm Eaton Vance Corporation.) They were major backers of Alcon's drilling program, as were the Stuart siblings of Bartow, Florida. J.K. was a little red-headed firecracker of a guy, clever and full of beans, and W.H. was a tall, quiet gentleman. I developed such a bond with the Stuarts that I wound up representing their petroleum interests after they died, and continue to even today.

My job as president was to look for the prospects on which to spend this money. I took office space in a third-floor walkup in the Rio Building, where I'd worked for Canadian Superior, just across the street from the Bank of Commerce. I was across the hall from a friend, Harry Dernick, a petroleum engineer who had a drilling company. There was one employee, Eva Cooley, who'd been my assistant at the bank and wanted to come over with me. And it was my good fortune that the fellow who decided to set up an office across the hall from us was none other than Boone Pickens, my friend of two years. As he wrote—much too flatteringly—in the first of his two autobiographies, *Boone*, "I had made some friends in Calgary over the years. One of them, whom I first met in 1957, was Harley Hotchkiss. A former Michigan State hockey player, he was a ruggedly handsome geologist who had gone from bank officer to successful independent oilman. He later became a close adviser and a member of the Mesa board [Mesa Petroleum was his public company founded in 1964]."

Boone had launched a subsidiary, Altair Oil and Gas, to explore in Canada. He and I were of the same ilk, kindred spirits as young geologists and entrepreneurs brimming with ideas. His company and ours shared a common room to hold our well and production records, with never a thought about being rivals in the business. The only competition we pursued on his visits to Calgary was the old game of pitching coins to see which ones landed closest to a wall.

The first well that Boone ever drilled in Canada was a deal I'd put together after doing the geological due diligence. He took roughly half of the small 160-acre project at the southeast end of the burgeoning oil field at Joffre, a village near Red Deer that later became a major petrochemical centre. I had managed to get it as a farmout from a company called Scurry Rainbow and its hard-assed negotiator, whose response to my initial offer was, "I'm not going to give it to you for that kind of chickenshit deal." Dave Williams was the drilling and completion engineer and I was the wellsite geologist. I never wanted to operate the properties I found; fortunately, Boone had an

engineer, a geologist, and a landman to run what turned out to be four de-
pendable forty-barrel-a-day wells—not a barn-burner at $2.60 a barrel for oil,
but at today's prices of $50 to $100 or more, it would be nicely profitable.

Everything was much simpler in those days: our overhead and the
cost of wells were lower, the royalty and tax systems less complicated. I
could visit a prospect and almost evaluate its economics in my head—which
was my strong suit, outpacing the competition with the speed of my decision-making. If we had bills for legal services above $3,000 a year, I'd think
something was wrong.

Another venture with Boone a few years later—in the oil and gas
fields at Medicine River eighty-five miles northwest of Calgary—started
optimistically. After we'd tested the first oil well at significant rates of flow, I
told the investors, "Hey, I think we've got a nice one." For the first ten days,
it was producing about eight hundred barrels a day. Then it began to yield
water and soon went to 100-per-cent H_2O. That was a tough one to explain
to our backers. But we screwed up our courage and drilled a follow-up well
to produce at a much lower rate; maybe we'd been trying to pull the original
one too hard. Our second try—and about seven other wells in its wake—
were successful and two have each produced more than two million barrels
a day on eighty-acre spacing and are still producing today. Highly competent
engineers had evaluated their potential at maybe three hundred thousand
barrels at most. The only time you really know what a well will produce is
when it's abandoned at the end of its life. In the case of Medicine River, we
were simply at the right place in the reservoir.

The Stuart brothers were part of that project. Orange growers, cattle
ranchers, and significant landowners in central Florida, they were looking
to create some expenditures to offset their profits from the sale of valuable
phosphate deposits on their land. As a banker, Harry had known one of J.K.
Stuart's six daughters and through her convinced her father that Alberta was
a potential hotbed of petroleum investment. Harry and I met him many
times on his visits to New York, forming a relationship that would have me
overseeing the brothers' estate's properties after they died in the early 1990s.

Not long before that, W.H. Stuart had taken a terrible financial hit.
Though the brothers were religious and gave generously to church schools,
the younger Stuart was a bit too trusting in some of his investments. A son
of his convinced him to put money into what a promoter claimed were oil
and gas schemes in the U.S. that guaranteed a 20-per-cent return because of
secret deals with petroleum companies giving him preferred terms. W.H.
asked me to look into the supposed deals and after talking with the promoter, who wouldn't disclose any details, I told W.H. that I didn't believe

anybody could do that well in that industry. I advised him not to invest any more but only play with his profits if he wished. A couple of years later, he asked me to come down to Florida because the promoter now wanted him to invest millions in a new venture. The day before leaving Calgary, I got a call saying the man had been arrested. Though I never did hear the details, he might well have been running a classic Ponzi scheme, paying outrageously high "profits" to investors with funds from subsequent backers. I could have cried when I heard about it.

Of course, during the Alcon years I had some of my own problems and sleepless nights because of dry holes—which then could cost about $100,000—and in one case a lawsuit. In 1960, our second year in business, I had a call from a friend at Canadian Superior: "Hotch, we've got this land we're about to farm out and I think our company should be drilling it, but we're not going to."

"I'll come right over and look at it," I said without hesitation. The land was in the Crossfield area northwest of Calgary. The leases controlled there by his company and Home Oil were about to expire if they didn't drill on them or farm them out. Studying the geology, I realized this could be a good natural-gas play and told Doc Seaman, who replied, "Let's take it."

But when I called Canadian Superior the next morning, they said, "Well, it's gone."

"I just looked at it yesterday. Who took it?"

The buyer was a subsidiary of American Metal Climax (later Amax Inc.), an American mining goliath. I knew the geologist in the Canadian office, Neil McKenzie, a husky, superbly conditioned fellow from Barbados. "Neil," I said, "I went and looked at that Canadian Superior deal. And you took it. I'd like to come in with you as a partner."

"No, we don't need a partner—we've taken it, we like it, and we're going to drill."

"We'll pay you some edge on it." When he was still reluctant, I said, "I don't want to make you mad at me, but I'm going to New York in a couple of days and don't want to go around you, but I do really want to talk to your boss there. Can I?"

"You can talk to him, but my recommendation is still going to be No." I just happened to be visiting Harry Van Rensselaer in New York, where American Climax had its head office. I went to see Neil's superior, Walter Scott, the company's chief of exploration, whom I'd known casually. And, in a bit of luck, he agreed that the proposed well was an expensive proposition—drilling seven thousand feet to the Mississippian formation—and yes, they'd let us partner on it. In the end, his company and ours, and Canadian Superior and Home, each had a 25-per-cent interest in a really nice discovery, a wet-gas well that became part of the trillion-cubic-feet Crossfield gas field. (Wet gas is a natural gas that contains natural-gas liquids, such as condensate and propane.)

However, after hitting paydirt, we evaluated the well's potential by taking core samples and running electrical logs, rather than doing the more conclusive drill-stem testing. The owner of the lease sued all of us to have her petroleum rights returned, claiming that we had not established there was commercial oil or gas on the land. The only way we could keep the lease was to prove production. A major court case ensued—which we wouldn't have won except for a single intriguing fact. The owner had earlier settled a dispute over a long-ago version of this lease with the forerunner of Canadian Superior, Rio Bravo. At that time, she had also wanted to have the lease revert to her. The issue was settled for about $15,000 and other minor considerations. And by the owner's agreeing at that time to a revised lease, which we inherited, it seemed that our lease hadn't expired either. The judge concurred, and so the little bit of cash and considerations she'd received would save our bacon in the early days when Alcon needed all the help it could get.

While we were drilling that first important well, I called Harry every day to update him. He had a chart in his office, where he carefully plotted the progress of all our operations. We had a whole variety of our own plays in Alberta and shallow gas wells near Lloydminster, Saskatchewan, and bought some properties from others. In Ontario, we acquired rights to some producing wells in the Rodney field west of London and the Gobles field near Brantford.

In our first few years, I flew regularly to New York to court investors, occasionally joined by Doc. Harry's office was on Wall Street, but we stayed at his home in Greenwich—really a nice apartment above a garage on a big Connecticut estate—and took the train in every day to meet and massage the money people. Harry being Harry, we followed the same hectic routine every morning, with him brushing his teeth with one hand and shooing the dog out the door with the other, yelling at Sue to get breakfast ready, and then all of us jumping in his little Volkswagen at the last minute ("We can't be late!" he exclaimed) to drive the five miles to the commuter train out of Greenwich, arriving at Grand Central Station in Manhattan and then hopping a cab to our meeting ("You gotta hurry!" he told the driver). If things were going smoothly, Harry had to stir them up; he thrived on chaos. I'd be worn out after two or three days in his presence.

He was seldom fazed by the unexpected. At one meeting, I was telling investors and their associates what was happening in Canada and suddenly lost my train of thought. There was a painfully long silence until I finally got on board again. "Harry," I said later, "you could see I was struggling there. Why the hell didn't you step in?"

"Oh, Harley," he said, "that was a really nice pregnant pause."

In the end, I was the guy who had to tell them whether their investment was a productive well or a dry hole sucking up their money. I was backstopped with solid annual evaluations by Calgary petroleum engineer Rod McDaniel, who went on to co-found Western Research and Development in 1965, became part of Doc Seaman's Rat Pack of friends, and later was a mentor on energy issues and a fundraiser for Premier Peter Lougheed.

Our two-person office grew over eight years to include Lloyd Bebensee, my fellow geologist and faithful friend from Canadian Superior. Itching to get out of the oil company, he had to tell Art Feldmeyer he was leaving. Knowing that Art hated to lose good people, I wasn't surprised one day to get a phone call from him after Lloyd had joined me. This soft voice said, "What did I ever do to you that you'd stab me in the back?"

"Art, you know as well as I do that no one can influence Lloyd to do something that he doesn't want to do." We talked and it ended up with him wishing us both well.

Lloyd was that valuable a geologist. He made the maps for us and pinpointed places to drill. We paid him a consulting fee as a retainer and gave him a small royalty interest in any project we pursued

As we increasingly sourced producing wells, I hired Cliff Fiesel as a landman, Roy Fisher as an engineer, Dave Young as head accountant, and Colin McDonald as his assistant. To this day, Cliff continues to consult for one of our investors, Harris Clay. Colin later worked for BP and Panarctic Oils and eventually for Doc, who retained him as a right-hand man after all those years. Counting office staff, we had as many as a dozen people at one time on the Alcon payroll.

More and more, instead of hunting for oil and gas—studying land maps, driving out to wellsites, reading rocks through a microscope—I was spending my time administering the business and managing people.

In 1962, the Seamans' Hi-Tower Drilling had become Bow Valley Industries and two years later, Harry Van Rensselaer left Henderson, Harrison & Struthers and, to my great pleasure, moved to Calgary. That year, Alcon was producing more than one thousand barrels a day as Harry attracted $3.7 million from the American investors. Important as that financing was, I wanted to expand our in-house production income instead of depending so heavily on investment from the U.S.

At this point, Bow Valley released a Manifesto for Growth that refocused on its investments in petroleum-hunting rather than its drilling operations. By 1966, when exploration and development spending reached nearly $1.5 million, Doc and his brothers were talking about cleaving the company into distinct halves and swallowing its subsidiaries—including Alcon—into the corporate fold. I would come under this broad umbrella. As our business philosophies diverged, I became restless, rethinking my future to envision running my own show—even if it was much smaller and riskier than staying with my associates and friends at Bow Valley.

Our growing family had moved in 1965 to a more spacious two-storey colonial home we'd had built in Lakeview Village. Another new neighbourhood in southwest Calgary, it offered vistas of the Rockies and the expansive Glenmore Reservoir, a great recreational spot for water sports on the dammed-up Elbow River.

Now it was 1967, the centennial of Canada's birth as an independent nation. There was a mood of optimism across the country as we celebrated ourselves and welcomed the world to Expo 67, the magnificent Montreal exposition. As Pierre Berton wrote in *1967: Canada's Turning Point*, "It was a golden year, and so it seems in retrospect—a year in which we let off steam like schoolboys whooping and hollering at term's end." In Alberta, commercial production of the oil sands began at the Great Canadian (later Suncor Energy) plant in Fort McMurray. "No other event in Canada's centennial year is more important or significant," Premier Ernest Manning announced on opening day. The federal government, meanwhile, established the public and privately owned Panarctic Oils to explore for petroleum in the Arctic islands. The Canadian economy was hitting its post-war peak. Maybe it was a good time for me to declare my independence as an oilman.

ENTER BARON CARLO VON MAFFEI. LIKE MY FRIEND Boone, Carlo has his critics. I'm not one of them. The intensely private but life-loving scion of a German-Italian industrial family came along at this critical juncture in my career. I'd met his father first, a big Prussian-looking businessman named Hubert von Maffei, when I was still at the Bank of Commerce and he was taking a get-acquainted tour of Canada with his West German banker. I drove them to see a well that Canadian Superior was drilling an hour outside Calgary and thought nothing more about it. Then about ten years later, in 1965, I got a call at Alcon from an associate at the Commerce saying they had a young fellow from Munich named Carlo von Maffei working for CIBC in Toronto who was visiting Calgary. Could they come over and have me give Carlo a little background on the oil business?

He was no more than twenty then, nearly half my age, with sandy hair and, at six-foot-six, tall like his dad. The elder von Maffei obviously thought Canada was a land with a future and had sent his only son to soak up some financial basics here. Carlo had worked briefly for National Trust in Toronto before joining the bank as a teller, which seemed a lowly position for a titled European. As I was to learn, he came from a distinguished corporate lineage: the von Maffeis were a prominent merchant family in nineteenth-century Italy (there's still a Palazzo Maffei in Verona). They left to run a tobacco wholesale business in Munich, where a son named Joseph Anton was born. He later helped found a private railway and locomotive and steamship works in Bavaria. The company Joseph created went bankrupt in 1930, long after his death, but merged with a competitor to form KraussMaffei. After the Second World War, it began producing more than ten thousand Leopard tanks as well as artillery, all heavily used by NATO, and developed successful process-engineering and plastics-machinery divisions.

Carlo's father, a direct descendant of Joseph Anton, had a comfortable fortune and bore the title of baron, which the son inherited (though in Germany there's no legal privilege associated with the honorific). Carlo's only sister, Huberta, was a countess, married to Count Karl von Maldeghem of Germany. And in 1970, Carlo would abandon his bachelor life to marry Karl's sister, Christina. (With Ferdinand, the Duke of Hohenlohe, I'd be one of his two best men at the three-day wedding on the von Maldeghem estate at Niederstotzingen on the Danube River). They all moved in rarefied circles of European royalty as companions of the king of Sweden, Carl XVI Gustav; his wife, Queen Silvia, the half-Brazilian daughter of a German businessman; and his sister, Princess Birgitta, who married the prince of Hohenzollern-Sigmaringen, Johann Georg von Hohenzollern—"Hansi" to his pals. Birgitta was the only one of four sisters to marry royalty and retain the title of Her Royal Highness.

For many years, Becky and I became friends with the royals through our relationship with Carlo (*see* A-Huntin' We Would Go, *page 128*). The king and queen would come to Calgary during the 1988 Olympics Winter Games and we invited them for dinner at our Eagle Ridge home, which had almost six thousand square feet of space. "It was scary," Becky remembers. "We had secret-service men all over. We flew the Swedish flag and we had a Flames flag up there too. There were twelve of us, including Kiki, the son of Hansi, who had a property outside Calgary. Kiki was going with a banker's daughter, and the banker and his wife came. The king and queen were very nice, enjoyed the dinner, and the guys went downstairs to play pool. The ladies were just gossiping upstairs in the living room. The king was pretty down-to-earth when he was in our home. I think they enjoyed having dinner in a private home rather than all the protocol that they have to go through."

All heady stuff initially, I guess, but on our first meetings Carlo himself had never put on any airs with me. He asked a lot of questions about the petroleum industry and I drove him up into the mountains for a look around. Over the course of the next year or two, we kept up with one another. I visited him in Toronto, where he had a swank bachelor's apartment and a Jaguar and that's when I told him I was thinking of leaving Alcon to launch a new company to invest in oil and gas.

"Well, why don't we do it together?" he suggested. "I've got money and I'd like to invest in the business."

That was a surprise. At first I didn't know how I felt about this guy—with no background in petroleum, so very young and relatively new to Canada—becoming my partner. Selling my shares in Alcon would probably yield me enough seed capital to attract other, more mature investors with better grounding in my game.

The more I considered it, though, the better Carlo's offer sounded. Finally I approached Doc and said, "Look, we have a great working relationship and I'll stay as long as you need me, but I'm going to go in another direction."

He wasn't the kind to plead with you. "We're sorry to lose you," I recall him saying. "Good luck in what you do, and I appreciate you staying a while."

Which I did, but Doc soon hired Gordon Darling, a geologist-turned-executive with Imperial Oil, who replaced me as head of an Alcon that was now rolled tightly into Bow Valley as an oil and gas exploration division. Gord would take the company into the Arctic—the Mackenzie Delta and Beaufort Sea areas. And later the Seamans would be smart enough to get out of their investments there with good timing and profits while other companies suffered.

I had a buy/sell agreement with Bow Valley and Doc acquired the 66,972 minority shares of Alcon, most of them held by Harry Van Rensselaer and me. Doc's board agreed to purchase them for a total of $630,000. My piece of that payout gave me a decent stake to invest in what would be my new company, with Carlo holding 60 per cent of the stock. Harry would go with Bow Valley, where he was on the board, and become an important fundraiser and vice-president of finance. He stayed into the mid-Seventies until becoming disillusioned with the dispute over energy between the federal government and Alberta that led up to Ottawa's much-loathed National Energy Policy.

By the early 1960s, our family was booming along with Calgary: (seated left to right) Richard, Jeff, John, and (standing) Brenda and Paul.

IN 1961 BECKY HAD GIVEN BIRTH TO JEFFREY ALAN, FIVE years younger than his nearest brother and a well-behaved kid ("he never did anything wrong," his mom says). So now, six years later, we had five children to be cared for, Jeff aged six and Paul the eldest at fifteen. It was a little nervous-making to take everything I'd built up in Alcon and gamble it on another fresh venture. But I had Becky, the glue in our family, who had enough faith in me to endorse any decision I made. And by now I had confidence in my abilities and knew that if things didn't work out, I still had my head and my hands to get me out of a hole and on to solid ground again.

Carlo and I decided to call our venture Sabre Petroleums. The name had a dashing quality to it, referring to the sword with a large hand guard that cavalrymen carried; in many armies, sabres often signified high rank. As we set Sabre up, Carlo's lawyer was Maclean Everett (Mac) Jones, senior partner of Calgary's Bennett Jones and a director of such blue-chip companies as the Commerce and Simpsons-Sears.

I went to Jim Palmer of Burnet, Duckworth & Palmer, who had consulted on my will while I was estate-planning. He was a judge's son from Prince Edward Island, where his grandfather had been premier and a

Jim Palmer, who in 1961 would become my lawyer and confidant for the next four decades.

great-grandfather a (reluctant) Father of Confederation. Jim would become chairman of his firm, chancellor of the University of Calgary, and a federal Liberal candidate in a very Conservative town (despite our differing political philosophies, I gave him financial support). One year younger than me, he is a heckuva tennis player, having been the Maritime junior champion, and a great hiker on tough trails around the world, even while wearing a leg brace in later life. Jim has done all my legal work in the forty years since we met. If I ever had a problem in the middle of the night and needed somebody to talk to, Jim Palmer would be at the top of my list—not just as a lawyer but as a personal friend whose judgment I respect and who has deep empathy.

We formed Sabre as a private company with two partners, capitalized at about $900,000, with Carlo investing about two-thirds while I contributed the rest along with my expertise and experience. He also committed to putting in another $3.5 million in three interest-free shareholder's loans, although we used only about half of that. While taking space within the Sabre office, he never did have an active part in the company, travelling as he did so often to Europe and caught up in his own pursuits. By now, he had property in Calgary, a half-section of land with horse barns and a small house where he lived. He was a horse breeder and during the Stampede threw memorable parties with a huge side of beef barbecuing for a horde of guests.

Before we had our own office, I borrowed a room on 7th Avenue from Harry Dernick, who was then representing American oil and gas investors. And that's where I met Doreen Agnes Warren, who would loom so large in my life. She replied to an ad I put in the paper for an assistant to work in a startup company "with European money." I learned this tall, slim, raven-haired thirty-seven-year-old had grown up on a grain and cattle farm near Okotoks, south of Calgary, where she rode horseback four miles to school. After her mother died when Doreen was seven, her dad had unwed mothers come in to cook and care for her. At fourteen, she moved in with the family of her older brother in Calgary.

Following high school, she took a business course while waiting to take nurse's training, She apprenticed with Texaco and then did office work for Calgary Power (now TransAlta) before studying to be a nurse at Calgary General Hospital. But living on $7 a month wasn't appealing after she'd been earning $125 as a secretary. Doreen left school to work for a new petroleum consulting company. That was in 1951, the year I arrived in town, and she heard of me then because her bosses consulted for the Bank of Commerce (though she confesses they never knew if my name was Hotchkiss or Hitchcock).

Her employer was acquired by Colorado Oil and Gas, which had an active drilling program in the province. Doreen was executive assistant to the three owners, handling heaps of financial work, including bank loans. Colorado sold out later to Great Plains Development (now Norcen), where she worked in accounting, in charge of authorizing expenditures and managing the pool of stenographers. Disgruntled at dealing with all those personalities, she joined an economic consulting firm, which proved frustrating too ("doing all the accounting and billing and also typing these horrible economic reports"). Two years later, she saw my ad and decided to escape. By now Doreen was married to Don, a low-key guy with a nice sense of humour. He'd been a good junior hockey player before becoming an electrical mechanic for Westinghouse, working on transformers that ran generators on dams for companies such as Calgary Power As a couple, they came to be part of our extended family, spending Christmas and other occasions with us.

The young Doreen Warren and her husband, Don, relaxing on a cruise during one of the few times when I haven't run her ragged in all the years since.

In our first meeting, I had to ask only a few questions to realize that Doreen was an extremely competent woman with a straightforward if somewhat shy manner—yet oozing self-confidence—and a resumé that squared nicely with my needs. A couple of days after our interview, I offered her $400 a month.

"No," she said, "we don't know each other and I'll start at $350 and we'll review it in six months."

Her first meeting with Carlo was not auspicious. He showed up in our borrowed office, took one look at her and demanded, "Who are you?" She wanted to say, "Who the heck are you?" but held her tongue. She thought he expected her to stand up and salute. Getting to know Carlo, Doreen found him unpredictable—hard to make appointments for—and fond of extravagant gestures, such as organizing African safaris for his friends. The flip side of this conspicuous consumption was his generosity in bringing wine and flowers to Doreen when she was in hospital and inviting her and Don, Becky and me, to dinner with his new wife on the ranch he soon bought.

AFTER BORROWING SOME ROOMS AT THE MAIN BRANCH of the Commerce, we moved within a couple of months to our own space on the seventh floor of the Crown Trust building at 8th Avenue Southwest and 3rd Street. The suite of four offices was handsomely decorated, much to Carlo's taste: substantial traditional furniture, wood-panelled walls, an oak-lined boardroom with a map soaring to the ceiling. Shortly after we settled in, I arrived one morning to find Carlo already there, which was unusual. He had pulled out the corporate ledger and was studying an investment I'd made in a new project.

"Well, Harley," he said, "this is a fairly large investment and perhaps I should be signing cheques along with you."

"Carlo, I've got all my resources and reputation here and I'm committed to make this work. You're not here very much and it won't work if you don't have confidence in me signing cheques."

The next day, he came in and said, "You're right. That's the way it will work."

My game plan was to focus on buying producing properties to provide ongoing cash flow. Because Carlo and I were using after-tax dollars, I didn't want to invest in high-risk exploration. We bought an interest in active oil and gas wells near the fabled Pembina field and in several other areas. We used our capital to develop production income from those properties and only then took some risks drilling exploratory wells. We were fairly evenly split between oil and gas. At the time we launched, prices were still on the plateau they'd settled at for many years—in the case of oil, generally a wellhead price of $2.50 to $2.70 a barrel, out of which we had to pay our operating costs, such as royalties and overhead. Gas was anywhere from ten to fifteen cents per thousand cubic feet, depending on whether it was sour or not.

The autumn before we started Sabre, Boone Pickens had come back into my life—and to Calgary. His Canadian manager, Lawton Clark, had been fishing with his wife at Seymour Narrows near Campbell River, B.C., when a whirlpool capsized their boat and Sally drowned. After that tragedy, Boone suggested swapping houses temporarily, with Lawton moving to his place in Amarillo and Boone running Canada, where Mesa Petroleum was finding more oil and gas than in the U.S. ("It was my turn in the barrel," he says about his move north.) Over the nearly two years he lived here, we developed an even deeper rapport as Boone and his first wife, Lynn, came over for some of Becky's satisfying dinners or he and I might end up a long evening at work with a fat steak at Hy's, one of the few posh restaurants in town.

In the late Sixties, he called to say he had a problem. He'd bought a gas well up in the Yoyo field in northeastern B.C., near the Liard Highway between Fort Nelson and Fort Simpson. "It's a big well and a good deal, but Lyndon Johnson has put on some currency restrictions—and I can't get the money out to pay for it."

I went over to look at the high-quality prospect. He and I visited Westcoast Transmission in Vancouver to discuss the contract to ship the gas. The fellow in charge there didn't know our relationship and thought that Boone was my geologist, an impression we didn't bother to correct. Coming back on an Air Canada plane to Calgary, two flight attendants picked up on Boone's Texas accent and after we kidded back and forth, they brought each of us a little toy. Boone got a rubber duck. When we got off the plane and were walking through the crowd in the terminal, we heard a voice calling out behind us. It was one of the attendants: "Mr. Pickens, Mr. Pickens, you forgot your rubber duck!"

Boone had paid about $1.7 million for the well. "I like the deal, Boone," I said during our negotiations. "But you're the one that's in the corner here. Now you want $1.9 million."

"Well, I did all the work on it," he argued.

"Okay, let's saw it off." So Sabre bought it for $1.8 million.

Because it was such a major transaction for us, I told Boone I'd had to bring in a partner. I went to my old pal Harry Dernick. "We'll take half," he said.

Then little more than a week later, Boone called and said President Johnson's restrictions on moving currency out of the U.S. had been lifted. "I want to get back into the Yoyo deal."

"Boone, there isn't any room anymore. We've completed the deal. I've laid off half to Harry Dernick."

"You mean you're not going to let me back in my own deal?"

"I told you I was going to take a partner and you got me to pay another $100,000 for it."

He still ribs me to this day about the Yoyo deal. Though the price of gas was only about ten cents per thousand cubic feet, that one well produced about twenty million cubic feet a day (and I suspect it's still providing income today for Harry's widow, Glenda).

As we geared up our operation, Lloyd Bebensee joined me again on retainer, bringing his deep knowledge of exploration and an ability to visualize things underground in three dimensions that far exceeded mine. He did yeoman's work when we became substantially involved in the eastern high Arctic, alone and with others. Both Panarctic and Dome Petroleum, under the flamboyant Calgarian Jack Gallagher, were active up there and it looked like the activity was going to continue. We filed exploration permits on fairly extensive offshore holdings and did some geophysical work in the very remote Lancaster Sound area. We put some of our properties together with a dozen other companies into one big entity called Magnorth Petroleum Ltd., the most active landholder in the Northwest Passage (Cliff Fiesel, my landman at Alcon and then Sabre, later ran Magnorth for a while).

A bunch of us once flew into Resolute, Northwest Territories, and then out on a helicopter, staying aboard a seismic vessel overnight to view the geophysical work in Lancaster Sound, the passage linking Baffin Bay with the Barrow Strait between Devon and Baffin islands. The shortest water route across northern Canada to the Beaufort Sea, it was teeming with polar bears, whales, walruses, and millions of breeding seabirds. The next day, we drew straws to see who would fly to shore first across that spectacular seascape. I was the last to go and had the longest to travel as the ship drifted further into the sound. And the copter had a damaged pontoon. I thought, *Man, Hotchkiss, if you go down in that icy water, you won't survive.* But we got there fine. On another expedition, just to get a feel for the country, we chartered a plane and flew over the Beaufort to the hamlet of Sachs Harbour, where the Inuit were still hunting muskox and caribou. All the petroleum prospects looked promising, but in a high-risk way. In the end, our explorations there didn't mean a whole lot financially during the time we ran Sabre.

Our most interesting play was in northeastern Alberta, where the geology indicated real possibilities for natural gas. Western Minerals, owned by the legendary oilman Eric Harvie, had once drilled and completed a well there in the Colony sand a hundred feet thick and at a depth of two thousand feet. On an intermittent basis, it had produced 15 billion cubic feet over a long period. I don't know who came up with the idea that some strange things we were seeing on the geophysical records—bright spots—were somehow connected to that well. We were operating up there with Houston Oils, run by a long-time friend, a landman named Al Whitehead, who'd worked with Boone Pickens in Mesa Petroleums. Al had tried unsuccessfully for several months to negotiate a farmout with Western Minerals. "Well, let me try," I said. At first, the people I knew at Western told me they weren't interested but they called me one day: "Look, you've been pretty persistent in talking to us and maybe we could make a deal."

We did. Sabre and Houston committed to drill two wells and earned an interest in three or four sections of land. And darned if we didn't get that same sand, old channels that filled with the sand and then gas, anywhere from a quarter to half a mile wide. Because the channels were narrow, you had to be pretty accurate in your drilling. We thought, *Boy!*, and negotiated more farmouts in the area and did more geophysical work—only to find more channels establishing a pattern. Then Al negotiated a farmout from Amoco Canada of about three hundred thousand acres to the north. We probably drilled thirty wells over three years, completing all but one— a good success ratio. Along with Lloyd Bebensee, we had solid guidance from Harvey Robinson, Houston's top geologist, and Bill Chilton, a friend from my Tillsonburg High School days who became our capable consulting geophysicist. Some wells could produce up to four million cubic feet a day. And at two thousand feet deep, they weren't that expensive to complete. It was an exciting play and we had a headstart of a year or more on our competitors. For Sabre Petroleums, this was a lucrative project.

We drilled other wells in Alberta and southeastern Saskatchewan that were good producers and gave us cash flow. For instance, there was significant oil production from the Cardium and Belly River zones in the Pembina area of the Alberta Basin, seventy miles southwest of Edmonton, where we participated with Ed Koetsier of Leddy Exploration, the most capable and efficient petroleum engineer I've ever worked with.

American Metal Climax, whom I partnered with at Alcon, had left Canada by now and supposedly wanted to sell its interest in a high yielding oil field in the Rainbow Lake area of northwestern Alberta. We had Rod Mc-Daniel do an independent evaluation of what turned out to be a top-quality property drawing interest from five other companies. But all proposals to buy it, including ours, were rejected. Curious, I called Amax's local manager, Lloyd Parks: "Lloyd, we made a bid and I understand you've turned down all the offers. Well, if we were a hundred miles out, fine, but were we anywhere close?" He told me roughly how much. "Lloyd, let me come over and talk to you." And we negotiated the deal. Sabre had to move up only $100,000 to about $1.9 million. It seems I was the only bidder who bothered to follow up. The property proved to be a long-term, stable field and while some people would have said we paid top dollar for it, oil prices rose dramatically over the next few years. So if oil was $2.70 a barrel when we bought, it was more like $20 when we sold in 1976.

CARLO, MEANWHILE, WAS FOLLOWING HIS OWN QUITE different drummer. In *The Acquisitors*, Peter C. Newman, the chronicler of the Canadian business Establishment, called him "Alberta's most mysterious big-money man." Carlo *was* that to many people, despite being friends with Conservative Premier Peter Lougheed, federal Liberal cabinet minister Jack Horner, Alberta Social Credit leader Rod Sykes, the legendary construction and energy entrepreneur Fred Mannix, and Doc Seaman. By the end of the Seventies, Carlo was reportedly worth $100 million as he invested in various ventures, including a sporting-goods store; began developing office real estate in Calgary through his Mico Developments; and bought thousands of acres of good agricultural properties. At least twelve thousand of those acres were ranch and farm land just north of the city near Airdrie, where he moved his thoroughbreds to run on his private racetrack.

When Carlo acquired race horses in Europe, Becky and I accompanied him on that trip with a veterinarian to fly them back in a big Hercules transport plane. There I saw his father again after our brief meeting in Calgary a dozen years earlier. The von Maffeis were hospitable and after dinner and schnapps, we sat in their large living room when I commented on the fact that the fireplace had no screen—"in Canada we'd have one."

"Oh, here the wood is perfectly dry," The senior von Maffei said. And at that very point, there was an explosion and the sparks flew out on the expensive rug. Given our surroundings, I was discreetly silent.

Becky recalls a huge home full of beautiful china, breakfasts with Carlo's friendly mother dressed in a Chanel suit, trading tips about makeup in her fluent English while the men were away, and elegant lunches beneath a great vine-covered trellis on the back patio.

We could see where Carlo, who was close to his mom, got his taste and appetite for good living. He built a home on his ranch for his wife, Chris-

Becky and her dancing partner—Carlo von Maffei—in a typically splendid environment the baron enjoyed.

tina von Maldeghem, and their three children. This was a multi-room mansion framed in steel and concrete, with gym, squash court, a vault to hold his art collection, a trophy room with full-sized polar and brown bear and various African big-game animals, a big cellar for his family's German white wines, eight fireplaces, and a master bedroom of twenty-four hundred square feet (Newman referred to it as "the world's largest bungalow"). There were separate servants' quarters for maids, nannies, and a cook. As Doreen said after dining there, "You could hardly see the person sitting across from you." Carlo had sports cars for the city, but he loved the Subaru wagon he drove around the ranch. He entertained the king and queen of Sweden here, among many other prominent folk.

All this would start to unravel in 1982, some years after selling Sabre. Carlo's and my birthdays are just one day apart and we usually got together to celebrate and exchange small gifts. When I was on the road that year and sent him a hunting book, he called to thank me and said he had something for when I returned. A few days later, Becky and I were in Ontario to visit her mother when he phoned and in a frantic voice said, "The bank has suddenly closed in on me."

"It couldn't be that serious," I said. "I'm coming back tomorrow and I'll come and see you."

I realized right away that he'd continued to buy acreage around his ranch and commercial land in Calgary at high prices as the inflationary spiral of the Eighties sent interest rates rapidly soaring above 20 per cent. To help him out, I bought a piece of land he'd optioned, but it was just a drop in a holey bucket. The bottom line is that Carlo stayed the course and

fought the battle with courage. It wasn't enough: in 1985 the Commerce—
my old bank—put his holdings into receivership, including some industrial
property, farm lands, and his country estate that went on to the market for a
$7-million price tag. On his final night in his baronial home, Becky and I had
a sad dinner with him and Christina.

They returned to Germany, to his mother's estate at Karlsruhe on the
Rhine, where he helped the Baroness von Maffei develop her valuable property. And though she has since died and he and Christina divorced, Carlo
eventually got back on his feet financially as a successful and capable German land developer and still lives in the family home. Some of the people
he associated with in Canada were fairweather friends who abandoned him
during his crisis, but many others who were supportive found it difficult to
maintain contact with him. To this day, Carlo von Maffei and Harley Hotchkiss remain close comrades.

BUT ALL THAT WAS IN THE FUTURE. ONE YEAR INTO THE
decade of the Seventies, the Alberta economic landscape began undergoing
convulsive change. A new Conservative government, under a dynamic Calgary lawyer named Peter Lougheed, shocked the province—me included—
by ending the thirty-six-year reign of the Socreds (then led by Harry Strom).
While I didn't vote for Peter's resurgent party then out of respect for Ernest
Manning, I came to know and support the premier in later years. He un-
settled the petroleum industry almost immediately by increasing the provincial royalties that companies paid on their production. As Peter says now,
"We held a public hearing and allowed the industry to give their points of
view. But we were pretty determined that we would change that maximum
royalty of 16 2/3 per cent to no maximum on future leases. It was very, very
controversial." But some of the pain of that policy waned within a couple of
years: the Organization of Arab Petroleum Exporting Countries declared an
embargo on shipping oil to the U.S. in retaliation for the American support
of Israel in the Yom Kippur War against a coalition of Arab states. One side
effect was to attract major investment in oil-rich Alberta and turn it into the
wealthiest province in Canada.

The embargo began in 1973, six years after Sabre's launch. Doreen
and I were the only direct employees and she was bearing a heavy workload,
looking after our office, our land, and accounting. Carlo and I were realizing that we'd developed substantial production and would soon have to
increase our staff and perhaps even go public. This would be a logical move
because we really had minimal capital of our own in the pot, the rest being

modest shareholders' loans. On my side, there had been a progression from Alcon, where I'd had a relatively small financial interest, to Sabre, where I was essentially my own boss yet still a minority partner with about 40 per cent. Amid Alberta's boom, the next step for me might be to go entirely solo—calling my own shots, reporting to no one else. Carlo had proved to be a great partner, but if we were a larger public company, I wasn't sure what that would mean for our business relationship.

Finally sitting down to talk about such things, we mutually decided to sell Sabre. Was it a wise decision? In hindsight, maybe not: the company had strong support with consultants such as geologist Lloyd Bebensee and landman Cliff Fiesel, a good solid base of assets in oil and gas properties, and some fascinating exploration plays. Given the economic climate, there was no reason to believe we couldn't increase our profitable projects. But the truth was, I had never had much appetite to run a public company, preferring to make deals with a minimum of bureaucracy. In a small office, the endlessly efficient Doreen Warren kept all the financial detail off my shoulders (as she still does all these years later).

Carlo and I talked to a number of potential buyers and eventually fashioned a deal with Sun Oil of Philadelphia, which had drilled its first producing well in Alberta back in 1949. Much of its Canadian exploration focus in recent years had been on its pioneering Great Canadian Oil Sands project in Fort McMurray. Sun agreed to buy us out for nearly $13 million.

There was only one big catch. The deal had to be approved by Ottawa's new Foreign Investment Review Agency—FIRA. Pierre Trudeau's Liberal government had enacted the legislation in 1973 to screen foreign corporations acquiring Canadian companies or setting up new ventures in this country. The idea was to protect indigenous industries from the dominance of outsiders who might pose a threat to national sovereignty. But for too many Canadian companies, there was nothing to fear but FIRA itself—as we soon learned.

The next couple of years were the worst in my oil and gas career. We had to face the nightmarish bureaucracy of the review agency. I believe we were the first energy company to apply to them. Sun, having bought subject to FIRA approval, was very good in leaving me alone. But while I managed our existing assets, my hands were tied in terms of seeking new petroleum plays. It was an awful dilemma for someone with an exploration bent. The Sun people and I made several trips to Ottawa to answer FIRA's questions about our deal—which was really one of the simplest transactions in the world. Sabre was a company with only two shareholders; there was nothing complicated about us.

Though the agency was supposed to make a decision within a reasonable length of time, it could defer its ruling by demanding more information, as it did with us. At one tough, all-day meeting, its representatives—many of them Brits brought over to administer the new agency—had peppered us with questions. Don Kennedy, a lawyer for Sun and a patient, helpful guy, finally said, "Look, we're happy to co-operate with you people. We know this is a new agency and you're new to the oil and gas business, and we're happy to try and help you understand."

"Oh, Mr. Kennedy," one of the FIRA fellows said, "we know all we need to know about your business."

Afterwards, I wished I'd just tipped the table over and said, "Go ahead and figure it out." I thought, *Of all the gall. They'd caused us so much trouble and to put a guy like Don down when he was trying to co-operate while we were at their mercy.*

Many months passed. In February 1975, when Becky and I were in Orlando, Florida, I sat stewing about the deal until telling her, "I've had enough. I'm going up to Ottawa myself." The guy running FIRA was called Murray; I'd met him because his daughter and ours had gone to Balmoral Hall, a girls' school in Winnipeg. He'd worked for the Hudson's Bay Company there and then joined FIRA. I went to his office early in the morning and sat outside as people started filtering in and staring at me. "Do you have an appointment?"

"No, I'd like to see him for just a minute to see when we could make an appointment."

There was scurrying around and finally a woman came out and said, "Mr. Murray will be here, but you don't have an appointment."

I told her the basics of my plight. "This is my life's work. If Mr. Murray can't see me today, I want to know when he can and I'll stay here or come back, but I need to get this settled."

She told me to return to my hotel and she'd make sure he saw me. That afternoon he and I did meet. He spent a lot of time telling me about all the problems he had running this new agency. I actually managed to get my complaints off my chest. But in the end, none of it did Carlo and me any good. A few months later, the feds turned the Sabre-Sun deal down. They didn't have to give any defining reason, and they didn't. So at what was likely one of the most productive times in my career—I was in my mid-forties when we started the negotiations—they took more than a couple of years out of my life when I couldn't really do anything expansive with the company. The review process was frustrating, time-consuming—and to absolutely no purpose. It wasn't until the mid-Eighties that the heavily criticized FIRA was rechristened as Investment Canada and the Conservatives transformed it to actively promote and facilitate investment in the country by both Canadians and foreigners.

But a decade earlier, we had been forced to sell to somebody else, presumably a pure-blood Canadian. We found Gary Last, an engineer who'd co-founded a petroleum consultancy in Calgary. He put together a consortium of investors, including an insurance company and a brokerage firm, and we closed the deal in February 1976, less than nine years after Sabre's birth. The company had grown from a dead start to daily production of about seven thousand barrels of oil equivalent, using $900,000 of equity capital and a portion of Carlo's shareholder loans. The buyers paid cash—about $24 million—and I walked away with about $8 million. That was a lot of money for me, with my background, but then I'd put a lot of myself into the company. The irony is that with FIRA's delaying tactics and eventual rejection of the Sun Oil bid, Sabre had risen in value as oil prices increased—which left us with a much richer payout when we did sell and made me look smarter than I really was.

Last and his investors didn't do as well with the company as they hired more people and increased the overhead from our exceedingly lean operation. Three years later, Sabre was sold to Dome, which split it into two components, mainly to maximize Alberta royalty tax credits. One of the units ultimately moved to Amoco Canada Petroleum (which acquired the embattled Dome in 1988). The other was bought by ex-Domer Jack Pirie, who still runs its today as the successful Sabre Energy. I'm sure some of its assets still have my fingerprints on them, including wells in the Pembina field that keep producing.

It felt good to sell Sabre Petroleums. My main business would continue to be in oil and gas as the involvements I pursued on my own expanded to Texas, Oklahoma, Michigan, and both onshore and offshore Louisiana. I wonder if my Scottish mother ever read Robbie Burns' lovely line about "the glorious privilege of being independent." Being free of Sabre gave me a sense of total independence for the first time and set me up for the next act of my life: operating personally and within a single-shareholder company nostalgically named for my old college hockey team—Spartan Holdings.

A BOONE COMPANION

A year after Boone Pickens moved to Canada in 1966 as an aggressive petroleum explorer, his newly public Mesa Petroleum did a hostile takeover of
a Kansas gas venture thirty times larger. Hugoton Production was named for
a field that held the most onshore natural gas outside Alaska. In the decades
he ran Mesa, it has produced well over $1 billion worth of hydrocarbons from
that field and along the way became the biggest American gas producer.

Ever since we met, Boone and I have maintained a friendship so close
that I'd been on his corporate board, invested in projects with him, contributed to some of the same philanthropic endeavours—and still invest with
him and exchange phone calls an average of once a week.

During the 1980s, he was considered the consummate takeover artist,
with his face on the cover of *Time* and *Fortune* magazines and his reputation as a shareholders' champion that encouraged him to think of running
for the American presidency. Along with his many ups, he has gone through
some dizzying downs, including accusations of being a greenmailer after
he and those he represented had profited from the sale of shares in huge
companies he'd failed to take over. In 1996, he resigned from a debt-heavy
Mesa as gas prices plummeted, but the following year launched BP Capital,
an energy hedge fund. In 2006, BP and other investments earned him $1.5
billion, making him more money than in any year since he'd become an entrepreneur. And the previous year, he'd been named the fifth-most-generous
philanthropist in the U.S. as he gave away almost $230 million (*see page
293*). No wonder he's been called both a King Lear and a Robin Hood.

I played a small role in his Canadian operation as a trustee for the
employee pension plan of Altair Oil and Gas and participated in several oil
and gas ventures. Although the company was flourishing as the most active driller in western Canada, in 1979 Boone sold Altair to Calgary's Dome
Petroleum for $600 million and future royalty payments. He hired me to
handle the bidding process. Mesa was charging the eighteen or so interested
companies $25,000 each to study its financial data (that's $450,000 just
to let them look). Dome president Bill Richards was among the bidders who
came to my office.

In the early Eighties, I also participated with Boone in offshore gas
exploration in Louisiana. The operator was the well-respected Cockrell Oil
Corporation of Houston, headed by his friend Ernie Cockrell Jr. Boone and I
took a small interest in what began as an exciting two-zone deep gas discov-

ery at 17,200 and 17,400 feet—at a time when such gas was selling at more than $9 a thousand cubic feet and the wells were capable of each producing eight to ten million cubic feet a day. But they were expensive, costing about $10 million each, and one well, drilled to twenty thousand feet to unsuccessfully test lower zones, cost $20 million.

Although our wells produced more than forty million cubic foot a day at their peak, problems soon surfaced. Ours were on State of Louisiana lands while offsetting federal lands were owned by Kerr-McGee Corporation of Oklahoma City. We became rivals in a race to drill these high-priced wells, but, in the end, the gas reservoirs were over-drilled and production started to decline rapidly. And that—combined with a sharp drop in natural-gas prices—made what we thought would be a highly economic project only modestly profitable.

Boone had asked me to become a director of Mesa. This was during the era he attempted takeovers of petroleum giants such as Gulf Oil, which drove up the stock and netted Mesa a $404-million profit, Phillips Petroleum, and Unocal, which led to lawsuits that cost his company $42.8 million. Boone would say, "We got a bloody nose on this one, let's see what we can salvage out of it and move on." Like Doc Seaman, he's a guy you'd want sitting next to you in any tough situation.

Because my background was small business, and Alcon and Sabre were privately run, all the high-level legalities that haunt big public companies like Mesa concerned me. I was at a deposition in New York once when Boone was attempting the Phillips hostile takeover. High-powered lawyers for the other side were questioning me about a small private real-estate company I owned; I didn't realize anybody even knew anything about Colony Developments—though there was absolutely nothing to hide. They knew so much about me that I wondered what was coming next. Mesa's lawyers, meanwhile, were telling me not to volunteer anything, which went against my nature: my inclination was, "Ask me and I'll tell you." After a morning of this, I decided to skip lunch with our team and go for a long walk just to clear my head. I stayed on the board until 1986 when Mesa changed to a limited partnership and I felt there wasn't much need for a Canadian director.

I've had an intimate look at this extraordinary guy through my time on Boone's board, our investments together, and our quail-hunting expeditions on his beautiful, fifty-thousand-acre Mesa Vista ranch on the Canadian River in the Texas Panhandle. At Mesa, he gave stock options to everyone, including the secretaries. He always employs a lean staff—and I don't mean their weight, but the size of his payroll. Yet he believes in corporate aircraft, largely to get his people back to their families faster following a road trip. He has long been a fitness buff, working out with a personal trainer, but also funding an in-house fitness centre for his young employees, and playing racquetball better than any of them. Boone is a serious basketball and football fan; he gave his alma mater, Oklahoma State University, $165 million, much of it to enhance its sports programs, especially football. I once got him to a hockey game when the Calgary Flames were in the Stanley Cup finals, but he observed, "Why would you want to own a hockey team and lose money year after year just to hold a trophy?"

Boone has married three times since Lynn, with whom he had four children in their twenty-two-year union. He was with his second wife, Beatrice, for twenty-four years, and then one day he called me to say: "Bea and I are getting a divorce."

"Come on, get serious."

"Yeah," he said, "I've got an eighteen-year-old girlfriend."

"Now I know you're not serious. No eighteen-year-old would even look at you," I said. Well, he was—about the divorce, if not the reason. The only advice I gave him was to end things quickly and, as he would say, move on. It didn't wind up that way: the divorce was long and messy. He then married a nice woman in her fifties named Nelda, but that was a brief relationship. His last wife (he swears) is Madeleine, the widow of Allen Paulson, owner of Gulfstream Aerospace. She is smart and successful in her own right, once running a business to supply flight attendants and equipment for private jets and now the owner of California's Del Mar Country Club and a string of winning racehorses.

I'm not surprised that Boone likes Becky and she likes him. She's as plain-spoken and straightforward as he is and, whenever they're together, Becky seems to keep him a little bit grounded (just as she does me). As Boone might say of her, "If she tells ya a goose can pull a wagon, I'd say load the wagon."

And that's one of the many reasons Boone and I have been friends for fifty years.

Boone and Becky are like-minded pals in their forthrightness and he enjoys her down-to-earth approach to life.

Mike Carr-Hartley, my personal hunter from Kenya, with a Mrs. Gray's lechwe (neither rare nor endangered) in the Nile swamp area in southern Sudan.

A-HUNTIN' WE WOULD GO

It was the summer of 1976, not long after Carlo and I had sold Sabre Petroleums. Here I was at the far northern border of Botswana—on the scorching sand and amid thick reeds along the mighty Chobe River—when the lions leapt out of the tall grass, roaring and charging at me furiously.

I wasn't alone. There were three native trackers, two of them Bushmen who could stalk a wild animal across a cement floor, and a professional hunter, a calm, quiet third-generation white Kenyan named Pat Carr-Hartley. He lived in the northwest corner of Botswana, was an honorary game warden for the Chobe National Park there, and later became a wildlife consultant for filmmakers. We'd had a few days on a safari with the king and queen of Sweden and the king's princess sister and her husband at the Chobe camp. Then we moved on with Carlo's other friends, Fred Eaton, the Toronto department-store heir, and his wife, Nicky, to settle into a camp at Saile, where I began tracking lions.

You can hunt these legendary kings of the beasts in three ways: catch them resting at noon, wait for them from behind a blind over such bait as antelope, or track them. I elected to stalk them. There were days of 115-degree Fahrenheit heat and on the fifth one, the Eatons were out on their own with another guide when Pat and I took off early in the morning aboard a Toyota pickup. Several times in the first four days, we had walked, following distinctive four-toed paw prints into the brush, only to hear guttural growls as the lions fled. Pat and the trackers communicated in the Swahili dialect, which left me always on the edge, never knowing how close we were to the animals. In light khaki long pants, toting heavy .460-calibre rifles, we were walking behind the trackers when Pat whispered, "Be really on your guard here. There's a lioness and cubs in this pack."

It was just about noon when we traced them down to the reedy river and back out on the sand of this arid country, where thorn bushes nicknamed "wait a bits" snag your clothing with their angled long spikes. The Bushmen motioned us to move up. We could see where the pride had been lying in the midday sun.

The five of us were standing quietly, whispering—and then from a patch of grass thirty yards away, a lioness came charging with a snarl, followed by half a dozen other animals. A full sized mature male was the last to emerge. Raising my rifle, I yelled to Pat, "Which one?"

"That one!" he cried, pointing to the menacing, shaggy-maned beast racing away to the right.

I wheeled and fired. Surprisingly, given the controlled panic of the moment, it couldn't have been a better shot. The bullet slammed right behind the lion's shoulder and into the heart and lungs. As he fell, I looked around. After a false charge, the lioness and two other mothers had escaped with their offspring. Pat hadn't had to pull the trigger.

We were about five miles from our vehicle. "Look, Harley, it's a hot day, I'll go back and get the truck," he suggested. "You wait here." Waiting with the trackers for a couple of hours, I thought, *There was only one male with the lionesses and their cubs and they're not going to be very happy with you, Harley. What'll you do if they come back?*

They didn't, and Pat did. And bagging that trophy lion was the highlight of my first African safari. Carlo had arranged the three-week trip as an all-expense-paid gift to me in the wake of the Sabre sale. In the past, he'd invited me on several hunts on the Alaska Peninsula and Kodiak Island for caribou, moose, and Kodiak bear. This time, though, it was country-club camping. The baron always travelled first class, with fine food and wine and pedigreed hunting partners. In Africa they included not only Fredrik Eaton

The honeymooning King Carl XVI Gustav and Queen Silvia of Sweden during a safari in 1976 that Carlo invited me on.

("the unofficial dean of Canada's family dynasties," to quote Peter Newman) and his wife, but also the Swedish and German royals. King Carl XVI Gustav was on a honeymoon with his bride, Queen Silvia (following the first wedding of a reigning Swedish monarch since 1797) and his princely brother-in-law Johann Georg (Hansi) von Hohenzollern and his sister, Princess Birgitta. She and Hansi had been married for sixteen years by then (at their wedding, she'd worn a tiara once owned by Napoleon's Josephine).

All of us, royalty included, slept under canvas in a comfortable camp with a cook tent and reed-enclosed showers—a bucket of hot water above you and a tap to let loose a two-minute soaking. The king was open and affable as he sat around the campfire with a drink and a cigar. Birgitta was a slender, attractive woman and the friendliest of this well-born lot. Her Hansi was a happy, life-loving companion, who was a director of the Bavarian state art collections in Munich after they separated in 1990. Birgitta would move to the island of Mallorca in Spain.

During my baptism of big-game hunting, the lion-tracking expedition was the toughest of all. I'm now somewhat embarrassed to admit that during our safari, I shot eighteen magnificent specimens of wildlife in all. They ranged from zebras and warthogs to the small deer-like sitatunga living in the swamps and large antelopes, including the dark-hided, barrel-chested sable, with vertical horns that curve back, and gemsbok, a heavyset tan antelope with long, straight horns and black-and-white face markings. I had all the trophies shipped back home for mounting (the lion became a rug) and eventually donated them to the Calgary Zoo.

On that trip, we allowed ourselves a sidetrip of sheer luxury. After some hard days of tracking, Fred and I began feeling a bit bushed and sneaked away on a small chartered plane to what was then Rhodesia (now Zimbabwe) to view Victoria Falls—by some measures the biggest and most beautiful cascade in the world—and had a luxurious dinner in a casino.

In my future were two more of Carlo's big-game safaris (which I insisted on paying for). One a couple of years later took me to the southern Sudan with him and another Swedish princess, Birgitta's sister Desirée, a dark-haired beauty with a wide smile and a talent for textile design, and her husband, Baron Niclas Silverschiöld, an officer in the Swedish army reserves. A count came along too: Axel Douglas, the lanky scion of a Scottish family that moved to Germany.

Since the 1950s, Sudan had been in a permanent civil war, which was on pause when we were there. Hunting from three camps—one called Bo River—we saw abandoned villages and missionary schools still bearing the scars of machine-gun fire. I hunted the giant Lord Derby eland, the fleet Coke's hartebeest (kongoni in Swahili), the antlered wildebeest (or gnu).

The main trophy in this rainforest area was the plentiful bongo, a beautiful member of the antelope family with orange hide and white stripes. After several days, we were on our last morning of hard hunting with only glimpses of bongo. Deciding to call it quits, I was walking ahead of the others when a large bongo bull came out of the trees in front of me, seventy-five yards to my left. When I pulled up to shoot, our guides behind me yelled, "Don't shoot!" The bongo heard them and broke into a gallop ahead and to my right. That's when they

Sudan 1978: Swedish Princess Desirée, and her husband, Baron Niclas Silverschiöld.

cried, "Shoot!" I picked an open spot ahead of it and when it reached that point, I fired. The bongo dropped instantly with a broken neck. It was a lucky shot because I was really aiming for the left shoulder. Afterwards, I learned that if I'd shot at first, a native man in our vehicle up the trail would have been directly in my line of fire.

This time I was with Pat Carr-Hartley's brothers Roy and Mike. On one expedition, Mike had deliberately antagonized a herd of elephants with his truck and a couple of days later had us climb out and gingerly approach what turned out to be the same cows and calves. Suddenly catching our scent, one elephant turned and thundered towards us. We were still a couple of hundred yards from the vehicle. Mike fired one shot from his double-barrelled .470 rifle in the dirt ahead of the animal, who didn't slow for a second. He shot again and this time the cow hit the ground, but then got up again and fled. Mike had purposely aimed for the bony structure of the skull, simply stunning the elephant.

My only regret was shooting an elephant myself. My family had asked me not to, but in the excitement of that first Botswana hunt, I did. It was a mature bull downed with a single shot to the brain. I still feel remorse at killing such a magnificent animal; I resolved never to repeat that deed.

Later, not learning our lesson about startling wildlife, we tiptoed up behind a rhinoceros in savannah country. I was photographing the rhino when it swung around and chased us—my final, shaky picture, taken from behind a tree, shows a plume of sand bursting in front of it from Mike's bullet.

After our Bo River camp, Mike and I drove to Lake Nyubor in the southern Sudd, a swampy part of the Nile system. Passing through a few towns, including one called Wau, with a population of perhaps four hundred thousand, we saw people with legs grotesquely swollen from elephantiasis and limbs lost to leprosy. On the last road into the camp, we started meeting tall, rangy men and women carrying their possessions. They were Dinkas, fleeing from another group in an ongoing battle between tribes. At Nyubor, some of them—bearing spears and hide shields, and their faces smeared with ash—killed a man in the water in front of our camp. With Mike and me the only whites in the area, I was frankly frightened. I took all three of my guns into the bucket-of-water shower and kept them beside me in my tent that night. Our government game scout found the spear that had slain the victim and gave it to me to take home, to tranquil Calgary, where it was a vivid reminder of the horror that the largest country in Africa was enduring.

At another point, two badly frightened young Dinka boys came into our camp after one had been bitten in the hand, probably by a puff adder.

Spear-bearing Dinka warriors with shields of hide gather after a tribal battle near our camp at Lake Nyubor.

His arm was swollen right up to the shoulder. The only thing we could do was load them into a vehicle to take them to a small village several miles away. Although we never know what happened to him, he would likely have lost him limb and maybe his life.

As I wrote to Becky in a long lovelorn letter:

This is an unbelievably primitive area. Yesterday we hunted in the swamps— waded in mud and water at times up to our waists. Occasionally there are slightly higher spots where people live—whole families in an area smaller than our living room. They live on fish, roots & whatever animals they can spear.

This is the last trip of this kind I will make—I really don't have the desire to hunt animals anymore & it is far too long to be apart from you.

Despite my vow, in 1980 I was lured to Africa again with Carlo, Baron Niclas and Princess Desirée—to the Kalahari (meaning "great thirst"), the scrub-brush semi-desert that covers more than three-quarters of Botswana. A small single-engine plane landed us beside a dried-up pan where we set up camp. Our guides, diminutive Kalahari Bushmen, took us to see some others nearby who hunted bat-eared foxes for their meat and skins. There were two couples, including a mother nursing a baby. And you could almost hold all their belongings in your two hands. One of the young girls was at a "sip well", a small hole dug in the fine yellowish sand and filled with fine grass to collect traces of moisture that seeped in. She was sucking on a bamboo reed and spitting the water into an ostrich eggshell that she then balanced on her head to their camp. Others were roasting a bat-eared fox in the ashes of an open fire for their supper. Maybe I was projecting, but despite what seemed to be abject poverty, they looked happy, healthy, self-reliant—and I wondered, *Who's got things right, them or us?*

I came back home with two bites from a scorpion on my right hand. At first I thought it had been a snake, which could have delivered instanta- neous death. The bites had swollen my arm up to the elbow so much that I couldn't move the safety catch on my rifle. One guide had laughed and said I might lose the hand; the tingling lasted for at least a month. But I also returned from this trip with a decision never to hunt big game again. At the time I was there, more than one hundred thousand lions roamed through- out Africa. And into this century, game censuses show that the numbers of wild animals in Botswana are still plentiful. So I never had the feeling that the well-managed safaris I went on were part of any wholesale slaughter of dwindling species.

Charles Dickens, one of the classic English writers I read as a boy, once wrote, "There is a passion for hunting something deeply implanted in the hu- man breast." Some modern writers (Ernest Hemingway, for one) glorified big-game hunting in their prose. But I'd never had any great wish to kill wild animals other than the rabbits and squirrels we ate on the Hotchkiss farm.

In the beginning, going on safari seemed novel and exciting; I was caught up in the challenge of it—pursuing only mature trophy game that took hard work to track and find, travelling with highly skilled professional hunters, obeying all the game laws strictly. Yet I was suffering pangs about this kind of hunting. I took Becky on an expedition to Botswana in 1982 and again three years later I went with Joe Mathes, an Alberta hunting guide and co-owner of our favourite Calgary restaurant, La Chaumière. The only targets I went after were birds, and when I once went to retrieve some ducks, a man in a khaki outfit stepped out from the bushes in front of me with a machine gun. You can imagine what went through my mind. He turned out to be a border guard with the Zimbabwe army—who liked the birds, which I promptly gave him. And in Botswana in '87, I brought Boone Pickens and his third wife, Bea, who fell in love with shooting animals in later safaris even though he never enjoyed the sport. But aside from a wild-boar hunt with Carlo in Austria, in the quarter-century since my African safaris, I've never shot anything bigger than a bird again.

Some of those shoots were with Carlo and his royal pals, including the king, Princess Birgitta, and Hansi. There were pheasant hunts in
Austria, Czechoslovakia, and England. Becky was sometimes along—
though never hunting—and recalls the women in fur coats and Hermes
scarves as they tramped through the mud. Telling the story now, she says, "I
just walked around and sat behind them on a little stool. They spread all the
nice lunch out on the field for you under a shelter and served champagne. It
was black tie every night for dinner, where they talked a lot in German. We
grew up as farm kids; their way of life was totally different from those of our
families."

For my first European pheasant shoot, Carlo took me to a prestigious
gunmaker in London, Holland and Holland, where in a moment of weakness
I ordered an expensive pair of their Royal shotguns. Meanwhile, Becky had
outfitted me with a tweed shooting jacket with matching knee-length trou-
sers and knee socks. In Austria, between the guns and my attire, I attracted
some attention from Carlo's group of elite guests. Each of us had a loader,
who reloads your second gun while you're using the first. I couldn't communicate with my Austrian loader, which became a problem when the second
barrel in each of my guns failed to fire. By the end of the day, I was a basket
case. I had to borrow a pair of guns to finish the three-day shoot. When I
took the Royals back to Holland and Holland, a partner in the Establishment
firm was flustered and suggested that it might have been damp in Austria
at the time. "Not really," I said. When I later told this story to Boone Pickens, he retorted, "Aw hell, tell him I've got a Remington pump that shoots
under water."

The firm eventually found that each gun had a different defect. I lost
confidence in the repaired Royals and sold them to Fred Eaton. And now I
rely on my old reliable Brownings.

More suited to our background have been the outings with family
and friends in North America. I'm one of about seventy members of a hunting club on Griffith Island in Lake Huron's Georgian Bay in Ontario. After
General Motors used it as a corporate retreat, this private game reserve was
acquired by a group headed by John Robarts, the province's former premier.
On a twenty-six-hundred-acre outlier of the Niagara Escarpment, the beautiful treed island had white-tail deer and wild turkeys, an introduced stock
of pheasants and partridge, and a range for skeet and clay-pigeon shooting.
Our family joins me there annually in the summer with our grandchildren for
swimming and fishing and I bring guests in the fall to shoot pheasants.

On one winter trip, I took Becky's brother, Don Boyd, to fly into Griffith
on a four-passenger Cessna; he'd never flown before. A direct cross-wind

was blowing snow across the island runway and when the pilot cut the power to land, we went out of control, missed the runway—and luckily, a large grove of trees ahead of us—did a complete end-over-end flip, and came to rest badly damaged upside down. Saved by the deep snow, none of us was seriously hurt. My brother-in-law was hanging head down from his seat belt with a bump on his head. As I hurriedly helped him out, while fearing fire, all I could say was, "Don, I'm sorry—we don't normally land this way."

But in the fall of 1978, Fred and Nicky Eaton joined Becky and me to visit Griffith with several guests, including Carlo and his wife, Christina, and Boone and his wife, Bea. In late afternoon, we were on the island's sturdy, but loaded, diesel-powered boat from the mainland when the full blast of a storm hit us. Big waves washed over the bow. The club manager, Bud Tripp, was an efficient skipper, but in this case hadn't predicted the squall in the main channel. It took us an unnerving thirty minutes—the scariest waterborne trip I've ever endured. Finally landing, our subdued group wondered what the headlines would have read if we had all gone down.

In recent years I've invited a group of hockey friends—Glen Sather of the New York Rangers, Brian Burke with Anaheim, and Harry Sinden from Boston. Other regulars have been the Seaman brothers, Fred Eaton, and Boone Pickens. Jim Palmer tells the story of Bea Pickens joining the menfolk one day on Griffith: "We were all going out shooting and Bea came along and said, 'You fellas mind if I join you?' Of course, there was the usual shuffling of feet and then we said, 'No, no, not at all.' And the first four birds that flew up, Bea knocked them down. Then she said, 'Aw, I think that's enough for me today.' She just wanted to show us that she could do it."

Boone returns the favour by inviting me to his Mesa Vista ranch in Texas to hunt the wild quail he prefers. A crack shot since boyhood, he has top-of-the-line hunting dogs and gathers some exceptional people to hunt with him. One of them is Walter Stark of the Wilmer Eye Institute at Johns Hopkins University, among the world's leading eye surgeons. (He removed the cataracts of King Fahd of Saudi Arabia when the monarch was in his nineties.) Walter is entirely without pretence and loves what he's doing; he always brings a little eye kit with him and checks our eyes.

Hunting with friends you like and enjoy being with is the kind of camaraderie that is the true measure of the sport.

Hockey buddies showing off the pheasants on Griffith Island in 2008: Glen Sather of New York, me with the bird dog, Brian Burke of Anaheim, and Harry Sinden of Boston.

Relaxing after the hunt on Griffith in 1978: Jim Palmer, me, and Fred Eaton.

Doreen takes dictation in our office at Spartan Holdings, where I went out entirely on my own and got involved with some major companies, from the petroleum business to telecommunications.

CHAPTER 6

CORPORATE CONNECTIONS

Conwest, NOVA, and Telus

ARTIN CONNELL IS AN EXTRAORDINARY GUY. Which might not be that remarkable, given his extraordinary ancestor. He's the grandson of Fred Connell, a far-sighted Ontario mining engineer who became a great finder and builder of mines, producing everything from precious metals to lead, zinc, and uranium. In 1930 the Irish-Canadian Fred and his brother Harold founded Connell Mining and Exploration and eight years later Conwest Exploration to pursue its activities in western Canada and Alaska. Along with Kerr Addison in northeastern Ontario, once the country's biggest gold mine, they developed United Keno Hill mines in the Yukon, which at one point produced the most silver in Canada, and the Cassiar Asbestos Corporation mine in northern British Columbia, which had a successful forty-year run. Much later, I met Fred Connell, who still came to Conwest's Toronto office and stayed sharp as a miner's pick until his death at ninety-seven.

Martin was a latecomer to the family business. In the mid-Sixties the McGill grad was in his mid-twenties, a bond salesman with McLeod Young Weir and an investor in Toronto's nightlife haunts. After helping finance the Boiler Room bar and then a half-dozen other watering holes, including Ports of Call and Bemelmans, he also backed the bank loan for 21 McGill, the city's first modern women's club. By 1974, he'd joined Conwest and become president. A mass of seeming contradictions, this sophisticated, business-suited executive loved baking bread so much that he opened the Ace Bakery in Toronto with his second wife, Linda, to supply numerous restaurants. This full-bearded man who made his money in the capitalistic mining and petroleum industries had a strong social conscience, inspired by his wife, that much later led him to establish a charitable foundation, Calmeadow. It micro-financed the poor as they built bootstrap enterprises in Third World shantytowns and Canada's northern native communities. "Our role is catalytic," he explained at the time. "We're creating a new mechanism for lending money that is cost-effective and low-risk." He's also been on the board of the Salvation Army and the Canadian Save the Children Fund and chaired the Canadian Centre for Philanthropy and its Imagine Campaign to promote charitable giving. For his efforts, he would earn the Pearson Medal, awarded by the United Nations Association in Canada.

By the late Seventies Martin Connell became chair of Conwest Exploration and was transforming the public company into an independent natural-resource heavyweight through exploration and friendly acquisitions and mergers. That's when Martin and his president, John Lamacraft, decided

to become serious about investing in oil and gas properties in western Canada. And when they first approached me.

After somebody gave them my name, they came out to Calgary to pick my petroleum brain. I took to both of them. John Lamacraft was from Sudbury, an accountant who'd specialized in tax matters. Martin, seeing the quality of his work, had hired John, given him a lot of elbow room, and watched him grow into a highly capable entrepreneur. Over drinks at the Four Seasons Hotel, I was just trying to be helpful as they peppered me with

John Lamacraft

intelligent questions that led into a good general conversation about prospects. Not much more than a week later, they came back to say, "We want you to go to work for us."

"Well, look, I am not going to do that," I said. "I've been doing that all my life, and now I'm doing my own thing."

But knowing I wanted to pour some of my proceeds from the Sabre sale back into oil and gas, they suggested we invest together while I sought potential projects. They would give me better terms in the deal because of my experience. At that time, if you bought an oil or gas property, the cost was a 100-per-cent deduction; you didn't have to pay any tax on the asset until you got paid out. So you could afford to pay more buying it as an asset than by buying shares in the company. In late 1977, we made a a very simple deal in a two-page agreement and that began a seventeen-year relationship, the best corporate board experience I've ever had.

Going solo a year earlier had given me the freedom to pursue my passions without worrying about how they would affect others—whether bosses or partners—either financially or in terms of the time I devoted to any activity. Indulging myself, I could put substantial money into a sports team, chair the National Hockey League, donate some of my corporate and personal earnings to philanthropies of my choice, and get involved in businesses with my family—all of which I describe in the following chapters.

But being my own master also meant I could invest in and join the board of any company that interested me and wanted me as a director; there was nobody to second-guess my decisions. Starting with Alcon and then Sabre, I had decided I would never serve on a board without a significant investment in the venture. If I was to represent shareholders, I wanted to hold stock too; if my actions affected the corporate welfare one way or another, I should suffer or profit from my impact. In 1979, I became one of Conwest's eight directors. Among them was Martin's uncle, Earl Connell, and executive vice–president Colin Coolican, who'd been a partner in McCarthy & McCarthy of Toronto, one of the largest law firms in Canada.

Conwest's first western office was my new digs on the twelfth floor of the Dome Tower, which (as Doreen says) looked more like a den than a business setting with its burgundy leather chairs and the Canadian art I brought from home. At first, Conwest's only staff working with me there was an engineer, Randy Pawliw.

Because we soon began chasing petroleum plays that were right up my alley, I felt I was really contributing. And participating financially in most of the projects, I was looking after my own interests at the same time. The corporate style was more informal than a bank's or a big oil company's. Though Martin ran a good meeting, not much time was spent on corporate governance. But, boy, it was exciting—and he and John got things done.

Our first acquisition was two companies, Scottfield and Myrol, which had half a dozen oil and gas properties in Alberta. I did a lot of evaluation work on the deal, stickhandled an outside appraisal, and after Martin and John went over it with me number by number, we put in a successful bid for about $5 million, with me investing about a quarter of that. Some old friends in the Oil Patch were also bidding on it and thought we'd overpaid. But it turned out to be an outstanding acquisition as petroleum prices rose.

Within a year, Conwest moved to its own office space and started staffing up. Our game plan—echoing my role at Alcon and Sabre—was to set me loose to find enough acquisitions to generate cash flow to take more risks. In 1978, net income was $4.65 million and within a year grew to a still-modest $6.2 million. Conwest concluded an agreement in late '79 with a subsidiary, International Mogul Mines, to commit $10 million over three years to petroleum exploration and to take a ten-per-cent piece of an $11-million private drilling fund co-managed with Polaris Petroleums of Calgary. By 1980, with petroleum production a top priority, profits reached a record $14.1 million—healthy enough to issue dividends for the first time in eight years.

Early in the new decade, I introduced Conwest to Ernie Cockrell Jr. of Cockrell Oil, who'd participated with Boone Pickens and me in offshore developments in Louisiana and Texas. We took a small working interest in a $15-million program involving seventeen prospects. We had only moderate success with those gas plays and in one case could have lost our shirts by bidding on existing wells. I was in Houston when we bid on them without having a final, crucial piece of information from our evaluation process: the measurement of pressure that would tell us how fast their production was declining. The data, when it did arrive after the fact, was scary. The pressure was dangerously low; our bid had been much too aggressive. Our lawyer said our only chance was to hope that the well's owner hadn't yet accepted our offer. Rather than writing a formal letter withdrawing our bid, I hopped into a cab and took a sweaty drive to the fellow's office—and learned to my relief that he hadn't quite got around to dealing with it.

Conwest grew rapidly over the next ten years. It amalgamated its subsidiaries International Mogul and the Central Patricia and Chimo gold mines, which gave it a net asset value of about $86 million. It got Petroleum Incentive Program (PIP) grants from the feds—80 per cent of development costs—for its 8.5-per-cent interest in an all-Canadian venture for offshore exploration on the east coast. In 1986, Faraday Resources, which had direct interests in producing oil and gas properties in the West as well as a uranium mine in Ontario, became Conwest's major shareholder with an 18-per-cent equity interest and 49-per-cent voting interest. Conwest, in turn, owned 27 per cent of Faraday.

Three years later *Oilweek* editor Frank Dabbs was praising Martin, John, and Colin Coolican as "the Quiet Irishmen of Conwest" and "among the most unobtrusive men in Canadian petroleum." Operating eight different companies, he noted shrewdly, they had an agenda of long-term capital appreciation, the discipline to stay within their investment parameters, and the cash to support first-class assets:

> Among recent deals was the $24.25-million restructuring of Colonial Oil & Gas Ltd.'s debt two weeks ago. [Calgary-based Colonial had producing properties in Montana and Texas.]

> Another was the friendly takeover in September of 70 per cent of Bar-

ons Oil Ltd. [a Lethbridge, Alberta, oil and gas producer] by Mineral Resources International Ltd. [a zinc and silver miner in the Northwest Territories]; this month, MRI raised its stake in Barons to 84 per cent

Last summer, Conwest invested $4.7 million ($3.3 million in treasury share purchases and $1.4 million on the open market) to acquire 16 per cent of Altex Resources Ltd. [a low-cost junior explorer and producer].

Conwest has also been a strong supporter of Mical Capital Ltd., merchant banker Michael Cooke's rescue of Paragon Petroleum Ltd. (formerly Warren Explorations Ltd.). In turn, Paragon has sponsored the development of Alterio Resources Ltd., a junior capital pool.

There are three common denominators to these activities. First, Conwest does only friendly deals.

Second, companies drawn into orbit around Conwest invariably become healthier.

Third, minority shareholders always make gains after Conwest moves into the picture. . . .

Conwest is, today, a $300-million independent Canadian natural resource major with three business paths. It has western Canadian oil and gas interests on its own account as well as direct and indirect mining interests. It also holds the portfolio of investments in other public companies through which it carries on sponsorship activities.

If anybody built Conwest into a heavyweight, I'd have to say it was John Lamacraft. On first meeting, you'd think he was as imposing and gruff as a grizzly. John was someone who looked you square in the eye and spoke his mind, yet he was a large-hearted guy. From a business perspective, he was a true roll-up-your-sleeves leader. He and Colin also benefitted from the leadership of Jim Kalman, who ran the Calgary office, and the expertise of John Stephure, a petroleum engineer who became vice-president of Faraday and senior VP of Conwest. Smart and solid, John recognized the potential of a gas field near Sexsmith, in the Peace River Arch area of northwestern Alberta. While I and others in the company had reservations about the discovery, he aggressively pursued what turned out to be the sixth-largest gas pool found in the province since 1980. Within five years Conwest opened a large sour gas plant in the Sexsmith area.

In the mid-1980s, Conwest launched a sour gas plant amid a huge gas discovery in the Sexsmith region of northwestern Alberta.

Conwest, meanwhile, was diversifying. In 1990, it was an investor in Aber Resources, one of the largest landowners near the great discovery of diamonds in the Territories, where Aber went on to develop its own diamond mine. Two years later, Conwest was putting another $75 million into a series of small hydro-electric generating projects in Ontario after already spending $24 million. These projects were a nice balance, offering a stable flow of income.

I was now on the boards of both Conwest and Paragon Petroleum, counselling and questioning more than actively seeking petroleum plays. Paragon had plenty of Ontario acreage, which was naturally of interest to me, and emerged out of a mid-Eighties slump to become a reasonably successful producer. My stockholdings in both companies were significant. I held 250,000 Paragon shares when a company called North Rock Resources paid $134 million for it in 1998. By the mid-Nineties, my Conwest shares were worth $5 million.

In 1991, Conwest had suffered its first loss in history—$15.8 million. Four years on, it was profitable and essentially debt-free and its share price had doubled in the past year. At that propitious moment, Alberta Energy Company came calling.

AEC was the brainchild of Peter Lougheed's first-term Conservative government, a nearly all-Albertan public-private enterprise, partly backed by the Alberta Heritage Fund the Tories had created to save and invest revenues from provincial oil and gas. Half the initial capital of $150 million came from local investors, none of whom could hold more than one per cent. The company got some great baptismal gifts: an option to acquire up to 20 per cent of the enormous new Syncrude oil-sands project in Fort McMurray, the right to construct two-thirds of a power plant and to build its oil pipeline to Edmonton; and the exclusive petroleum permit to exploit the untapped thousand square miles of the Suffield block near Medicine Hat, where Canadian, British, and NATO forces had trained since the Second World War. Thousands of wells later, Suffield ranked among the continent's largest centres of natural gas.

AEC's first head was Dave Mitchell, a strong presence, an engineer from Great Plains Development, a subsidiary of Britain's Burmah Oil. His right-hand guy was Gwyn Morgan, who built a team to get Suffield up and running and then took over a diversity of divisions, from fertilizer plants to forest products. When Dave retired in 1993, Gwyn became president as Premier Ralph Klein (the successor to Peter Lougheed and Don Getty) sold the government's remaining shares in the company. Gwyn soon stripped AEC of its non-core assets, focusing entirely on oil and gas. But sensing it was vulnerable because the stock price wasn't indicative of the strength of the petroleum assets, he went looking to bulk up with a friendly acquisition.

I'd long known Gwyn from my days on the Independent Petroleum Producers Association, where he was an aggressive attacker of the monopolistic TransCanada Pipeline. The fourth child of a homesteading farmer near Carstairs, he'd graduated in mechanical engineering from the University of Alberta and worked as a reservoir engineer for the Alberta Oil and Gas Conservation Board under George Govier. He's been described as "thin as a blade of wheat" (from ninety-minute daily workouts) and "more like a school teacher" (with his small round eyeglasses) than a tycoon. An ardent Canadian with a healthy ego, he had the vision to see Conwest Explorations as an incredible opportunity to consolidate forces and create the largest domestic producer of North American gas and the continent's largest independent gas-storage operation.

Conwest's executives and directors realized that our company was faced with major capital needs to continue growing. When Gwyn approached Jim and me about a friendly takeover, we were prepared to listen. By now, Martin Connell was actively pursuing his philanthropic interests and as chairman and major shareholder was prepared to sell. John Lamacraft and

Colin Coolican sat on the front line of negotiations. It quickly seemed to make sense to pool the two players' resources, which would double AEC's assets. But the bargaining was hard when it came to weighing the value of our people and properties. In the end, though, the price was an eminently fair $1.1 billion. (At the time, I had roughly $10 million in AEC shares.)

The sale boosted Alberta Energy's market capitalization to $2.2 billion, its exploration land by 56 per cent, natural-gas reserves by 49 per cent, conventional oil reserves by 84 per cent, gas production by 55 per cent, and conventional oil production by 96 per cent. More important, the merger gave Gwyn and his team even more confidence, the courage to leap to the next level. And leap they did: "From there on," he recalls, "we got things moving. We got some momentum and the stock started showing it, and we just kept on going from there."

I was invited to become an AEC director, along with John and Martin (who stayed on the board only briefly). Over the next four years, I had a ringside seat as the company doubled petroleum production and expanded its midstream business (processing, storage, and transportation). It became the dominant foreign oil producer in Ecuador and a prominent gas producer in the U.S. Rocky Mountain area, which reflected Gwyn's growing focus on North American operations. In 2000, AEC posted a record $950 million in earnings.

That was the year I retired from the board—reluctantly, though not bitterly. I was seventy-three that summer, clearly beyond the upper age limit for a director of AEC. I don't agree with such an arbitrary age barrier. Obviously such restrictions are designed to allow a corporation to clean house of deadwood. But I felt strongly that my mind was still sharp and my interest and sense of involvement were still keen. By imposing an artificial, dogmatically applied age ceiling, a company can lose people with experience and good judgment.

It was too bad I wasn't there to see first-hand the next act in the Alberta Energy saga. That's when Gwyn went calling on PanCanadian Energy of Calgary, which led AEC as the country's largest overall petroleum producer. PanCanadian had boomed after the Canadian Pacific conglomerate (railways, ships, hotels, real estate, and coal-mining operations, among others) spun off its various parts, including the energy company. And following hush-hush talks led by Gwyn and David O'Brien—the Montreal lawyer who'd become chair of CP Ltd. and interim CEO of PanCanadian—shareholders agreed to a $9.8-billion, all-stock merger of equals. Rechristened EnCana for "energy" and "Canada" (Gwyn was a fierce Canada-firster), it instantly became the nation's third-largest industrial company and the world's largest independent oil and gas producer.

The rest is the stuff of Canadian economic history as EnCana overtook the Royal Bank of Canada as the top company on the benchmark domestic stock index. Its winning ways have continued since Gwyn took early retirement in 2005 and left his hand-groomed lieutenant, Randy Eresman, to become CEO.

ONE OF THE KEY DIRECTORS WITH Alberta Energy, who helped shape the AEC/PanCanadian merger, was Dick Haskayne. In conversa-

Dick Haskayne

tion with me, he'll recall that "you were quite choked up when you left the board, Harley." If I was, it's in part because I was leaving behind a corporate connection with people of quality like Dick. Both he and I were the only directors there who'd objected to the description of a payout that was essentially a pension plan for board members in all but name. Instead, it was officially labelled something like a "consulting allowance," to be paid when we retired. Coming on the board, I discussed the issue with Dick, who said, "Harley, I've run this thing down and I've kind of given in because technically it's legal, but I don't agree with the wording." That kind of concern about even the most obscure ethical questions was typical of him.

It's hard to do a shorthand summary of Richard Francis Haskayne. A compact guy who stands much taller than his size, Dick radiates great cheer and oozes commonsense intelligence wherever he goes. And he's gone many places in a career spacious enough for six men. In all of them he has distinguished himself with his business acumen and personal integrity, his caring private philanthropy and sterling corporate citizenship. A proud Canadian, he has fought to keep domestic companies in domestic hands—preaching this in the boardroom, on the lecture circuit, and in his recent, well-regarded book, *Northern Tigers: Building Ethical Canadian Corporate Champions*.

You get what you see with this straightforward fellow; to use that old British expression, there is no *side* to him. He reserves any anger for the dishonest and the greedy in the world of free enterprise. Over the years, he's encountered the likes of Dome's Jack Gallagher, Olympia & York's Reichmann brothers, and Hollinger Inc.'s Conrad Black. Responding once to my comment that you can't legislate integrity, he wrote, "You may not be able to legislate it, but you *can* set standards of ethical behaviour in the business environment and do your damndest to make sure the people around you and those running companies that affect our society hold true to them."

He knows this from front-row experience as the chairman or a director of such corporate giants as Manulife, CIBC, TransCanada Corporation, TransAlta Corporation, Fording Coal, and MacMillan Bloedel—where he was, to his great regret, the last chair of the built-in-B.C. lumber company when it was sold to its American rival Weyerhaeuser. With the birth of EnCana, he served on the board for three years and, at the urging of non-executive chairman David O'Brien, became chair of the human-resources committee and vice-chair of the corporate-governance committee.

One thing that endears Dick to me, of course, is his hockey prowess as a teenager, when he was invited to try out for the Medicine Hat Tigers, a Junior A team that sent many grads to the NHL (he passed and went to college instead). Another thing is his storybook humble roots. A self-described butcher's son from the hamlet of Gleichen, an hour east of Calgary, he put himself through the University of Alberta to earn a commerce degree. An accountant, he worked for the legendary Canadian petroleum company Hudson's Bay Oil and Gas and eventually became president. When HBOG was swallowed up by Dome Petroleum, he ran Home Oil, Interhome Energy, Interprovincial Pipe Line, and eventually NOVA Corporation.

I'd known Dick casually since the late 1950s, when I was at the Commerce and HBOG was one of the bank's best clients, though he never dealt with me directly. He and I worked together for the first time and got to know one another—became friends—in the Seventies while raising funds for Peter Lougheed's election campaigns (*see* Giving Back, *page 343*). But we never had a business relationship until the early Nineties when we were both involved in NOVA.

I'd joined the board of Alberta Gas Trunk Line—my first major one—in 1979, the same year I became a Conwest director. NOVA Corporation was the successor to AGTL, a 1954 creation of Ernest Manning's Socreds. The public utility was designed for the near-monopolistic transport of natural gas by pipeline within Alberta to the federally regulated TransCanada line (a move that would help keep Ottawa's hands off the province's natural resource). Almost from its start, I'd scraped some money together to buy shares in the company when I was still working for the Commerce and even bought some for my brother Ralph. It looked exciting and it was a truly Alberta venture.

Bob Blair had joined AGTL as executive vice-president in 1970 and became president and CEO the same year—touting his nationalistic dream of a pipeline from Prudhoe Bay, Alaska, to Alberta, through the company's transmission lines, and on to the rest of North America. Later he pulled out of the Alaskan consortium to propose his own all-Canadian pipeline from the Northwest Territories.

Blair—who grew up in Trinidad, where his father operated a refinery—was an anomaly in the Oil Patch: a Liberal in a Conservative province; a Canadian-firster in a town dominated by American corporations; a capitalistic joint venturer with Petro-Canada, the state-owned oil company. Highly intelligent, but a little offside with his peers, as in his early concern over environmental issues. He was a shy, almost morose-looking man in an industry teeming with extroverts, stocky of frame and round of face with long, unruly hair, a monk's bangs, and a thick moustache. He showed up only rarely at the Petroleum Club or the Ranchmen's Club (though he had a family ranch). He'd attended Connecticut's private Choate prep school and then Queen's University for his chemical-engineering degree. At one time, he'd boxed semi-professionally.

When I knew him best, he was a bachelor, divorced after a twenty-five-year marriage. I got along well with him, though I don't know if anyone was close to him. His political friends included both Conservative Peter Lougheed and Liberal Energy Minister Marc Lalonde, who brought in the notorious National Energy Program. Bob was probably motivated in part by his feeling of powerlessness as CEO of a Canadian branch of the American gas utility Pacific Gas Transmission. Peter Foster, in *The Blue-Eyed Sheiks*, wrote, "Blair's ego, AGTL's corporate objectives and the best interests of Canada—as perceived by Bob Blair have become rolled into one. This metamorphosis, in which Blair seems to have assumed an almost Messianic mantle, is somewhat disturbing to other executives."

The Blair I saw up close in my early days as an AGTL director was, I knew, a fierce nationalist. Yet Doc Seaman, who was on the board, said the CEO was truly altruistic: "He firmly believes that corporations should take a national stance and lead in situations even when they don't make money." That last phrase would loom large and ominous in the decade to come. But in '79, optimism reigned among the management and directors as the company came off another record year—$1.2 billion in operating revenues—and Bob forecast it would grow to $2 billion in 1980.

He had come to my office at the Dome Tower with an interesting invitation to join the board—which was an absolute powerhouse of people. It included four government appointees: Doc from Bow Valley; Don Getty, the former provincial energy minister and future premier, who became a director when I did; the legendary Bud McCaig, who founded Trimac, the huge trucking and waste-management corporation that had recently gone into oil and gas; and Joe Healey, a major Edmonton Ford dealer. Others with impressive credentials were Art Child, co-owner of Burns Foods, Canada's second-biggest meat packer; and two prominent Queen's Counsels and power brokers, Bill Howard of Calgary and Peter Macdonnell of Edmonton. Those with deep backgrounds in petroleum were Ron Southern of the highly successful and expansive family-operated ATCO group of companies, with products ranging from prefabricated housing to natural gas; Fred McKinnon, a former senior exec with British Petroleum Canada; and Ernie Pallister, a geophysicist and experienced oil consultant in Calgary. Management representatives, besides Blair, were executive vice-president Bob Pierce, once a key Liberal fundraiser in Saskatchewan, and senior VP Robin Abercrombie. The capable chair was Hugh Sanders (Sandy) Pearson, who had a private industrial-supplies company in Edmonton and sat on numerous other boards, among them the Bank of Montreal, TransAlta Utilities, and Mutual Life Assurance.

All of which makes it surprising that these savvy directors—and I —failed to see the scary handwriting on the wall after AGTL became NOVA, an Alberta Corporation, in 1980 and began to implode as the decade progressed. During the '70s, the company had launched numerous petroleum-related businesses: Alberta Gas Chemicals Ltd.; Algas Resources (which became Noval Enterprises), Algas Engineering Services (now Novacorp Engineering Services); and Novacorp International Consulting. It created Alberta Gas Ethylene and Algas Mineral Enterprises (now NovAlta Resources), which did gas exploration and development). Foothills Pipe Lines was an alliance with Westcoast Transmission to develop the northern pipeline project—but though the Canadian and U.S. governments would approve it, that line was never built.

In the early Eighties, Peter Lougheed pressed NOVA to build the province's first petrochemicals and plastics plants. Our board supported its participation in a three-company scheme: it agreed to build a plant near Red Deer to produce ethylene for use in plastics and supply it to Dow Chemical of Canada while Dome Petroleum would build a pipeline to carry any surplus chemicals to eastern Canada and the U.S. NOVA also built a polyethylene plant in Joffre, the foundation of its petrochemicals division, Novacor Chemicals, which ran the plants.

At the same time, the company was diversifying even further. Partnering with Doc Seaman, it acquired the Canadian operations of Western Star Trucks, an American manufacturer. It did a joint venture with the provincial government to run NovAtel Communications, a cellular telephone company. NOVA was even experimenting with growing tomatoes with waste heat from greenhouses. We directors were becoming uneasy about this veering into fields so unrelated to its core businesses. This was all happening against a tumultuous backdrop as the National Energy Program played havoc with the Alberta petroleum industry.

But NOVA's most significant stretch—and the one that wounded it grievously—was the acquisition of Husky Oil, a public company. Because Dick Haskayne devotes an entire chapter in *Northern Tigers* to his later role at NOVA and his dealings with Husky, I'll summarize the events leading up to his arrival there.

Husky was originally a Wyoming-based refining operation, which moved to Lloydminster, Alberta, in 1946 and became so successful it acquired all the shares of its American counterpart fourteen years later. It expanded into heavy-oil reserves around Lloydminster and bought Union Oil of Canada's refining and marketing operations, including its western retail gas outlets (rebranded as Husky stations) and a refinery in Prince George, B.C. Overseas, it was exploring for oil in Asia, Africa, and South America. Petrocan had been eyeing the now-booming Husky Oil as a possible acquisition.

But in 1980, the year after I came aboard, NOVA finalized its quiet creeping takeover of Husky, cemented with a 69-per-cent interest. (In typically contrarian moves, Bob named former federal NDP leader Tommy Douglas to the Husky board and his son Jamie Blair would become a senior executive and then co-chair.) NOVA's directors had some concern about a potential conflict of interest for a company that now controlled this major petroleum producer while serving other producers with our gas transmission.

But there were other, more immediate worries. The petrochemical industry was soon in decline and in 1982 Canada was smacked with recession, sinking NOVA's share price to $6 from more than $14 two years before. Husky, meanwhile, was able to post more than a $500-million profit after selling some assets in '84.

A year later, crude-oil prices sagged and NOVA had its first-ever loss, $192 million. *The Financial Post* reported that Bob "was lambasted for autocratic investment decisions, involving gas producers and shareholders' money, that had turned a public utility into an unprofitable conglomerate." Bob himself told reporters, "We have not been very wise about predicting commodity prices." Senior management (who took a 15-per-cent pay cut) discussed solutions with the board and together we made one major decision—to take Husky private and realize some badly needed cash from the deal. The buyer of a 43-per-cent share, for $855 million, was Hutchison Whampoa, owned by Li Ka-Shing, the storied Hong Kong multibillionaire.

It and Husky went on to buy Canterra Energy of Calgary for $375 million, strengthening Husky's presence in Arctic and East Coast frontiers, among other areas, while increasing NOVA's debt load. Trying to revive corporate fortunes, Bob replaced Bob Pierce, now president, with Jim Butler, the chair of Novacor Chemicals, which was then swallowed into what was renamed NOVA Corp.

Husky wasn't the end of Bob's buying spree. In '88 NOVA did a long, hostile takeover of Polysar Ltd., the Crown-owned petrochemicals company in Sarnia, Ontario, for almost $1.92 billion—a hefty price tag and exactly what Polysar had demanded. The company had a flourishing North American and overseas rubber trade and refinery and petrochemicals holdings in its home province. NOVA was now the continent's second-largest ethylene producer and by 1988 the overall company had net income of $424 million.

Unfortunately, a year later petrochemicals were in free fall and the times were recessionary again. That, along with the Polysar debt, left NOVA's financials and its stock price at half the value of the previous year. With the board's approval, the company sold such subsidiaries as Western Star Trucks, NovAlta Resources, and NovAtel Communications. Stock prices were down once more and in '90 Jim Butler left as president, not to be replaced; everyone now reported to Bob. NOVA's net income was a disappointing $185 million.

The strength I'd brought to the board was my knowledge of oil and gas exploration from the perspective of both the geologist and the entrepreneur running two businesses in the industry. Doc has credited me with having a good memory for detail and keeping meticulous notes as a NOVA director. Of course, I wasn't all that familiar then with the hierarchy of large corporate structures. Though I did my homework and served on committees, my voice wasn't strong enough in debates about, say, major international deals. But I hope I offered the same sense of integrity the others displayed, of not wanting to cut expedient corners, of protecting shareholders' interests.

It wasn't enough. Bill Dimma, a Canadian expert on corporate governance, writes in his book *Tougher Boards for Tougher Times*: "Directors individually and boards collectively must have the conviction and strength to say No more often than they do." The NOVA board had continued to attract big names from various fields, including Willard (Bud) Estey, the retired Supreme Court of Canada justice, and Sir Alastair Morton, former managing director of the British National Oil Corporation, co-chair of Eurotunnel, and chair of Britain's Strategic Rail Authority. As loyal directors, we balanced our growing unease with the feeling that this was a powerful

Alberta company with a strong leader. It seemed most of us were generally confident that we would work our way through the setbacks. Not all of us had such trust in Bob: Ron Southern had reluctantly left the board of what he considered a pivotal Alberta company, telling friends he found its CEO too difficult to work with and believed the company had turned from "a thoroughbred to a plough horse."

Fortunately, at this crucial point, Dick Haskayne arrived on the scene. Bob had begged him to join the company, intending to split it into separate chemicals and pipeline divisions and make Dick president on the pipe side. Dick had just left Interhome Energy, which had made a similar move to divide Home Oil and Interprovincial Pipeline (IPL). But he was also in the midst of caring for his beloved wife, Lee, who would die of Lou Gehrig's disease in 1993. In a one-on-one meeting, I had encouraged Dick to get involved. He refused any employment contract with NOVA but became a director—and began to see the extent of the problems, as he writes in *Northern Tigers*:

> *Until my first board meeting, I didn't appreciate that NOVA was now a shambles, laden with $4.2 billion in debt. It had diversified into a host of activities totally unrelated to its core businesses, manufacturing things like trucks and cellular phones. One director, Bill Howard, whispered to me, "Dick, I bet you're sitting here wondering why you took this job"—which is exactly what I was thinking. That year, the company would lose $937 million. It was bleeding about $15 million a month in the chemicals business alone and yet the executives and directors were listening to investment bankers pressing them to send the two divisions out on their own as separate entities. They wanted to free the pipeline, with its guaranteed returns, from the chemicals arm that was hurting the collective credit rating. At Interhome it had taken us years to split Home and IPL and here NOVA was about to leap into a similar venture with very little forethought. A third-year Commerce student would have known better than to make chemicals a stand-alone, no longer relying on the strength of the pipeline's balance sheet.*

By the autumn of 1991, realizing he'd exhausted his options, the beleaguered Bob Blair bowed to the inevitable and retired as chairman and CEO. Doc was appointed interim chair—interim because he was never comfortable in that role outside his own companies. NOVA went looking for someone to head Novacor Chemicals and found the distinguished Ted Newall, who'd been chair, president, and CEO of DuPont Canada, with thirty-three relevant years at the Canadian subsidiary of the U.S. chemicals, materials, and energy corporation. He was now chair of the Business Council on National Issues and had headed the Conference Board of Canada and served on boards as varied as the Royal Bank and the Molson Companies. Dick acted as special adviser to Ted on the petroleum side of the business and they became fast friends. With Dick's great reputation and Ted's experience and exuberance, they were a good fit.

The details of the subsequent story are all in Dick's book: how he became Husky's co-chair; how he and Ted visited Li Ka-Shing in Hong Kong to unload NOVA's share of Husky for $375 million; how Ted presided over all of NOVA and Dick took over as its non-executive chairman; and how eight top executives working with consultants then restructured the company. A key decision was selling Polysar's stand-alone rubber division to Bayer AG of Germany for about $1.3 billion, which generated a writeoff of $923 million—the largest in Canadian corporate history to that time. Doc Seaman posed one big question: "Are you sure you've got it all?" Ted was, and by 1992, NOVA had rebounded with a profit of $164 million, giving shareholders a 24-per-cent return. A year later, Ted's senior-executive peers across the country voted him CEO of the Year.

The company prospered over the next several years, taking a quarter stake in Methanex, the globe's largest methane producer, and more than a third of Natural Gas Clearinghouse, a Texas-based gas marketer and vendor; and acquiring a polyethylene plant in Sarnia owned by DuPont Canada. Even though the 1996 earnings were NOVA's third-largest, a year later the shares were languishing because the company was seen as an incompatible mix of pipelines and petrochemicals. American vultures were circling in hope of a takeover.

This time, one of Dick's old business colleagues appeared on the horizon: Gerry Maier, formerly of Hudson's Bay Oil and Gas and now non-exec chair of TransCanada Pipelines, which had grown into a huge and profitable transmission network across the continent. He'd been on the DuPont board and came to be pals with Ted, who consulted him before taking the NOVA job. Gerry and his president, George Watson, liked the logic of marrying NOVA's Alberta pipeline business with TransCanada's national one. That was especially appealing after Ted announced in late '97 that he was now seriously thinking of making his pipe and petrochemicals divisions separate public companies.

He and George Watson met in secret to discuss the overall parameters of the deal. We all soon realized this would become Canada's largest-ever such merger in the energy field. Both sides chose three-member committees to oversee the work of the lawyers and financial people negotiating the details. TransCanada's representatives were Gerry; Allan Taylor, the former chair of the Royal Bank; and Harry Schaefer, the ex-chief financial officer of TransAlta and and a longtime TransCanada director. NOVA's were Dick; Ced Ritchie, a new director and the former chair and CEO of the Bank of Nova Scotia; and me.

In my early years on the board, as a small private entrepreneur I'd felt a little in awe of Bob Blair and icons of the Alberta Establishment like Ron Southern. But as we ran into problems, I was able to play a more meaningful role with my background of experience and age—maybe you do get a little wiser with age, or as Ralph Waldo Emerson philosophized, "The years teach much which the days never knew." Later I became chair of the audit and finance committee, and while having no formal accounting background, I could analyze a balance sheet with some skill—and had invaluable support from financially experienced committee members such as Harold Milavsky, Janice Rennie, and Bill Comrie. So I got to know the company and the people and that may have been one reason I was chosen to be on the oversight committee for the merger.

For the next couple of months, we met—a lot—in Calgary, often in Dick's Bankers Hall office and a few times at the airport in Toronto. Our big challenge was to help analyze the structures of both companies and shape what would be a merger of equals, a pooling of interests with no controlling shareholder. The two committees had to balance personalities and hopes and wishes and emerge with the best directors for both the pipeline and chemicals divisions, the best corporate framework, the overall best solution for the shareholders of NOVA and TransCanada. Balancing the boards was particularly tricky, as Dick remembers: "That's where some people were ticked off. They wanted to be on the TransCanada board and got on the NOVA board, or the other way around."

We knew our responsibilities and there was no real posturing during our debates; everyone acted in a wonderfully businesslike way. Which sounds like motherhood, but in this case it resulted in the birth of a Friendly Giant: the fourth-biggest energy-services corporation on the continent, with sixty-three hundred employees, annual revenues of $16 billion, and assets of $21 billion. As part of the no-cash deal—valued at $14 billion and finalized on January 24, 1998—NOVA Chemicals was set up as an independent company with Ted as non-executive chair and moved to Pittsburgh a year later. (While I shared some critics' reservations about the loss of a Canadian company's headquarters to the U.S., proponents argued that was where its customers were.)

At a NOVA board meeting even before the deal was finalized, Ted presented Dick, Ced, and myself with large Inuit carvings of polar bears and said, "This team has been ferocious in what they've done for us."

Dick took over as chairman of what was now TransCanada Corporation. I went on the board for a year until my age—seventy-one—forced me to step down. From the sidelines, I saw TransCanada mature into a tremendous success story under the strong leadership of Dick Haskayne, Doug Baldwin, and Hal Kvisle. It became one of Canada's most respected corporations, which it remains today.

IF MY NINETEEN YEARS WITH NOVA ULTIMATELY HAD A happy ending, my seven years as a director of Telus were much less satisfying. I was surprised to be asked on its board in the first place. Fred Stewart, the province's technology, research and telecommunications minister, called with the invitation in 1991.

"No, Fred," I said, "I don't have the background for this." In truth, I was busy serving on the boards of NOVA and Conwest and deeply involved in all things hockey (as I'll describe in the next chapter).

Fred persisted, calling back to say, flatteringly, "Look, Harley, this is important for the province and we'd like some people who can be good, useful directors."

So, despite my lack of knowledge of the telecommunications industry (aside from NOVA's cellular-phone subsidiary), I succumbed. The year before, Premier Don Getty's government had created Telus Corporation, headquartered in Edmonton, as a partially private company born out of a three-decade-old Crown corporation, Alberta Government Telephone Commission. AGT, in turn, had evolved from the province's launch of a phone system in 1906. It had assets of $2.8 billion and the previous year a profit of $56.6 million. The new Telus was a no-brainer for investors: the sale of $896 million in shares was Canada's largest initial public offering to that time. Within a year, the provincial government sold its remaining interest for $870 million. Telus, with more than 13,000 employees, became Canada's third-largest group of telecommunications and information-management companies.

The chairman was Neil Webber, a former college administrator who'd been Alberta's Associate Telephone Minister as well as minister of energy and of social services, and the president Hal Neldner, who'd served in that role at AGT. Among the fifteen board members were some confidants of the previous premier, Peter Lougheed, including Harry Hobbs, a former heating and plumbing contractor and Conservative fundraiser, and Chip Collins, the former Deputy Provincial Treasurer who'd worked with Peter in the private sector. The board also had, or would have, experts in telecommunications, among them Jack McAllister, former chairman and CEO of the US West telephone system with forty-plus years of experience in the industry. Saskatchewan-reared Harold Milavsky may have been best-known as chair and president of Trizec Corporation, the giant Bronfman-Reichmann real-estate venture, but his directorships included the energy companies Dome, Amoco Canada, TransCanada Pipelines, and NOVA.

But there would be others like me with no track record in this highly specialized sphere. One of them was my friend and legal counsel, Jim Palmer, who came in as non-executive chairman in 1995. The previous year, I was on the selection committee that hired George Petty, vice-president of global business service for AT&T, as president and CEO of Telus. Now the board was headhunting a chairman from outside and when Jim's name came up as someone with a lot of corporate-governance experience, I was only too happy to support and encourage him—though I didn't think he'd really want the position. In fact, he said at the time, "When I first was approached, I really didn't think I was very interested. I thought of it as a sleepy telephone company. And I'm somebody who can't work the VCR very well." But he asked to meet the plainspoken George, with whom he got along, and decided to accept—with one caveat:

"I knew nothing about the bloody business," Jim recalls, "so I said to George, 'I've got to get up on all this' and he arranged for me to go down to UCLA and have three days there to get started on learning things. And I thought he said I'd be in a class. I said, 'How many will be there?' 'Oh, just three or four.' What he didn't say was that there were three or four people *teaching* me; I was the only student. I'm a person who took first-year physics three years in a row in college and never got through it. So I had all this stuff coming in at me and after two days, I said, 'I've got to go home.' It was just too much. But you know, I picked it up. And I had a reasonably exciting time."

Even though I sometimes felt uncomfortable as a director, it *was* an exciting era as the telecom industry exploded during the Nineties. Just after I'd joined the board, Telus launched North America's first digital cellular network. Now the market was witnessing the fallout from deregulation. There was long-distance phone competition in the province from the likes of Rogers Communications and Bell Canada and such innovations as fibre-optics networking and high-speed Internet service for consumers offered by Shaw Communications and others.

Amid all the national and global currents, more local issues surfaced. When Telus acquired the arms-length telephone subsidiary of the city of Edmonton for $467 million, a protest group called Friends of ED TEL gathered more than thirty-five thousand names on a petition in an unsuccessful attempt to force a civic referendum on the sale. And as directors, we always had to deal with the criticism that our executives were being overpaid—especially at the annual meeting in 1993 when angry shareholders raised executive salary issues as the company planned to lay off 1,240 employees. Even two years later, George Petty's compensation was $440,000, which Telus argued was moderate compared to the $2 million paid a year earlier to Jean Monty, president and chief executive officer of Northern Telecom and the $1.6 million total payout to Red Wilson, chairman and CEO of BCE Inc., Bell Canada's parent.

I served on some committees in areas where my experience could be useful, such as compensation and human resources, and even chaired a couple. Yet while I liked the association with the industry and enjoyed the board members, I was probably relieved in 1998 when my stint ended, again because of age. Not having the fundamental grasp of the business itself, I'd often wondered whether I was reflecting on all the technological challenges deeply enough.

The year I retired, Telus and its larger neighbour, BC Tel, a subsidiary of General Telephone and Electronics in the U.S., announced a proposed merger. It happened early the following year as the two companies joined forces to compete against their big eastern rivals. The headquarters moved to Burnaby, B.C., while many administrative matters were handled in Alberta, where taxes were lower and workers less unionized. In the years since, Telus has only continued to grow exponentially—with a virtual monopoly in western Canada and bulking up to the point where it tried (but failed) to take over its arch rival BCE in 2007.

These days I don't bother to follow the telecom news as carefully. And I'm still too technologically challenged to ever use the Blackberry friends recommend.

FOR MANY YEARS, I HAVE BEEN A STOCK-MARKET investor, mainly in oil and gas and mining where I can better use my knowledge and experience. As part of my investment program, I've often participated in higher-risk startup projects where I knew the people involved and was excited about the risk and potential rewards. One venture was in Kazakhstan, deep in Central Asia, the world's ninth-largest country by size. Once a state of the Soviet Union, it won its independence in 1991. The republic has significant petroleum reserves and during the 1950s and '60s, Russians conducted exploration and some development there but never followed up. My son-in-law, Jamie Mackie, has a geologist brother, David, who was a partner in a company with oil and gas rights on lands acquired from the Kazakhstan government. David's lead partner in Altius Energy Corporation was Mike Volcko, an experienced petroleum engineer. Their program was to re-complete old wells, drill new wells, and put three shallow undeveloped oil pools into production.

I asked my friend Ed Koetsier to look at the project. Back in the recession-battered year of 1984, a *National Geographic* writer doing an article on Calgary described him as one of the city's "surviving millionaire independents . . . a blond man with a childlike smile and a Dutch accent." In 2000, he decided to take a significant financial interest with me in Altius. Because Kazakhstan has poor roads, inexperienced oil-field workers, and old and unreliable equipment, we wanted to see the operations there first-hand and offer any assistance where Ed's background could be helpful. That August, he and I flew from Calgary to Almaty, Kazakhstan, twelve time zones away (with only one stop, in Frankfurt). From there we went to Atyrau, a city on the Caspian Sea, close to Altius's main office and its three oil fields in the barrens.

At one field, the locals decided to hold a celebration for us in a typical round tent called a yurt. We sat on the rug-covered floor at a long, low table abrim with food and Georgian wine. The culinary attraction was a sheep butchered on the spot with its head served on a large platter with rice and vegetables. I was sure I'd get an eyeball but ended up with a piece of the jaw. While Ed was manfully chewing away, I couldn't handle the gristle and during one of the many speeches slipped it out of sight under the table.

Altius faced many operating and marketing challenges and finally sold to a larger, Dutch company experienced in trading oil. Ed and I gradually sold our shares in the open market. As well as making a good profit, we shared in the adventure of an oil play in a strange new country so far from home.

I'VE SERVED ON SEVERAL LOW-PROFILE BOARDS OVER the years, small oil and gas companies including Triquest Energy and Sebring Energy, with smaller boards where my background and experience would let me play a productive role. The only directorship I continue to have outside that realm is on the board of Sanatana Diamonds of Calgary. In 2005, Jamie Mackie told me about an exciting mineral-exploration project in the Northwest Territories that he and two partners had put together. After they'd filed on about twenty million acres with a focus on diamonds, they were now exchanging their interests for stock in the new company. He asked me to serve as a director and, though trying to simplify my life, I was intrigued with the risk-taking of this geological venture.

I'd had some knowledge of the diamond game through Conwest's involvement with the mine in the Territories owned by Aber Resources, a company in which I held shares. Sanatana's geologist is Buddy Doyle, who had worked with Kennecott Exploration of the Rio Tinto group of companies when it and Aber discovered the world-class Diavik diamond mine. Kennecott now owns a 15-per-cent interest in Sanatana. The company was first listed with AIM, the Alternative Investment Market of the London Stock Exchange, and then the Toronto Venture Exchange.

Sanatana has a large exploration program of soil sampling and airborne and ground geophysics to establish drill-target potential for diamonds. After unsuccessful results in 2006, a diamondiferous kimberlite was found a year later just north of Great Bear Lake. Named Dharma, it held numerous small diamonds and two larger ones in four drill cores. Further drilling is required to determine how significant the discovery is. In this and other areas, drilling will continue through the 2009 summer season. The high-risk challenge will be to locate "pipes" of kimberlite of sufficient size and diamonds of sufficient quantity and quality to create a commercial mine in these remote regions. And because I always have a sizable shareholding in any company in which I'm a director, I'm sharing the risk with the other investors.

Investing in diamonds might seem to be a venturesome prospect with a daring, unpredictable result. But then, I know about taking such a gamble—after all, for nearly thirty years I've been a founding owner of the Calgary Flames.

Joseph D'Angelis of La Chaumière and Vineyard South

A MODEST WINE SELLER

The Calgary of thirty years ago was a relative desert for anyone who wanted to experience fine dining. Of course, there was always Hy's for a swell steak and Trader's in the Four Seasons for more cosmopolitan fare. But it wasn't until La Chaumière opened in 1978 next to a commercial garage in a tired stretch of 17th Avenue Southeast that the city truly had an oasis of elegant French cuisine. The first issue of the old *Calgary Magazine* called it "refreshingly authentic and meticulous in quality and service." And not long ago, after the restaurant named for a thatched cottage moved to a chateau-like building down the street, the *Calgary Herald* described it as "one of the originals of the best of the best . . . excellent food beautifully prepared and presented in a contemporary style in comfortable surroundings at prices that have not taken advantage of overblown expense accounts."

Joseph D'Angelis, with two partners, founded the restaurant; a year later he bought them out and brought in Joe Mathes and Herbert Sattlegger, Austrian-born and -trained chefs from Trader's, where he'd worked with them as maître d'. In their new space, they served traditional Gallic dishes like coq au vin but also (a rarity in this beef-happy town) coquilles St. Jacques and a seafood platter of smoked and poached salmon, prawns, and Alaskan lobster claws (all for $5.25). By sheer chance, the night they opened, July 10, was my fifty-first birthday and Becky and I celebrated it there. We've never stopped going back.

In the decades since, the attentive Joseph has maintained the food quality and exacting service; seeing a fork out of place, he'll straighten it himself. He and Joe later brought in another partner, a superb local executive chef named Bob Matthews. We became such friends that Becky and I gave Herbert and Joe our vacation home in Naples, Florida, for their honeymoons after each of them got married.

And Joseph and I became so close that we applied for a licence to operate a wine store in Calgary—a process involving a thorough evaluation of applications by a recognized outside accounting firm. Even before the Alberta government decided to turn alcohol retailing entirely over to the private sector in 1993, there were about fifty non-government wine and beer shops. While no connoisseur, I enjoy wine and thought it would be an interesting avocation to own a shop and maybe get to visit Italy and France as a part-time vintner. I was pursuing the idea on my own when Joseph said he'd been approached to join a group also applying but would rather collaborate with me.

With his knowledge of the grape, he was a natural fifty-fifty partner when we opened Vineyard South in a shopping mall on McLeod Trail. Joseph got it up and going and his wife, Marissa, did the books; at one point, my daughter, Brenda, worked there. They'd have tastings and demonstrations of wine-and-food pairings and eventually ran an agency representing wineries around the world selling to local restaurants and individuals.

When the province did privatize all alcohol sales, more and more wine shops opened and we had to compete with the liquor stores by adding beer and spirits to our mix and moving to a larger and more visible location in the same mall. Some of the fun went out of the business for me, while my partner found it taking up an increasing amount of time away from his real love, La Chaumière.

After a decade together, we decided to sell. Joseph, an excellent partner, retained the wine agency as a hedge for his retirement. Vineyard South had returned a little profit to me every year without my doing very much. I certainly came to know a lot more about wine and appreciate it the way Robert Louis Stevenson did when he wrote: "Wine is bottled poetry."

But I never did get to Italy and France posing as a wine merchant.

A REAL-ESTATE FLYER

As Mark Twain once wrote, "No real estate is permanently valuable but the grave." That was certainly true in the case of the downtown Calgary commercial projects I first got involved in about 1978 with Clive Beddoe.

In the mid-1990s, he would become a co-founder of what became the very successful airline WestJet. I hadn't known him until he approached me about investing in real-estate ventures but soon learned that he was an English chartered surveyor who moved to Calgary in '70. He'd worked as a development manager for Alan Graham of the Cascade Group of Companies, which operated in construction and real estate, and had taken the business into building office towers. Clive later went on his own with Hanover Management, buying older central properties to hold the land for eventual office developments.

I agreed to put up some capital through my wholly owned private company, Colony Developments Ltd., in several projects, the main three being: the Hanover Building at 6th Avenue and Centre Street Southwest, the Lougheed Building at 6th Avenue and 1st Street Southwest, and the Herald, Herald Annex, and some neighbouring buildings, covering a half-block along 1st Street between 6th and 7th Avenues. I brought in my friend and lawyer Jim Palmer for a percentage of my investment, and later buddy Bill Siebens of Siebens Oil and Gas participated for a majority interest in the bigger Herald Assembly.

Clive did a good job assembling the land for the Hanover Building and in 1982 we completed a twenty-six-storey office tower with Cana Construction. Through his efforts, the Canadian Pacific Pension Fund became a partner. With Calgary booming, we found good tenants, including Petro-Canada, at attractive rents. When Canadian Pacific believed even higher rents were on the horizon, we turned down long-term commitments in the tower. And then the local economy fell out of bed. PetroCan had a rent-review provision in their lease, which was taken to arbitration, and when the decision cut our rent by about 75 per cent, we lost our equity in the project. What had been a well conceived and executed development became a tough reminder of the importance of timing in the real-estate market.

During the boom time, our group also purchased the Lougheed Building, constructed in 1912 by Premier Peter Lougheed's grandfather and once home to the famous Grand Theatre of the vaudeville era. In our first couple of years of ownership, we could have sold for a significant profit but had future development in mind. When the economy sharply deteriorated, our acquisition didn't look so good. We carried on under Clive's management through many challenging years of low rents and high operating and maintenance costs. He was adamant that renovating and preserving the building made no economic sense. In the end, we sold it to a group in 2003 to carry out their plan to restore and rehabilitate the building and theatre, which have since been declared a Provincial Historic Resource. Taking into consideration all our time and efforts over two decades, it had been a marginal investment at best.

The Herald Assembly of buildings, which had been occupied by the *Calgary Herald*, its printing presses, and adjoining structures, was a prime downtown location with the Light-Rail Transit running along its south boundary. With the city bustling in 1980, we had grand plans for the land. Clive negotiated a deal with the Hudson's Bay Company, which owned the Bay Parkade in the remaining half-block, for a joint office development with two high office towers—until the dramatic downturn nailed us. Despite the development approvals, we couldn't proceed with our plans and again the rents were paltry and the maintenance costs were high as usual with an older, lower-class building. We made efforts to sell the property with no success. Clive helped by locating his Career College there to stabilize our situation.

Though we continued to rely on him, he'd now started WestJet and had less time to focus on our real-estate partnerships. We had to subsidize the projects from time to time and provide guarantees to renew mortgage financing. Although Clive and Bill Siebens had occasional differences on the Herald project, our relationships were generally strong and we co-operated well to meet the many challenges.

In 2005, we received an offer from a pension fund. Jim Palmer and I were willing to sell the Herald package, as Clive was—with reluctance. While Bill believed we should find an experienced commercial developer to work with, we couldn't make a deal with interested parties. Because of our lack of experience and other personal issues, Jim and I were not interested in participating in a long-term development project and were concerned about the disagreements Clive and Bill were having. In May 2006, Clive approached Jim and me to buy our interest slightly above the pension-fund offer. Clive told us he believed the property had good potential for higher long-term values, but Jim and I discussed it and accepted his offer, which closed in June. In August we heard that the property was being sold and I'd find out that it had been concluded that fall at a price about 50-per-cent higher than our sale to Clive. We asked for a meeting in early 2007 with Clive, who pointed out that he had warned us that the building would be worth more. So that was the end of it—a sad finish for Jim and me to lose our profits after a twenty-seven-year relationship that had worked well to keep the project alive through many setbacks.

Clive and I had other business relationships, participating with him in Career College and putting him into some successful oil and gas plays. But I was never involved in WestJet and when I asked him later why he hadn't approached me, he said he was embarrassed after our poor real-estate ventures.

So in spite of a lot of time and financial outlay, my buying into that trio of buildings between 1978 and 1980 proved to be a mediocre commercial investment. As it turned out, I had a lot more fun as the decade of the Eighties began when I jumped at the chance to join close friends in acquiring a National Hockey League team.

CHAPTER 7

CATCHING FIRE

Our Flames Blaze into Being

ALL THROUGH MY CORPORATE AND ENTRE-preneurial career, and my more important life as a husband to Becky and father to our five children, my love for hockey never flagged. I played pickup games as a young geologist in Calgary. I coached kids' hockey for many years when we lived in Glendale and Lakeview Village, shovelling snow, flooding the rink, tying skates, wiping noses, and driving to games in other communities. And I was a regular at matches of whatever professional or semi-pro teams were current in the city. When I arrived in town in 1951, the Calgary Stampeders of the new Western Hockey League were playing in a $1.2-million Stampede Corral the community had recently built especially for them. At the time, there were only the six original teams in the National Hockey League, none of them in the West. That young Harley Hotchkiss couldn't have foreseen in his most far-fetched pipe dreams that one day he'd be co-owner of an NHL club, that it would begin competing in what was now the *old* Corral—and then find a home in a new saddle-shaped arena.

Few other Calgarians in the Fifties—or even twenty years later—would have ever imagined the city had much of a chance to land an NHL franchise. The Stampeders had long since folded, so we locals were excited when the World Hockey Association was cobbled together in 1971. Competing for players against the senior major league, it authorized a team called the Calgary Broncos. But the Broncos never survived to start the first

Red-bearded Lanny McDonald—about to retire but not very retiring as he clutches the Stanley Cup—joins president and general manager Cliff Fletcher and the Calgary Flames as they celebrate our 1989 win against the Montreal Canadiens.

season—though a team in Edmonton called the Oilers did. It took another four years for the WHA to move the Vancouver Blazers to Calgary as the Cowboys. They played only one more year before low turnouts in a lacklustre season bucked them into oblivion. The league itself died two years later.

As John Davidson, a local junior player who's now president of the St. Louis Blues, once observed, "The people in Calgary had spent their lives with a taste for a Stanley Cup but unable to have the chance to ever drink from it. In fact, they'd been staring at it from a distance for so long, they'd begun to hallucinate about it." Yet against this backdrop of dashed dreams, some Calgary friends of mine—and an outsider I'd never met—conspired to resurrect the prospect of bringing the National Hockey League to town and lassoed me into their scheme.

Not that I was in any way reluctant. I still held on to a little of the hero worship, born in my boyhood, of hockey players like Syl Apps (to be honest with myself, that awe still exists even now). And I'd already invested in one team, a friend's local junior club in the Western Hockey League (originally the Western Canada Junior Hockey League). At the time, the Canadian Hockey Association considered the seven-team league an outlaw organization ineligible to compete for the Memorial Cup. In the inaugural season of 1966, the team was called the Calgary Buffaloes and then played as the Centennials until moving to Billings, Montana, in 1977. The major investor was Bobby Brownridge, who'd been a real hockey hopeful before the Second World War and was now running a drilling company aligned with Doc Seaman. Both Doc and I put in money, attended many of the games, and likely came out even financially at the end of it. The Centennials (named for Canada's hundredth birthday in 1967) produced some interesting graduates: goalie John Davidson played for the New York Rangers and St. Louis before heading the Blues; right-winger Bob Nystrom went on to a fine career with the New York Islanders; and another right-winger, Lanny McDonald, would come to figure prominently in my life.

REMINISCING, DOC SEAMAN SAID THE STORY OF THE Calgary Flames really began in the late 1960s when Charles Hay was the second president of Hockey Canada, the national body newly organized to govern the game. Charlie had been a goalie for the University of Saskatchewan Huskies in 1921 when they played for the Allan Cup, the senior amateur trophy, and his son, Bill, became a centre and top goal-scorer for the Chicago Blackhawks when they won the Stanley Cup forty years later. Charlie, a successful executive in oil and gas, had well-honed organizing skills. He used them to co-ordinate the efforts of amateur and professional hockey administrators to build programs that would ultimately result in a national team to best represent Canada in international competition.

Doc went on the board of the Hockey Canada Foundation to help raise money. "It was at the time when we were falling behind the Russians in hockey, particularly in the Olympics," he said. "Charlie's idea was to put something back into our game at the grassroots level. And that put a spark in my mind." Doc decided to approach Peter Lougheed. Brother B.J. had been on the premier's finance committee and Peter's family had deep hockey roots in Alberta: his uncle, Clarence Lougheed, was goalie for the Calgary College team in 1898.

"Calgary was getting ready to host the 1988 Winter Olympics and I went to Peter and said, 'You'll need a showcase facility for the Olympics. I'll see if I can get a hockey franchise that would be a long-term tenant for the rink.'" He added that, inspired by Charlie Hay, he wanted to invest in hockey development in this country through an ambitious project to be called Project 75 (*see page 235*).

Peter, reflecting on events more than a quarter-century later, tells the story from his side of the fence:

"So I'm premier and I'm looking at the situation. We'd held the Commonwealth Games in 1978 and built a stadium for them up in Edmonton. I'd been long involved in the Olympic bid and knew the competition we faced. And I'm thinking to myself, *Now what are we going to do in Calgary? Because we were able to finance the Edmonton Coliseum as part of those summer games. We've got to build a stadium in Calgary.* But I knew that if you're going to build a facility like that, you've got to think about what happens after the games are over. What are you going to put in it? And—magic! The phone rings. Doc Seaman phoning. It was *that* coincidental. Four days later, Doc came in and said, 'I think we can get an NHL franchise in your home city, Premier.' I said, 'Okay, why don't we go do this together? The province will build the stadium.'"

Doc had already been talking to Alberta's colourful Peter Pocklington, a major Ford dealer, meat-packing magnate, and owner of the Edmonton Oilers, who'd moved into the Commonwealth Games legacy stadium as their home rink. Originally with the rival World Hockey Association, they were one of four teams absorbed by the NHL when the WHA folded after the 1978-79 season.

As Doc related, "Peter Pocklington had the rink and came to me saying, 'You know, you guys should have a franchise here and I can help you if you'll help me get in the oil business. I can give you the names of the people you should contact who have teams that I think are available for sale.' So I advised him about doing something in the Oil Patch and he gave me a couple of names. One of them was Tom Cousins of the Atlanta Flames."

Cousins was a speculator in real estate during the late Seventies when that market was struggling in the U.S. He'd owned the Flames for eight years, but the team had lost $8 million in a southern city with no hockey history. During a desperate season-ticket drive, Atlantans committed to 13,000 of the 15,000 seats in the Omni Coliseum that Cousins and his partners had originally built to house the National Basketball Association's Atlanta Hawks. That was still not enough to keep the failing team in town—and, luckily, the Flames were the only club that did not need the unanimous consent of the league to move to another city.

Doc picked up the story: "It was just B.J. and I then. So in 1979 we started a dialogue with Tom Cousins back and forth and got the bid started at $10 million because they were in bankruptcy. Tom said, 'How are you going to pay for it?'

"'Well, I'll pay you cash.'

"'In U.S. dollars, I don't want Canadian dollars.'

"So this went on for the better part of a year, and then he said, 'I've got this guy Jack Kent Cooke interested; he'll pay me $12 million for it.'" Cooke was the Canadian-reared entrepreneur who moved to the U.S., where he eventually owned the National Football League's Washington Redskins, the NBA's Los Angeles Lakers, and the NHL's Los Angeles Kings. "But Cousins said, 'I'd like to see you guys get the deal; I think it's better for you.' And we said, 'Okay—$12 million.' Then Coca-Cola, who have their headquarters in Atlanta, were interested. So now the price gets to $14 or $15 million. And even Glenn Ford had looked at the financials and said No." At one point, the Canadian-born actor suggested he'd pay $8 million for the Flames.

As it turned out, it was another fellow Canadian who finally trumped Doc and B.J.: the flamboyant Nelson Skalbania of Vancouver. Nelson was a structural engineer who became Canada's highest-rolling real-estate trader, buying and selling—and flipping—hotels and office and residential buildings across North America. He'd also owned the Indianapolis Racers of the WHA and at one time held a $500,000 mortgage on the Oilers when they played in that now-defunct league. Not only that, he'd had a personal-services contract with a seventeen-year-old junior star named Wayne Gretzky, whom he peddled to the Oilers in 1978. Skalbania was a swashbuckling guy with two Mercedes and four Rolls-Royces, an executive jet that cost him and a partner $600,000 a year to run, and hundreds of pieces of fine art.

Now he wanted his own NHL team, which *he* would buy for $16 million—the highest price yet paid for one—and move it to Calgary. Which was a big surprise to the Seamans. In March 1980, they'd met with Tom

Cousins in Calgary, and their proposed deal hit the media; in April, B.J. met with him in Atlanta to finalize details. Early the next month, Pocklington, acting as a middleman, announced that the brothers had reached agreement in principle with Cousins. "Atlanta Flames cook with gas," *The Globe and Mail* headlined on its front page May 8. "Three Calgary oil and gas millionaires will announce today that they're buying the Atlanta Flames."

And then, little more than two weeks later, the bombshell burst: Skalbania had clinched a deal to buy the Flames.

But not if Doc and his family and friends could help it. I was one of the buddies he had approached early on. When we met on the street one day, he confided, "Hotch, we're talking about getting an NHL franchise here. Between us, we're working with Atlanta and just starting down the road with them. Would you like to be a part of it?" Doc was not a man of many words, but he sketched out the negotiations with the provincial government and Cousins so far.

It took me the blink of an eye to reply: "Doc, sure, count me in. I'm happy you're leading the parade here and I don't need to have any role. I appreciate the opportunity." Doc Seaman and Peter Lougheed were involved— that was enough for me. Doc then carried the puck; I never did meet Tom Cousins.

Now, with the news of Skalbania's deal, I thought we were finished, our dream had died aborning. It was a bad week. Doc remembered being "disappointed that I hadn't been smart enough to figure Cousins out." We soon realized, though, that Skalbania had a problem. Getting a stadium built by the government was politically correct when major local investors were involved in the team and committed to support grassroots hockey. But backing a project led by an outsider like Skalbania was another matter. He had brought in some Calgarians: Ralph Scurfield, a one-time school teacher who founded and ran the multibillion-dollar Nu-West Development Cor-

Ralph Scurfield

Norm Green

Norman Lim Kwong

poration; Norm Green, a prominent developer of shopping centres and a Lougheed confidant; and Norman Lim Kwong, the revered China Clipper of Canadian Football League fame.

Normie was a great catch for Skalbania: the first Chinese-Canadian in the league, he was an all-star fullback for the Calgary Stampeders and then the Edmonton Eskimos until retiring in 1960. He'd scored ninety-three touchdowns, played on the winning Grey Cup team four times, and was named Canada's Athlete of the Year in 1955. At this time, he was working with Gerry Knowlton's Knowlton Realty in local commercial real-estate sales. His Vancouver brother-in-law had introduced him to Skalbania and they'd discussed some potential deals. "Nelson thought that I'd know the major players in Calgary and might introduce him to you and the Seamans," as Normie recalled for me recently. "I barely knew you and them, except by reputation and running into you at different functions. I knew Ralph because he was a neighbour." Normie was intrigued to get involved again in sports, this time from the owner's side, especially since his young sons were deeply involved in minor and college hockey. He also liked the idea of Doc's Project 75. Skalbania gave Normie, a long-time Calgarian, a one-per-cent piece to make the introductions as well as be a high-profile partner and promoter.

Apparently Skalbania had approached Norm Green on his own but quickly realized the need for more hometown backers—particularly the people who'd been talking to the premier about securing provincial financial support for a city-owned coliseum and about making the Flames a community venture that would invest in the grassroots game. About a week after sealing his deal, he invited Doc, B.J., and me to Norm Green's office. We had no idea why. A lean guy in his early forties with a wraparound beard, Nelson had bought the Flames in typical wheeler-dealer fashion. He put down only about a $100,000 deposit and then negotiated $6 million in loans (getting his deposit back) and peddled TV rights for that amount to the Molson brewing conglomerate. I was furious that he'd snookered us. At the start of the meeting, his attitude seemed to be, "Too bad, fellas, I know you wanted this deal, but we got it."

It's a good thing I held my peace. If it had just been me in that room, I probably would have blown any chance of a deal. Just as I was wondering if the only reason he'd asked to see us was to gloat, he proposed that we come in for 49 per cent. We would have to put up some earnest front-end money, about $1.2 million towards our $8-million share. Then our group—which now consisted of Ralph Scurfield and Norm Green—would have 49 per cent, Normie his one per cent, and Skalbania 50 per cent. Not surprisingly, when Skalbania firmed up the offer following the meeting, we all agreed to the terms.

When the smoke cleared, here I was—the Depression kid playing on a frozen pond, the very average college hockey player—now part of a consortium of investors in a franchise at the senior-most level of the sport I loved.

My kids hadn't even known I was buying into the Flames. The first our grown-up son John learned of it was while working in Edmonton and a friend said, "I hear your dad bought a hockey team."

"Aw, B.S," he replied. When he called to confirm it, I explained, "We wanted to keep it hush-hush." John was later heard saying, "Of all the things my dad has done, this tops them all."

MY PARTNERS AND I HADN'T GONE INTO THIS VENTURE blindly. At the time, there were twenty-one teams in the NHL, generating collective gate receipts of more than $95 million while expending about $46 million on their payrolls. In 1979-80, a good nine of them had lost money: the Flames at least $2 million, the Colorado Rockies more than $2 million, and the Los Angeles Kings, Pittsburgh Penguins, Washington Capitals, Chicago Blackhawks, and the Edmonton Oilers $1 million plus. Edmonton was carrying a hefty debt—although it had enjoyed a healthy gate of roughly $6 million, the same amount it had paid to join the league that season as an expansion franchise. Even the Detroit Red Wings, with revenues of $5.5 million, were in the red for the year because their ancillary businesses, such as concessions and parking, didn't meet their costs. Among those in the black were the Minnesota North Stars, who'd made it into the playoffs, and the Boston Bruins, who owned the Boston Garden.

John Ziegler, the league's president, had cautioned, "The cost of operating an NHL franchise varies from a minimum, bottom-line $4 million to $6 million. Additional burdens are placed on clubs that don't own their own arenas or control concessions." And we would neither own the community run, non-profit Corral nor have any concession income. Despite these sobering figures, our group of investors was optimistic about our chances; there wasn't a cynic among us. (It was Bob Edwards, the witty nineteenth-century publisher of the *Calgary Eye Opener*, who once described cynicism as "the art of seeing things as they are instead of as they ought to be.")

We formed a twelve-member board, with Nelson as president and Doc chairman. The other directors were me and our contingent (with whom Normie Kwong was very empathetic), as well as Fred McNeil, CEO of the Bank of Montreal; Tom Sterling, a Molson executive; and Skalbania's business friends Peter Saunderson and Cas Hyciek and Nelson's lawyer, Grant Macdonald. Part of the agreement at the time was that all of our group's share of half the net profits would go to Olympic and amateur hockey pro-

The cramped old Corral was the Flames' first home for three years and drew sell-out crowds hungry for the NHL.

grams while Skalbania would contribute 25 per cent—effectively making the Flames a 75-per-cent non-profit organization.

After that, things moved like lightning in a prairie storm. While the fans wanted to keep the team name, we changed the emblem to a flaming "C." From the start, we knew the club would have to play for at least a couple of years in the Corral, a pretty humble home for an NHL team—the league's smallest arena. The building was so small that the Flames office had to be shoehorned into an Atco construction trailer on the site.

Our first new hire was Al Coates, an Ontario dairy farmer's son who had parlayed a business-administration degree and his hockey career into a job with the Detroit Red Wings organization. He went overseas to tour a team of North Americans to see how Europeans would react to pro hockey. (It played against an amazing Swedish fifteen-year-old named Kent Nilsson.) After returning, Al became the Red Wings' public-relations director. He came to Calgary in the same role and moved into an office with the only other staff member, western scout Ian MacKenzie. I would come to appreciate Al's dedication and loyalty in the next two decades, when he rose to be our executive vice-president and GM. If you wanted something done, this personable guy would do it even at some personal sacrifice. Beyond that, he was a passionate supporter of the wider community.

Al has since recalled that at the Flames' first press conference, reporters were asking when ticket sales would start and Skalbania replied. *"Now, I guess."*

Al Coates, looking down at the action on the ice, was our first hire, a public-relations director who moved into many other roles.

"There was a drove of people descending on the Stampede Corral to line up at the ticket windows," Al has said. "We sold out the season in six or seven hours. We had deposit cheques for $300, $400 or $500 all over the place [a single-game ticket was $25, highest in the league]. The place only held sixty-three hundred fans and we had fourteen hundred standing-room season-ticket holders." In fact, there was so much pent-up demand that all the tickets sold before the Monday morning they were supposed to go officially on sale.

All we had to do now was put a club together—the thirty-ninth team in the twenty-seventh city in the NHL's sixty-fourth season of continuous operation. In buying the Atlanta Flames, we inherited some good people, including their first and only general manager—the astute, committed, and well-respected Cliff Fletcher. Cliff was forty-five then, straight-talking and with a nice sense of humour; like me, he went prematurely gray, which helped explain his nickname, Silver Fox. Based on his record

Cliff Fletcher

alone, he was as sharp as a fox, a guy who inspired confidence among the players and in the community. He started his career as a scout for Sam Pollock, the brilliant architect of the Montreal Canadiens, where Cliff worked for ten years before becoming an assistant GM with the Blues when St. Louis joined the NHL in 1967. In his four years there, they reached the Stanley Cup finals three times in a row.

Arriving in Calgary from the Georgia capital, he soon realized he was back in a real hockey town when, on his first day, a fan buttonholed him on the street: "It doesn't matter how well you do—as long as you beat Edmonton." And so began the rivalry between the Oilers and the Flames.

Cliff brought along his assistant, David Poile, whose dad, Bud, had played in the 1940s on a line called the Flying Forts (with fellow Fort William natives Gus Bodnar and Gaye Stewart) for what was now my *second*-favourite team, the Maple Leafs. David himself was an outstanding college player, a business-admin grad, and another quality person.

Our head coach was Al (Chopper) MacNeil, who had eight seasons on defence as a workhorse with Toronto, Montreal, Chicago, Pittsburgh, and the New York Rangers. He'd been Atlanta's coach for only a year when the team moved north. Cliff had known him in Montreal, where Al jumped in late in the 1970-71 season to coach the Habs to the Stanley Cup. After receiving death threats for benching the wildly popular Henri Richard, he fell out of favour and ended up returning to his roots in Nova Scotia, taking the Canadiens' farm-team Voyageurs to the Calder Cup in the American Hockey League. And in 1976, he was assistant coach when Team Canada beat the Soviets. Chopper returned to Montreal as director of player personnel in 1978 and 1979 when the Canadiens won two more Cup championships.

In Calgary, Al would find a home in various roles over a quarter of a century as a salt-of-the-earth mainstay anchoring the team. His first assistant was Pierre Pagé, a Quebecker who'd worked with him and the Voyageurs in Halifax, where he was head hockey coach at Dalhousie University, ranked number two among Canadian college teams during his tenure.

Cliff and Al had been nurturing some talented players in Atlanta who came with them. All the focus at first was on getting the guys and their wives and families settled. In one-on-one encounters, Becky and I got to know and like them. There have been thousands of newspaper and magazine articles and at least a couple of books written about our team's first decade in Calgary, so I won't start making long lists of all the Flames who thrilled us in those early days. But I do want to mention a few of my many favourites.

AMONG THEM WAS BIG, FRIENDLY ERIC (THE TRAIN) Vail, the left-winger who'd tallied the most career goals of any Atlanta player. The equally likable, all-round Swedish forward Kent (Magic Man) Nilsson, the Wayne Gretzky of European hockey, who in his first season here would earn 131 points, to set a team record that still stands and trailed only Wayne and Marcel Dionne in the league. Popular right-winger Willi Plett, our high-scoring, scrappy heavyweight who'd held the team penalty record

Al MacNeil, our first head coach, joshing with one of our most engaging players, Jim (Pepper) Peplinski.

in Atlanta but was also an NHL rookie of the year—he had long blond locks that flowed freely in this era when helmets weren't mandatory. Paul Reinhart, a skilled twenty-year-old defenceman from Kitchener, Ontario, who during his first season in the league with Atlanta led the defence in assists and points. Guy Chouinard, a Quebecker who used finesse rather than physicality to be the first Atlanta Flame to reach fifty goals in regular season. And the incomparable Jim Peplinski, a strong, tall junior for the Toronto Marlboroughs whom Atlanta drafted in 1979. Pepper (or Pep) wasn't afraid to mix it up in Calgary, where he was a solid two-way centre—and off the ice his charm and community involvement made him a beloved local fixture.

There were so many others—including goalie Pat Riggin, centres Don Lever and Bill Clement (who had a successful career as a TV colour commentator), right-wingers Bobby MacMillan and Ken Houston and defencemen Pekka Rautakallio of Finland, Phil Russell and captain Brad Marsh. All thirty-three players would become high-profile in our town when they hadn't been in Atlanta. People recognized them, stopped them on the street, and gave them either hell or a big hello. Down south there'd been a kind of country-club, golfing-in-January atmosphere, which changed with Calgary's frigid winters (aside from the odd chinook) and a knowledgeable fan base putting them on their mettle.

They got a pass on the first regular-season game, on October 9, 1980, against the Quebec Nordiques. The only complaints the fans had were the introduction of paid parking and the gridlock traffic around the Corral.

The 1980 Calgary Flames pose for a team portrait in their inaugural season, ending third in their division, seventh overall in the league.

They didn't care that seven hundred tiny squares had been painted on the floor to mark season-ticket standing room. They certainly didn't mind that the players had to walk from the cramped dressing room through a roped-off hallway to the rink, where everyone could see them passing by, near enough to touch. And it was exciting to watch a game where you sat so close to the play—creating an intimate home-ice atmosphere that intimidated visiting teams. We owners were part of the crowd in our own little seating area and had to squeeze into a room under the stairs to socialize between periods.

With the Corral sold out, as it would be for the next three seasons, ticketless fans had to watch on CFAC-TV or listen on CHQR. Nelson got a semi-standing ovation, which may have rankled some of the investors in our group. In the stands, sprinkled with white cowboy hats and tuxedos, was a passel of Calgary-bred ex-NHLers, well-known players including Bill Hay, Ron Stewart, Bill Gadsby, Bert Olmstead, and Merv (Red) Dutton. Some of them were in the Hockey Hall of Fame and a lot had been Maple Leafs, who still had a place in my heart. Red, a former league president, did the ceremonial faceoff, witnessed by John Ziegler. Covering the game along with excited local reporters was the dean of Canadian sportswriters, Jim Coleman. The game program predicted (hopefully and accurately): "In the Eighties the Flames will bring the Stanley Cup to Calgary." Its cover had a

Our guys played tough hockey from the start, winding up in a 2-4 series against Minnesota in the Stanley Cup semi-finals.

cartoon specially drawn by Charles Schulz, the hockey loving creator of Peanuts, showing the team's fiery logo chasing Snoopy, who's thinking, *These guys are tough!*

Not quite tough enough. After Flames goalie Dan Bouchard crashed through a poster of the team emblem to launch the season, things started well. The visitors had the first power play, but the home team out-shot them 3-0. We took a 3-1 lead in the lively first period on two goals by Guy and one by Willi. Kent got one in the second while Quebec scored three and then he added another in the third, which was matched by the Nordiques. We had to be happy with a respectable, if frustrating 5-5 tie. "When you have a 4-1 lead at home, you should be able to hold it—that's the bottom line," Al MacNeil grumped.

But Al was as surprised as we all were when the Flames caught fire during the rest of the regular season. Five days after the inaugural game, coming off losses to the Colorado Rockies and Chicago, we had our first win, at home against Los Angeles, and promptly defeated both Boston and Minnesota. Then we lost on the road in our initial matchup with the team that became our reviled rival, Edmonton. We didn't succumb to the Oilers again that season, beating them in our next two encounters and tying once. Our guys blasted into the playoffs, establishing sixteen team records and collecting ninety-two points, their highest ever. Even the rookies shone:

Paul Reinhart, a power-play wizard, garnered the most goals and assists ever by a Flames defenceman. We trounced Chicago 3-0 in the preliminary playoff round (with Willi beating Tony Esposito in double overtime to put it away) and Philadelphia 4-3 in the quarter-finals—returning home in the middle of the night to a mob at the airport. The final match in the Philadelphia Spectrum had been a heart-thumper. As forward Jamie Hislop told the *Herald*'s Jean Lefebvre not long ago, "We went into that game and nobody gave us a hope in hell and we ended up winning." Guy and Kent were the offensive leaders when our sweep ended in a 2-4 series with Minnesota in the semi-finals of the Stanley Cup (which the New York Islanders won). Yet we finished a heartening third in what was then the league's Patrick division and seventh overall.

GOING INTO THE 1981-82 SEASON WITH ALMOST THE same cast of on-ice characters, the Flames organization experienced a major change backstage. Nelson, ever the flipper, decided to sell his majority interest. Among other things, he didn't much like the idea of ploughing profits into Project 75 to develop the game at the grassroots level. "That's one of the reasons he got out as quickly as he did," Normie says. Just before Christmas 1980, Ralph Scurfield met privately with Nelson and made a deal to buy part of his interest. Ralph was a good partner but an impatient fellow who just bulldozed ahead with an idea. What he'd forgotten was that we had a buy/sell agreement that any such deal had to be offered to the rest of us, *pro rata*. He said he *might* divvy it up with the other investors—in fact, he had no other option but to do that. So those shares from Nelson were divided proportionately among Ralph, Doc, B.J., Norm Green, and me.

The following August, Nelson announced that, without consulting us, he was selling the remainder of his interest to one of his appointees on the board, Cas Hyciek. "You can't do that," we reminded him. "We're partners here and we have the right of first refusal." After some debate, he capitulated and the five of us now shared 90 per cent of the club—18 per cent each—while letting Normie increase his token stake to ten per cent. ("It was a big investment for me at the time," he says, but his friendly, open personality and insider's knowledge of how professional athletes think made him a good partner.) In the two separate transactions to buy out the Skalbania investment, however, we had to pay well above the original share price, bumping the final cost of the Flames up to about $18 million.

Once again, Nelson had made money by reselling a property with the ease of a short-order cook flipping a flapjack. A year later, burdened by debt, he was in bankruptcy court but managed to convince his 120 creditors to let him pay off $39 million within five years. (In 1996, convicted of stealing $100,000 from a potential partner, he served his one-year sentence at home wearing an ankle monitor.)

A few years after we purchased Nelson's last interest in the team, a problem surfaced about American antitrust legislation against the Atlanta Flames predating his purchase. While the litigation involved several teams, all the claims for the other franchises were dropped or settled. At the time, we weren't aware of the problem or the court hearings—until out of the blue, we found that we were liable for about $4 million US. Had we been represented at the hearings, the claim against us would likely have also been dismissed. When I attended the hearing before a judge in Rockport, Illinois, it was a long, hard day. We ultimately paid the claim but recovered a significant part from our lawyer's insurance. It was all a lesson to be vigilant in closing any major financial transaction.

But the happy end result of all our negotiations with Nelson was that he was out of the picture and our quintet could now run the Flames with our own style, as we would for the next ten years. Taking over, we made Cliff Fletcher president and general manager and had him represent the organization as a governor with the NHL. He had a lot of latitude. As directors, we served on finance, marketing, and hockey committees. We kept a weather eye on our investment with regular management meetings where Cliff and Lynn Tosh, our capable controller, presented the financials and we checked the performance numbers. Doc headed the hockey committee, which he described as having some influence "if management wanted to spend a bunch of money to trade a player, but we wouldn't tell them how to coach." Of course, there was always talk of the game around the table—coaches giving us a rundown on the current roster and answering our questions—but we never interfered in the running of the team.

From the first, we'd decided on a hands-off approach to the actual day-to-day hockey side of the business. In a meeting, we might ask, after the fact, "Hell, why did you do that?" But we wouldn't approach a coach and say, "Why aren't you playing so-and-so?" Nor would we allow players to dump their problems on us owners, to squeal on their coaches.

Where we did get involved, along with our spouses, was in welcoming the team members to the community and, without intruding in their personal lives, making sure their loved ones were being recognized too. The owners reached out to these young people, many of them just out of their teens, one of them an ocean away from his home. Doc would host events at his ranch, for instance, and Norm Green held tennis tournaments.

Because of our own close family relationships, Becky and I threw autumn barbecues at our roomy Eagle Ridge home before training camp for all the coaching staff and the current and hopeful players and their wives, girlfriends, and children. It was our last house in the city, once more in the southwest near Glenmore Reservoir, where only our teenaged Jeff lived with us. The big, beautifully landscaped backyard had two lots for players' kids to scamper in. They got little toys and there was always entertainment for the grownups, including a few appearances by Alberta's folksinging icon, Ian Tyson. The chefs at La Chaumière cooked the steaks and served nugget potatoes and other vegetables fresh from my big garden while Becky always made four or five kinds of pies the guys would devour.

Knowing the women in their lives were often ignored, living in the shadow of glamorous athletes, Becky invited them to elegant Christmastime luncheons at La Chaumière (while their husbands stayed home to babysit). My thoughtful partner also included the women in the Flames office and the wives of the trainers and equipment managers and the team doctors. Over the years, we were guests at the weddings of many of the players. As she recalls, "We grew up with hockey—it was a huge, huge thing to bring the NHL here. Those first years were so wonderful. We lived and breathed hockey."

She and I got into the habit of taking an annual eastern road trip with the Flames during that decade. We joined the team as they flew by commercial jet and sat discreetly in the stands of the arenas just to see how things happened on the road. Walking around these cities, we ran into some of the players and had a chance to bond a bit, talking about their families, and on a free night took the coaches and trainers and the Calgary media people out for dinner. One day on a New York trip when our team was playing the Islanders, we were surprised to learn Cliff was trading defenceman Steve Konroyd and Richard Kromm for a big-name New York left-winger, John Tonelli. Becky, who had come to know Steve and his parents, cried when she heard he was leaving. That was typical of how attached she got to many of the Flames. Our sons also became diehard fans. John says now, "It was almost unreal because you'd grown up with hockey and NHL players were like gods and all of a sudden you're walking in the dressing room and meeting these guys."

Calgary became so comfortable for some team members that they decided to make it their permanent home. Jim Peplinski was among those who not only settled and found interesting post-hockey careers in town but also contributed mightily to the community. Pepper married Cathy Esplen and they raised four children while he bought a franchise in her family's business, turning it into a large auto-leasing company. He became heavily involved as a volunteer for such charities as Big Brothers and the Alberta Special Olympics and as co-chair of the United Way campaign. Other well-known players who've stayed on or come back include Colin Patterson, Joel Otto, Jamie Macoun, Theo Fleury, and Lanny McDonald.

MEANWHILE, IN OUR SECOND SEASON, THERE WERE A few intriguing changes out on the ice. Eric Vail was gone, traded to the Detroit Red Wings, where he'd soon end his career. Kari Eloranta doubled our European content overnight by joining his fellow Finn, Pekka Rautakallio on defence for nineteen games. He then went to the minors before returning the following season and stayed for four years. (Pekka, after his best season in '81-'82, making the league's All-Star squad, would return to Finland for the sake of his children.) Bob Murdoch, a defenceman with Montreal and Los Angeles before being traded to Atlanta, became our playing coach to work with young defenders. And in *Countdown to the Stanley Cup: An Illustrated History of the Calgary Flames*, Bob Mummery offers a nice summary of the biggest move the Flames made that season:

> *Within the first month, Phil Russell became the new captain when Brad Marsh was dealt to Philadelphia. In return, Calgary got versatile Mel Bridgman, the former Flyer captain. But it wasn't too long before president and general manager Cliff Fletcher was consummating a major acquisition— Lanny McDonald was coming to town. The November trade saw Bobby MacMillan and Don Lever go to the Colorado Rockies in exchange for the goal-scoring right-winger from Hanna [Alberta]. It would turn out to be one of the most astute, and most popular, trades that Cliff Fletcher ever made.*

Lanny instantly brought increased credibility to the club (*see* Lanny, *page 203*). He also brought his down-to-earth, almost boyish charm and the incredible bushy red walrus moustache that his own dad described as a corn broom. His career with the Leafs had been exceptional—in the 1978 playoffs, with his nose and a wrist bone broken, he scored in overtime of the seventh game to beat the Islanders and send Toronto to the Cup semi-finals. He was an Alberta boy to boot, who appreciated the Flames' warm family feeling and the fact that they were locally owned (the Rockies' owner lived in New Jersey). And Lanny McDonald didn't have a phony bone in his body nor did he ever bad-mouth anybody. Looking back, Cliff himself says getting The Moustache was the best trade he ever made: "Lanny basically changed the face of a franchise."

On and off the ice, Lanny was a classy leader admired by the other players. At six feet and 195 pounds, strong and solid, if not huge, he was a

Lanny McDonald—the inimitable number 9—joined us in our second season from the Colorado Rockies, hampered by a separated shoulder.

grinder on the forward line with a blistering slapshot. While playing clean and fair, he never backed away from a bully. Despite all this, his debut with us was less than spectacular. With a separated shoulder still healing, he had a slow start and didn't start clicking until he teamed with Pepper and Jamie Hislop, ending his abbreviated season with an impressive thirty-four goals. In his second year, he would score sixty-six, setting a club record no one else has come close to, and over his career became one of the top hockey players Canada has produced.

For the Flames generally, 1981-82 was lacklustre. We lost to Vancouver 0-3 in the semi-finals of the Smythe division, where we were now grouped. As Lanny wrote later in his autobiography, "The media was reporting that the Flames players were doing their best to get Coach MacNeil fired. What I do know is that they weren't happy about anything: Calgary, MacNeil, housing prices, not being in Atlanta, hockey, everything." That would surprise me when I read it, because as an owner I'd been isolated from the dressing room and didn't hear those kinds of gripes. At season's end, however, Cliff did decide to move Al into the office as his assistant general manager. Lanny (who became a good friend of Al) later said this was "probably the best thing that ever happened to him."

Coach Bob Johnson

In came a whole new contingent. There were only eight players who'd spent all of the previous season with us. In the 1982 off-season, Pat Riggin, Willi Plett, Bill Clement, and Ken Houston, all of them former Atlanta Flames, had left as some stalwarts arrived, including Buffalo Sabres goalie Don Edwards and the superb centre Doug Risebrough, who'd played for five Cup winners. At the management level, David Poile left to be GM of the Washington Capitals, Pierre Pagé went to coach our Calgary farm team—and our new coach was the brilliant Bob Johnson.

He looked like a rough draft of Spencer Tracy. The players called him CJ, for Coach Johnson, or Badger—probably because before joining the Flames he'd coached the University of Wisconsin Badgers but maybe also because he was such a relentless motivator. Al Coates recalls him as a gifted communicator and "the most positive person I've ever met. He never had a bad day. He wouldn't let other people get down, either." His favourite phrase, which he voiced virtually every day, was, "It's a great day for hockey!" Another Bob—playing coach Murdoch—became his assistant.

Bob Johnson, a hockey star at the universities of North Dakota and Minnesota, in his hometown of Minneapolis, had enjoyed a terrific coaching career at the collegiate and national-team levels down south. In 1976, he oversaw the U.S. Olympic team and five years later emboldened the young players of Team USA to an unexpectedly strong performance in the 1981 Canada Cup series. That caught the eye of the NHL and in particular Cliff Fletcher. "He probably thinks more like an NHL coach than any other coach who came into the league without an NHL background," Cliff said at the time. "The biggest problem he's had is that he's used to having four or five practice days to prepare for two weekend games in college." It was a bit of a gamble bringing a coach of American college players to a league where a lot of the guys had grown up on farms, without much education, and fought their way up the ranks.

As it turned out, the fifty-one-year-old Bob Johnson was a godsend for the Flames, with his optimism and the ability to inspire even veteran players. Tugging the long nose of his long face, he'd tell Kent Nilsson in his throaty voice, "This is a big game for us, Kenta."

"I don't know if I've got the legs tonight," said Kent, who never seemed to think he was as good as he was.

"You got what it takes to do it for us," the coach insisted. "You're the guy we're counting on." And at least once, Kent played well after such a pep talk but fell apart later in the game and said something like, "See, I knew I wasn't up for it."

The *Calgary Herald*'s George Johnson (who was no relation) has written of the day Bob had a fitness expert in to give the team stretching exercises.

"We're going to be like the lion, the King of the Beasts. The lion does what he wants, takes what he wants. He's the Lord of the Jungle. And first thing in the morning, what does the King of the Beasts do?"

Kent's voice piped up from the back of the room: "He licks his balls."

At a Molson's Cup lunch, honouring the three-star award winners, a fan asked why in a tight game, down a goal with two minutes left, Bob didn't put his best player—meaning Kent—on the ice. Before Bob could reply, Kent retorted, "Because he doesn't want to be down two goals."

Lanny, who excelled that season, was Bob's biggest fan: "He absolutely loved what he did. He was like my father, who'd been a farmer who loved every day and what *he* did. Bob helped to change the overall philosophy and atmosphere, not only in the dressing room, but in how the team played. He understood the game inside out." And, in Normie Kwong's words, "he was always looking on the high side."

Under his leadership, we made the divisional playoffs, downing Vancouver 3-1 in the semi-finals but falling to damn Edmonton in the finals 1-4. Losing to the Oilers always hurt most. One commentator called our rivalry "the most uncivil war in Canadian hockey history." It was more like two feudin' families in the Ozarks. Reflecting the antagonism the cities felt for each other in every other area—Edmonton being the provincial capital, Calgary the energy capital, and both having antagonistic CFL teams—the competition got more intense and bizarre with every passing year. An infamous sign that once popped up at a Calgary home game captured the typical tone: "I'd rather have a sister in a brothel than a brother who's an Oilers fan." Things weren't helped by the fact that Edmonton had arguably the best player in the world, Wayne Gretzky, along with such superstars as local boy Mark Messier, defenceman Paul Coffey, goalie Grant Fuhr, and Finland's Jari

Kurri, the league's highest-scoring European. Adding our own superheroes over the years, Stephen Cole wrote in *The Canadian Hockey Atlas*, "turned an idiosyncratic family feud into what was the most thrilling Canadian hockey story of the decade."

At one point, the conflict became nicknamed "the Battle of Alberta." The military term worked because some of our matches descended into bouts of violence that mortal enemies would wage. The ill will was apparent when Doug Risebrough lost a fight to Edmonton's Marty McSorley, the most penalized player in the league, but then yanked McSorley's jersey off and shredded it to pieces under his skates. In his autobiography, Lanny (who didn't mind "a good clean one-on-one battle") wrote:

> There was a time when the games were getting out of hand. It wasn't just a battle to see which team won or lost; some nights, it was a battle to see who survived. The fights became more frequent, the stick work more evident. . . . you don't forget incidents like Mark Messier sucker-punching Jamie Macoun from behind or Dave Semenko kicking Tim Hunter. You don't forget the brawls, which both teams participated in."

AT LEAST BY THEN WE HAD PRIDE OF PLACE IN OUR NEW home, the Olympic Saddledome, a lavish cut above the Oilers' Northlands Coliseum (and both were superior to Maple Leaf Gardens). As Al Coates says, "We were supposed to move into the Saddledome in two years, but there were construction problems and we were in the Corral for three." We could never make money in the Corral: there weren't enough seats, any food and beverage profits, and our large bank loan carried interest rates reaching as high as 20 per cent. Doc recalled that we lost close to $10 million there.

At the time, Calgary's oil-fuelled economy was enduring a downturn, so the launch of the Saddledome as the Flames' expansive arena was a welcome diversion. It opened on October 15, 1983, at the east end of the Calgary Stampede grounds, under its innovative roof, the largest free-span concrete structure in the world—an inverted hyperbolic paraboloid of precast concrete panels suspended by cables and shaped like a stylized cowpoke's seat. *The Globe and Mail* noted that the saddle was "delicately sited so that what would be the horse's rear does not point at anything that might be embarrassing to city fathers."

The building cost $100 million—a $16.5-million overrun from the previous year's estimate. The province and the city were the biggest investors in the project, with the federal government agreeing to pay a third of the original budget. Graham McCourt Architects designed the aluminum-

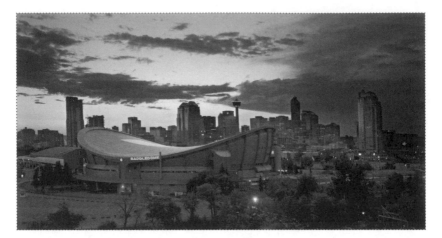

In 1983, fans welcomed the impressive new Saddledome on the Calgary Stampede grounds, with 16,700 permanent padded seats on international-sized ice.

sided structure while Jan Bobrowski and Partners engineered it and Cana Construction built it. This was the first major arena in North America that could host hockey on the international-sized ice sheet.

None of the 16,700 permanent padded seats was more than two hundred feet from centre ice. The thirty-three corporate boxes, holding another 354 fans, were located at the top level. They were being leased for between $180,000 and $480,000 for five years—half that revenue going to the team. And while the rent was initially costing us about $1 million a year (depending on the gate) in a twenty-year lease, the dome could hold more than twice the seating of the Corral. We were profitable every season for the next nine years. In 1983-84, with great community support and a boost in ticket prices, the Flames were the highest-grossing team in the history of the NHL, at $280,000 a game compared to the second-place Oilers at $270,000 (the two New York teams weren't far behind).

Unfortunately, in our first game in the Saddledome, the fans watched us lose by a heartbreaking score of 4-3 to—who else?—Edmonton. Then though we defeated Vancouver 3-1 in the Smythe Divisions semi-final play-offs, the Oilers edged us 3-4 in the finals and in 1984 went on to win the first of four Stanley Cups they would bring home over five years. The following season was equally maddening: after losing six games to Edmonton while winning only one and tying one, we got into the semi-finals against the Winnipeg Jets, who knocked us out 1-3.

In 1985-86, our frustration level was peaking, especially when it came to the Oilers. As Lanny tells it, "Bob's whole philosophy was finding a way to beat Edmonton. And so even in '86, when Montreal, Toronto, and ourselves were three of the favourite teams to go all the way, Bob knew that the only way we were going to get there was to find a way to compete with the boys up the road."

By then we had Joe Mullen from St. Louis, the Flame with the most goals and assists for the season, followed in points by centre Dan Quinn, Lanny, and newcomer John Tonelli from the Islanders; rookie defenceman Gary Suter (who'd win the league's Calder Memorial Trophy); Joel Otto, a six-four bruiser of a centre, among the few who could take on Edmonton's powerful Mark Messier; right-winger Hakan Loob, our response to Montreal's Swedish star Mats Naslund; and Al MacInnis, the seven-time victor in the Hardest Shot contest at the annual NHL All-Star game. Al had played a few games with us in two previous seasons before joining the Flames blue-line full-time in 1983-84.

In late '85 and early in the New Year, the Flames suffered through an eleven-game losing streak. After a not-very-good Hartford crushed us 9-1 in a home game, media from all over pounced on us, certain we could never recover. I didn't want to be there when Bob held a press conference—*migod*, I thought, *what can he possibly say?* But he put the most positive spin on a disastrous defeat I'd ever heard: "I don't understand people talking about our so-called slump. . . . Did you see that power-play goal that Peplinski scored? We haven't had one in weeks."

Seeing the hockey world through rose-coloured glasses seemed to work: 1986 was the year we went to the Stanley Cup. While the Flames bowed to the Oilers six times during the regular season, our guys outfoxed them 4-3 in our divisional finals. When we came home to Calgary, about 25,000 fans showed up at the airport, wowing newcomers like John Tonelli—"we never had anything like that in Long Island." We moved on to the Campbell Conference finals to beat St. Louis 4-3. And suddenly, almost miraculously, we were on our way to meet Montreal in the Cup. It was the first time in our brief history that we'd gone so far. Our Cowtown upstarts were facing the fabled Habs—Les Habitants, Le Grand Club, the team with the winningest Cup record ever.

This proved to be the spark plug that ignited our fans, who'd earned the rap that they were an unemotional lot. Some local sportswriters had complained that the Saddledome seemed mostly "a sterile and silent theatre of a building." Maybe—though we'd tried to jazz things up with mascots, bands, organ and rock music, nothing seemed to take until that season, when Calgarians became more and more excited at our winning ways. And then, till the end of the decade, the demand for tickets became so great that we would seriously flirt with the idea of featuring our games on pay-per-view television, which the NBA's Portland Trail Blazers had pioneered in North America.

The series with the Canadiens *was* emotional, intense—draining. One factor was that both Cliff Fletcher and Al MacNeil had worked for the Habs. For another, Doug Risebrough had been key in helping Montreal take the Cup four years straight in the eight seasons he'd played there. Despite my early love of the Leafs, I'd always had a grudging admiration for the Canadiens, the *bleu, blanc et rouge*. Now we were facing what some people (especially its coach, Jean Perron) described as the best defensive team in its history, one that had a fast-skating flair and were generally as tough as they had to be without being outright mean. They were captained by career Canadien Bob Gainey, one of the best all-rounders in the game. And our guys had to get past the seemingly unbeatable Patrick Roy—Saint Patrick to the locals—who in his rookie season as a twenty-year-old goaltender would win the Conn Smythe Trophy. But we'd hired the masterly Glenn Hall, retired as goalie with Detroit, Chicago, and St, Louis, in the role of "netminding consultant" to our talented young Mike Vernon.

It was the first all-Canadian Cup in nearly twenty years. The weather was appropriate for the first game between the northern clubs, with twenty-five inches of snow covering Calgary. The Flames won the opener by a re-sounding 5-2 but lost the second home game 3-2 in overtime. The next two matches were in the nostalgia-steeped shrine of Montreal's Forum, where the Canadiens beat us again. The fourth encounter featured a bench-clearing brawl as the 1-0 game ended with a fight between Jim Peplinski and Mario Tremblay that flared into a free-for-all. The league assessed a total of $42,000 in fines against the teams and the players.

The final contest, back in Calgary, was all Montreal's until the middle of the third period, when we were trailing 4-1. Then in a rousing rally, Steve Bozek got his second goal for us and Joey Mullen scored with forty-six seconds left, with Mike out of the net. As the clock ticked down, Joe fired another shot, but it rebounded to Jamie, and Roy made the split, stopping the puck with his pad and smothering it in his glove.

We'd lost, 4-3, yet our team and city had won something intangible. In the last couple of minutes, the fans kept chanting "Thank you Flames!" Lanny was among the many of us who left the Forum with welling tears— but when we got back home, a civic parade for the players arrived at the Stampede grounds as at least twenty thousand people waved "No. 1" fingers and wore red McDonald moustaches. As Cliff made a moving speech to the crowd, I felt the Flames were becoming legends in their hometown. A very special thing happened afterwards: a group of anonymous local business people created scholarships at the University of Calgary in honour of the Flames and we owners all got plaques. I've added to the scholarships and every year since received letters of thanks from the students receiving these endowments.

(Flash forward more than twenty years to early 2008 when Bob Gainey, now Montreal's GM, had his number 23 retired in a ceremony at the cavernous Bell Centre, the Forum's successor. He was surrounded by retired players like Mats Naslund, Doug Jarvis, and Guy Carbonneau—with a video appearance by Patrick Roy. The *Globe*'s Stephen Brunt wrote: "They were members of the 1986 Stanley Cup winning team, a group that can easily get a little bit lost, sandwiched as it is between the 1970s dynasty and the miracle champions of 1993." The irony was that at the very time Bob was being honoured, his Canadiens were languishing in their division. The Maple Leafs were being managed by a veteran GM called in to rescue their season, a fellow named Cliff Fletcher. And the Calgary Flames had then come from behind, like the troopers they are, to lead their Northwest Division.)

The Flames organization had been tempered in that '86 series—had learned that a six-year-old team in a small western city could come within sight of "the top of the mountain," as Bob Johnson would say. We needed to take only one more step to achieve the summit.

THE PLAYOFF SERIES HAD BEEN GOOD FOR OUR BOTTOM line too. Though we were then still tenants paying to use the Saddledome, our dozen matches in Calgary sold out and, among other revenues, we earned an estimated $25,000 a game in souvenir sales. Despite the fact that our payroll was among the highest in the NHL—about $5 million to Montreal's $4 million—our post-season earnings meant gross revenues of about $19 million for 1985-86.

Clare Rhyasen, whom Cliff had hired in 1984 as a financial officer, recalls, "When the team was playing well, we used to budget aggressively for revenues from two playoff games and we could certainly break even with them. If we went beyond that, we were going to make money." Clare was a young fellow I'd known first as a twenty-year-old articling accounting student who went on to help audit the financials of Sabre Petroleums until Carlo and I sold it. He'd then worked directly for Carlo before joining the Flames, where he moved his way up to being an accomplished and loyal VP of finance and administration.

A tall, wiry amateur hockey player from Nanton, Alberta, he'd found his dream job with us. As essentially a CFO, he reported to the owners monthly and particularly got on with Normie Kwong and me. Clare dearly loved Cliff, who'd bring him into his office on days when the team was making trades. "For a hockey fan, it was great—are you kidding?" He soon came up with innovative ways to compensate players, among them programs that deferred salary payments by giving them high-yielding annuities over a period of years.

Our financial success in 1986 cheered us owners mightily. We had a new partner now, the widow of our friend and hockey compatriot Ralph Scurfield. A year earlier, to our great regret, he'd died in an avalanche on a heli-skiing trip in B.C.'s Cariboo region. Ralph, founder of the giant Nu-West Development, was a steadfast supporter of community projects in the city and province, whose spirit later earned him second spot in *AlbertaVenture* magazine's list of the fifty greatest Albertans. As Normie Kwong says, "It was a major blow to us because we admired and respected him and he was a valuable part of the organization."

Sonia, Ralph's wife and the mother of their seven children, took his place in our ownership group. She was usually represented by her brother, Charles Tittemore, a former executive VP of Abitibi-Price (the world's largest newsprint company) who was now executive-in-residence on the University of Calgary's management faculty. We found him compatible in temperament as well as obviously knowledgeable about business. And the gracious Sonia was a firm believer in our ten-year plan to invest $5 million of our profits in Project 75 for the development of amateur hockey. "It might sound like a motherhood and apple-pie type of thing, and maybe it is," she said. "But I think we all got into this simply because we all love sports."

In the indifferent 1986-87 season—when the only memorable highlight seemed to be Joey Mullen's winning the Lady Byng Trophy for sportsmanship as well as skill—we lost in the first playoff round. And sadly, that May we lost Bob Johnson and his sweet wife, Martha, to his other love: non-professional hockey. Badger left us to go home and become executive director of the Amateur Hockey Association, which under his leadership became USA Hockey. But as we suspected, he couldn't stay away too long from the NHL. Craig Patrick of the Pittsburgh Penguins lured him back to coach a team shaped around the remarkable Mario Lemieux. In 1991, Bob's debut season there, he took the Penguins to their first Stanley Cup.

Back in Calgary after he'd left, we thought it was a shame he hadn't stayed with the Flames, especially since the team he'd built had gone on an exciting two-year roll. Our new coach was Terry Crisp, who'd been a leading scorer with the Boston Bruins farm team in Minneapolis after he turned pro in 1963. Two years later, when the NHL doubled in size to twelve teams,

PREVIOUS PAGE: On the ice with Lanny, having scored the final goal of his career in the 1989 Stanley Cup series.

The Cup-winning Calgary Flames and our ownership team pose with pride for the formal photograph following the six-game series with the Montreal Canadiens.

To
Becky & Harl[?]
Thanks for all ? ?
the kindness you ?
shown to me and my family.
God bless the both
of you. Yours truly,
Joe Mullen #7

Becky and I are delighted to share the joy with Joey Mullen, who had been a giant in
the '89 finals with Montreal.

I gave up hunting for wildlife decades ago, but in my younger years these trophies included a Kodiak bear in Alaska on a trip with Carlo von Maffei and a bongo of the antelope family on safari with Carlo and the Swedish king and queen.

Boone Pickens and I (opposite page, top) are after pheasants on his Mesa Vista Ranch in Texas. (Below) A rainy trail ride in 2003 on Doc Seaman's OH Ranch in Alberta with Doc, former Premier Peter Lougheed, and me. (Top, this page) I'm studying a report from the Hotchkiss Brain Institute, and our son Jeff and I are thanking Boone for his generosity in supporting the institute.

My Order of Canada (opposite) at Ottawa's Rideau Hall in 1998, with Becky, Governor General Romeo LeBlanc and his wife, Diana Fowler LeBlanc. My Alberta Order of Excellence the same year, at Government House in Edmonton, with a certificate of the Order with a border of images reflecting stages in my life.

Becky and my executive assistant, Doreen Warren, and her husband, Don, are with me in my ceremonial robes in 1996 for my honorary Doctor of Laws from the University of Calgary, with which I've had many involvements over the decades in the health-care fields.

Michigan State University, where I graduated in geology and played college hockey, awards me an honorary Doctor of Science degree in 2000. Becky and I are with George Leroi, dean of the College of Natural Science, which has given me an Outstanding Alumnus Award.

Gardening has been a passionate avocation ever since my days on the family farm in southwestern Ontario. In Calgary, I started growing everything from tomatoes to cucumbers in our son Paul's modest greenhouse and now at Hotchkiss Herbs and Produce, operated by him and his wife, Tracy, I can raise a variety of vegetable delights—like this wonderful sweet corn.

Coach Terry Crisp

the new St. Louis Blues claimed Terry and he helped them get to the Stanley Cup finals in three consecutive years. He moved on to the Islanders briefly and then the Philadelphia Flyers, where he was among the Broad Street Bullies who clocked the most penalty minutes as they won a surprise Cup victory in 1974. They got another the next year before losing to Montreal in the third final in a row.

Terry then retired to coach juniors in his home province of Ontario. By 1985, his Sault Ste. Marie Greyhounds took the Ontario Hockey League playoff championship before representing the OHL at the Memorial Cup, where they lost to Prince Albert of the WHL. His coaching prowess intrigued Cliff, who hired him to oversee our American Hockey League farm team in Moncton, New Brunswick. He had a good record there and two years later became our head coach.

Terry was a rough-and-ready, in-your-face redhead with a dressing-room vocabulary that would make your ears sizzle. As Lanny recalls, "Because Crispy had played in the league, we thought he would understand more of the players' side, about what we were possibly going through. But his job was to coach and he had tough decisions to make. He was totally the opposite of Bob Johnson. Bob was all about preparation—New Wave. Crispy was all about yelling and screaming—Old Style. Not that one is right and one is wrong; they were just miles apart." The free-spirited Terry himself has said, "People think I'm a loud, raving lunatic who goes completely off the wall. I'm one of the more calculating people in the game. To be a great coach, you've got to be a great actor."

In early 1988, the Flames had to play many more away games as the Saddledome hosted events in Calgary's stunningly successful Winter Olympics. Our progress in the second half of the season was overshadowed as the whole town became galvanized by the global Games. On our roster for fifty-seven games, we had the impressive rookie Brett Hull, son of the legendary Bobby, who went on to score 741 career goals, third on the all-time list. Meanwhile, we won the first of two consecutive President's Trophies awarded to the NHL team finishing with the most points in the regular season. But though we were six points ahead of our old antagonists, the Oilers, they blanked us 0-4 in the divisional finals and ultimately captured their fourth Stanley Cup in five

Joe Nieuwendyk came to us as an All-American college star and in his first season netted an astonishing fifty goals as a rookie in the league.

years by sweeping the Boston Bruins by the same margin.

The following season—1988-89—was all ours. There were only eleven players left over from the '86 Cup series. Among the new names on our rolls was Doug Gilmour, a sterling junior defensive forward in Cornwall, Ontario, who went to St. Louis and led the league in post-season scoring—though the Blues didn't even make it into the finals in '86. That was the year Joe Nieuwendyk and his boyhood friend Gary Roberts joined us. Joe had played junior in Oshawa before attending Cornell University and being named an All-American hockey star there. In Calgary he became only the second NHLer to net fifty goals as a rookie (Mike Bossy was the first). Gary did his junior apprenticeship in Ottawa and Guelph and as a Flame proved to be a solid left-winger on a line with Joe and Hakan Loob. Mark Hunter, the youngest of three southern Ontario brothers to make it to the NHL, came to us with four respectable seasons in Montreal and three in St. Louis.

And then there was Theoren Fleury. Theo was a feisty little guy from Russell, Manitoba, who played in Moose Jaw, Saskatchewan. Standing all of five-six, he twice played on Canada's World Junior team. The first time, he duked it out in a melee that lost the championship and, in the second, played it cooler as the Canadians came home with the gold. We selected him as our ninth-round pick in the draft, figuring he'd be good enough to play for what was now our farm-team club in Salt Lake City. In his first full season there, he racked up so many goals that Cliff moved him up to the majors as a right-winger and centre. Over the next dozen years, he'd surpass Joe Nieuwendyk as the top Flame in career goals, a figure that stood until Jarome Iginla overtook him in the '07-'08 season.

Our 1988-89 season began with a tie, a loss, and then four wins in a row, one of them 11-4 against Los Angeles. We never looked back, earning the best home-ice record in the league, the second-best on the road, and another President's Trophy with 117 points, two more than the eastern powerhouse, Montreal—which delivered two of our four home losses. Our Joes, Mullen and Nieuwendyk, both scored fifty-one goals in the regular season. Mike Vernon led all goalies with thirty-seven wins during the year. And in March, even while on the ice less often, Lanny earned his one-thousandth career point against the Winnipeg Jets and his five-hundredth

The small but scrappy Theoren Fleury, a consistent goal-leading forward.

goal against the Islanders. I can still see him circling behind the net and scoring in one of those pretty wraparound plays—to the warm acclaim of the hometown fans.

Behind the bench, backing up Terry, was Doug Risebrough, now our assistant coach. Just to make things even more interesting, late in the season Cliff introduced the first Soviet in the league during a game against the Jets on March 31, 1989. Sergei Priakin was a pleasant twenty-five-year-old from Moscow. The four-year veteran of the Soviet national team became the first player the Soviet Ice Hockey Federation permitted to sign with the NHL. He'd play right wing for the Flames before going home.

Along with our Flames partners, Becky and I would attend every game in the playoffs. To reach the Cup final, Calgary would first have to get by Vancouver, Los Angeles, and Chicago. Vancouver—which had lagged forty-three points behind us in league play—should have been no problem. It's worth remembering this series in a little detail because the odds-makers had been saying that a Canucks' triumph over the Flames would be the second-biggest upset in playoff history (after seventeenth-place Los Angeles downed the high-flying Oilers in the 1982 semis).

Sergei Priakin was the first Soviet player signed by an NHL team—the Flames.

Obviously, nobody had told Vancouver. In the Smythe semifinal opener, former Flame Paul Reinhart shot through a mess of legs at 2:47 of overtime to give the visitors a 4-3 win. We rebounded in the next two games, taking them 5-2 and 4-0. In the fourth encounter, Vancouver had four power-play goals to lead 5-0 and eventually finished 5-3 to tie the series. Again we rallied in the fifth for another decisive 4-0 victory. The sixth was in the Vancouver Coliseum and the shorthanded Canucks, trailing 1-0 on a goal by Al MacInnis, did some terrific puck work that led to a rookie centre named Trevor Linden tying it. While Pepper and Hakan scored, Vancouver fired five more goals—three in little more than two minutes late in the second period—to humiliate us 6-3.

Going into the seventh and deciding game in the Saddledome, the Flames were limping emotionally. We led on power-play goals by Joe Nieuwendyk and Joey Mullen until Robert Nordmark and that guy Linden connected on Canucks power plays. Gary Roberts gave us our third. But for much of the three periods, the Canucks simply outplayed the home team on our own ice. Only Mike's coolness in the net kept us in the game. After booing in the second period, our fans erupted with standing ovations when he stopped two sure goals with pad and glove saves and shut down Stan Smyl on a breakaway. Then Vancouver tied it 3-3 at the end of the third when one of their defenceman's shots deflected off a Calgary stick. We went into overtime and it took us until the 19:21 mark before Pepper's shot bounced off Joel Otto's skate and flipped into the net past the Canucks' Kirk McLean. *Phew!*

Now we faced Los Angeles—and Gretzky, whom the Oilers had traded to the Kings in a shocking move the year before. But on our side we had defensive forward Doug Gilmour, of whom the generous Wayne would later say, "I think Dougie is the Flames' leader. He's not only good offensively, he's good defensively." That certainly proved true as we put Wayne and the Kings out to pasture in four straight games—winning one of them 8-3—and sent Doug well on his way to collecting twenty-two points in twenty-two playoff games.

He was key when we met our next target, Chicago, coached by a man who'd someday figure prominently in our future: Mike Keenan. The Blackhawks' sixty-six points were the fewest of the sixteen playoff teams and the fewest of any Cup semi-finalist since 1970. We opened the Campbell Conference finals confidently, shutting them out 3-0 in the first match, but they came back 4-2. We retaliated 5-2. In the fourth game, Keenan moved Denis Savard to another man because Doug had been harassing him so well. Then Doug forced the game into overtime on a power play; we took it 2-1. And in the final, our Flames put the series away, 3-1.

The gutsy Gilmour's most dramatic goal was yet to come as we moved on for a climactic rematch—the showdown—with our nemesis, Montreal. The Habs, coached by the gruff Pat Burns, were fresh from losing only three games as they put away the Hartford Whalers, Boston Bruins, and Philadelphia Flyers. Here we were, about to get our second chance to seize Lord Stanley's coveted silver-and-nickel trophy from the club that had robbed us of it three years earlier. Again this was one of the rare all-Canadian finals; the expanded NHL hasn't seen one in all the years since.

Our fans had been up for the whole playoff series, helped along by the players' wives and girlfriends who painted inspirational posters that hung around the arena. It was a folksier, less security-conscious era, when kids could collar the players for autographs as they came out of the Saddledome. Right from the opening semi-final game, in Calgary, the place was wall-to-wall bonfire-red—the folks in the stands ablaze with the "C" of Red or the Red Sea, as the sportswriters were calling it. Backed by our bad-boy mascot, Harvey the Hound, the home crowd was on its feet roaring as the guys stepped on the ice and then howling at every Flames goal or an opponent's decking.

On May 14, the Cup opener in Calgary began badly at 2:43 when Stephane Richer scored while we were shorthanded. Then Al MacInnis connected twice in the first period, once on our power play, to beat Patrick Roy. A pass that bounced off Jamie Macoun's skate deadlocked the game. In the second, Theo Fleury had the third, winning goal—to another standing O—while Mike kept the Habs out of our net for the rest of the game to cries of "Mikey, Mikey, Mikey!"

In game two, again at home, we were sideswiped by defenceman Chris Chelios. Even as we controlled play in the first forty minutes—and despite Joe Nieuwendyk and Joel Otto scoring—Chris set up two goals, stole one from us, and popped in the winner. Them 4, Us 2.

Moving to Montreal for the third match didn't help. In what was the longest overtime Cup game since 1931, we outshot the Canadiens 28-17 during regulation time. The Canadiens scored at ninety-two seconds into the game, but by the second intermission Joey replied with a pair of goals. Montreal balanced things 2-2 early in the third, then we were up 3-2 when Dougie Gilmour capitalized on a rebound from Tim Hunter's stick. As we held our collective breath, Mats Naslund forced sudden death with forty-one seconds left. Centre Ryan Walter got the Habs' winner at 18:08 of the second overtime.

We exacted our revenge in the Forum in the fourth game. Russ Courtnall and Claude Lemieux got by Mike, but Dougie had a breakaway for our first goal and little Joey Mullen was a giant again with two shots that outfoxed Roy. In between, Al MacInnis got our third goal at 18:22 of the final period. Us 4, Them 2. The series was tied 2-2.

It was Al MacInnis's turn in the fifth battle, back in Calgary. We leapt out of the starting gate with a 2-1 lead thanks to Joel and Joey ("Joey Mullen? Hey, I'd like to adopt the guy. Joey Mullen Crisp," Terry told reporters). Bobby Smith evened it up for the Canadiens. Then, with twenty-nine seconds remaining in the busy first period, Al sent a bullet of a puck fifty-five feet into the Montreal net. Their Mike Keane sank one in the second period, but nobody scored in the third. The game score and the series stood at 3-2 in our favour—just one win shy of the Cup.

The atmosphere on that Thursday night of the sixth opening faceoff in the Forum was supercharged. Becky and I were intoxicated with the excitement, knowing that no visiting team had ever won the Cup inside the sixty-five-year-old temple of hockey. Most Calgarians knew that the thrill of the game itself would be tempered by the thought that this might be Lanny McDonald's last appearance on the ice; The Moustache was retiring, age thirty-six. He'd been benched for the last three games and hadn't yet scored in these playoffs.

Doug Gilmour set the spunky tone of the evening when he kissed Hockey Night in Canada's Don Cherry for good luck. During the entertaining first period, we were being outshot 9-4, yet Colin Patterson scored the only goal. Chris Chelios had stopped a dump-in by Dana Murzyn in the Canadiens zone when Colin snagged the loose puck and beat Roy. At 1:23 of the second, Claude Lemieux came back for the Montrealers with a mediocre shot, just inside the blueline, that somehow lofted over Mike's shoulder. Then three minutes later, Lanny came off a holding penalty and on his aging legs joined a rush for a three-on-one breakaway, taking Joe Nieuwendyk's pass and potting the puck on Roy's glove side. I'll tell you, there was joy in

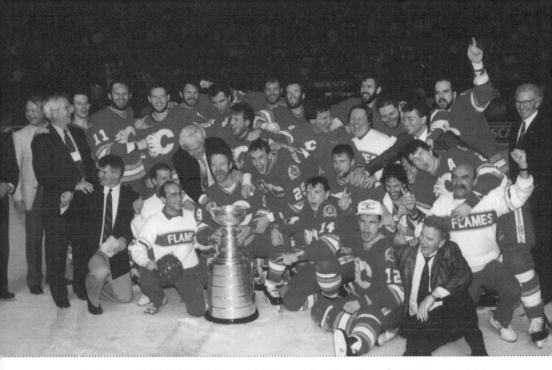

On the ice of the hallowed Montreal Forum, we're all exultant (me with a grin, third from left) having taken the Stanley Cup from the Habs.

Cowtown. Doug sealed the score with two in the third, one on a power play at 11:02. Habs defenceman Rick Green scored fifty-one seconds later. It was 3-2. In the dying minutes, Patrick Roy had just been pulled to beef up their attackers when at 18:57 Dougie did it again.

And we'd done it, downed Les Canadiens to capture the Cup, for the first time ever. And the first and last team to win it in the Habs' own home, the Montreal Forum, long since gone.

In the last two minutes, I'd told Becky, "We've got this one won" and slipped out of our box seats to go downstairs. When the final buzzer went, I was standing by the boards, debating whether to step onto the rink, when Al MacNeil said, "Get on the ice—you don't get this chance very often!" So I did, and stood beside the full-bearded Lanny, both of us beaming, as he hoisted the Cup in one of the great feel-good photos in Calgary Flames history.

Al MacInnis, the first defenceman to get at least one point in seventeen consecutive playoff games, had broken Bobby Orr's record and won the Conn Smythe Trophy as the most valuable playoff player. Without taking anything away from him, it could just as easily have gone to Doug Gilmour, Joe Mullen, or Mike Vernon. Mike had the most playoff wins and Joey the most playoff goals—sixteen in each case. (Good ol' Pepper got the most penalty minutes—seventy-five).

For a brief time, the Cup gets pride of honour in our backyard, where so many players and their families have come for barbecues.

It was a grand day all around for Becky and me. Our guys were not only taking home the trophy, but we also learned that morning our son John's wife, Joan, had just given birth to our grandson, Matthew. Life doesn't get better than that.

As we flew back to Calgary on the plane with our partners, the Stanley Cup was supposed to be stowed safely in the luggage compartment. On board with us were Jim (Bearcat) Murray and his son, Allan, who worked together as our trainers. Allan managed to sneak down below and smuggle the Cup into our cabin where we could all fondle it with pride and sheer pleasure. As Lanny remembers, "There was this huge family on the plane for five hours celebrating with the Stanley Cup. When you think that there were all these people responsible for it: owners, management, coaches, training staff, players, wives, girlfriends. It was phenomenal!"

Back home, we heard reports of the pandemonium that had prevailed here on the Thursday Cup night. Thousands of people spilled out of bars to celebrate along the entertainment strip on the well-named Electric Avenue. They waved signs and banners, put on "No Parking" hoods borrowed from meters, set off firecrackers, and even tried to kiss the police on hand to control what turned out to be a boisterous but orderly crowd. In future seasons, the action would move elsewhere, to the Red Mile on 17th Avenue, but this playoff series was the real birth of the very public Flames phenomenon that would attract media attention across Canada.

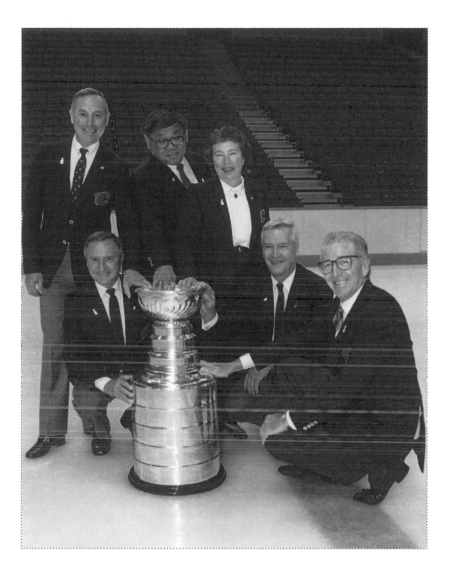

The partners get their own hands on Lord Stanley's trophy on our own ice: Doc, B.J., Normie Kwong, Sonia Scurfield, me, and Norm Green. We shared in the joy that our players experienced with Calgary's victory. As Lanny McDonald had said, "There is no feeling like it." And Theo Fleury announced: "This is the greatest day of my life. I love everybody in Canada."

B.J., Doc and I goof around in fur hats in Russia during a Flames exhibition tour after the Cup win to help promote the NHL.

There was a victory parade on Saturday. The more than 20,000 umbrella-bearing fans who braved the freezing rain made it feel like the whole town was lined up along the 9th Avenue route or tossing ticker tape and hollering down from office towers. Teenaged girls scurried into the street to present flowers to their heroes. The floats wended their way to the Olympic Plaza amid cries of "Lanny!" and "Thank you, Flames!" Mayor Don Hartman handed out plaques, Terry Crisp did a jig, and provincial Environment Minister Ralph Klein and deputy House leader Jim Horsman sported false red moustaches. I spoke for the owners, but Lanny said it for all of us: "We all may be a little cold today, but you have made us warm on the inside."

Al Coates says flatly, "Our greatest team was the 1989 Stanley Cup champions. It didn't matter if you wanted to play a skill game or be the Broad Street Bullies—we could play either way and beat you and did both during the playoffs that year." In Doc's opinion, "It was really Bob Johnson's team." I agree that it was the legacy that Bob had left us. But it was also Al MacNeil's team as well as Terry's and Doug's, the culmination of a decade of development.

That fall, the Flames trained in Czechoslovakia (by that time, we'd signed Jiri Hrdina, a thirty-year-old Czech forward) and then did an exhibition tour of the Soviet Union, all of this to raise the NHL's profile in Europe. Becky and I, along with other owners, attended games in Moscow and Leningrad, Russia, and Kiev, Ukraine. With hockey our common denominator, we found the Slavic people warm and courteous. But it seemed as if we had chicken Kiev every night until a friend of Doug Risebrough's at Safeway in Calgary sent over a shipment of food, including pasta that our people prepared for one welcome dinner in Moscow. We were fascinated by the big women who acted as stern floor guardians in the rundown hotels. The most moving moments were our visits to war memorials; just to see the sheer numbers of soldiers killed in combat and civilians starved to death in sieges was heart-wrenching.

Along with winning the Cup, that absorbing trip was a wonderful windup to the Eighties. They had been our glory years. We couldn't have guessed that the Flames' next decade would be such a hard slog—like skating on dull blades on mushy ice, with almost every step a struggle.

LANNY

Lanny took off his skates and put on a suit to represent the Flames in the community.

When Lanny McDonald came to us from the Colorado Avalanche in our second season, he might have been the only Flame who didn't mind playing in the old Corral. "I played junior in the building for the Calgary Centennials and the Medicine Hat Tigers and absolutely loved the Corral," he recalls. "So now all of a sudden you were playing where you not only had some success, but in junior hockey that was *the* building. The boards were high and the people were jammed in—it was kind of like a gladiator pit. They were right on top of you and you didn't want to let those people down. It was good."

It's this genuinely positive attitude, right from the get-go, that made Lanny the player who has best personified the Flames for most Calgarians over the years. His optimism and sense of joy in life translated off the ice into a compassion for others, especially participants in the Canadian Special Olympics, which offers sport training and competition for those with mental disabilities.

Coming into the NHL from an outstanding junior career, he was one of Toronto's first-round draft picks. In 1976-77, he and his buddy, team captain Darryl Sittler, ranked among the top ten scorers. A couple of years later, coach Punch Imlach returned to the Leafs and began battling with Darryl, eventually trading away his friends—even high-scoring Lanny. At the end of 1979, he and another player went to the Colorado Rockies and coach Don Cherry.

By now he and his teenage sweetheart, Ardell, were married and had the first of their four children. "The hockey team was horrendous, but it showed us what life could be like south of the border and gave us a two-year hiatus—especially after Toronto—that really helped set it up to come back to a hockey centre like Calgary and to be able to handle the pressure that goes with that. And I still have all the time in the world for Cliff Fletcher."

He also appreciated the involvement the Flames organization had in the community. "Project 75 is a classic example," he says now, "but no one really knew about it or a lot of things that the ownership group was doing. Because they just wanted to do it quietly—no big deal. But it came back to hurt them later in negotiations with the city to take over the Saddledome because people looked at them only from the business standpoint and not the overall picture of what they were trying to accomplish."

One philanthropic cause that Lanny has been supporting since his days as a Leaf is the Celebrity Golf Tournaments for the Special Olympics. Even when he was in Colorado, he came back home to Alberta to do a commercial for the newly formed Canadian Special Olympics. Lanny has travelled throughout Canada and the U.S. to appear at events to promote the movement. In Calgary, he became an active volunteer and fundraiser and in 1986, when the Games came to town, he and other players, including Jim Peplinski, were front and centre in working to make them a success. He's written that being involved has changed his approach to pro sports: "I see competition differently now. Maybe I'm more able to accept defeat than I was before. I think I was better able to handle a blow like our Stanley Cup final loss [in 1986] after having worked with the Special Olympics."

Three years later, Lanny was thinking he was on his last legs as we went back to the Forum for another crack at the Cup. He'd been off the ice for three games when Terry Crisp played him in the sixth match. "I'm sitting in the penalty box, and being the good Catholic boy, I said about two hundred Hail Marys the whole time I was in there," he reminisces.

"The team had killed off the penalty, I jumped out of the box and went right into a three-on-two rush. Hakan Loob passed the puck over to Joe Nieuwendyk on the left side and I joined on the right side—he threw it all the way across in one motion. I knew Patrick Roy was coming across and that he spread-eagled—you had to go high, it was the only chance to score—and the puck went top shelf just over his shoulder. *Like okay, can this game end now?*"

After we took the game and the Cup, he said, "I don't know if the storybook has ended on my career, but this is a great final chapter." It was the last goal of his career; he retired as a player the following off-season. He was named the NHL's Man of the Year, won the King Clancy Memorial trophy, and was later inducted into the Hockey Hall of Fame. The Flames have since retired his number 9.

But he didn't retire from either hockey or philanthropy. The Flames hired him as vice-president of community relations, cementing the team's reputation in Calgary, while also having him mentor young players. Later on, he ran the marketing department after taking a course at the University of Western Ontario. He went through some rocky times as we renovated the Saddledome, forcing some people out of their traditional seats. But his worst experience with us was during the period in the late Nineties when he was head of corporate development under a new president, Ron Bremner (*see next chapter*). He disputed Ron's way with people and was one of many in management let go during that era, to the great displeasure of me and Doc, among a minority of dissenting owners.

Lanny bounced back, as he always does. He went to work in marketing and business development for the local office of Baker Hughes Canada, an international petroleum-services company. But even then, he returned to help us promote the sale of season's tickets to corporations when the Flames were in financial trouble. He was also a director of player personnel for Team Canada in the 2001 World Hockey Championship and the 2002 Olympics, when the Canadians won the gold medal.

And he continues to do charitable work for organizations such as Big Brothers, Ronald McDonald House, the Calgary Children's Hospital, the Kids Help Phone, Canada's only toll-free, twenty-four-hour, bilingual and anonymous phone counselling and referral service for children and youth.

What all of these causes have in common is their concern for family. In interviews and at award ceremonies, Lanny always said, "I'd like to thank Ardell and the kids." It's a heartfelt sentiment. "Family means everything to us," he says. "It's one of those things you learn as an athlete: when all is said and done, when it's all over, all you have left is family."

THE HEART OF HOCKEY

There's another side to current and former Flames players in what they do, much of it quietly off the ice behind the scene. They work with our Flames Foundation for Life and have helped raise millions of dollars for a cornucopia of community causes. They're the heart of our business.

Our idea was always to have the team make a positive impact on the quality of life in southern Alberta. The Flames Foundation has directed more than $32 million to fund education, medical research, health, amateur sport, and recreation.

In 2006, Calgary's Rotary Club joined with us in the Rotary Club/ Flames Gift to the Community as a joint effort to heighten fundraising. Over five years, the partners are donating $10 million. And the players and their wives and our staff get involved in the cause by taking part in community events. It might be a Texas Hold 'Em Tournament against 320 poker players to raise $300,000 or the Flames' Better Halves Ultimate Ladies Night Out, when hundreds of women see a fashion show with the players' spouses modelling local fashion to generate funds for the Rotary/Flames House.

That's Calgary's first free-standing pediatric hospice and respite cen-tre for terminally ill children up to age eighteen and their families. Opened in 2008 near Alberta Children's Hospital, it has patient rooms, therapeutic-activity centres, and a classroom. The kids might have progressive degen-erative conditions such as muscular dystrophy and cystic fibrosis; malignant diseases, major organ failure, and resistant autoimmune deficiencies; or trauma-related injuries demanding end-of-life care.

A year earlier, the Ronald McDonald House opened on two acres next to the Children's Hospital as a home away from home for out-of-town fami-lies with critically ill kids. Our foundation and Rotary contributed $750,000 to create a park as a wonderful outdoor haven of greenery and flowers for family members staying at the House.

Meanwhile, Flames for Medical Advancement has given $5 million to the ambitious Reach! campaign (*see page 293*) of the University of Calgary and the local health region. As well as funding the pediatric hospital, the donation backs the Markin Institute for Public Health's target of improving disease prevention and health promotion; the Libin Cardiovascular Institute of Alberta providing an integrated heart-health program with patient care, research, education, and health promotion; the Hotchkiss Brain Institute's neurological and mental health research and clinical care; Project neuroArm's surgical robot, supported by Doc Seaman (*see page 282*); and the McCaigs' Alberta Bone and Joint Health Institute's research, treatment, and advanced prevention and wellness.

Meanwhile, the Flames are deeply supportive of our own sport in the community by encouraging minor hockey. A financial assistance program offers hundreds of kids from low-income families each winter the chance to play as part of the national KidSport Canada initiative. It pays sport registration fees and provides equipment. The team has given well over half a million dollars to the program since 2000.

I'm often asked which NHL players I would have on my list of all-time greats. Some like Wayne Gretzky, Gordie Howe, Bobby Orr, Mario Lemieux, and Maurice Richard are obvious choices because of their great records and unique skills. But even these skills differed widely—for example, Wayne's superb ability to anticipate and "see the ice" and Gordie's superior strength and durability. My group would be larger and my net wider. A fundamental attraction of our game is the quality of our players and the important role they perform with our young people and in our communities. So my list would include players such as my boyhood hero Syl Apps, Jean Beliveau, Lanny McDonald, Steve Yzerman and, from today's players, our own Jarome Iginla.

Jarome has reached out with his heart to KidSport in Calgary. He was there from the start by donating $31,000, deciding to give the organization $1,000 per goal over a full season for local kids and later to double his contribution, with half to the national KidSport. In the first seven years, this magnanimous man—a symbol of the best of the Flames—has contributed close to $400,000.

CHAPTER 8

TOUGHING IT OUT

The Team's Dark Years—and Bright Future

N RETROSPECT, THE NINETIES WERE A DECADE OF departures, of folks I had come to like and admire while they took their leave in many different ways. It's a truism in professional sports that you shouldn't get too attached to any player or coach or general manager—or even a franchise, for that matter. Yet it's still darn hard to say goodbye to those with whom you've shared intense moments of excitement and joy, loss, and victory. Over the next ten years, we would lose a lot of people and come close to losing the Flames themselves. But as Theo Fleury has been known to philosophize: "It's hockey—and life goes on."

The first to go was our business partner Norm Green. In 1990, he announced that he was acquiring the Minnesota North Stars (now the Dallas Stars), who'd been failing on the ice and at the box office. Norm was viewed as the Stars' saviour and under his ownership the team would improve so much that it went to the Stanley Cup finals the following year, beating St. Louis and Edmonton before losing to Pittsburgh.

Doc, B.J., Normie Kwong, Sonia Scurfield, and I had agreed to take up his 18 per cent of the Flames. But while we'd identified two sterling potential partners, it would take till 1994 to seal the deal to bring them in with other owners.

The next to leave the team after Norm Green was Terry Crisp. He'd taken us to back-to-back President's Trophies and then the Cup. The Flames had renewed his contract for three years in June 1989. The following season,

Washed in a C of Red, our fans erupt in 2004 as we went to the Stanley Cup again, this time against the Tampa Bay Lightning—after the long decade of the Nineties when the Flames and other Canadian teams were beset with financial woes.

he led the club to the first round of playoffs, only to lose to Los Angeles. We'd already lost to the Kings at regulation season's end, in a double-over-time game during which—in full view of the crowd and the TV audience—Terry blew his nose dramatically in disgust to protest a referee's decision over a disputed goal by Doug Gilmour. It wasn't only his loose temper with officials; it was also his over-the-top theatrical style that some of our players and sports reporters found hard to take. His wife, Sheila, had a point when she said, "It's quite obvious he wasn't treated fairly by the media."

In 1990, Cliff demoted him from head coach to a scout. Liking the guy, I felt for Terry. But one thing that a good owner learns early on is that you can't keep second-guessing an experienced and respected senior execu-tive. We did have one of our two consulting team psychologists, Max Offen-berger, work with Terry in an attempt to help ease the abrupt transition and loss of face. In the long run, he landed on his feet: two years later, he was an assistant coach of the silver-medallist Canadian team at the Winter Olym-pics in Albertville, France. He then coached the NHL's new Tampa Bay Lightning from its birth in 1992 until '97. Terry has since been a commenta-tor for TSN in Canada and Fox Sports in the U.S. and is now a colour analyst for the the league's Nashville Predators. The friendship Becky and I have with him remained strong and we enjoyed our occasional visits together.

Replacing him was Doug Risebrough, who had become Cliff's assis-tant general manager. Playing for five Cup-winning teams, Doug had shown his skill as a centre; now he had to prove himself as head coach. His first season, with many of the same stars who'd played under Terry, we made it to the Smythe's semi-finals, where the Oilers edged us 4-3.

Becky and Doc Seaman, who shared the love of our Flames through the team's good and tough times.

It was during the '91 playoffs when Doug—and the team—suffered a crushing body check. Cliff Fletcher had spent nearly two decades as the only general manager of the Atlanta and Calgary Flames and ranked among the finest ever in NHL history. Now he was leaving us as both GM and president. Not only that, he was heading east to be president of the Maple Leafs. Only partway into a recent contract I'd helped negotiate, he wasn't going for the money. When I asked him, one-on-one, if there were any problems we weren't aware of, Cliff said he and his wife, Boots, simply wanted to live in eastern Canada, where their family was, and to be closer to their Florida vacation home. There was also the challenge of reviving the ailing Toronto club.

It was a great loss. In the last four seasons, the Flames had earned two-thirds of the points available to us, more than any other club in the league. At the time, Jim Proudfoot of the *Toronto Star* commented, "For a decade, there was no NHL executive with authority like Fletcher's. The folks who bought the Atlanta Flames in 1980 and moved them to Alberta weren't looking to make a lot of money. Profits were to be handed over to worthy projects like the Olympic squad and hockey research. Fletcher's mandate was to beat the hated Edmonton Oilers, first of all, and to win as often as possible. What it cost was pretty much irrelevant." Well, not quite, but his point was well taken.

To replace Cliff at the top, we brought in Bill Hay as president and chief executive officer. Bill had been a scoring leader on the Chicago Black hawks' Million-Dollar Line with Bobby Hull in their 1961 Stanley Cup win. Retiring to Calgary, Bill—or Red, for his ruddy hair— gained a wealth of business experience in the Oil Patch, especially while working for the Seamans' Sedco Drilling and then as senior vice-president of their Bow Valley Resource Services, the service and supply arm of Bow Valley Industries. Red left in 1990 and briefly became president of the Hockey Canada organization his father, Charlie, had founded (his mother had been a goalie with the University of Saskatchewan women's team).

Under Bill's presidency, the intense and often stubborn Doug now became both our general manager and coach in May '91. As it turned out, that was not fair and a huge mistake on our part, giving him just too much, too soon to handle in the tough times. A GM has to deal with the coach's concerns, owners' questions, media critiques, players' injuries, the farm team's health, as well as the major tasks of negotiating with athletes' agents and trading players with other teams. And now, there was a president between the general manager, the coach, and the ownership group, a level of potentially second-guessing management that Cliff never did have because he'd always acted in both roles.

One of the first major moves Doug made was a ten-player trade with his mentor, Cliff. Doug Gilmour, one hell of a gritty, skilled, determined hockey player, had been unhappy during his salary arbitration negotiations—he wanted a long-term contract and $450,000 more for the season—and was champing to go elsewhere. There was friction between the two Dougs that took on a personal tone. In what was then the biggest trade in league history, Risebrough swapped Gilmour and four others (defencemen Jamie Macoun and Ric Nattress, left-wing Kent Manderville, and goaltender Rick Wamsley) for a leading Leaf scorer, right-winger Gary Leeman (along with left-winger Craig Berube, defencemen Michel Petit and Alexander Godynyuk, and goalie Jeff Reese). Gary would get only nine goals as a Flame. Toronto, meanwhile, flourished with their new blood. Describing the deal, Jim Proudfoot said Cliff "hoodwinked his former protégé in about as lopsided a trade as you're apt to see. This was the Silver Fox at his most cunning."

Doug stayed on as coach for the first sixty-four matches of the 1991-92 season. One of them was the 12-0 drubbing we took from the Vancouver Canucks. We relieved him of his coaching duties but retained him as GM for the next four years. "Funny thing in athletics," Bill Hay reflects, "they think the better you play, the easier it is to be a coach or a general manager." Doug was replaced by Guy Charron, who'd been his assistant since 1990. Guy, a former forward with Detroit, the Kansas City Scouts, and the Washington Capitals, filled in as head coach as we had to settle for fifth place in the Smythe Division. He then went back to being assistant until 1995.

Guy was followed by Dave King, who came off a great career at the college and international levels. He was head coach of Team Canada in five International Ice Hockey Federation world championships, winning the gold at the 1987 Isvestia Cup against some strong European teams, and as its coach in three Winter Olympics, taking silver in '92. Compared to Terry, he was more analytical, more a pure student of the game. In Calgary, he had the help of a suddenly sensational Theo Fleury, who collected 100 points in the 1992-93 season. Yet we missed the playoffs—a first for the Flames since 1975 when they were still in Atlanta.

As Clare Rhyasen points out, "This was Dave's first attempt at coaching professional hockey players. In all of his coaching career up to that point, he'd had the ultimate hammer: if you don't do it my way, then I'll get someone to replace you. Well, you can't do that with pro players and so his hammer was gone."

And he proved to be much more reserved compared to the enthusiastic Bob Johnson. Late in 1991, word had come of Bob's sadly premature death; he was only sixty and had coached for thirty-two of his years. In the

1990-91 season, Badger had pumped his Pittsburgh Penguins to the Stanley Cup—and not long after, he was operated on for a brain tumour. Travelling in the U.S., I called his wife of thirty-eight years and Martha said he'd love to see me in hospital in Colorado Springs. In a way, I wished I'd never gone; he didn't know me.

When he died, Martha asked if I'd speak at his funeral. Al Coates and Cliff Fletcher were among the pallbearers and all the Penguins were there, including Mario Lemieux and Joey Mullen (whom we'd now traded to Pittsburgh, much to my regret). Giving an eulogy was a tough assignment. One of the stories I told was calling Bob after his team had won the Cup and getting his answering machine, on which he said, "Well, we've climbed the mountain." Then in the middle of the night, he called me back, and as I came out of a sound sleep we talked for half an hour about old times and favourite players. As Becky and I discussed the call the next morning, I said, "Who else in the world could call in the middle of the night, talk hockey that long, and make me feel good about it?"

Another Badger story I enjoyed concerned his well-known thriftiness with money. Becky and I were down in Pittsburgh one evening with Al Coates and Al MacNeil. We invited Bob and Martha out for dinner and Coatsey had pressured me not to pay for the meal when the tab came. As Al MacNeil tells the story, "Badger was shuffling around, kind of half-heartedly reaching for it. So we sit and sit, the bill sitting there in the middle of the table. And finally Coatsey says: 'Oh, it's okay, Badger.' So Badger kind of sat back and relaxed. And then Coatsey says: 'You and Martha can split it.'"

At Bob's funeral, a soloist sang "Wind Beneath My Wings"—and this inspirational man was exactly that for all of us who knew him.

THE NATIONAL HOCKEY LEAGUE WAS CHANGING. I KNEW this first-hand now by becoming Cliff's successor as the team's NHL governor on the league's board. The most obvious marker of the change was the steady escalation in players' salaries. Two examples close to home were Doug Gilmour's recent exit to get more money from the Leafs and Brett Hull's negotiations after he left us in 1988 to join St. Louis. Though Brett scored a hefty seventy-two goals in 1989-90, he was making only $125,000. His agent, Bob Goodenow, then landed him a three-year, $7.3-million deal with the Blues, a contract that became a major propellant in boosting salaries throughout the league. It wasn't long after this deal that Bob became executive director of the NHL Players' Association and began transforming the economics of the league—in a revolution I detail in the next chapter.

One of the unfortunate spinoffs of this demand for higher salaries was the short-lived players' strike of 1992. (There hadn't been a labour upset over salaries since the Hamilton Tigers refused to play in the NHL finals of 1925.) The league had gone into the current season with no collective bargaining agreement (CBA) and by that March there'd been no real movement from either side. The owners were betting the players would back down. The Stanley Cup series were looming, but the players now voted overwhelmingly to strike on April 1.

Bob was very good at telling his members that they had an obligation to save younger players from what he saw as abuses in the system. I agreed then, as I do now, that pro hockey can be a tough business with short careers and its participants have to maximize their earnings. In their skates, I would likely shoot for the most money I could get too.

Even so, I was surprised and disappointed that our guys walked out, as I told the *Calgary Herald*: "I can't take it any way other than personally. When we brought the franchise here, we put up the money and guaranteed the loans. I don't want to sound self-serving, but we've taken a lot of pride in what the Flames have brought to Calgary. The personal side is where the enjoyment is. If that isn't there, then this is just another cutthroat business. . . . We told our players to come in and verify our figures and bring in someone to help them assess the figures. All we would ask for is confidentiality. We're not going to sit here and watch this go from a strong franchise to a faltering one. We're willing to take the risk of a bad season and the consequence of that, but we're sure as hell not going to go down and enter into a planned program to do that. Why would we do that?" That was the beginning of my role as the prime spokesman for the ownership group.

Less than a week later, the NHL's John Ziegler and the NHLPA's Bob Goodenow were meeting seriously, horse-trading over terms that gave the players small increases in playoff remuneration and let them keep the rights to the lucrative hockey trading-card business, among other things. The owners, while happy to have their teams back in time for the playoffs, began girding themselves for a much more crucial round of negotiations coming up in a couple of years.

On the happier side, one of the top Flames during the first few years of the Nineties was our second Soviet player named Sergei—Sergei Makarov, Russia's Gretzky, its leading scorer who'd played in the Olympics, the World Championships, and a couple of Canada Cups. During the pre-season in 1989, we'd sent him back to compete against his countrymen for a Friendship Tour in the Soviet Union. During our season, he amassed eighty-six points and the Calder Memorial Trophy as a thirty-one-year-old rookie of the year (after that, the league lowered the age limit for the honour to twenty-six or younger). As Al MacNeil says, the veteran Sergei helped develop both Joe Nieuwendyk and Gary Roberts: "He made them understand what is was like to work as a line." He stayed with us until joining the San Jose Sharks in 1993.

IN '94, THE NHL FACED A FULL-FRONTAL LABOUR ACTION that followed the players' strike. This time, the owners took the decisive step. The following chapter about my time with the NHL describes how Bob Goodenow was pitted against the man who eventually succeeded John Ziegler: Gary Bettman, the league's first executive to be named commissioner. The lockout lasted 104 days and 468 games, from October 1 to January 11, 1995.

By then, with expansion to twenty-six franchises, including the Anaheim Mighty Ducks and the Florida Panthers, the character of pro hockey was being reshaped. In Calgary, the nucleus of our ownership group had been transformed as players' salaries continued to climb. Our two partners who decided to take their leave in this yeasty ferment were Sonia Scurfield and Normie Kwong. They were strong partners and we understood the reluctance both of them had to keep investing in the club during these uncertain times.

Normie, who went to all the playoffs with his wife, Mary, recalls that his involvement with the Flames "was a real highlight of my life. It was great being an owner because of the privileges, the respect, and the success we had—at a time when it was new and everybody in the city seemed to jump on the bandwagon." But now, he realized, "hockey was just about to change. Realizing that and understanding that there were going to be some huge cash calls—which I wasn't prepared to do, or couldn't do—we decided to bow out." He became president and GM in revitalizing the Canadian Football League's Calgary Stampeders for a few years with a new coach, Wally Buono. In 2005, he became Alberta's distinguished lieutenant governor.

Looking on the fate of the Flames after he left, His Honour can sagely reflect "that things hit the skids" for more than the next half of the decade. At first, things appeared positive after our small ownership group—as early as late 1991—had begun courting two key investors. John (Bud) McCaig of the Trimac transportation and drilling group (where Doc was a director) had been on the Alberta Gas Trunk Line and NOVA boards with me. Alvin Libin was vice-chair of Crownx Inc., which had major stakes in Crown Life Insurance and Extendicare, Canada's largest supplier of health care services. Bud,

Al, and I had been directors and chairmen of Foothills Hospital and along with B.J. Seaman were on finance committees to raise money for the Peter Lougheed government.

In 1994, Bud and Al formally became partners in the Flames. Both sterling citizens as well as astonishingly successful businessmen, they were a comfortable fit with us. Peter C. Newman once described Bud as "a staunchly loyal Lougheed adviser with very real power but a pleasant, laid-back manner, still not afraid to admit that he enjoys being a member of the Petroleum Club." I second all of the above. Al has been a solid partner, a tough, shrewd businessman yet with a depth of caring for people and a feeling for the community that's right at the top of the heap. When Bud encouraged him to get involved with the Flames, he had little hesitation: "I always believed that if you're going to be an important city in North America, you need to have an NHL hockey team, especially when you come from hockey country." His marvellous wife, Mona, as deeply involved in philanthropic ventures, remained a passionate Flames fan until her recent, untimely death; we miss her terribly in our lives.

There were four others joining the partnership that summer of '94. The most controversial was Ron Joyce. A Maritimer, he'd once worked during his teens in Ontario tobacco fields and had been in the Navy—two arenas close to my own background. Later, his interests veered from mine as he joined the Hamilton police force before taking over a doughnut shop and then becoming a co-owner in 1967 in a chain started by Maple Leaf blueliner Tim Horton. After his partner died, Joyce would build the Tim Hortons into a thousand outlets and by 1990 was looking to involve himself in hockey with the involvement of the restaurant group. We'd met before while he was hot on securing a Hamilton franchise. But, during his bid to the NHL, he hadn't agreed up front with the neighbouring Leafs in Toronto and the Sabres in Buffalo on how much to indemnify them for intruding on their exclusive territories. The other factor was that he wanted to pay the league's franchise fee over time. Not surprisingly, he failed to get approval—while Tampa and Ottawa were accepted into the league.

It was in 1993 that Doc, B.J., and I met Ron Joyce at the All-Star game in Montreal and, knowing his strong business career and interest in hockey, we discussed getting him involved with our club. He'd bought a house in Calgary a few years earlier. We recognized that, as we grew older, one possibility could be his taking over the ownership at some future point. But nothing came from these discussions. Later, after much backing and forthing with his people doing their due diligence, he agreed to become a partner in October '94. Doc, B.J., and I, Murray Edwards, and Joyce took 15.1 per cent of the shares and left equal minority pieces to Bud McCaig, Al Libin, Allan Markin and Grant Bartlett.

Murray was a lawyer, who'd been a protégé at Burnett, Duckworth & Palmer of Jim Palmer. As Jim pointed out, "Murray and I have been close really from the day he articled here as the best young lawyer we've ever had. In fact he became a partner after four years, which is unusual in a firm our size." Murray eventually graduated to become a major financier of Canadian Natural Resources (CNQ), the country's third-largest gas producer, and Magellan Aerospace, among the largest Canadian tech companies. (Jim serves on the boards of both companies.)

Murray's other partner was CNQ's chairman, engineer Allan Markin, who rebuilt the company and made the junior oil and gas company into what eventually has become the $30-billion giant, with a significant footprint in northern Alberta's oil sands. It also holds petroleum assets in the south of the province, Saskatchewan, West Africa, and the North Sea.

Grant Bartlett, a Nova Scotian, taught geological sciences at Queen's University in 1980 before coming to Calgary to enter the Oil Patch with Cities Service Co. and Canterra Energy Ltd., and then ran Archer Resources, Apogee Capital, a private investment management company, and Maken Energy. As he complained to people about the team not being a real business in a small centre like Calgary, "A business is something you do to make money."

From the first, our new group was confronting serious financial challenges. To garner some of the revenue in operating an arena, we original owners had considered building our own structure in 1992, even talking seriously of an option on some land in the downtown behind the Calgary Inn. In the end, we realized it wouldn't be right to compete with the community-owned Saddledome. Instead, we paid about $20 million up front to buy out the management contract from the Calgary Exhibition and Stampede Board that had run the Dome.

There was a political uproar in 1994, during the lockout, when we intended to renovate the building, but for months critics delayed civic approval of $12 million in federal infrastructure funds for the work. In the summer of '95, the total spent between the taxpayers and us was $36.6 million—the majority contributed by the Flames—to gut the lower bowl and add forty-five executive suites (as much as $96,000 a year) and 1,250 plush club seats ($3,100 annually plus $1,500 membership fee). The suites were perhaps the best in the NHL. Also added were exclusive dining and lounge facilities and improved public washrooms. Al Libin, with his expertise in a national nursing-home business, helped us in the renovation. "Hockey guy I'm not," Al reflects, "but we got the job done—some of it good, some of it not good."

We made one huge error by electing to install that row of suites at row 14 and bring the upper bowl down to the top of those suites. As a result, we cut down the number of fans in the lower bowl by half from 9,000. When they were moved to the upper bowl, even though the views were excellent, most felt disenfranchised in losing their long-standing lower-bowl season's tickets. The public-relations fallout was terrible.

Lanny McDonald was running the marketing department then: "One of the toughest parts about that whole scenario is that the building had to be changed for the survival and the success of the franchise, period. Over maybe four months, we needed to meet with every season ticket-holder, from 6 o'clock in the morning until 10 o'clock. It was a huge deal for them. Some people you made extremely happy, other people hated you with a passion." And along with this kerfuffle, we suffered significant lost income from the lower-bowl seating as some fans dropped their season's tickets.

At the time, we needed every buck available as the exchange rate between the Canadian and American dollars had become so unbalanced. Our loonie went poof—dropping into the low sixty cents compared to the sturdy greenback the U.S. teams enjoyed. As described in the next chapter, I became chairman of the NHL in 1995 and pushed for currency equalization. At the start of the following year, with Gary Bettman's firm guidance, the board of governors was convinced to approve an enlightened plan to assist smaller-market Canadian clubs with contributions shared by all of the franchises.

A team at the bottom half of the league was measured by its payroll, revenues, and the size of the currency differential. The Flames were ideally positioned to benefit up to an initial $5 million U.S. per year. We had to generate 80 per cent of the league revenue average or sell 13,500 tickets, plus all our luxury suites, which we did. Over the nine years, the equalization scheme solved about 30 per cent—more than $30 million—of our problem. We wouldn't have survived without that transfusion and neither would Edmonton, Ottawa, and possibly even Vancouver.

In 1997, we acquired the Calgary Hitmen of the Western Hockey League from its eighteen investors, including wrestler Bret the "Hitman" Hart, Theoren Fleury, and Joe Sakic. The idea was to have the junior team help bump up our revenue by playing in the reconfigured Saddledome, as it still does. There were obvious economies of scale in operating the building while the Hitmen also offered us the potential to test coaches and managers in a training ground in the minors.

But through the later Nineties. the fans of the Flames who saw us failing on the ice were becoming disillusioned. Between 1997 and 2003, we never made the playoffs. Management changes were inevitable. Bill Hay had left as president in 1995, unwilling to step into a lesser position and eventually went on to do a superb job as head of the Hockey Hall of Fame. The versatile Al Coates, who'd been general manager, then filled in as acting president the next season. Over the next couple of years, he traded two of our pivotal players: Joe Nieuwendyk and Gary Roberts.

Talking to Joe before he decided to leave us was one of only two times I've ever discussed contracts with players as an owner. As our captain, he was a superior, well-spoken symbol of the team who, among other things, had helped me in some philanthropic work for the Foothills Hospital fundraising campaign. Involved in a contract dispute, he called me from Ithaca, New York, to say it was probably time for him to move on. "Well, Joe, if you're under any illusions that you're not wanted in Calgary, I'll tell you you're not only wanted, you should be here. I'd be really disappointed; I think you'd be making a mistake."

"Harley, I've enjoyed the relationship, but...."

"But if you've come to that place, I'd be very sorry."

Though he agreed to talk it over again with his agent, in the end he was traded for Jarome Iginla to the Dallas Stars, where he went on in his outstanding career to help win the Stanley Cup before joining three other teams.

The only satisfaction that most of our fans (and I) could feel in the 1996-97 season was in welcoming Jarome, who'd starred on two Memorial Cup-winning teams. Jarome Arthur-Leigh Adekunle Tig Junior Elvis Iginla, with West African heritage on his father's side, is a right-winger from St. Albert, Alberta, who has graced our team with his leadership and skill ever since—becoming all-time leader in goals scored and games played by any Flame and named team captain in 2003 (the first black captain in NHL history).

Knowing the organization needed a new leader to revitalize our sapping strength, we went through a candidate-review process to bring in another native of Hamilton in the spring of 1996 as president. Ron Bremner had started as a radio salesman with Standard Broadcast Sales in Toronto and moved to the west coast to work his way up to president and CEO of the very successful BCTV in Vancouver. Murray and Grant encouraged his hiring and I was in favour of his appointment—as it turned out, to my regret.

Ron decided to start housecleaning early on. Before his first summer was out, he'd fired Clare Rhyasen, saying he couldn't work with the chief financial officer. Inconsistent with how we'd traditionally treated our staff, I thought Ron was especially unfair to a guy so loyal and efficient. When I told

The superb Joe Nieuwendyk, whose knee problems prevented him from playing early
in the 1995-96 season, was traded to the Dallas Stars. In return, we got another star,
Jarome Iginla.

Clare how sorry I felt about his abrupt dismissal, he said, "I thought I was
going to be there until they decided to retire me." Fortunately, he wound
up as CFO with a prominent McDonald's franchisee in southern Alberta
and the Seamans and I reconnected with him when he became a leader for
our Project 75 grassroots-hockey movement. Clare was succeeded by his
assistant, Mike Holditch, now a top-notch VP of hockey administration and
CFO. But under Ron's regimen, there wasn't much feeling of management
togetherness.

That was reflected in the lack of progress with the team. In the 1995-96 season, Pierre Pagé came back to us, this time as head coach, a decade and a half after being Al MacNeil's assistant during the debut of our Calgary franchise. Pierre was with the Flames for only the following lacklustre year when a native Albertan replaced him: Brian Sutter. He was one of the astonishing Sutter dynasty of six brothers from a farm in Viking who went on to play for the NHL. They were all cut from the same impressive mould, with a strong family affiliation, hard workers who shared a talent for the game. (By 2008, we would have Darryl Sutter as general manager, Duane as director of player personnel, Ron as the western scout, and Darryl's son Brett as a freshman left-winger.) Brian had a great career with St. Louis and then coached the Blues before going on to coach the Bruins for three seasons. Taking two years off the job, he joined us in 1997. I respected Brian as he slowly tried to build the team despite a shortfall of money and mixed messages from the leadership at the top.

One of the stars Brian lost was the volatile little dynamo, Theo Fleury. I had a lot of time for him despite his cocky stance and all his contretemps on and off the ice. I remember being with Theo at the Nagano Winter Olympics in 1998 when he expressed his disapproval of the NHL's upcoming decision to have two referees officiating together in 1998. "I don't like it Harley. When there's just one referee, and he's got his back turned, that's when I get even."

Given that he stood at the top of our points chart yet again in the 1998-99 season, my partners wanted to hold on to him if we could possibly afford his demands. So for only the second time, at their urging, I talked to a player about his contract. "Look, Theo, you know that we can't match what New York or some others can pay you, and you know why, but you're well liked in this town, you've made a real name for yourself here. You're going to face a long life after hockey and this may be a place best suited for that."

"Well, Harley," he said, "I've always honoured my contracts. But I've got a chance to hit a financial home run for my family. I think I owe it to myself and to them to take it."

"I know and I understand that too, Theo. I'm just trying to say balance that out with what you're going to do with your life. Because maybe we can't give you $10 million, but we can go a long way down the road." At most, we were probably offering him a contract for about half that.

By February 1999, he was just too expensive for us and, rather than let him go out on his own as a free agent, GM Al Coates announced that we were trading him to the Colorado Avalanche. In return, we got the relentless, rugged Robyn Regeher, our most solid defenceman and a strong participant in the community.

Theo was the final remaining Flame from our 1989 Stanley Cup winners. The irony is that after being briefly with Colorado, he did go to the New York Rangers and the Blackhawks and never did play as well as he had done for the Flames. Today, he's back living in Calgary again, running a successful small business and realizing that he's in a true hockey town. We meet occasionally and despite the challenges he has had to overcome, I've always appreciated his big contribution to the Flames and his big heart.

But when we dealt him away, *Sports Illustrated* noted, "And with that, the Flames' all-time leading scorer was off to Denver as a rent-a-player for a Stanley Cup run. No pomp. No circumstance. Just a brief press release that made Fleury seem but a minor part to Calgary's deal for three players and a draft pick." When Theo left, the *Calgary Sun* said, "this was the dawn of the apocalypse" for the franchise.

There was good reason for gloom. As players' salaries soared, we were beggared by a sixty-three-cent Canadian dollar. The Rangers' payroll was $62 million; ours was $25.6 million. Reporters were quoting me as saying, "We're determined to stay in Calgary," but if we didn't escape the fiscal straitjacket, "our only recourse is to leave." I did add, for public consumption, "And that's not on the radar screen—at least not at the moment."

One of my few happy Flames moments at the end of the Nineties was a reunion Becky and I had with some members of the 1989 Stanley Cup team in town for a ten-year celebration. We invited them and their wives or girlfriends to a dinner in our backyard the way we'd done over the years. During all the wonderful reminiscing, the players gave me an actual seat from the old Montreal Forum where we'd won the trophy. They all autographed the back of the seat, which became one of my most treasured mementos.

But behind the scenes then and throughout the next two years, our owners and managers were embroiled in backbiting and buck-passing because of the fear the franchise could fold. Most of those of us with the money reacted predictably. It was a bad night at the Country Club in early April 2000. Led by president Ron Bremner, two newcomers to our partnership fuelled the dissent: Ron Joyce and Grant Bartlett, aided strongly by both Murray Edwards and, surprisingly, B.J. Seaman. They all wanted to wipe the floor clean, from the general manager to the whole coaching roster.

The GM, of course, was the dedicated Al Coates, who'd been with us for our entire two decades. Assistant to the president (1982-89), director of hockey administration (1989-91), and assistant GM (1991-95), now executive vice-president as well as GM and alternate league governor from 1995 to 2000. I had such a strong admiration for his contributions. Yet knowing there had to be a change in our fortunes, I realized from the start of our discussion that he'd be the prime target. What I hadn't realized was how deeply Ron and his supporters were mounting a purge to rid the club's entire core.

Now Brian Sutter was getting the chop too. Shocked by this decision, I rejected the idea that his three years of team-building should be dismissed so cavalierly in what seemed like a desperation move. Doc, Al Libin, and I argued against it—especially when Brian's most vocal detractors were also cutting loose key people who worked with him, including assistant coach Rich Preston, who'd once been the backup to the Chicago Blackhawks' Darryl Sutter and Mike Keenan (two coaches who would later be part of our history). I felt that you just didn't snap your fingers and rebuild a hockey team that was starting to climb out of our deep cellar.

At the time, the knowledgeable veteran Al MacNeil said Brian "knows how to handle a dressing room and how to get things across to his players.... Give him good players, he'll make them great. . . . Anybody who's coached could see what he's done with this team. I defy anybody to go into that dressing room and find one guy who will say Brian Sutter was wrong."

So much of the bad will with the franchise seemed to spring from Ron's office. As Lanny has since described it from within, "Bremner burned so many bridges with both people outside the organization and people inside who were working their ass off to try and make it work. It was like we were being undermined all the time—or our good intentions were going sideways because of some of the things he either did or said." Lanny left the following August after nineteen years with the Flames. I know he'd wanted to have a more important hockey role with the Flames. The consensus was that he needed more experience at a lower level, and I'm saddened because he would have had a great deal to contribute in a closer day-to-day relationship with the team.

We hired the young Craig Button as GM, who'd been with the Dallas Stars as director of player personnel (his father had started the NHL Central Scouting Bureau). His tenure proved disappointing over the next three years as the Flames continued to miss the playoffs every season. We had a revolving door of four head coaches moving in and out. The first was Don Hay, who'd been an assistant coach for us before briefly becoming head coach of the Phoenix Coyotes and then a coach and GM of the Tri-City Americans of the Western Hockey League. Letting him go after his single season, Craig bumped up Don's assistant Greg Gilbert in early '01. Greg was an American Hockey League coach-of-the-year and had played on the Cup-winning New York Islanders. With us, he was suspended for two games during a role in a

Darryl Sutter—the second of his family's hard-working brothers to break into the NHL as a player—became our head coach after stints with Chicago and San Jose and eventually took over as general manager.

brawl with the Anaheim Mighty Ducks. By the depressing end of 2002, we let him go. Among other candidates was the just-retired legend Scotty Bowman of the Red Wings, who at sixty-nine passed on the job. We pulled in Al MacNeil again as interim head coach while we sought a replacement.

And this time we landed Darryl Sutter. Brother to Brian—and Duane, Brent, Ron, and Rich, the band of siblings who've played in more than 5,000 NHL games and won six Cups. On the ice, Darryl had been with the Blackhawks for eight seasons, five of them as team captain, until injuries sidelined him. He later coached Chicago for three seasons before helming the San Jose Sharks over six years. Soon he'd also become our GM, replacing Craig.

BUT BEFORE GETTING THIS LUCKY AGAIN, WE HAD TO suffer those dark years into the new century, my most difficult time with the team I love. There was no fun. This was our worst span of ill fortune on the rink, in the front office, and within the ownership group—all of it reflected in the public perception of the Calgary Flames.

The brutal reality was that our image sagged lower than a dachshund's belly as we lost fans with nothing to cheer about. They told us that as guardians of the team it was our job, not theirs, to solve the money problems. The business of hockey had spun out of financial control and we were failing as leaders. Most of all we lost the sense of importance the Flames held for the community. I felt more and more that we bore such a fundamental obligation to make it work for the city and the game despite the crippling monetary considerations.

The pervasive feeling seemed to be that we just might not be able to compete in a centre the size of Calgary, that we were forever doomed to be second-class. In the end, I became the public spokesman to challenge fans to get behind us again. It was a role I disliked. My friends in other places wondered why I was pursuing the dream when the franchise was falling apart. In Toronto, John Lamacraft, the president of Conwest Exploration, asked me, "Harley, what the hell are you doing this for? You don't need the money." In Texas, Boone Pickens said, "I hate to see you spending your time and energy on this."

In the middle of some restless nights, I was wide awake to hear Becky ask, "What's the matter with you?" and I'd answer, "I'm trying to figure out whether we can get this damned thing solved."

Soon after the purge of our senior management and coaching staff, we owners held an emergency press conference. What I said baldly was if we couldn't boost season's ticket sales to fourteen thousand by June 30, the Flames would be offered for sale. We'd sold fewer than nine thousand this year. I laid out the hard facts: financing salaries in American dollars cost us $12 million in foreign exchange alone. And selling too few seats meant we wouldn't qualify for the $3.4 million currency-equalization share from the NHL kitty. We had the lowest ticket prices in the league. Any long-term answer to capping escalating players' salaries wouldn't be possible until the collective-bargaining negotiations upcoming in 2004. Right now, we needed stronger business sponsorship and lower Saddledome lease terms from the city. As the *Calgary Herald* concluded, "the countdown is on."

By mid-May, I was reporting publicly that a business colleague in Houston—Chuck Watson, owner of the International Hockey League's Houston Aeros—had indicated his interest in buying the Flames. "We're committed to staying in Calgary," I told him. Meanwhile, we announced a new corporate campaign to generate ticket sales through four hundred major local companies and made a renewed plea for the fans to get beyond the ten thousand season's tickets sold to date as the six-week deadline loomed. "We're not threatening anybody. We're facing a situation that wasn't going to work here. I'm cautiously optimistic."

By July 1, our believers purchased fourteen thousand of the tickets in seventy-seven days. The corporate sponsors agreed to pay more for luxury suites. The arena was also renamed the Pengrowth Saddledome, thanks to the generous financial backing of Jim Kinnear, leader of the Calgary-based energy income trust. Meanwhile, we were still after a renegotiated lease and leaning on the provincial government for revenue from sports lotteries and marketing deals. Yet despite the fan support, I couldn't promise there were iron-clad guarantees that the team wouldn't be put up for sale. "No," I confessed to the media, "this isn't much fun."

The ugly truth was, some of my partners were very anxious to sell. In particular, Ron Joyce. In some ways, I couldn't blame him and others like Murray Edwards and Al Markin who wondered what the hell their business deal was all about. Though we'd had our auditors Peat Marwick make as accurate predictions as possible for the future of the team, the new owners came in as the league-wide costs of running a franchise started erupting in salary demands. They didn't have the benefit of those earlier years when we were leaders on the ice and making money.

One of the side effects was a sense of loss between the ownership and the players we once met socially. For the first dozen years of the franchise, Lanny remembers, "There wasn't the hockey players over here and the owners over there. They were friends. And Becky especially was very good. She'd have dinners for the players and looked after our wives, helped them out. And of course it's changed now."

Meanwhile, the new partnership sometimes ruptured with rancour while the Seamans and I felt the old feeling of friendship we'd experienced with fellow owners had deteriorated. Ron and Grant Bartlett bonded with one another as fellow Maritimers and—as more of our funds had to prop up the team—they began to push to sell the franchise. In recalling them, Doc said, "They both thought we were doing things all wrong. I mean, Joyce was cruel. I had to tell him to shut up a few times. It was vicious because he thought the entry fee we charged him and Bartlett was too much—and it wasn't a helluva lot. And with these derogatory remarks, it wasn't a happy time."

In his autobiography, Ron Joyce accused me of being too aggressively hands-on in the management. He'd got several other things wrong in describing my involvement. Mistakenly, he wrote that I was the one who had secured the franchise for Calgary—when of course it was the Seaman brothers who had first engineered that move. He argued that I didn't treat the other partners equally, even to taking the best seats in the owners' box. In fact, I never had such special seats set aside for me. From the beginning, everyone was treated equally, regardless of share ownership, as Doc or Normie would have quickly confirmed. With a workable system, we had an understanding with our partners to allocate seating of our own guests beside us when possible. In the past, there had been no friction.

In December 1997, when the NHL was holding a semi-annual meeting in Florida, Ron went after me publicly during dinner at the Palm Beach home of Jeremy Jacobs, the owner of the Boston Bruins. I was there as the league chairman. Ron came in late and we invited him to join our table with Flames and representatives from other teams. Out of the blue, in the middle of dinner, he exploded, loudly proclaiming that I should get out of the hockey business, that I had made a criminal deal with him and others to invest in the Flames. I was flabbergasted. "Ron, stop it. I don't know what this is about. This is absolutely the wrong time and the wrong place."

But walking outside later, we got into it again. He accused me of misrepresentation.

"What you're saying is just totally false," I said. For a while the tone was so combative that I was imagining we'd might come to blows. I found it hard to forgive his blustering remarks made in a private home in front of my friends and colleagues.

Things became progressively worse between us, especially after he stopped attending many of our ownership meetings. He was not a man who enjoyed being in a minority position. By 2001, it was mutually agreed that the only course we had was to buy him and Grant out of the group. Because my relationship with them was fractured, Murray Edwards capably did most of the negotiation to buy their shares.

In one way, it happened at the best possible time to save the team and the partnership. Yet it came when the business was deeply in trouble and our bank was viewing us with jaundiced eyes. I was absolutely committed to make it survive with concerned yet solid support from Doc, B.J., Al Libin and Bud McCaig. For Murray and Al Markin, there was much more skepticism.

Former local publisher Ken King succeeded Ron Bremner as our president.

Late that year, we asked Ron Bremner to leave as president and CEO. While trying hard, he was handicapped by never being fully accepted in Calgary in these challenging times. I'll quote the statement he made to the media: "At a recent meeting with ownership it was apparent to me that I did not have the full and unqualified support of the group. Without that mandate, it is impossible to provide the kind of leadership necessary in these difficult and challenging times. Therefore, in the long-term best interest of the organization I am tendering my resignation in order to allow someone new a fresh start."

Fortunately, we hired a superb successor, Ken King, to stickhandle the ongoing, ominous challenge. Growing up in small-town Saskatchewan (like the Seamans), he had a thirty-year career in the newspaper business and, unlike Ron, was a strong local presence. Ken had been advertising director and then general manager of the *Edmonton Sun*, publisher of the *Calgary Sun* and a VP with Toronto Sun Publishing, and then president and publisher of the *Calgary Herald* before briefly heading Pacific Press, which publishes the *Vancouver Sun* and the *Vancouver Province*. He's a big guy with a lumberjack's handshake and a big heart that led him over the years to community and philanthropic ventures, such as co-chairing the Reach! medical fundraising initiative (with my daughter, Brenda) and earning an Alberta Centennial Medal for outstanding contributions to the province. As a local publisher, he'd brought his talent for marketing and his sure knowledge of corporate relationships.

We needed all the help. The young, whip-sharp, and tough-minded Murray Edwards and I tangled a few times over his criticism of the operation and his questioning the future of the Flames. Once when we had words, I was angry enough to walk out of our meeting and went to see Jim Palmer to discuss our confrontation. Jim, who'd long ago turned down any idea of investing in our partnership himself, now had his firm acting for the Flames.

As he describes his involvement with the franchise's original founders, "Going to the meetings then, I was generally keeping everybody happy with each other; it wasn't easy. You were all Type-A people." Of the new batch of owners, he understood Murray the best: "He's a smart and volatile person. As he just flat out said, 'This is not a game—we've got to get this thing going properly.'" Ultimately, that insightful reinforcement from a friend sympathetic to both Murray and me helped our relationship. I'm pleased to say that our bond as owners has strengthened in the years since.

It was after that head-butting that the rest of our group wondered if it was time to sell after all. I was still thinking then that there was no enjoyment if we couldn't work effectively together—it was almost distasteful. At one point, despite my despair about selling the club, I stood aside to see if there was any interest out there from a potential buyer. Ken had already talked to some people in Portland, Oregon. They represented Paul Allen, the former partner of Bill Gates in creating Microsoft, who now owned the Portland Trail Blazers of the NBA and the Seattle Seahawks of the NFL. His name had come up in the last couple of years, but as it happened, he didn't bite for a team in such a troubled league. I look back and imagine how heartbroken I would have been then and would be now if he had taken the bait.

LUCKILY, DARRYL SUTTER ARRIVED IN DECEMBER 2002. It was little more than a month after he'd been let go by the Sharks after an 8-12-2 start to their 2002-03 season. Yet Ken said from the first meeting, "Every ounce of intuition told me that this guy was the kind of person we needed." And in Darryl's first year as our coach, the media were calling him the master of the Flames ship who was doing the best coaching job in the NHL. The day he arrived, surrounded by management and coaching personnel, he walked into the dressing room in his trademark cowboy boots. After being introduced to his young team, he announced curtly in his bass voice that everyone but his players should leave.

From the first, blunt and tough, he took command. By also becoming general manager the next April, he was drafting good prospects to back up a small core of dependables, including the valuable Jarome Iginla— earning the top salary of $7.5 million. Among the newcomers were rightwinger Shean Donovan, experienced on four teams, from San Jose to Pittsburgh; centre Steve Reinprecht, via Los Angeles and Colorado; veteran left-winger Chris Simon, who'd played for the Cup with Colorado and the Washington Capitals; and a perhaps-unpromising goalie stuck on the third string for the Sharks, Finland's Miikka Kiprusoff. But Darryl had to replace our ailing netminder Roman Turek and knew the promise of the cool, acrobatic Miikka. Grabbing his chance in the first season, Kipper set a modern record (since the mid-1940s) with only a 1.69 goals-against average in the regular schedule.

Finally, all things were falling into place for the Flames. Backstage in 2003, Clay Riddell had joined us as a partner. A native Winnipegger, a geolo-

Finland's Miikka Kiprusoff came to us in the 2003-04 season and promptly registered a modern NHL record with his goals-against average, and within a couple of years won the Vezina Trophy as the league's best goaltender.

gist like me but younger, Clay is the down-to-earth founder of Paramount Energy a massively successful natural-gas-focused trust with assets in western Canada. I identified with his decision to involve family in the business as the patriarch partner in petroleum ventures with his son, daughter, and son-in-law. In philosophy, he has the same view that we share of the community and the symbolic value of the game. We'll be forever grateful to Clay because he took a big risk in putting up his cash along with his faith in the Flames, who'd lost $50 million over seven years.

A risk that was about to pay off, for all of us.

THE 2003-'04 SEASON WAS THE FIRST TIME WE'D MADE the playoffs since 1996. With Kipper defending the net, the team had exploded with a collective vigour led by Darryl's obsessive attention to detail. The players had melded as a unit: since October, Craig Conroy had introduced the plastic green hard hat given to the overlooked hero of each game and this working man's symbol came to honour these hard-scrabble winners. As *Sports Illustrated* remarked of their passionate play, "their grinding style won't win any beauty contests." Our first quarter-final series, the square-off with the top-of-the division Vancouver, set our compass.

We lost the first in Vancouver 5-3, squeaked by with a 2-1 win there, then lost by the same margin in Calgary. (Their third-period game winner came from Matt Cooke, who had been in the forward spot that until recently had been held by Todd Bertuzzi, suspended in March for the rest of the season after he jumped on the back of the Avalanche's Steve Moore, who was driven into the ice and has never played since.) We took the next two at home and away 4-0 and 2-1. The sixth was a strange, long game that went into a triple overtime to 12:29 a.m. Our guys looked overwhelmed in the first half as the Canucks scored four times in the first two periods until we rallied with the stickwork of two left-wingers. Oleg Saprykin (a Russian import returned to us after a couple of years on our AHL farm team in Saint John) and Ville Nieminen (the Finn who'd recently arrived from Chicago and Pittsburgh) connected in the second. Then Marty Gélinas and Chris Clark tied it in the third to move us into the improbable overtime. The first two sessions went scoreless before Vancouver won early in the third for a 5-4 win.

The final, away game went into a brief, wonderful overtime when the Canucks tied at 5.7 seconds left in regulation. Jarome had opened scoring in the second period with a breakaway and, after the Canucks responded in the third, got his second goal.

With little less than a minute to go, Doc Seaman told Becky, "We've got this one."

"Never, never say that," I said.

A Canuck knocked Jarome's stick out of his hand and Markus Naslund went scooting up the boards, squeezed his way through our defence, and scored.

We were into overtime. There was a carryover Vancouver penalty. On the power play at only 1:25, rookie goalie Alex Auld had made two saves when Marty followed up and just seemed to throw the puck in, as he said later.

As Al Libin still says, "The whole turnaround with our franchise came on that overtime goal in game seven." Playing above their heads, our Flames had just survived the series by the raw skin of their teeth. For the first time in fifteen years, our underdog, blue-collar club had moved into the second round of the playoffs.

Before reaching the Stanley Cup, Vancouver was the first of the teams leading three divisions that we had to dare beat. We had to go six games against both the Detroit Red Wings—who had the best record in the league—and then the San Jose Sharks to sizzle through to the final with the Tampa Bay Lightning. The San Jose mayor—who had a personal bet with our mayor, Dave Bronconnier—declared his city hall the world headquarters of Flames fans.

By now, our Cowtown was Flamesville—and so was Canada. As we were in the last minutes of overpowering the Sharks 3-1 in that final, Ken King got a call on his cellphone to say the prime minister's office was calling. Ken said, "Yeah, I'm Daffy Duck and I've got to watch a hockey game to watch here"—and hung up. The PM's people phoned back and Paul Martin sent his warm wishes to the team, Jarome, and Darryl as the first Canadian club to reach the Cup final in a decade.

The fiery C was blazing all over our town, from thousands of Flames flags waving on cars and folks painting the logo on their vehicles, houses, and front lawns. The new red home sweater was unveiled to became one of the hottest ever to launch in league history. The jersey was being worn as everyday dress in upscale offices—even some priests were spotted wearing it in church. One judge briefly interrupted a robbery trial to let the jury watch the first game in the series. The Calgary Zoo named a bighorn lamb Kipper. A couple named their brand-new son Miikka. A rap song commemorating the team was unavoidable on radio ("You can find me in the Dome/Chilling with Jarome/Got my eye on the Cup baby we gonna bring it home"). The local papers simply shouted: "YES." And of course that famous five-block stretch of 17th Avenue was again "a C of Red" in what became a massive block party along the Red Mile of pubs. There were thirty-five thousand snuggling together on that post-game night after the San Jose series, chanting "Go Flames Go!" in their ocean of crimson jerseys (with some women lifting them up briefly to flash their breasts).

That late May, Becky and I were brimming with the Calgary-brand excitement in Tampa, about one hundred and seventy miles north of Naples, our vacation home on the Florida coast. The glittery downtown arena, the St. Pete Times Forum, was controlled by the Lightning's owner, Bill Davidson, the glass-manufacturing magnate who also had the NBA's Detroit Pistons (they were about to win that league's championship the next month). The nicknamed Bolts had first taken the ice a dozen years before when our Terry Crisp became head coach for the first five seasons. Now it was John Tortorella, a graduate assistant coach with the Buffalo Sabres, Phoenix Coyotes, and New York Rangers.

Our series looked as if it would be a lopsided contest between the sixth-seed Canadians and the first-seed Americans. They had stalwarts such as centre Vincent Lecavalier (who'd go on to be Most Valuable Player of the winning Canadian National Team in the 2004 World Cup of Hockey); centre Brad Richards (winning the Conn Smythe and Lord Byng trophies); right-winger Martin St. Louis (the compact Quebecker who took the Lester B. Pearson Award as the league's most outstanding player); and left-winger Ruslan Fedotenko (the import from Ukraine who would star in the final game).

In fact, we went all seven games, with us taking the first on foreign territory with a resounding 4-1. The clubs alternated win-loss in each of the first four games. In the second, the Lightning reversed the score there, then at home we blanked them 3-0 before they did the same in the next one, 1-0. We were back in Tampa for an end-to-end, up-and-down match when, deep into overtime, Oleg slipped by them 3-2. In the sixth encounter, they came back with that very score during a second overtime to even the series. But there was justifiable controversy when the game was tied 2-2 and Marty drove the net as the puck hit his skate and appeared to cross the line before goalie Nikolai Khabibulin kicked it out with a pad save. We were rapturous—for seconds, until the refs discounted it. Even video replays seemed to show the goal. But NHL director of hockey operations Colin Campbell said replays were inconclusive from various camera angles. (Well after the series, I went to see Gary Bettman at the league office in New York to look at the replays again, for my peace of mind. After the technical guys had recreated the supposed goal, the puck looked as if it was only half-way across the line.) We felt robbed, but after a second overtime, Tampa evened the series.

Throughout, we were playing the chippy approach that sometimes got penalized, sometimes not. Robyn Regehr managed to get away scot-free after slamming Fedotenko into the boards to open a gash in his face in game three. But in game four, Ville was suspended one game for bashing Vincent Lecavalier's head into the boards and Marty Gélinas got two minutes for an elbow to the head that kept Pavel Kubina out of the match.

In the final, on Lightning ice, we got our lumps back when two of those victims retaliated. Fedotenko scored on a power play at 13:31 of the first period on a rebound. His next at 14:38 of the second was another wrist shot as Lecavalier worked the puck with determination in the left corner and drew three Flames towards him. Midway through the third, Craig Conroy got one for us on a power-play slap shot. With about five minutes left, the Lightning's beleaguered Khabibulin made his best save against Jordan Leopold. But our comeback crumbled when, with 1:01 remaining, our defenceman Andrew Ference took a charging penalty for battering St. Louis into the boards, leaving his face bloody. We wound up at the sorry end, 2-1. As Darryl said later, "We just ran out of gas." Jarome said, "Every guy in this room wanted to win that Stanley Cup. It's very, very, very hard to take."

Yet back home in Calgary, we were winners—as the Flames had been through our whole astonishing run of playoffs. Despite the loss, thirty thousand fans packed into Olympic Plaza to celebrate the players. At year's end, the national annual poll of sportswriters and broadcasters named us the Team of the Year, beating handily Wayne Gretzky's victorious Team Canada at the World Cup.

In 2004, the Flames had fought their way to the very top and, instead of just being a bunch of players, become a team again. And they'd done it with "guts to burn," to borrow the words used by Conn Smythe to describe his players of the Forties and Fifties on the team that I grew up with, the Maple Leafs.

We owners had won too. Our partnership group had, with late-season acquisitions, boosted our payroll to just below $38 million for the season. Yet by the Cup finale, the fans had come back and our bottom line was significantly fattened after being so thin so long. Finally, we might start recouping some of our losses over the past decade. It was vindication, redemption, showing our newest partners that even if we hadn't netted a hat trick yet, the franchise could make some real economic sense. And it was fun again. Look what can happen, I thought, if we all work together with such harmony.

There was only one big problem, I knew so well as the current NHL chairman: the league's next season could soon be a black mark indelibly staining the history of professional hockey.

PROJECT 75

In 1980, Doc, I, and B.J. launch Project 75 for grassroots development of players and coaches and training for officials.

In the late 1960s, Doc Seaman became more and more concerned that Canada was lagging so embarrassingly behind the Soviet Union in world hockey competition. Then came the famous Summit Series in 1972 between the two rivals when Paul Henderson—with only thirty-four seconds left in the final game—scored the winning goal that elated Canadians.

But our slim victory had never been a sure thing and (as *The Canadian Encyclopedia* says) the decline of our game "was tantamount to a national identity crisis." Doc still liked to quote the farsighted words of Charlie Hay, then the founding president of Hockey Canada, the governing body of the non-professional game: "We have to put something back into hockey at the grassroots level."

Doc had taken Charlie's warning seriously. After the Flames came to town, we acquired some producing oil and gas properties specifically to fund a foundation that would help foster the skills of young hockey players across the country. Because 1980 was the year Alberta celebrated its seventy-fifth anniversary as a province, we called our creation Project 75.

More recently, it's known as the Seaman Hotchkiss Hockey Foundation. In the nearly three decades since, it has donated $4.42 million to support new research and development, and the current value of its investments is $9.55 million. Helping to keep the Canadian game a dominant force internationally starts by teaching youngsters the skill and fun of hockey in communities across the country.

I was among the core of the original Flames partners who bought into Project 75 financially, and since 1994, Doc, brother B.J., and I were its sole backers. At the start, the properties weren't yielding much revenue. "We went through some tough times when there were high tax rates and gas prices fluctuated a lot," Doc recalled, "so we didn't have a lot of cash flow in those early years. But we certainly did into the Nineties."

Heading the not-for-profit foundation was Doc's executive assistant, the dedicated Ken Stiles, working with lawyer John Poetker of Borden Ladner Gervais and Clare Rhyasen, then our Flames CFO. All three volunteered their time as the only members of the board (none of us financial partners in the project have been directors). Rob Moffat, president and CEO of Bow Valley Energy, has since joined them and when Ken died of leukemia in 2006, Clare became president.

Consulting with us, the directors sold the petroleum properties in 2001 and, with some wise counsel from the owners, put the proceeds into the market early the next year. "And what a fortuitous time to do that," Clare says. "Our market value is since almost triple what we invested, while giving away $1.46 million in that period."

Almost all of the funding has gone to programs delivered by Hockey Canada. In 1985, Bill Hay—Charlie's son—led a group of Calgary businessmen with Ken, the Canadian Hockey League's Ed Chynoweth, and Hockey Canada director Norm Robertson to launch the first Centre of Excellence.

Bill describes its modest beginnings at the Saddledome: "Dave King, our Flames coach, would bring in coaches and make videos that we would circulate. We had groups of parents, some of them single parents, to bring their young teenagers and we'd talk to them about playing the game, staying in school, moving beyond—but you don't have to go to the NHL. More parents came up and thanked us for helping them out."

Over the next ten years, as our Centre developed in sophistication, others opened in Toronto, Montreal, Vancouver, and Saint John, where we had our farm team. They were supported by NHL and local teams to help transfer technical knowledge to the grassroots level. In 1995, the foundation also gave $400,000 to move the national headquarters of Hockey Canada from Toronto to the Father David Bauer Arena in Calgary, with the able Bob Nicholson as president and CEO.

The range of R&D that our investment has helped seed has been boggling in its breadth. An annual Program of Excellence Coaches Seminar instructs national and regional team coaching staffs and a bi-annual International Coaches Conference ranks among the world's biggest, with more than four hundred delegates from ten countries. A national computer-based system tracks injuries among junior players in the Canadian Hockey League; the data helps leagues at all levels respond in their policies and playing rules. A Trainers and Safety program aimed at teams' qualified safety people teaches them risk management and appropriate tools and information to prevent injuries. Officiating seminars help recruit referees and linesmen and sharpen the skills of the thirty thousand registered officials in the minor leagues. And Ken Stiles Officiating Scholarship Awards—the first of their kind in Canadian amateur sport—are given annually to young women and men who participate in these seminars.

A handbook to educate parents about their kids playing the game is distributed through the minor hockey system. Hockey Canada's website lets coaches connect on-line and reap the latest information. And instructional DVDs created in high-quality production facilities for players, coaches, and officials are part of the Charles Hay Memorial Library, the largest such hockey educational resource centre in the world.

Beyond the support through Hockey Canada, the foundation has donated $100,000 to Project Motion with Foothills Hospital and the University of Calgary for research into joint injuries suffered by athletes, established athletic scholarships to the U of C and the University of Lethbridge (matched by the Alberta government), and provided funding for the Jim Kyte Hockey School for the Hearing Impaired.

We'd given $1 million towards construction of the Lakeshore Lions Arena, a community facility for youth hockey in Toronto, the first to be built in the city in a quarter-century. By the fall of 2009, it will be the future practice rink for the Toronto Maple Leafs and its AHL affiliate, the Toronto Marlies. Other partners in this project are the Hockey Hall of Fame, to house its Hockey Resource Centre and Archives in the arena, and Hockey Canada, to run their Ontario regional offices there and use the Olympic-sized pad for training and development of Canada's national teams.

There's another, much smaller arena that delighted Doc, B.J., and me. Doc had long wanted to create a model of the kind of rink that would be reasonably priced for communities lacking enough ice time for young people. The Calgary area alone could use as many as ten more rinks. As a first step in developing such a project, Doc chose Black Diamond, a town in the foothills southwest of the city. Built in six months, it operates now as an outdoor artificial-ice surface with a service building next to an existing facility; the staff and a Zamboni serve both rinks. "This is a fantastic opportunity for young Canadian players to get more time on the ice to develop and improve their skills," says Bob Nicholson. "There's the strong possibility of a number of rinks such as this one being constructed across Canada."

Doc donated $500,000 for the prototype and our Seaman Hotchkiss Foundation matched it. The new facility is called the Scott Seaman Sports Rink, named in memory of his grandson, an enthusiastic athlete who died tragically at age eighteen.

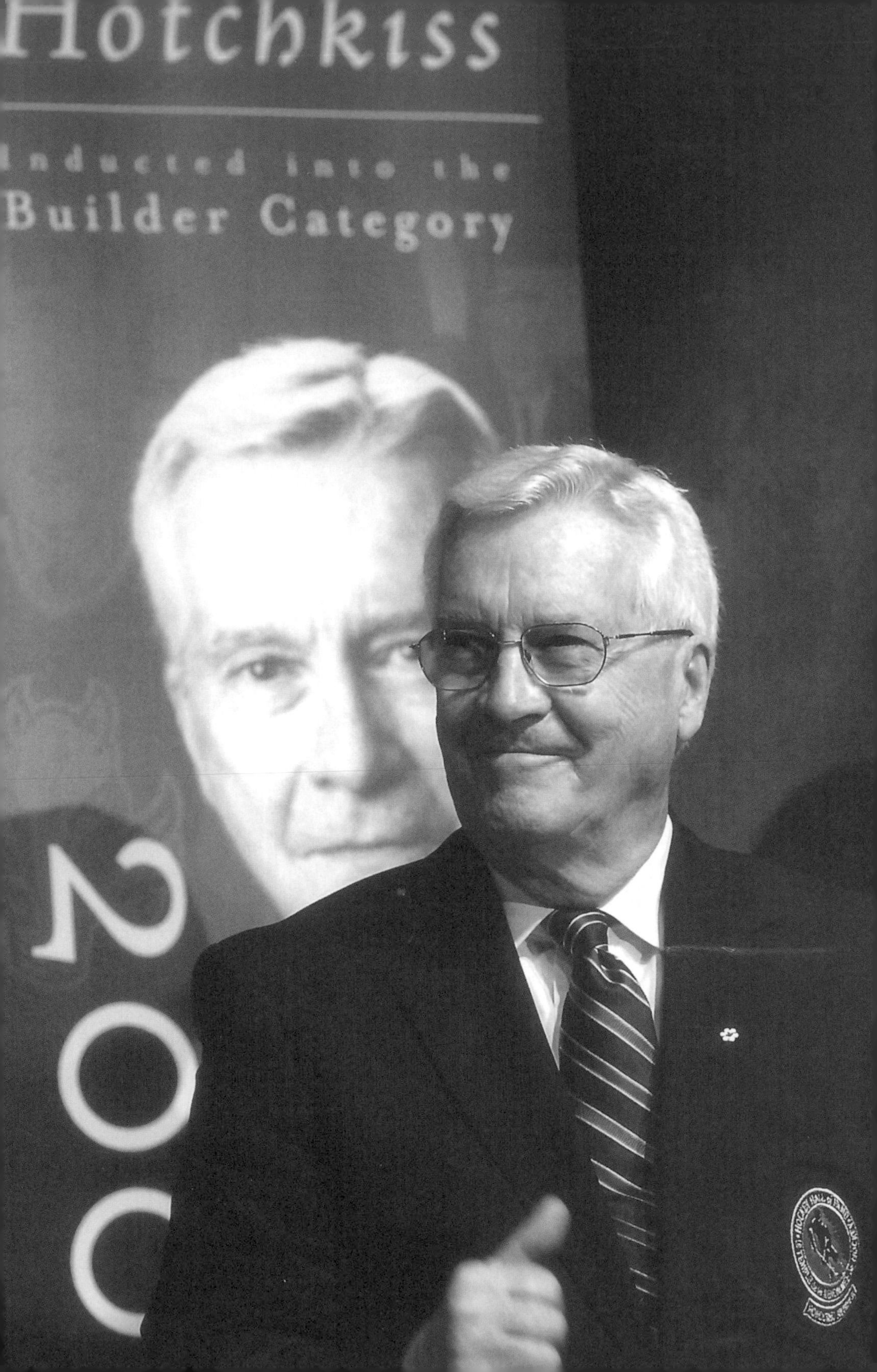
Hotchkiss
nducted into the
Builder Category
200

CHAPTER 9

THE PUCK STOPPED HERE

Chairing the National Hockey League

ORLEY CALLAGHAN, THE CANADIAN novelist, once wrote, "Hockey is our winter ballet and in many ways our national drama." When I became the chairman of the NHL in 1995, the league had endured a dramatic existence for nearly eight decades, slowly evolving into what I believe—presented through its players—is the best product in professional sport, in Canada and the United States.

It grew out of troubled beginnings, an offspring of the National Hockey Association of six teams in Ontario and Quebec that competed for the Stanley Cup. While potential players were fighting overseas in the First World War, the NHA dissolved in 1917 when a Toronto team owner had angered his rivals with shady shenanigans. Meeting in Montreal to freeze out their antagonist, they formed the National Hockey *League*, with the Montreal Canadiens, Montreal Wanderers, and Ottawa Senators as founding members. They recruited the existing Toronto players to form a new, nameless club that in its first year would win the Cup. After the team was later threatened by the ex-owner's lawsuits and briefly went into bankruptcy, it emerged as the St. Patricks and over the next few years—despite the threat of moving them to Philadelphia—attracted local investors. One was the legend-to-be Conn Smythe, who became coach and general manager and in 1927 the sole owner of what he named the Maple Leafs.

One of the highlights of my life happened in 2006: being inducted as a Builder, along with legendary players Dick Duff and Patrick Roy, into the Hockey Hall of Fame. During the ceremony in Toronto, I was rubbing shoulders with Ted Lindsay, Yvon Cournoyer, and Jean Beliveau, one of my favourites.

Smythe reigned over the Leafs for five fascinating decades as the NHL matured. In 1924, the Boston Bruins was the first team from the U.S. and within a couple of years six of the ten teams were American. The Depression era of my boyhood wracked the league as franchises folded in Montreal (the Maroons), Pittsburgh, Philadelphia, and Detroit, which was revived from bankruptcy as the Red Wings by James Norris (whose name resonates today on major players' trophies). In the early wartime Forties, when I was serving on a Norwegian merchant ship hungry for news about the Leafs, only six clubs survived: Toronto, Montreal, Boston, Detroit, the Chicago Black Hawks (as spelled then), and the New York Rangers.

They would be the the the NHL until 1967, just as I was going into business with Carlo von Maffei in Sabre Petroleums. That year, the league admitted six American clubs: the Minnesota North Stars (later owned by Norm Green), Philadelphia Flyers, Pittsburgh Penguins, St. Louis Blues, Los Angeles Kings, and what became the Oakland Seals. By 1974, the number had exploded to eighteen, but only a trio of them were Canadian, including Vancouver. Four years later, when the World Hockey Association imploded, the league absorbed three more from Canada: the Quebec Nordiques, Winnipeg Jets, and Edmonton Oilers. And in 1980, our Flames arrived from Atlanta to launch the perennial rivalry with our pesky northern neighbour. In the decade and a half that followed, there were twenty-six franchises, with one Canadian newcomer, the Ottawa Senators, and the loss of the small-market Nordiques to Denver, with the Jets soon to move to Phoenix.

IT WAS IN LATE 1991 WHEN I SUCCEEDED CLIFF FLETCHER as the Flames representative on the NHL's board of governors. As a governor among the owners and senior executives, I was eyeballing up close the inner workings and outside influences remoulding the league so drastically through this decade. Our chairman then was William Wirtz, the powerful, cantankerous owner of the Chicago Blackhawks, whom the fans gave the nasty nickname of Dollar Bill for his tight-fisted approach to player negotiation. He wanted to hold an equally firm hand on running the board— as he did for eighteen years until stepping down from its helm in '92. Although Darryl Sutter, in his time with the Hawks, would say Bill was kind and considerate, Wirtz and I would later have differences on several major issues.

The NHL's president was John Ziegler, a Detroit lawyer who acted as counsel to the Red Wings before becoming president of a league bleeding cash badly in 1977. Along the way, he'd negotiated the amalgamating of teams from the collapsed WHA and had a reasonably smooth tenure until he ran smack into a flinty new object: the president of the National Hockey League Players' Association, Bob Goodenow.

In '91, Bob had just replaced the executive director, Alan Eagleson, the NHLPA's autocratic union boss who later pleaded guilty to stealing hundreds of thousands of dollars from international hockey originally destined for the players' pension fund. The Eagle's successor was the motivated, competitive Detroit native who'd played on the U.S. national hockey team in the 1970s and, after studying labour law, became a players' agent. As I've mentioned, this formidable guy as their leader touched off the fireworks to send salaries soaring and in '92 organized the league's first players' strike, the ten-day walkout in April during the race for the Cup. In the negotiations that led up to the action, Goodenow was clearly looking for a fight and Wirtz became a hard-nosed chair refusing any concessions to the players—even threatening that during a strike he'd fill his own team with replacements from the minor leagues and Europe.

Of course, with Bob Goodenow firming the players' resolve against this kind of attitude, the strike happened. Outside observers have weighed its effects, as authors Richard Gruneau and David Whitson wrote in *Hockey Night in Canada* a year later:

> In one reading the players made important gains in the areas of pensions, playoff money, insurance, and arbitration; they also held on to the status quo with respect to [collectible] playing card revenues, which the owners wanted to share, and salary caps, which the owners wanted to introduce. Conversely, on the most important financial issue of all—the rules regarding compensation for free-agent signings—the changes did not open the doors to free agency very wide, and many players were reportedly unhappy that their "final" offer had already conceded too much.

A new governor still trying to get up to speed, I was simply relieved that the labour dispute was over. Whoever supposedly won, all this unprecedented turmoil caught the attention of a hardball bloc of embittered owners: they made sure John Ziegler was gone by the end of the resumed playoff season. In came an interim president, Gil Stein, a Philadelphia lawyer who'd been the CEO of the Flyers and since 1978 a vice-president and general counsel for the league. On the plus side, he was the first in the job to visit every NHL city and made some fan-friendly changes, such as encouraging players to warm up without helmets. But as a finalist for the presidency during his first year as acting leader, he failed to win the support of most team owners and bowed out to his successor. Gil's own reputation would be later sullied during a controversy about his jockeying for a spot in the Hockey Hall of Fame.

Gary Bettman became commissioner after a sterling career in pro basketball.

The man who followed him was a surprise to the league at large. In February 1993, Gary Bettman was named the first commissioner in NHL history. He wanted the broader title instead of merely president to conform with other major sports leagues. A select search committee of owners given the responsibility of finding a new leader had recommended him to the board. It approved him as an outsider from the hockey world—even though that was one of the raps against him in the beginning.

Who was this compact lawyer who really didn't know the game from the inside? True, he wasn't an experienced student of the sport. But growing up in a single-parent family living in Queen's, New York, he watched the Rangers in Madison Square Garden, loved the Islanders, and went to Cornell where he'd sleep outdoors in the ticket lines over four years just to get a season's seat for the university team (on which Ken Dryden would later play goalie). More important, with his degree from New York University School of Law, he was a senior VP and general counsel with the National Basketball Association under David Stern, its longest-running commissioner who built it into a market-wise colossus.

He'd started with the NBA in 1981 when the office had a staff of twenty-five. A dozen years later, there were as many as nine hundred overseeing a sport that had become a major marketing vehicle and media property. "I also learned the complexities of the business and the politics of running a professional sports league," Gary says now. "It ultimately led to what I consider the fundamental truth in my role as commissioner: you must always do what you think is right because every decision you make can and will be second-guessed."

As Gary announced on his first day at the NHL, "Basically, everything is under review." I came to learn that he had a tremendous mind and a high energy to handle unbelievable pressures while developing a real understanding of the Canadian-bred game. And he's become a friend.

"I welcomed the challenge and the opportunity to do something I believed in, to make the league grow and be bigger and stronger—and to be, in effect, the CEO." His executive team included chief operating officer Steve Solomon, legal advisor Jeff Pash, and Brian Burke, whom he'd hired as the VP in charge of hockey discipline.

After Gary arrived, a later independent investigation showed that Gil Stein had been placing his own employees as directors on the Hockey Hall of Fame to engineer his election as an honoree. *Sports Illustrated* would call Gil "a Hall of Shame candidate." A raw newcomer to the board, I'd really had no idea of what he was doing.

Meanwhile, Gary was dealing with the equally larger-than-life board chair who'd followed Wirtz: the short, chubby, always-smiling Bruce Mc-Nall. The owner of the Los Angeles Kings, Bruce had snatched Wayne Gretzky from the Oilers in 1988 and helped open up the American west to hockey. Like Nelson Skalbania, he lived a flamboyant life, owning homes in six centres, several luxury cars, two planes and a helicopter, hundreds of race horses, two film companies, and was a partner in the Canadian Football League's Toronto Argonauts with Wayne and actor John Candy. All of this was based on being a broker of expensive antique coins, artifacts, and sports memorabilia.

Arriving at the NHL meetings in a stretch limousine, Bruce was pushing expansion with more wealthy owners than those who had recently brought Ottawa and Tampa Bay into the league. He convinced Michael Eisner, who was running the Disney Corporation, to launch a team where Disneyland was based in Anaheim (the Mighty Ducks, named for a Disney film). Meanwhile, he did a similar sales job on Wayne Huizenga, the chairman of Blockbuster Entertainment and the owner of the NFL's Miami Dolphins and baseball's National League Florida Marlins, to create the NHL's Florida Panthers. Wayne paid the league $50 million as an entrance fee, but while Eisner gave only half that amount to the league, the rest was an indemnity fee to Bruce for the Ducks' sharing of the Kings' territory. Recognizing the name value of Disney and Blockbuster as NHL owners, the board approved the deals in his first meeting as chairman.

As Gary says, "It was clear that there were a lot of things going on in Bruce's world, which was making his life increasingly complicated." In the end, what none of us governors had known before about Bruce was that his so-called fortune was based on a crumbling house of misdealt cards. In late 1993, he defaulted on a $90-million loan and, half a year later, the bank forced him to sell control of the Kings to two buyers, who soon understood how badly managed its finances were and, as part of the transaction, the team was taken into bankruptcy. Denver oil billionaire Phillip Anschutz and Los Angeles real-estate billionaire Edward Roski then bought the team but, in its rebuilding, traded Wayne Gretzky. As Bruce's fate unrolled over the next three years, he was sentenced to nearly six years in prison because of a scheme to defraud banks, a securities firm, and the Kings for more than $236 million US.

When Bruce resigned in disgrace from our board in 1994, we'd been taken in by a scandal that reflected badly on the NHL. The governors decided not to replace him immediately, letting Gary manage the operations without a chairman. And at this pivotal point as commissioner, he now had to carry the ball for the owners who were intent on ensuring cost certainty for their teams—even if the league had to force a lockout of the players.

Gary came to know Bob Goodenow as "very focussed, determined, and somewhat ideological in his beliefs. One on one, we always got along well; there was never anything personal. But Bob had a view that the weaker the league, the stronger the players."

The labour action began in the fall of 1994. Its essence was dig-in-your-heels disagreement over such issues as the NHL's salary cap, a heavy tax that would penalize teams exceeding a set ceiling on its total players' payroll; at least a salary cap for rookies; the league's wish to end arbitration to solve salary disputes; a Players' Association proposal that its members become unrestricted free agents at age thirty-one, not thirty-two; and the owners' demand for a limit to a player's movement during the peak of his career. Hovering over everything was the plight of small-market franchises, with the league wanting salaries linked with revenue to subsidize the weaker teams while the players wanted the owners to carry the revenue-sharing load themselves. The owners debated this as some more prosperous teams didn't necessarily want to share gate receipts and local TV, sponsorship and advertising revenues.

There was no rush of public support for the players—perhaps because, three decades in the past, a typical player making $19,000 was earning about three and a half times the average American salary and now a player taking home $800,000 was getting more than forty times that average. But the owners were facing their own pressures: a dozen of them had new arenas opening and the Fox network was planning to start televising games in the coming January.

The lockout lasted 103 days and 468 games, until January 11, 1995. In the end, there was no overall salary cap and salary arbitration had survived, but there was a partial cap on rookie salaries and unrestricted free agency was set at age thirty-two until 1999 and only then at thirty-one. Bob Goodenow was pleased with the collective bargaining agreement that emerged, one that would be extended for almost a decade. As Eric Duhatschek argued in the *Herald*, "By getting a deal without a salary cap/luxury tax, the players effectively put the onus on owners to run their businesses efficiently." (A luxury tax is another way of saying that if the average team payroll exceeds a cap by a certain amount, this tax is paid to the league to redistribute to teams with lower payrolls.)

Gary recalls, "There were people who were writing that we had gotten a great deal and accomplished everything we needed to—ultimately, though, that turned out not to be the case." At the time, I was quoted as saying, "We should have been tougher. We needed to get a solution for everyone, a system that works if you run the thing well."

AT THE BOARD LEVEL, WE STILL HAD NO OWNER IN PLACE as chairman. More than a year after Bruce McNall resigned, I took on the job. It was John McMullen, the crusty, straightforward owner of the New Jersey Devils, who had called me on my cell phone one day when I was in Edmonton.

"Harley," he said, "an executive committee has put your name forward as chairman of the board of governors."

I was totally flabbergasted. Though we weren't close at all, and didn't always agree on things, John was usually commonsensical and down to earth. "Oh, John, this was not on my horizon at all. Quite frankly, I've got a lot on my plate. I'm on a number of corporate boards."

After we talked for a while, he said, "I'd like you to think about it. Canada's important and you guys have developed a franchise there with a good reputation." After three Americans in the chair, I'd be the first Canadian.

"Well, I need some time to think." I called Gary, whom I didn't know that well. I hadn't been dealing with him on any committee—he'd eliminated all the many committees under his purview except for Executive and Audit and Finance. Yet he too encouraged me to run for the position. "One of the great things about having a chairman," he's said, "is having somebody you can have very candid and private conversations with to discuss and think about things, to get feedback in a straightforward, unpolitical, unvarnished way."

At the next board meeting, there was some discussion during which Bill Wirtz, not unexpectedly I thought, offered an alternative candidate, Dick Patrick, a fine guy and a part-owner of the Washington Capitals. But Dick didn't want the job and in June 1995, I became what some folks described as the sacrificial lamb.

Fortunately, there was some public support for my decision, especially from locals who knew me from my association with the Flames. In an editorial, the *Calgary Herald* wrote in part:

> *The NHL did itself a huge public relations favor by naming Flames' part-owner Harley Hotchkiss chairman of the league's board of governors—at least among hockey fans across Canada.*
>
> *And while it would be overly optimistic to expect that Hotchkiss will be able to wield his new-found powers to insure the future of NHL franchises in so-called small market cities, the appointment does confirm that the issue is of some concern to league owners.*
>
> *And it should be. . . . it is a reasonably safe bet that Hotchkiss' appointment also reflects the NHL's need to heal the deep internal wounds created by last season's lockout. . . .*
>
> *Choosing a moderate, intelligent individual like Hotchkiss to help them get their ducks in a row may have been the smartest thing NHL owners have done in recent memory.*

It was far over the top in its praise, but I was heartened by the confidence in me.

The ill will of the lockout the previous year had troubled the atmosphere among the owners, players, and fans. We'd had the Quebec club fold and debt-ridden Winnipeg on life support, with financial concerns about Ottawa, Edmonton (Peter Pocklington thinking of moving the Oilers to Minneapolis)—and certainly Calgary. Facing us was the threat that the bigger franchises might use their higher revenues to create what would become a two-tier league with haves and have-nots. With the loonie plummeting against the greenback, the weaker Canadian teams had been hemorrhaging. More might not survive. I believed there should be a broader, while still limited, revenue-sharing scheme among the teams. Done well to contain inflationary trends, we'd have a stronger NHL with more competitive teams and a more exciting product. And then there'd be more expansion opportunities.

Based on research by Murray Edwards and our Flames finance committee, we were suggesting the league should adopt adjustments to Canadian-currency shortfalls. The idea was to have all the franchises contribute to a pool of forty per cent of both their gate receipts and local broadcasting revenues to generate transfers to us have-nots. As I put it as a Calgary owner in an August 15, 1995, memo to Jeff Pash, the NHL's senior legal and policy adviser:

Calgary continues to believe that the growing discrepancy between franchise revenues must be addressed. Every franchise, *assuming it is in a market that has demonstrated its ability to support a National Hockey League franchise and runs its business well, should have an opportunity to have a competitive team on an economically viable basis.* As revenue disparities increase, there will be a growing temptation to use higher revenues in an undisciplined way. We believe there is a real danger of a "two tier" League developing and the League's ability to present a competitive and entertaining product for fans in all our NHL cities will be impaired. Ultimately historically strong franchises in smaller market areas will not survive. It is this concern that prompted Calgary to suggest we consider a broader but limited revenue sharing. Benefits would include a stronger League with more competitive teams presenting a more exciting product, restraint on inflationary trends, a positive message to our fans and players, increased expansion opportunities and franchise values, and encouragement to work together on League growth.

But when I did recommend such sharing to the governors in one of my first meetings as chair, my proposition was not exactly welcomed. (Gary remembers it as a contentious executive-committee meeting at the Admiral's Club conference room at Chicago's O'Hare Airport.) To put it mildly. Bill Wirtz looked as if he would leap across the table at me. That may have been where he began nursing his personal grudge with this upstart Hotchkiss. And strangely enough, even Rod Bryden, the major owner of the Ottawa Senators, pooh-poohed my concept, essentially saying "We're big boys, we can handle things." Yet financially, he was on the most fragile ground himself. I can recall only Dick Patrick speaking up for the idea. But it got nowhere then. As I mentioned in the previous chapter, it wasn't until 1996 that the currency equalization plan finally happened, with Gary's leadership, helping save the Flames and other Canadian teams.

In mid-'96, there was another disagreement between Wirtz and me. Late the previous year, the board had unanimously decided to extend Gary's term beyond his January 31, 1998 contract. But when the audit and finance committee proposed retirement plans for him and senior executives—including his executive VP and COO Steve Solomon and Jeff Pash—Wirtz wrote me to say he couldn't vote for the terms because they hadn't yet been approved by the board. He said our committee had accused him of being an obstructionist in "the worst tirade I have witnessed since being a member of the NHL." In fact, he had been a member of the executive committee that was fully aware of the retirement plan and was free to raise the issue at the board meeting.

Our differences, as he developed them, would deepen—even five years later when most of us governors wanted to again extend Gary's term. We followed the same process we did in 1996. Wirtz objected that it was Gary's appointed executive committee that would decide the fate of his contract, and the other board members hadn't been notified of the revisions. In fact, I'd contacted all of them and had their unanimous support in dealing with the contract in an extraordinary executive session. The vote was 29-1 in favour.

After I explained this in a letter to Wirtz, he replied with a particularly nasty letter accusing me of showing copies of his letters to other board members. My first reaction was one of anger and the instinct to make an issue of it by involving other governors. But the last thing we needed in those difficult times was open conflict between the chairman and a senior governor. And respecting his long service to our league, I had the feeling that at the time, Bill Wirtz was not acting in a rational way.

Curbing my resentment, I wrote in response: "I did not share letters from you with any other member and I have no idea why you would think that I did. . . . You can have any personal view of me you care to. In my responsibilities as Chairman, I have one overriding objective—to act in the best interests of our game, our League and all member clubs. While you and I may disagree on some issues, these disagreements should not lead to challenging each other's integrity."

As John F. Kennedy once said, a crucial question to measure our own success or failure is to ask, "Were we truly men of integrity?" My integrity has always been my touchstone in business and personal dealings. It was particularly relevant in acting as chairman to a group of owners with dramatically diverse personalities and backgrounds as well as the size of the wealth in their wallets. And Bill Wirtz, long may he rest, just never challenged my integrity again.

AS CHAIR AS WELL AS A TEAM OWNER, I PLAYED A LOW-key role in the board meetings when a hundred or more franchise proprietors and executives met regularly around a huge table in a midtown hotel. Gary ran the agenda, backed by savvy colleagues who emerged, such as Bill Daly, chief financial officer Craig Harnett, and Colin (Coly) Campbell, senior VP of hockey operations. A brief sampling of the teams' owners I got to know well was a trio of larger-than-life individuals.

One was the Boston Bruins' Jerry Jacobs, who lives in Buffalo, headquarters of his Delaware North, the global hospitality and food-service corporation and among the continent's largest private companies. First encountering him, I realized how much time and energy he contributed, such as chairing the vital audit and finance committee, and how faithfully he did his homework to make sure he was well prepared while attending every meeting. In the hockey world, he's known as among the hardliners in terms of player negotiations.

The Philadelphia Flyers were controlled by Ed Snider, a passionate, strong-minded man. He was building what became a sports and entertainment company in which he's also a partner in the Philadelphia 76ers of the NBA, the Philadelphia Phantoms of the American Hockey League, and a regional broadcasting sports network. His Spectator Management Group not only manages and markets his town's Spectrum arena but also nineteen facilities across the U.S., including the Los Angeles Memorial Coliseum. Ed's full in your face and you know precisely where he stands. As he says, "most all businesses are the same—they just do different things. I couldn't be the chief scout of the Flyers, I have to get the best scout." With his practicality, he and I have always had a good relationship.

I hold great respect for Mike Ilitch, who owns the Red Wings as well as the Detroit Tigers of baseball's American League. After playing ball in the minor leagues, he started a chain of thousands of Little Caesars pizza franchises in North America and even in Europe. Even now, Mike doesn't come to many of the meetings—he sends his managers—but he revitalized Detroit as the American Hockeytown. He had been able to develop a stability and loyalty with the team under coach Scotty Bowman. When I became chair in 1995, he was only a couple of years away from his back-to-back Stanley Cups. He calls himself "a fan with an owner's pocketbook."

As I got to know Gary, these were just three of the conglomeration of characters he encountered as commissioner. He was a quick study and a strong communicator, who grew increasingly fearless in dealing with the governors and their teams. Over the years, for instance, he's fined Toronto coach and GM Pat Quinn for critical comments about the league's free-agent policy, and imposed a $100,000 levy against our Flames for lack of discipline in a playoff game—as well as separate fines for the coach and the goalie, who also got a five-game suspension for stick-slashing.

In my role, I acted as a sounding board for Gary, jawboning any current issues often three times a week by phone when we didn't meet in New York or other places. He could most often count on a call from me on a Sunday before the week began. During the decade since his debut in 1993,

I saw him shepherd the NHL through a multitude of changes to improve the game, including four-on-four overtime, the two-referee system, and downsizing goaltender equipment. At one point, the league signed TV deals with ESPN and ABC (soon to change). By 2003, it grew from twenty-one to thirty franchises doubling to twenty-two American markets in such non-traditional areas as Texas and Arizona. The collective revenues would grow from $430 million US to nearly $2 billion, Over the same time span, player salaries would rise to $1.45 billion. So the reality was that the teams would now have to spend 76 per cent of total revenues on their salaries, compared to 64 per cent in the NFL, 63 per cent in major-league baseball, and 58 per cent in the NBA.

Obviously, costs had climbed to Everest altitudes for the franchises, often because of their poorly planned strategies in acquiring players at any price. A key propellant for this ascent had begun in 1992 when star forward Eric Lindros—who still hadn't played in the NHL—was traded by the Quebec Nordiques to the Flyers in return for six players, two first-round draft choices, and $15 million. In the dozen years since, the league-wide median annual salary had reached an astonishing $1.5 million.

The owners knew they had to contain the excess they'd created themselves. In 2004, the current collective bargaining agreement (CBA) would expire after the ten years it had endured. Meanwhile, a new one was being negotiated with cautionary and sometimes brutally frank dialogue between the league and the Players' Association.

The combat had really started at least five years before with opening shots that defined the battlefield. Gary had sent Bob Goodenow a confidential summary of the financial operating reports of each team for the previous season, while anticipating that the current 1999 season would be worse. He offered Bob the opportunity to have an accounting firm verify the information. He warned: "If the current trend continues, I cannot predict what shape the League will be in in 2004. I can, however, tell you with certainty that the potential for conflict will be greater because we would, under this scenario, be likely to insist on a significant re-trenching (not just limiting increases) of player costs."

Bob countered by asking for a small group from both sides to review all the economic and financial issues of four franchises. The league agreed to a joint economic study committee and, over the next twenty-two months, it met to weigh the results. In February 2001, Bob's senior director, Ted Saskin, replied to Bill Daly as executive VP and chief legal officer at the league. Bill, then in his late thirties, has a tremendous mind and a sense of fairness. Later I came to realize that Ted could be professional in seeing a broader pic-

Bill Daly is the league's fair-minded deputy commissioner and chief legal counsel.

ture, recognizing that healthy and competitive teams were in the players' interests. At that time, though, he was saying the teams had reported their revenues based on a Unified Report of Operations (URO), an unaudited document that supposedly failed to accurately describe the financial impact of owning a club. Bill replied that the effects of the figures in the UROs reveal "very real economic problems" and the Players' Association was attempting "to rewrite history and/or to manufacture a distorted and inaccurate factual record."

"In retrospect," Gary says of Ted's argument "it turned out to be a stalling tactic. When you don't want to acknowledge the fact, you throw up smokescreens."

It would take another couple of years before there was sincere action behind the scenes to start moving beyond the intransigent positions. Between March and June 2003, the league and the union met as part of a secret Project Blue Fin convened in various cities: Toronto, Philadelphia, Ottawa. "Bob had come to me, saying 'We were serious,'" Gary says, "and my guess is that he was beginning to feel some pressure—either from his own members or from the media about not doing anything."

Ted offered to have the players make an across-the-board pay cut of five per cent on existing contracts and a rollback of the salary cap for entry-level players to $850,000 from $1.295 million, among other changes. Bill said there had to be a general salary cap—salaries had to be calculated as a strict percentage of a team's revenues—with reductions in the wide gap between the high- and low-spending clubs. Again, the discussions ended. The Players' Association said flatly that if there was a cap, there'd be no season in 2004.

And the players continued to dispute the truthfulness of the league's financial reporting. To which our Ken King in Calgary told reporters, "The reality is grim enough. There's no necessity to take this information any other way. I consider it defamatory for anyone to suggest that we're not honest with the figures."

In the fall of '03, the adversaries had yet another a high-level meeting, which I attended as a member of the negotiating team. The NHL called it "Preparing for the Future." Along with Gary and Bill, there were the league's outside counsel Bob Batterman and general counsel David Zimmerman and owners Jerry Jacobs, the Carolina Hurricanes' Peter Karmanos (of Compuware, the software giant) and the Nashville Predators' Craig Leipold (of Rainfair Inc., protective clothing and footwear). The owners were pointing out that in 2001-02 the teams had lost $218 million and were expecting to lose $296 million the following year—and over the current bargaining agreement's first nine years, NHL clubs had lost a total of $1.5 billion. The league's revenues could support an average player payroll per team of only $31 million.

Despite the daunting figures, the two sides remained at loggerheads. Along with Bob, Ted, and other players' union executives was its president, Trevor Linden, of the Vancouver Canucks. I knew the six-foot-four, thirty-three-year-old captain was popular—known in his city as Captain Vancouver for his record as well as his charitable works off the ice—and his fellow players respected him for his sixteen years in the league. I'd be meeting him again.

IT WAS IN FEBRUARY 2004 THAT GARY LAUNCHED A BOMB-shell to release an independent report on the soundness of the league. He'd sought an investigator of impeccable integrity to be its author: "The same name kept coming up and when we were down in Palm Beach for the board of governors meeting in December '03, I went to see him at his home there after the meeting." That's when he and Bill Daly met Arthur Levitt, the longest-serving chairman of the U.S. Securities & Exchange Commission and the former chair of the American Stock Exchange.

As Gary tells the story, "At the end of the meeting, Arthur said to me, 'I don't take this retention unless I have complete unfettered access and I can do with the results whatever I see fit.'

"And I said, 'That's fine. It's your show to do with as you please and your findings won't be edited by us and you're free to make them public or do whatever you want with them.'

"That was point one. Point two, he asks me—I'll never forget this —'What if I find out that your clubs aren't in the condition that you're being told they are?'

"'I'd like to know that.'

"Finally he said, 'I want you to pay me in advance. I don't want there to be any issue that any payments are contingent on my work.' In other

Arthur Levitt brought financial wisdom to assessing the soundness of the NHL.

words, this shows how respectful he is in understanding integrity: if anybody questioned whether he did this or that, the answer would be that he got his money up front. That it was arm's length and his compensation didn't depend on any result. He'd already been paid."

In his exhaustive report, Arthur concluded that despite any alleged discrepancies in the UROs—which the Players' Association had suggested—they accurately measured the relevant revenues and expenses of operating the teams. In fact, the league had a combined operating loss of $273 million US for the 2002-03 season while nineteen clubs averaged losses of $18 million, putting the average loss among all thirty teams at $9.1 million. Of course, Arthur had carte blanche in investigating the true costs and revenues. The figures were all there. And paramount in putting the league on "a treadmill to obscurity" were "the rising labour costs."

The defusing report seemed to catch the union off guard. Despite how convincing it was, Bob Goodenow's people called it "another league public-relations initiative." Even a couple of our Flames said, "Accountants can come up with anything. They can cook the books." Bob refused to meet with Arthur to answer any questions.

On March 1, Gary sent the union written notification of the NHL's intention to terminate the current collective bargaining agreement as of September 15. The formal negotiation period had begun. Two days later, Bill and Ted met in Newport Beach, California, when the union said it would not retreat from its no-cap stance—until "the league brings the union to its knees, or until the picture of the business changes dramatically enough that players have no choice."

The volleying persisted that spring. The union proposed a guarantee that the league payroll would decrease by a defined negotiated percentage in the first year of the CBA, and if the guarantee was not met, the league would be repaid for the average amount above that target. The league replied that it would proceed only on a *multi*-year guarantee—which the union rejected. Into the summer, at a collective bargaining session in New York, the union conceded that the NHL has "significant losses, which are something less than what you tell us, but still total in the hundreds of millions of dollars."

By August, the parties did agree on the union's suggestion for a review of team and market performance, starting with six clubs, including our Flames. That process continued until early in September, the crucial month with the lockout looming. On the ninth, I was at the bargaining session in Toronto with all the key league and Players' Association executive. The union claimed, in its estimation, that the NHL's situation was less serious because only six teams accounted for $169 million of the league's then-calculated loss of $224 million. Repeating its earlier offer, the union proposed a five-per-cent, across-the-board salary reduction, entry-level salary changes, a luxury tax on player payrolls, and enhanced revenue-sharing among the clubs. But now it wanted to raise the payroll threshold to $50 million from the previously proposed $40 million when the tax took effect.

I was among those owners who argued that the union's offer, without realistic cost certainty, would simply mean that markets like Calgary would not have any future. We weren't even speaking the same language.

On September 16 (just the day after Canada won the World Cup against Finland in Toronto), the NHL lockout landed like the thud of a slapshot. Gary announced the board of governors' decision to suspend all games for the foreseeable future. What was supposed to be the first official day of the 2004-05 season, October 13, was put on ice of a different kind. The fans were hot-damn angry that thirty owners and 750 players couldn't agree on divvying up nearly $2 billion. The union members were seemingly united and determined behind a go-for-broke Bob Goodenow to squelch any suggestion of a salary cap—despite the fact that both the NFL and the NBA had one. For me, as an owner as well as the league chairman, there was a deep sadness and disappointment that the players weren't aware that the NHL was in dire trouble.

But some retired legends spoke out, among them Guy Lafleur and Jean Beliveau. As Jean said about the players, "They're making a terrible mistake. I've always sided with the players in the past, but this time I really believe they're completely wrong. Those who follow today's players will face a very serious situation because the game will be in very bad shape, financially and otherwise."

Early on, a national Ipsos-Reid poll found that 52 per cent of Canadian respondents blamed players for the lockout and only 21 per cent the owners. A month into the suspension, some Florida Panthers said they'd consider going back if the league ever decided to use replacement players. Even defenceman Mike Commodore of the Flames confessed in October he'd accept a salary cap if both sides agreed: "I'll risk the slap on the wrist [from the union]. I don't want to spend however long my career lasts playing here in the American Hockey League [playing during the lockout with the Lowell Lock Monsters]." Publicly accepting a cap were the Montreal forward Pierre Dagenais and New Jersey centre John Madden. By the end of November, more players were sounding like heretics in questioning the union's gung-ho stance and questioning the lack of any negotiations.

And then as this purgatory endured, the union surprisingly offered a one-time concession on December 9 that would be an across-the-board salary cut of 24 per cent for an estimated two hundred players who had current contracts. A six-year deal, to expire in 2009-10, would also include pay restraints for entry-level players, qualifying offers, and salary arbitration, along with a payroll tax and a revenue-sharing plan.

Looking back on that pay cut today, Gary says, "I was mystified that they had done it. I think the union miscalculated—not the players—by assuming that by agreeing to the rollback, somehow we'd be under this inordinate pressure to make a deal. But all it did was get us closer to the deal I knew we had to make."

At the time, Gary told the media, "I will acknowledge that one aspect of the proposal is very significant. That element is a recognition by the union of our economic condition, but it is a one-time element. We have said consistently that the focus must be on the overall systematic issue and the long-term needs and health of our game."

Yet simply put, there was no salary cap. And the following week, the league returned to reject the union proposal and insist on the cap, the end of salary arbitration, and a restructuring of the players' deep salary rollback. Yes, the cut would have had a significant, short-term effect, but there was nothing in the system to prevent a return to the same financial folly that got us into trouble in the first place.

The union turned this counter-offer down, but Bob Goodenow had already acknowledged, "The whole world has been adjusted downward by this proposal. . . . For negotiating and arbitrating, the world is 24-per-cent less—that is a fact."

For the next month, over Christmas, the first half of the wannabe season had evaporated. There was unemployment on both sides as the league headquarters had long since been thinning its staff by two-thirds. By now, Bob was telling his members to start looking for other work. And

Trevor Linden, head of the Players' Association, kept his members on goal.

then Trevor Linden surfaced to propose another negotiating session—but this time without the heavyweights Gary and Bob at the table. As Trevor reflected afterwards, "They're fighting and butting heads and they can't agree on what day it is or what colour the sky is. My point was let's get together—not in such a big group—and try and have some dialogue,"

The proposal was to meet on January 19 centrally at the United Airlines lounge at O'Hare Airport in Chicago. Trevor wanted me to be there with Bill Daly and Bob Batterman in my party and he brought Ted and the union's outside counsel, John McCambridge. Becky and I had flown up from our place in Florida. For Trevor and me, this was one of our first real personal conversations, face to face, one on one. I'd heard that he came from a good family in Medicine Hat, where he learned to play hockey on the frozen ponds, and was a serious young man of integrity. In earlier bargaining sessions, I'd seen him get disturbed about a point and say firmly, but without pounding the table, "Well, Harley, why are you so difficult on this?" He has said later that I struck him "as the type of guy who would do deals on a handshake."

For five hours that day in the informal setting, the two groups discussed the issues and, though we were a long way apart, the back-and-forthing was always respectful. One of the items I mentioned, which Trevor understood from his own longtime residence in Vancouver, was my wish to be able to hold on to Calgary's players and keep them in the community.

I felt the most important conversation he and I had near the end of the afternoon was on our own at his invitation. He thanked me for changing my schedule to come through Chicago. I said, speaking from the heart. "I would basically go anywhere and do anything within reason to get this solved. But there are a couple of things I have to tell you. I'm not making any threats, but unless we can find a solution that works for us—and for everyone in the process—we don't see Calgary surviving. And, Trevor, we are not a bunch of liars and cheaters."

He replied, "Harley, I don't doubt that. But there are some markets and some people on your side who don't report accurately and it's a problem for us."

"I know the history and I don't think that's an issue of any significance today. You guys make fun of the Levitt report, but you won't really deal with it. It's a pretty realistic evaluation of where we are in this league. I understand that you have to bargain hard. We expect that, but you have to understand that our businesses have to make some economic sense. But we really have a responsibility here to work together in what's the best interests of the game and the league. We can't be enemies like this. We've got to find a way to work together."

I had the sense throughout the airport session that Trevor was truly listening. Long afterwards, he told an interviewer, "Just that we broke down into a small group and started to build a little relationship, whether with Harley and me, or myself talking with Bill Daly, got some conversation flowing. It was just the fact that I could understand Harley's issues more. It kind of lowered the wall a bit."

Heartened by Trevor's report to the media of our "good dialogue," the group decided to meet the following day in Toronto, because Ted Saskin's mother had just died there. And I couldn't make the next session. Becky and I were flying home to Calgary for the funeral of our dear friend Bud Mc-Caig. Bud was more than just a partner in the Flames. He had been close to me as a confidant for so many years. As well as being buddies, we were deeply involved in the community: members of corporate boards, he being vice-chairman to my chairing at Foothills Hospital, and both of us on Peter Lougheed's political committees. Younger than me, he had been suffering from Crohn's disease. Now we came back home to help share the grief with his wife, Ann McCaig, a dedicated volunteer of her talents as the chancellor of the University of Calgary and a co-chair of fundraising for the Alberta Children's Hospital. In their enthusiasm for the Flames, the McCaigs often would host the annual fall picnic for the players and families.

After attending Bud's funeral, I flew for a restorative weekend quail-hunting in Dallas on Boone Pickens' ranch. When I came back to town, the *Herald* was calling me "Patron Saint of the Lost Cause, viewed by many as the last best hope of pumping life into hockey's flatlining EKG." The small eleventh-hour talks continued until January 27, but the hope faded despite our good intentions. In early February, there was another round of bargaining, the league re-insisting on a salary cap. What horse-trading we were able to offer was still happening on the 15th, as we raised our $40-million cap to $42.5 million and the union countered with $49 million.

Too damn late. The next day, Gary announced the cancellation of what would be the first professional sports league ever to lose an entire season. He'd spoken to me by phone about twenty minutes earlier. Recapping it since, he says, "Knowing that I was going to make this announcement in front of a room full of two hundred media on live TV and was doing something terribly historic—but in a very negative way—I knew there was no choice. I remember walking from our offices to the Westin Hotel on 42nd Street with Bill Daly and it was almost like an out-of-body experience. But after I did it, I was very much at peace because I knew even at that point the union leadership—meaning Goodenow—was not going to make any deal that was going to fix our problems."

Despite last-minute intervention by the likes of Wayne Gretzky and Mario Lemieux, the season was to stay irrevocably dead. It would total the most games lost (1,230) due to a work stoppage in sports history, and the longest-lasting shutdown (310 days). And it was the first time the Stanley Cup was not awarded since the global flu epidemic in 1919.

As Ken King said with a statesman's grace, "We failed, and to those emotionally and financially invested in this failed process, we apologize. I am confused and upset that we have not yet reached a solution. Everyone deserves better." I told reporters, "We want our fans to know we understand the impact this dispute has had on you. We want you to know how very much we appreciate the patience you have shown the NHL during this difficult moment in its history, and we want you to know we are deeply sorry for any hardship caused."

In fact, Gary told the NHL governors at our next meeting, "This is over. We're going to get what we need. I can't tell you how long it's going to take, but we're going to get it." What he understood was that the Players' Association executive had believed he couldn't hold the owners together, and they would cave at the threat of losing a season.

Meanwhile, both sides were at least looking with some hope to the next one—even though, as the lockout started, Bob Goodenow had warned that the NHL could be shuttered for two full seasons. As Trevor has explained, players were then considering that if the CBA was not settled before October '05, "It's payday number one on Year Two, and what kind of pressure are we going to be under? . . . The league is saying once we get into October, it's 'Forget it; see you in January.'" (At one of our governors' meetings, Gary had announced, "If we don't have a CBA, we aren't opening next season.")

Players such as Jarome Iginla were urging the union to get moving on negotiations. There were several insightful Players' Association reps at our sessions, guys like Bob Boughner, a combative ex-Flame defenceman, who was the son of a union leader in Windsor but could see the other side. At one league-union meeting, we had broken up into small groups and I was in a session with Trevor. We had a good exchange, but some of the others were just batting heads. Bob Goodenow summed up by saying something like "You've got no respect for us, we're not getting anywhere."

Looking at Trevor, I spoke up to argue with the others: "Our meeting didn't go that way. We didn't solve it, but we made some progress and I don't see any reason to get all pushed out of shape and go home." And they didn't leave.

In mid-March, the league offered a $37.5-million team-by-team salary cap and a deal linking revenues to payrolls. It was to be a fair proposal and I was surprised that Gary had floated this one as far as he did. The players caucused on it but returning to the meeting, they rejected it. Targeting their representatives, I said, "Do you really realize what you've turned down here?" A week later, the union was suggesting the idea of an upper and lower limit on team-by-team payrolls, which the owners found encouraging.

By early May, both sides were immersed in an aggressive series of thirty-one meetings over the next two months. I was on twenty-eight Air Canada flights during that month. The confrontations were hard, physically and mentally. At one point, after I made some comments about the importance of working together, Bob criticized me, saying that we'd done a lousy job in in our player drafts and running the Flames. Restrained, I replied, "Bob, we've made some mistakes and will probably make some more. But we're working hard to keep our team in Calgary."

Yet the tone was somehow becoming conciliatory now. And at the same time the hard bargaining was happening, the antagonists had actually come together in the background to improve the game with the creation of a competition committee—with players, managers, an owner, all under the direction of Coly Campbell—to evaluate and make suggestions to the NHL board of governors on matters relating to the game and the way it's played. It

Colin Campbell, director of hockey operations, spearheaded a committee to improve the game.

was a good bridge-building experience. One of its members was Detroit Red Wing's Brendan Shanahan, who was also invited to attend some of our latest contract negotiation sessions and brought both his enthusiasm and a welcome breath of fresh air to our collective love of hockey.

"Finally," Gary sums up, "what happened was the union asked not to see Levitt, but they asked to see the accountants who did work for him. We had this meeting— it wasn't just now Goodenow and Saskin, it was also players, including Trevor. They spent a day or two asking the accountants everything they could ask: How did they do their work? What about this, what about that? The accountants—because of how thorough Mr. Levitt was—were able to answer every single question they had. And it was clear to me after about the first three hours, the players understood that the Levitt report was on the level. They had ignored it for a year, but now understood there was no reason for them to be doubting it."

The truth that emerged later was that Bob Goodenow had lost his clout with his union members. Trevor, who had increasingly come to understand the economics of the game, was a key factor in the ultimate decision-making. He was asking his fellow players, "What are we fighting for now? We just lost a year, $1.2 billion in players' money—it's gone. And we're fighting for *what* now? Because of philosophies—cap, no cap. I mean, cap works for football, for basketball pretty well if you're making a lot of money. Is it really as bad as they're saying? . . . Let's just agree to take a piece and make it bigger. If we can make it bigger, everyone will be happy."

Gary has said, "I always believed that the players were so fortunate to have Trevor as the president. In addition to being extremely smart, he was passionate about the game and never lost sight of the big picture. And if he had his way, we would have made a deal sooner."

Then, in a crucial decision on June 2, the NHL and the Players' Association agreed on the introduction of what to the union had seemed the impossible sticking point: a salary cap. The two sides were in a conference room in New York for the better part of five weeks, with holiday weekends and some all-nighters. The lawyers wrestled over the fine-tuning of the details, translating the cap and the revenue-sharing into mutually acceptable words. At last, on July 13, after hammering out the final terms of the collective bargaining agreement, everyone reached a deal. More than six hundred pages long, it was reportedly the most complex CBA in the sporting world.

Among the major points, the salary cap was set at $39 million per team in 2005-06 and would be adjusted each year to guarantee players 54 per cent of total NHL revenues, with their share rising based on benchmarks geared to increasing revenues to a maximum of 57 per cent. The value of existing contracts was rolled back by 24 per cent. No one player could earn more than 20 per cent of the cap. Players could become unrestricted free agents at twenty-seven (rather than thirty-one) in the first year and then based on seven years' service as of 2008. In revenue-sharing, an unspecified pool of money of the ten highest-grossing teams would be split with the fifteen lowest on the rung. Entry-level players would be held to a maximum of $850,000 a year, with stiff limits on bonuses.

About 90 per cent of the players voted to accept the agreement. This wasn't a win-lose for anyone; the CBA would work well for all of us. As both chairman and a co-owner, I felt an enormous sense of relief. Franchises like ours could now be competitive and survive. Without this deal, Calgary, Edmonton, Ottawa, and Buffalo would surely have been among those to die.

Through all of this, Lou Lamoriello became one of my favourite hockey friends. President and general manager of the New Jersey Devils after a successful university coaching career, Lou was tough but fair and he and John McMullen created an atmosphere of player loyalty and trust among the Devils. As part of a four-man ownership group during the negotiations in the 2004-05 lockout (the others were Jerry Jacobs, Craig Leipold, and me), Lou was a key player in resolving the dispute.

In the years since the previous work stoppage in 1995, Gary had come to clearly comprehend all the issues—including how to ensure that his strong-minded governors stuck together—and he pursued the outcome with stiff resolve. There were at least a couple of times when I would have wavered a bit about going far enough to rescue the game, yet he didn't.

His staff was solid: the capable and unbelievable workhorse Bill Daly, executive VP and chief financial officer Craig Harnett, and senior VP of finance Joe DeSousa. The Levitt report, produced by a man beyond reproach, was a decisive instrument to give the owners credibility in making their financial case. Many teams too had firmer relationships with players and some of them felt enough trust in our integrity to spread the word to their union members. Meeting directly, as Trevor and I did at O'Hare and afterwards, appeared an important milestone along the way. And the new competition committee meetings gave hope that hockey could emerge despite the long bout of hard contract bargaining as a much better sport.

The seasoned members of the committee were players Jarome Iginla, Colorado's Rob Blake, Trevor, and Brendan Shanahan; team general managers Bob Gainey of Montreal, Kevin Lowe of Edmonton, David Poile of Nashville, and Don Waddell of the Atlanta Thrashers; and owner Ed Snider of Philadelphia. Analyzing the defects that were choking play, they succeeded well with thoughtful new rules to open up the game and return hockey to its essence of speed and skill, rather than obstruction and occasionally even outright hooliganism.

Among the many innovations were eliminating the centre red line for two-line passes, banning line changes by a team that ices the puck, reducing goaltender equipment by about 11 per cent, and moving the goal line two feet back closer to the end boards to create larger offensive zones. A player starting a fight in a game's final five minutes receives a game misconduct and an automatic one-game suspension (double for each additional incident), and the player's coach is fined $10,000 (double for each additional incident). There is now zero tolerance for interference, hooking, and holding/obstruction. And no more tied games: after a scoreless five-minute overtime, three players from each team participate in a shootout and the one with the most goals after those six shots wins. If the score is still tied, the shootout proceeds to sudden death. If a game is decided by a shootout, the final score gives the winning team one more goal than its opponent, based on the score at the end of overtime.

As the 2005-06 season began, there was a sense of expectation and some apprehension. We were fearful whether disgruntled fans, after being shut out for a season, would even return in large enough numbers. Well, they did. Then we wondered if they would consider the rule changes an improvement. By far the majority loved them. *The Hockey News* told the story by summarizing the season's first quarter of play: there was more scoring—6.32 goals per game compared to 5.07 in 2003-04—penalties were increasing to hobble aggressive players who now had to try taming their style, and the speediest skaters were performing better as the rules gave them the edge with the puck. At the end of the regulation season, *The Globe and Mail* said in an editorial:

Canadians who love hockey should rejoice. The old order in the National Hockey League is dying, as the first round of playoffs this spring has shown. The revolution has truly come.

In the older order, rich teams in Detroit, Philadelphia and Toronto could buy high-priced players that teams in smaller markets could not afford. And the hockey was lousy—virtually everywhere.

In the new order, the small or midsize markets such as Edmonton, Calgary and Ottawa can compete for talent with the big boys. And the hockey is wonderful.

THE HOCKEY I'D GROWN UP WITH COULD NOW BE THE sheer fun of old. As the following season was winding down in February 2007, the general managers met to measure the success of the modifications. They decided to keep everything the same. As veteran sportswriter Eric

Duhatschek commented, "In short, the GMs looked at what they'd created coming out of the lockout, decided they liked most of what they saw and weren't willing to do much to change things."

Meanwhile, I was disheartened about what was happening with the Players' Association. Shortly after the collective bargaining agreement was ratified, Trevor as president felt obligated to relieve Bob Goodenow as the leader who'd brought the union into the lockout. Goodenow and I had a cordial relationship but, believing negotiations should be between him and Gary, I never had any in-depth discussions with Bob of the problems our game was facing. Measured by the additional compensation his players received, he was highly successful. But we seemed to have different views on the importance of financially successful franchises and the value of hockey to Canada and its communities.

Ted Saskin took over Goodenow's role, but he would be ousted in the spring of '07 allegedly for accessing e-mail accounts of players who had challenged his hiring as executive director. Whatever the truth, Ted had done a good job in his years with the union. I was sorry about the events that felled the two men. I thought it was vitally important to have a healthy players' organization with strong leadership that shares our vision for the long-term future of the NHL. Ted has since been replaced by Paul Kelly, a Boston trial lawyer reputed to be an accomplished negotiator.

I knew then that the league itself had problems to confront in coming years. There was still pressure to spend more on the best players while trying to emphasize the developing youngsters who feed the sport. At the same time, you hoped loyalty to the team and community would keep the top ones despite other financial lures. While landing stars such as Sidney Crosby remained a big plus, you could go too far by glorifying the super players—for me, hockey is a true team game that should stress passing and playmaking skills over breakaways by individual players. And the other problem was that you could continue to create such salary disparity among members of the same club.

Then there was the massive challenge of building and rebuilding a league with American teams that often find themselves in states with no history of hockey in a nation with three other major sports. The NHL needed even more intelligent marketing such as new media initiatives, using technology as the league and local franchises promoted the game. While it was a stark wakeup that the final game of the 2007 Stanley Cup series between the Anaheim Ducks and Ottawa Senators on NBC had the lowest rating in twelve years, the figures for the '08 finals with Detroit and Pittsburgh were well up. And there was still room for expansion in the U.S. if the franchises were carefully chosen and brought in a wave of talent from other countries.

These hurdles all loomed—but for another leader of the board of governors to overcome with the owners and the league executives. After a dozen years, it was time for me to retire gracefully as chair in 2007. I'd always intended to pull the plug after ten years, but at that time the arduous negotiations were well under way and Gary and others asked me to stay on. Now, with that behind us, and after conferring with the commissioner, we decided to choose a candidate from owners rather than team executives and from one of the eleven people on the executive committee. I talked to them all and that June stepped down to welcome the Bruins' energetic, judicious Jerry Jacobs, who decided to take over the task. In turn, I succeeded him as temporary chair of the watchdog finance and audit committee. I suggested a vice-chair for the first time and we chose Tom Hicks, the owner of a newer franchise, the Dallas Stars.

Keeping me on even keel through my tenure as chair were my solid and close working ties with Gary. I developed a great appreciation of his leadership abilities and even more for his personal qualities of high energy, intelligence, integrity, and fairness. His warm and caring relationship with his wife, Shelli, and his three children (Loren, Jordan, and Brittany) added to my respect for him. Three things stand out as I reflect on his direction of the NHL. His efforts to help the many troubled franchises were untiring as ownerships changed during the two lockouts. The commissioner made several trips to Calgary whenever we needed him as the Flames struggled to stay in town. He was the leader in initiating the Canadian currency equalization plan and keeping it alive as it came up for review every year—when U.S. teams, several losing money, contributed to help their Canadian competitors. Our American partners feel good about supporting the scheme, which preserved Canada's strong, critically important presence in our league. And Gary's commanding role in reaching a new agreement with the players in 2005, and his skill in keeping such a diverse group of owners together during that challenging process, resulted in a solution that worked for all of us.

Leaving my post in 2007, I told the media, "Looking back, it was probably the toughest time in the league to be chairman. Our fans have come back, as they said they would. We've gone from survival to something that makes sense. I feel pretty good about it."

That year I was delighted when Doc, B.J., and I were accepted into the Alberta Sports Hall of Fame as Builders. I'd already been privileged the previous year by being inducted into the Hockey Hall of Fame. That November evening in downtown Toronto, I was all gussied up in tux and bow

Gary visiting with me at the Saddledome on one of his periodic trips to Calgary.

tie, squiring Becky in that grand, nineteenth-century stone bank, beneath the stained-glass dome of the ceremonial Great Hall. There I spotted a tribute on the wall to the man I'd worshipped as a kid, my hero Syl Apps. And now I was being honoured with players Dick Duff, who'd won six Stanley Cups with the Maple Leafs and the Canadiens, and Patrick Roy, who in playing for Montreal and Colorado had registered record numbers of wins and regular-season games played. And I was being named a Builder, along with a posthumous award to Herb Brooks, who'd been GM and head coach of the Miracle on Ice, gold-winning U.S. Olympic team. I had a friend from home who was being honoured as a media honoree: Peter Maher, the Flames play-by-play announcer, received the Foster Hewitt Memorial Award.

Gary Bettman introduced me with embarrassingly rich words: "I can assure you his work behind the scenes on behalf of the Flames and our league has been marked by impeccable integrity, exceptional commitment and energy, and a deep inner strength. His passion for the Flames knows no bounds nor does his passion for this game. Those two passions are surpassed only by his love of family, his love of community, and his pursuit of what is right. It is a privilege to work with Harley."

Bill Hay, my old pal and colleague and CEO of the Hall, brought me nicely back to ground. He pointed out that a member of the inductees' selection committee had noted—what with my record as a player with the

Michigan State Spartans—"this is one guy who won't go into the Hall of Fame on his scoring stats."

At the microphone, I fibbed, kidding Billy: "What you forgot to tell them is that I was a goalie." Mentioning that Becky and I had recently celebrated our fifty-fifth wedding anniversary, I said, "Becky is the solid one in our family and I'll tell you without the kind of home life that I have, I couldn't do a lot of the things that I do, so this is really a partnership award, Becky." After recalling my boyhood, I recognized Doc and B.J. in the audience for bringing our team to town and talked about our Project 75 programs to support grassroots hockey—including a million-dollar commitment that we'd just made in Toronto, involving the Hall of Fame, Hockey Canada, the City of Toronto, the Lakeshore Lions Club, the Maple Leafs, and the Toronto Marlboroughs. I also mentioned the Flames' well-known challenges along the way. "But now we've got a solid ownership group, we've got very strong and loyal fans. The Calgary Flames franchise is secure for way beyond my time."

I went on to pay tribute to all the guys who had come back after the lost season and put their souls right back into their work, their joy: "We've got the best product in professional sports. And by that I mean the people who play the game, our players. They provide all the excitement and enjoyment on this ice. There's another side to that: all the things they do in their communities, off the ice, and a lot of that is done quietly behind the scenes. . . . They're the heart of our business. I think it's important for the players to have a strong association, that they have strong association leadership, and they need that to look after their interests and bargain hard at the appropriate time. But we should always work together with respect and co-operation with an underlying focus on improving our game and keeping our league strong. It's a responsibility that we all share and we owe it to our fans."

Among the guests were great oldtimers—Ted Lindsay, Yvon Cournoyer, and Jean Beliveau, whom I came to know in his business career afterwards as a thoughtful and caring gentleman, remaining one of my favourite people in our hockey world. Before the ceremony, Lanny McDonald was interviewed for television and said warmly about me, "He welcomed every player into Calgary and their families with open arms, opened up their homes, and made us all feel like we were part of something special and that tradition still continues to this day. And it's part of why our alumni is probably the strongest alumni in the league. ..And [as NHL chairman] he made sure that hockey got back to where it was on the ice instead of in the boardroom."

I heard from other players of the past who congratulated me for the honour. Joey Mullen called me to say in his thick New York accent, "Hey,

Hawley!" Joe Nieuwendyk sent a bouquet of flowers to our home, reminding me again how central Becky has always been to the Flames. And our Flames captain, Jarome Iginla, and assistant captains Robyn Regehr and Rhett Warrener surprised me with a large photo presentation showing my 1950 Michigan State hockey team, Calgary's '89 Stanley Cup team, and the '04 cup final team.

AFTER ALL MY FOCUS ON THE LEAGUE AT LARGE SINCE 1995, I was pleased to be back in Calgary with our guys. At this writing, in each of the past four seasons we were one among only seven of the thirty teams in the league to qualify for the playoffs. Unfortunately, we fell to three consecutive first-round defeats.

Darryl Sutter was coach in 2005-06 when the Flames ranked the seventh-overall club in points. Miikka Kiprusoff won both the Vezina and the William Jennings trophies. Dion Phaneuf was nominated for the Calder Trophy as the league's best rookie. Jarome led our scoring in points (67) and goals (35), Daymond Langkow in assists (34).

As general manager, Darryl moved Jim Playfair to head coach the next season. In 2003, Jim had come in as his assistant, fresh from what was then our American Hockey League team, the Saint John Flames, where he'd led them to their first Calder Cup championship; *The Hockey News* named him minor professional coach of the year. Jim did some fine work for us, but when he became head coach in '06-'07, the pressures from the media—especially critical of a weak road record—might have got to him as the new man at the top. Maybe the Flames were a bit better as players than we were as a team. Doc agreed that Jim had done a good job generally. "One of the things we were deficient at was controlling centre faceoffs," he said at the time. "And I would have described the team as having a fragile personality—it didn't take much to get them off their game." In the conference quarter-finals, we lost the series to Detroit 4-2. Dion and Miikka were named to the All-Stars and Jarome got the most points (94) and goals (39) again.

I'd called Jarome in Kelowna, B.C. after the '06-'07 season about attending a gala event for the Hockey Canada Foundation in Calgary. Our team captain, our mainstay right wing, was amid negotiations for a new contract. During our conversation, he remarked in passing, "I'm so glad you want me back. I just want to be in Calgary, my wife wants to be there, and we just like the organization."

He, like many of our players, are family guys, valued in the community. A local business magazine, *CalgaryInc*, had recently asked branding experts to judge Calgary's best brands—the essence of a product, company,

Controversial coach Mike Keenan adds new energy and a wealth of experience.

or experience. In that ranking, the Flames were one of the three best brands: "Any brand that has a legion of fans who are willing to paint their torsos in a bright red and black flaming 'C' and run around a downtown street screaming 'Go Flames Go' at the top of their lungs has something going on."

That summer, Jim Playfair was retained as associate coach when Darryl brought in the pretty controversial Mike Keenan. Mike had a tough demeanour with his players that earned him the nickname Iron Mike and sometimes brewed conflict with management. He had been GM of the young Florida Panthers before leaving abruptly ten months earlier after coaching there for two seasons. When he joined the Flames, it was his eighth position, coaching the most teams in league history. He'd worked with Philadelphia, then Chicago, and in 1993 became head coach of the New York Rangers, leading to their first Stanley Cup win since 1940. As head coach and GM, he was with St. Louis, Vancouver, and Boston. And Darryl knew him well while working closely together with the Blackhawks.

Yet hiring him was a big surprise to us owners. We pay a lot of attention but don't get involved in those day-to-day operations After a lot of thought, Darryl discussed the idea thoroughly with Ken King, who came to us with their recommendation. You can bet there was a lot of discussion.

Mike brought us into the 2008 playoffs with the San Jose Sharks, who ended the regular season fourteen points ahead of the Flames. Despite the lopsided match, a lot of our players were optimistic. "We felt going into the playoffs we were a Cup contender," said left-winger Alex Tanguay. And we did persevere into the seventh game. As Jarome told reporters about their coach, "He brought a lot of confidence to our group and I think we probably played our best hockey of the year in the playoffs."

Darryl agreed that Iron Mike should be on the job for the 2008-09 season to keep on pushing the Flames to play with guts to burn. We owners accepted our general manager's judgment.

All of us knew, as *The Globe and Mail* headlined in early '08 about the NHL, "A new golden age cometh. . . . Spectacular plays have become common, the 'wow' factor is back." As for me, I would be in the Saddledome for every match, harking back to my childhood passion. And remembering the words of the legend-large Bobby Hull, who grew up as I did on a southern Ontario farm: "The game is bigger now, but it will never be bigger than a small boy's dreams."

CHAPTER 10

GIVING BACK

The How and Why of Philanthropy

I'D HEARD SAM WEISS'S NAME FOR SEVERAL YEARS while chairing the Alberta Heritage Foundation for Medical Research, an organization that has been around as long as the Flames. It was created by Peter Lougheed's provincial government but has always operated at a comfortable arm's length from politicians and bureaucrats while funding innovative world-calibre researchers who are enhancing people's health and quality of life. Dr. Samuel Weiss is a brilliant neurobiologist at the University of Calgary whose groundbreaking work has received many major grants and awards from the Foundation to pursue research in the neural stem-cell field, which has led to several patents and the creation of two biotechnology companies. Then in 2003 Dr. T. Chen Fong, head of the university's radiology department, and Jack Davis, chief executive of the Calgary Regional Health Authority, approached me with an intriguing idea. Would I support the launch of the first-ever brain institute to combine the fields of neuroscience and mental health—with Sam Weiss as director? I agreed to meet the man over breakfast at the Chamber of Commerce club downtown. What I didn't expect was that the first hour and a half of our meeting would be devoted to nothing but hockey. This compactly built, wiry guy walked in a little gingerly and when I asked him why, Sam explained he'd been playing beer-league hockey with friends the day before—and one of his more aggressive opponents was the Flames' physician, the surgeon Kelly Brett. "Even though it's a gentleman's league," he said, "you know, some-

Dr. Sam Weiss—amateur hockey player and a world leader in the fields of developmental neurobiology and neural regeneration—is the director of the Hotchkiss Brain Institute at the University of Calgary.

times gentleman can lose their cool and you find yourself crushed against the boards. And when you're getting close to fifty, that doesn't reverse itself as quickly."

It turned out that Sam was born in Montreal and raised as a Canadiens fan before switching allegiance to the Calgary Flames. So for most of the morning, we talked about the game—the Habs, Jean Beliveau, the Montreal Forum—while his colleague Dr. Greg Cairncross, who heads clinical neurosciences at the U of C, sat patiently by. Until I looked at my watch and said, "We'd better start talking about what you came for or it's going to be lunchtime."

MY INTEREST IN DISCUSSING SAM'S CONCEPT WAS BORN of my need to be involved in society—well beyond the worlds of business and sport, fulfilling as they are. At the risk of sounding awfully self-important and maybe self-serving, I believe philanthropy and community service should play an integral part of a person's journey through life. A couple of my altruistic friends have spoken publicly in interesting ways about contributing to the community. Boone Pickens, a brief resident of Calgary, said, "To give back, where I've made some money, it wasn't that hard. It's fairly easy to do. And I would like for others to feel that they enjoy, love living some place—Alberta and Calgary, Edmonton, wherever. But I don't like to put it on the basis that you owe something, I don't really see it I owe anything. It's what I wanted to do and felt very comfortable doing it." My friend Dick Haskayne talked of "the vital need for more of us who've done well in business careers to volunteer our time and pragmatic experience as well as our money to not-for-profit organizations."

The Calgary I adopted seems a place of such generous people who define the vitality of the city. With their traditionally conservative bent, they might not always trust big government to do everything for them and recognize that folks have to help themselves and others. That means not only funding good works but also getting behind the causes with their own active involvement and energy.

Yet some of us have realized that supporting a sensitive political regime in power would keep the economy boiling productively and offer citizens a deeper well-being of life. Before being enmeshed in health care, I was devoting time to back a government that would eventually make Alberta one of Canada's hotbeds of medical research and practice.

It began with the election of the Progressive Conservative administration led by Peter Lougheed. A lawyer in his mid-thirties in 1965, he'd headed the party without a single seat in the legislature. The no-nonsense Social

Credit government under Ernest Manning had a hammerlock on the province. It took Peter six years to get into government and become premier for the next fourteen. I didn't even vote for him during the 1971 election, when he beat Manning's successor, Henry Strom.

By the mid-Seventies, B.J. Seaman was a member of the southern Alberta finance committee for the Conservatives and I knew his friend and fellow fundraiser Rod McDaniel, the engineering consultant who'd founded the petroleum engineering firm McDaniel and Associates. It wasn't a big step to join them on that committee. Rod, who was chairman, had been on the original three-man group with lawyer Bob Black and this fellow named Alvin Libin. While Al and I would become partners in the Flames someday, we didn't know one another then. He had been apolitical until Peter, his childhood pal and neighbour, invited him on the committee. Others who became members were Norm Green and Bud McCaig—future Flame co-owners—and lawyer Jack Major, a partner in Bennett Jones, who later became a justice of the Supreme Court of Canada.

Peter, who didn't believe in unfettered free enterprise, refused to kowtow to the petroleum industry. As I pointed out earlier, he increased the existing maximum royalty rates to benefit the public purse and help small and medium-sized Alberta oil and gas companies rather than the giants based elsewhere. Then after his landslide re-election in 1975, he created the Heritage Savings Trust Fund with annual $1.5-billion endowments for commercial investments, diversified provincial businesses, and—so darn important—capital projects such as hospitals.

I was a member on the finance committee over the next several years. It gave all of us involved a unique insight into the political process with private sessions with the premier and his people. Today, Peter reflects about these informal discussions: "I'll bet there isn't a comparable set of circumstances of political fundraising to equal that in Canadian history. They never came and said, 'Peter, I want you to do something for me' because they knew it would be self-serving to them. You get to know what the people are thinking in a candid way."

During the National Energy Program and the battles with Ottawa in the late Seventies, he wanted to introduce incentives to keep the petroleum industry afloat. "They had to be smart incentive programs that would work," he says. "Where the hell do you think I could get that advice? Well, we'd go to Government House [used for high-level government conferences] and invite these people with the assistant deputy ministers and Treasury and talk about how to bring that incentive plan in. And there was no publicity about this at all, entirely behind the scenes."

In the runup to the 1982 provincial election, Peter invited me—at that time not a close confidant of his—to head the Calgary fundraising group. I told him, "I'm surprised you're asking me. I don't have a high profile here." By then I'd sold Sabre Petroleums and was operating on my own as an independent in the oil industry.

Taking the chairmanship on, I found it a lot tougher than predicted. First of all, the records were disorganized. Then, what with television advertising and sophisticated political marketing demands, the cost of running a complex election was much higher than in the past. Now, because of mandatory disclosure rules to identify donors, we couldn't just tap major support from two or three big hitters. In the old days, the committee would dig out the files from the previous election and pitch the previous contributors again. But I learned they were less responsive as they asked, "You come and see me only when you want money. Where were you last year?"

The Conservatives did win the election handily against four other parties, including the separatist Western Canada Concept. But I was still disturbed about the fundraising process. I cautioned Peter, "This isn't going to work anymore. It's just not politically smart or healthy. You've got to have a much broader base of support. A lot more people with more modest contributions; you can't just depend on these big $50,000 to $100,000 contributors. You do need to have a better relationship between your political system and the business community. And the only way you're going to get that is to be able to have some communication between the people who support you on a much more frequent basis and at times not related to money at all. So the business people can tell you what the issues are out there on the streets and you can tell them how you're dealing with them."

We expanded our committee to include prominent people such as Dick Haskayne and Harold Milavsky, president and CEO of Trizec, North America's largest public real-estate company. And we made sure that those who were involved in raising funds would have to dip into their own pockets first. After arranging to have the records updated, our committee went after new sources for financial support.

At one point, I told Jack Major, "We've got to get the legal firms involved."

To which Jack said, "Harley, you're not going to get them."

I pointed out that if Bennett Jones had eighty or so lawyers at the time, each giving $100, that would total $8,000. "You're not going to get them all, Jack, but they ought to be part of the system." Now was the time for all good men and women to come to the aid of the party they believe in, conservative or otherwise.

Alberta Premier Peter Lougheed led a government with a social conscience, creating the Heritage Savings Trust Fund for the future. I chaired his Conservative party's fundraising in the south of the province.

Our campaign continued between elections. We decided to seek donations annually rather than every four years so there were more frequent contacts and better relationships with donors. Like the others on the committee, I'd approach contacts based outside Alberta, companies such as the Bank of Commerce and National Trust. I'd write personal letters and make the phone calls myself to set up the appointments rather than handing the job off to a secretary. Locally, we would invite cabinet ministers and top mandarins from the capital in Edmonton for breakfasts and lunches to brief and answer questions from business and professional people. Peter recalls, "The advice from the committee members was that 'You've got to put this government more in tune with Calgary.'"

As Al Libin says, "Entrepreneurs were slowed down by the bureaucracy and the red tape, but Peter's government was always very approachable and if they saw something that made sense, you could get them to understand it or listen to it. We worked on developing a rapport with the community over twelve months a year. . . . Peter never had to worry about fundraising; it was in good hands."

I stayed on as chair for five years. In the mid-Nineties, I tried to resign, but then-chairman Brian Felesky prevailed on me to continue on the committee as a link between younger and older members. I was happy to keep helping while the province was being handled ably, not simply focused on the concerns of business. In 1980, for instance, the government created the far-sighted Alberta Heritage Foundation of Medical Research with an endowment of $300 million and later set up one of Canada's first technology-transfer programs to help researchers and private industry take innovations from the lab to the marketplace. In future years, I'd become chairman of the Foundation, but meanwhile I led up to that position by learning more about the health-care field.

IT'S PROBABLY ALL AL LIBIN'S FAULT. HE HAD BEEN THE chair of the board of Calgary's Foothills Provincial Hospital (now Foothills Medical Centre). Opened in 1966, it was the continent's biggest complete hospital built all at one time, which evolved from an eight-hundred-bed community facility into southern Alberta's university hospital as a regional referral, teaching, and research centre.

The Libins were highly supportive of the hospital. He and his wife, Mona, had created a private foundation with funds that led to a gene therapy centre, the Libin Theatre, and numerous pieces of medical equipment. Al was then the Foothills chairman and asked me in the mid-1980s to go on the board. I turned him down because I was a director with NOVA and Conwest and involved in my own businesses, not to mention the Flames. I don't know where he studied English because he's never learned what the word "no" means. He kept after me and a couple of years later, I succumbed to join the Foothills Hospital board of management. I was among other friends, including Jack Major, Bud McCaig, community leader Shan Cross, and Lanny McDonald's mother-in-law, the indefatigable Lucille Moyer—a warm, solid woman from Medicine Hat—and later Gwyn Morgan and John Simpson, head of CANA Construction.

With a wife who'd graduated as a nurse—and my natural curiosity about new things—I was now a small part of the health-care sphere. The board dealt with the hospital president, Ralph Coombs, who was doing a great job. However, it took only a year before Al wanted to retire as chair after a decade as he began to head the board of the Heritage Foundation for Medical Research. Now he invited me to replace him.

"I'm enjoying it, quite frankly, learning a lot and meeting interesting, fine people," I said, "but I don't bring the background experience."

Al replied, "That's simply not an issue"—at least, not in his mind.

Taking the post, I had the fortune of working with Ralph's successor, Clarence Guenter, one of my favourite people. Of Mennonite background from Manitoba, Clarence graduated as an MD at the University of Manitoba and took advanced degrees in the U.S. At the University of Calgary, he was head of the department of medicine and as a lung specialist became president of both the Canadian and American Thoracic Societies. At Foothills, he was the CEO. What impressed me even more was his activity since 1981 as a consultant in international health projects in Chile, Mexico, Russia, China, Japan, Laos, Nepal, the Philippines, and Thailand. At the U of C, he became director of the International Health Exchange Programs through the 1990s.

His humanity shone through when he once addressed a graduating class of medical students in the Philippines: "Why are some people healthy and others are not? What we learn is that people who have a good economic life, like Japan, have much better health than the poor do in Laos. We also know that poverty has its effect on health even within the same country. My country, Canada, is similar to Japan. We have very good health but even in my country the poorest people die about twelve years younger than those with good incomes do."

Clarence is a supreme human being with a good judgment and fairness in dealing with people in the hectic hospital environment. And, luckily, our Foothills board was something like Conwest's in its sane, measured way of operating even when hard issues surfaced. We had the heads of the medical advisory committee, the medical staff, and the nursing advisory committee all sitting in on our board meetings. Not as members, but these top people knew everything that was going on in that hospital and were a vital conduit between us and the hospital.

As chairman over the next half-dozen years, I probably learned more than I had to about the Foothills operations. I did ninety or so tours the staff would arrange. I saw how the incinerator and the carpentry shop worked. I also saw a cataract operation, and open-heart and orthoscopic knee surgeries. Clarence took me on one tour to view the heart procedure. The surgeon was Dr. Teresa Kieser, who'd paused while the patient was right there with his chest cavity open. Through the operating-room window, we saw the beating heart.

Clarence said, "Well, do you really want to see this?"

"I don't think I can handle this."

"I think you can," he said, leading us into the room while Dr. Kieser awaited to consult another cardiologist.

Then I went to see the cataract technique with the head of ophthalmology, Dr. Merv Kirker, whose two brothers were geologists I knew. Merv was sitting there inserting an instrument to suck all that stuff out of the eye.

A welcome interruption to my speech at the opening of the Neonatal Unit at Foothills Hospital in 1995 is our granddaughter Rebecca—Jeff's daughter— wandering up to the front for her own photo opportunity.

Finally, the orthoscopic surgeon was operating on a fellow's knee while I watched that technique on a screen. All of a sudden, with the doctor manipulating the probe inside, I started to lose it. Clarence grabbed me by the arm and it took us fifteen minutes walking me up and down as I threatened to faint for the first time in my life. Later, I reflected and thought, *Why the hell could I survive viewing an open heart, but not this? Maybe it was that Flames players like Joe Nieuwendyk getting the same procedure on their knees must have made me identify too closely with people I knew.* The interesting thing is that while I was chairman, Joe himself became a public spokesman for the hospital.

Making those visits gave me a much better appreciation of what was going on, but also I hoped that meeting all those people might let them realize they had a board that was vitally interested in them and cared for their well-being.

In 1992, with our health-care system under pressure, I went with Clarence to Finland and Sweden, where we had exchanges with hospitals there, to learn more about their systems. Becky and Clarence's wife, Marie, accompanied us as we also went on to Russia, where—with his concern for international health standards—he was seeing what help Canadians could offer to a nation just coming out of communist rule. The medical system was generally inadequate and dramatically underfunded. In visiting hospitals, we met one woman doctor in Moscow who revealed the financial hardships her colleagues were suffering by the reduction in take-home pay to perhaps 10 per cent of what it had once been.

Back at home, we were facing serious financial cutbacks during the new administration of Premier Ralph Klein. In 1993, he won the election by promising to eliminate Alberta's $3.4 billion deficit by '96-'97. Cut, cut, cut. In July, he announced health-spending reductions of $64 million, over and above previously reported reductions of $127 million. It wasn't a fun time to be involved in the health arena. Yet despite the inevitable discontent and the possibility of many professionals leaving one of the province's two leading hospitals, it didn't happen that way. With Clarence's compassionate leadership and the quality of the board members we had, Foothills rode through the storm. To discuss Foothills' challenges with the government, I had a buddy there, Health Minister Shirley McClellan, and never abused that friendship.

We didn't waste any time on politics. The board was so much of one mind that I can't recall in my years as chair that we ever brought anything to a vote except the minutes and the agenda. If there was a difference of opinion, we spent a bit more care to rethink an issue—mostly about funding—and then solve it. We really maintained the spirit and the sense of caring that otherwise would have plummeted.

Meanwhile, there was a Foothills Hospital Foundation, for which volunteers raised money. Its board was too large and wasn't accomplishing as much as it should have. We reshaped it as a smaller, select board with Bud McCaig, my vice-chairman, as foundation chair and me as his vice-chair. There were a couple of annual events that were spectacularly successful, one of them turning out to be the biggest health-care lottery in Alberta. I was skeptical about it in the beginning, but the first, in 1993, offered houses and cars as prizes and generated $1 million in profit. The following year, there were more than two thousand prizes, including three spiffy houses and nineteen cars to make $2 million. The other event was the Foothills Country Auction—entertainment, champagne, and prime rib—where hundreds of big spenders came in cowboy duds to bid on items such as dinner at La Chaumière and seats at a Flames game. And it also got the hospital people actively organizing the auction and feeling proud of being part of it.

By 1995, the government had created new regional health authorities in the province and with Calgary's in place, a specific board for Foothills was no longer needed, nor was I as the chairman. I experienced some regret because of the loss of that band of sterling members who'd helped guide the hospital through those financially straitened times.

Dr. Clarence Guenter, the respected president of Foothills Hospital, presents me with a memento of my chairing the board after the hospital came under the Calgary health authority.

Not that I would stay unemployed for long in the health-care industry. Shortly after I signed the papers turning the hospital over to the Calgary health authority, I got invited to lunch in Bud McCaig's office. And who was there but Al Libin and Dick Haskayne and others to hear a pitch for launching a public health-care campaign in Calgary. I'd talked about that as Foothills chair, but the university had a big overall campaign that Becky and I had played a small part in, and the hospital didn't want to compete with its fundraising. Everyone agreed it was time to revitalize the health system—and, my friends said, "We think you're the guy to head it."

"Hey, wait a minute," I retorted. "I've just stepped down from Foothills. I've had a pretty full plate of this stuff."

"Well, it needs doing."

Later, I thought about the task, realizing I probably knew as well as, or better than, anyone what should happen. "But," I insisted, "Dick Haskayne's got to join me as co-chair and I'm going to need support from all of you." We set a goal of $50 million after the doctors at Foothills had got together with Dr. Eldon Smith, the dean of medicine, to survey the greatest needs. He could point out that the province was facing an exodus of valued specialists such as a colorectal surgeon, a heart surgeon, a pediatric oncologist, several pediatricians, and emergency-room specialists.

Collaborating with the health authority, we designed a huge campaign for Calgary, called Partners in Health. For the most part, our challenge was that locals were simply not used to helping maintain health care—they paid their taxes and keeping people well was the provincial government's role. My argument is simple: Do we rely on government in the oil and gas business, for example? There are areas where the private sector has a responsibility to step up as a catalyst by supporting things that otherwise wouldn't be done—such as leading-edge medical research. When I went to public school, we had scarlet fever, diphtheria, measles, chicken pox, and later polio. And we don't have them now because researchers found ways to deal with the conditions

It was a hard sell to kick off this campaign because of all the negativity behind the cutbacks in the health-care system—"You're asking us to go and provide more beds and so on." Which wasn't what we were trying to do. Dick was a huge help because of his contacts and reputation. I was the guy who pulled it together and went after those fundraisers on our committee who weren't doing what they said they'd do. I had the list of the people who'd worked on the university's campaign, analyzed it with its chairman, friend Jim Palmer, and asked his honest opinion about those who produced results and didn't. We also selected several medical people as key to broadcasting the message; Dean Smith went on calls with us to define the specific needs in light of the government cuts. The vice-chairs were Mona Libin and Jack MacLeod, the former CEO of Shell Canada, working with a group of about fifty volunteers, none of them professional fundraisers. I know that many have enthusiasm and believe in the cause, but unless somebody's bugging them, other matters take priority. So it always winds down to a tight core of people.

Even before the campaign became public, we had $15 million in the kitty, mostly from business leaders each contributing from $500,000 to $1 million and more. It ran for three years. As Bud McCaig said nearly a decade after the campaign began, "Partners in Health was all about raising funds to help advance a vision to create centres of excellence in areas of core strength and, towards that end, the $50 million [actually $54 million] that was raised has, since 1995, generated $265 million in additional funds."

The funding was aimed at research, treatment, and education in heart disease, stroke, trauma, joint injury and arthritis, cancer, and women's health. It would also create a knowledge network, buy health equipment, and support superior health research. Among other things, it attracted world-class researchers and clinicians to Alberta and brought state-of-the-art medical equipment to the province. The campaign's funding led to the first intraoperative magnetic resonance imaging centre in Canada, including upgrades to the iMRI system to make interoperative surgery safer by monitoring the operation, right in the operating room, to minimize trauma to the patient.

I called on Doc Seaman to describe our campaign. He listened carefully and said, "So how much do you need?" Doc and his brothers, B.J. and

Don, with their interest in engineering, got intrigued by the innovative project and funnelled their main Partners in Health contributions to the work of U of C's Dr. Garnette Sutherland, who developed it. They had supported the Seaman Family MR Research Centre and then the neurosurgeon's astonishing neuroArm—the world's first MRI-compatible surgical robot capable of both microsurgery and image-guided biopsy. (Interested too, I helped back it financially.) The system, the most complex robotic device ever developed, is controlled by a surgeon from a computer workstation in conjunction with intraoperative MRI. Liberating the doctor's hands, neuroArm can move in increments the width of a human-hair strand. In May 2008, a historic operation at Foothills Medical Centre removed a tumour from a young woman's brain. Like the iMRI system itself, the neuroArm is destined to revolutionize neurosurgery around the world.

As an intriguing sidelight, my involvement with an inventor named James Klassen has had some bearing on a neurosurgery challenge since posed by Garnette. In the early 1980s, I'd backed some inventions of his—including an improved design for a snowboard (he'd been a North American champion in snowboard racing)—but in the end, because of financial mismanagement by his partner I had lost all my investment. A couple of decades later, I heard from James, who was now living in British Columbia. Initially hesitant about him, I did decide that his fertile mind might be of interest in projects Garnette and Doc were pursuing.

The neurosurgeon explained that brain aneurysms are usually "clipped"—small clips are installed to isolate and cut off blood supply to the aneurysm and remove the hazard of rupture. But the clips are made of titanium, which is MRI-compatible but masks the detail that allows a surgeon to see if the clip has been properly placed. In a few weeks, James came up with ceramic clips that wouldn't conceal the MRI results. Garnette was intrigued—as was I.

James now had a business associate, David Boehm of Kelowna, who was helping him with other inventions, including development of new kinds of engines. I agreed to lend their Concept Solutions $400,000 at first to move along their priority projects and then converted half of that to equity in the company. I've since invested $2 million to fully develop the ceramic clip and a new, improved clip applicator and secure the patent on one of the engine inventions. The clip was successfully developed and a paper about its attributes was published by Garnette, James, and David in the May 2008 issue of *Operative Neurosurgery*, a leading journal. The clip has been presented to prospective manufacturers in Germany, Japan, and the U.S. and at this writing we are awaiting their responses. Among James's other inventions are a hand- or foot-powered water pump that one person can operate in underdeveloped countries and a submicron rotary arm for robotic surgery capable of finer accuracies than anything available.

My son-in-law Jamie Mackie, Brenda's husband, and my grandson Jeffrey Mackie later met James and David and joined me in supporting two more of their inventions. While one is a cold-cycle engine designed to operate on temperature differentials, the other has health ramifications. It's a power disk, which is a plastic device installed in the heel of a shoe to recapture energy from stepping down and produce more efficient walking.

IN 2000, AL LIBIN HAD BEEN CHAIRING THE ALBERTA Heritage Foundation for Medical Research for a decade while the provincial government's original $300-million endowment grew to exceed $1 billion. As Al said, "It gave us an ability to recruit some top-notch research talent to Alberta. So we brought in medical scientists who would never have been in the province had this simply not have happened. It gave us a great recruitment tool to bring in some leading stars of medical science and build a huge research initiative here."

Peter Lougheed recalls that the medical deans of the two major Alberta universities approached his government for support of medical research bankrolled by the province's enlightened Heritage Fund. "We were struggling with the question of applied research or basic research," Peter says. "It was a hard decision: that no, we wouldn't go into applied research even though it would show the people tangible results earlier." Equally important, he points out, "We wanted to have it independent of the government." When the nine original trustees of the Foundation for Medical Research gathered at a launch dinner, the premier stood up before they'd finished dessert and said, "I'm leaving. And I won't see you for nine years as a group. You're on your own."

The foundation could have been merely an arm of government, but by being created arms-length from its political masters has carved its own path as an outstanding Alberta success story. I was to discover the strength of its independence after Al asked me to consider succeeding him to become a trustee, with the hope I'd succeed him as chair. He badgered me to accept the post: "I'm not leaving you alone. You're going to love this job." I'd finished heading Partners in Health with its heaps of work and told Al I was sorry, but couldn't take it on. A couple of weeks later, I was having breakfast with Becky when we were discussing how I'd become friends with great people such as Clarence Guentner and Eldon Smith. "I turned Alvin down and I might have made a mistake."

Sir John Bell, Oxford University's Regius Professor of Medicine, is among the remarkable scientific advisors to the Alberta Heritage Foundation for Medical Research, which I chaired.

"Well," my wise wife said, "I think you may have."

I had a nice warm seat as a trustee for only about a year when Al recommended me as chair. And once more the foundation was an absolutely enriching experience as I worked with first Terry White and then Harvey Weingarten as presidents of the U of C and Rod Fraser and Indira Samarasekera at the University of Alberta. As well as admiring these wide-open, intelligent minds, I came to know a scientific advisory council of world-class doctors as consultants. Among them have been the medical deans at McGill, Harvard, and Duke University and Sir John Bell, the Regius Professor of Medicine at Oxford University (a title, originated by King Henry VIII, once held by Canada's Sir William Osler, known as the Father of Modern Medicine). Dr. Bell, a former Edmontonian Rhodes Scholar, has contributed major research to the understanding of type 1 and rheumatoid arthritis along with the molecular interactions associated with immune activation.

The foundation awards lengthy multimillion-dollar grants for teams in all walks of research to help solve priority health issues. The thousand or so applications are evaluated in exhaustive peer reviews. Each is graded on a point system by two of the scientific advisors. I was privileged to attend the sessions where they discussed whose work was to be recommended to the trustees. The research might involve a couple of University of Alberta molecular biologists developing a drug to minimize damage done to the heart during a heart attack or open-heart surgery when cells are starved for oxygen. Or it might fund the Alberta Prion Research Institute, a network of scientists to investigate infectious agents called prions that transmit disease in mad-cow and other chronic-wasting diseases. It was all over my head, but these brilliant advisors were invariably congenial people with a sense of fun and liked to relax afterwards with a glass of wine.

When not being a fascinated fly on the wall at these get-togethers, I collaborated with our trustees to make sure the research funding was secure. But partway through my six years as chairman, our endowment's investment well was starting to run drastically dry. Our fund was managed by Alberta Treasury, which put significant money into an index fund that included Nortel, the Canadian telecommunications-equipment manufacturer. Unfortunately, Nortel had been collapsing since 2000.

The generally acceptable guideline for endowment spending had been 5 per cent or less over the long term. Now our negative returns from the markets in 2002 and 2003 had shrunk our investments by close to a third from its high of $1.2 billion. The foundation was forced to cut back expenditures.

It was a time of belt-tightening in the province. With our president and CEO, the accomplished Dr. Matthew Spence, I decided to see Premier Ralph Klein to discuss an injection of funding that our trustees thought we should seek. Still behind the scenes on the Conservative finance committee, I had a cordial relationship with him though I was not a confidant. While waiting to see him in Calgary, Matt and I noted Mayor Dave Bronconnier looking unhappy leaving a meeting with the premier. To add to the problem, Ralph was dealing with a mad cow incident in Alberta that prompted nations to reject Canadian beef.

In a tough conversation about our investment, he said, "You've lost all this money."

Explaining that our endowment was managed by his own government and that the whole market had taken a downturn, I said the trustees were requesting $500 million. He wasn't encouraging. "Premier," I said, "we think we've got a strong record to support it, and I want to tell you up front that I'm going to present our case to the cabinet ministers. If you tell me not to do that, I won't."

"Well, you go ahead and do that. I don't like your chances much."

So I did, meeting with several ministers, among them Victor Doerksen, the minister of science and innovation. I knew him without having a close relationship and, as I saw him and others, sensed that the foundation was not going to win this battle. I decided to bring Gail Surkan on my last government visits in Edmonton. Capable, diligent, with a degree in economics, she was mayor of Red Deer, had served as chair for the Provincial Health Council to evaluate health reform and report to the legislature, and was a trustee, head of the audit committee, and would succeed me as chair of our foundation.

We met with my friend Shirley McClellan, then provincial treasurer and deputy premier, who carved out time for us one Friday afternoon when she wanted to be back on her farm for the weekend. Shirley listened carefully, told us she was very aware of the foundation's great record, and thanked us for coming to see her. And when we followed up to see Ralph (several months later this time), the environment was different, entirely friendly.

It wasn't long after that, in January 2005—the start of the province's centenary year—we got the requested $500-million boost over three years to bring the endowment fund to nearly $1.4 billion. When I retired at the end of 2006, we were now giving up to $80 million a year for research. Since its inception, the foundation has supported health research with more than a billion dollars. It was one of the smartest things Peter Lougheed did and wise for Ralph Klein and his government to support.

At a farewell dinner for me, the foundation announced it was giving $350,000—with a further $150,000 eligible if matched—in total $650,000 in my name for the Provincial Program on Perinatal Determinants of Brain and Mental Health. It would be led by Dr. Bryan Kolb at the University of Lethbridge to bring together lab and clinical researchers from the U of L and the universities of Calgary and Alberta to better understand how brain development is affected by experiences from the gestation stage to the newborn period.

One heck of a legacy.

A NAME I'D OFTEN HEARD DURING THE FOUNDATION'S scientific advisory committee sessions was that of Dr. Samuel Weiss. Sam, who earned his PhD at the University of Calgary, was always graded right at the top as a superb neurobiologist. In 1985, with Dr. Fritz Sladeczek, he'd discovered the metabotropic glutamate receptor, a major target for pharmaceutical research and development for neurological-disease therapies. Seven years later, he discovered neural stem cells in the brains of adult mammals, proving that these cells exist in all stages of development. The finding led to new approaches for brain-cell replacement—regrowing neural tissue in brains and spinal cords damaged by accident or disease. I obviously knew he had a very healthy brain himself and, as I'd learn, had plenty of people skills too. That was made clear the day he came to pitch me for the Brain Institute.

I had more than passing interest in the subject. Half a dozen years earlier, I was visiting my son John's Riverbend farm near St. Thomas, Ontario. One day after picking morels, I came back to have a big dinner of my favourite mushrooms and couldn't keep my balance and started feeling nauseated. The upshot of all this—going to the local hospital in an ambulance, going home to consult with a specialist in movement disorders—was that I finally had an MRI. Garnette (in the days before he was focused entirely on his iMRI project) sat me down and said, in his straightforward way, "Well, Harley, you have this aneurysm in the brain. It's small and we could operate on it and correct it. Our recommendation is to monitor it and if it stays the same, leave it alone." I have an MRI every year. My brother Ralph had an aneurysm in his abdomen that was operated on successfully, but another one found on his aorta couldn't be—and he died of it just before his eightieth birthday.

Becky and I had made our Partners in Health donation to the neurology department at Foothills; Unit 13 at the hospital bears our name. Though I told Sam Weiss this was an area close to me, I never told him the specifics until we had later conversations. Yet—after our hour and a half swapping stories about hockey—I was all ears as he told me about his plan for a new institute. Seeing a PowerPoint presentation on his computer. I had the general idea of a centre of excellence in both neuroscience and mental health, one that would prevent, detect, and treat disorders of both the brain and mind.

When I asked what he and his colleague, Dr. Greg Cairncross, wanted from me, Sam said, "Truthfully what we want, and would hope to have, is your endorsement of what it is that we're trying to do. And your ability to work together with us in the community and give them a sense that you believe that this is important. Quite frankly, with all due respect, this is worth a lot more than anything that you might wish to contribute personally."

We met a couple more times and, in the end, I was overwhelmed by the ambition of the institute. It would bring together all the region's brain-related programs into one co-operative organization while both focusing on research and delivering its benefits to pragmatic bedside care. There were ramifications for such afflictions as stroke, Parkinson's, and spinal-cord injuries as well as psychiatric conditions. Our family decided to fund the Brain Institute with an immediate $10 million and then a further $5 million plus smaller amounts, some deferred through insurance programs. It didn't take long for others to contribute another $25 million in cash and pledges made through an enormous new Calgary fundraising campaign called Reach! that had another family involvement (*see next chapter*).

In October 2004, we were honoured to be at the official launch of the Hotchkiss Brain Institute. Involved with it to this day, I'm on a strategic advisory board chaired by Dr. Fong, who has retired as head of the university's radiology department but remains a professor there as well as being senior strategic-planning advisor to the chief operating officer of the Calgary Health Region (the former Calgary Regional Health Authority). The board includes six medical leaders from the U of C and the health region and two other businessmen, Dick Haskayne and the dynamic young entrepreneur Ron Mathison. We asked Dr. Guenter, with his great reputation and medical knowledge, to be chairman in our initial years. He was succeeded by Dr. Fong. I'm chair of a large community and partners advisory committee; its members include Becky, our daughter, Brenda, and our son Jeff's wife,

Sam Weiss and I observe the work of Dr. Kenichiro Muraoka, a post-doctoral fellow from Japan, researching at the Brain Institute.

Sheryl Hotchkiss, along with such friends as Barbara Palmer, Lois Haskayne, Marilyn Milavsky, and Sharon Siebens.

Over the months, I heard Sam selling the concept of the institute to many potential donors. With his captivating energy, he's like a superstar on ice in his skill with stickhandling the complexities of the project into understandable layman's language. Here's a sampling as he met with people in the community:

"First and foremost in making the institute unique is in its focus on translating new knowledge into real-world application. While believing we have excellence in both those domains, we think the value-added is actually bridging the science and the medicine and trying to bring new thinking, new approaches, new resources towards application. From a business perspective, it's the research that develops the pipeline. So it's the pipeline of ideas to turn them into practice—so you actually have a bona fide product that can be delivered. And we talk about two-fold applications. One is clinical, so taking an idea, testing it first in, for example, animals and then testing it in humans in clinical trials to become implemented as new models of care.

"Remember, we don't control the care, we can only inform delivery of care, which is handled through the health regions and government, which have to balance the economics with the outcomes. But it's also translating the knowledge into technology development and the commercialization of knowledge which has significant spin-offs in terms of being able to develop products and services that are of interest to the scientific and biomedical communities—that in turn will develop additional fiscal resources that can be ploughed back into the science and medicine.

"Number two is bridging the solitudes of neurology and psychiatry. So neurological and mental health have classically been considered to be two separate worlds. It has often been thought that neurological problems are very tangible—in a stroke, you bore a hole in the plug, open up the blood flow. In Parkinson's disease, you give them more dopamine. But at the end of the day, it's the brain and its structure and function. There is no real difference in terms of the disconnect or over-connect that manifests itself as a neurological disorder. In one case, it's much more obvious. The other case is a little more subtle and a little harder for people to grasp, accept, and talk about.

"We are in the infancy of bridging neurological and mental health. We're among a growing group of thinkers who believe that the two areas are essentially founded on the same underlying pathology and etiology [the study of the cause], but further that they mutually inform one another—and that the separation is at our own peril. Not only that, but it turns out that in many of the neurological disorders, mental health is actually a major component. So it's known that in two examples, Parkinson's disease and multiple sclerosis, depression is a major co-morbidity, which means that the diseases intersect. And if you're able to treat the depression, you can dramatically improve the outcomes for the neurological. So even from a very pragmatic perspective, there's reasons to have the two being very closely aligned from a research, education, and clinical care. So that's number two."

The institute's third way of uniqueness is in its competitive advantage, Sam says. "Now, I'm going to argue that with neurological and mental health in general, the need is enormous. Even just in mental health right now, 51 per cent or more of all disability—*all* disability—is because of mental health and addictions. Greater than cancer, heart disease, all of the above, in disability, not mortality. Then you plunk neurological in there, and you're in the 60-per-cent plus. So what's our competitive advantage in Calgary? Three things: one major research-intensive university, essentially one hospital called the health region that has between one and two million patients (and experimental subjects, if you'd like). And we have one community that is very knowledgeable—white-collar, affluent, and proud.

"In the sub-set of the U of C, we have more than a hundred excellent physicians and scientists in neurological and mental health, together with an even larger constellation of social scientists, social workers who are interested in being a big part of what we're doing. And they're all willing to sing from one song sheet. We have a health region that doesn't look to anyone else but us for neurological and mental-health research and education. And we are ready to serve the community as an institute that responds and reflects some of the areas that are near and dear to this city— although its borders, of course, are the ends of the earth. So I think those three elements make this institute unique as far as other such initiatives elsewhere in the world."

Asked for a good example of encouraging work, Sam might mention the identification of the hormone prolactin as being a potential weapon in treating multiple sclerosis, which has double the rate of incidence in Alberta than anywhere else. As he describes the origins of this discovery, "This was an idea actually that came out of my lab because we had been interested for a while in understanding natural mechanisms of repair of the brain and seeing if we could identify what causes them and apply them where there's been an injury or disease. We had a first report a few years ago that pregnant women have remarkable changes in their bodies that are called regenerative repair mechanisms that occur as they prepare themselves for the challenges of raising their offspring. It's very well known that certain organs, like the pancreas and liver, are stimulated during pregnancy and produce new cells. So we actually had a major finding that made headlines about the fact that new brain-cell production also occurred during pregnancy."

Working with V. Wee Yong, the Canada Research Chair in Immunology and co-director of the institute's MS program, "we took that finding a step further, coupled with the observation that pregnant women who have MS often show improvement in their condition during pregnancy. So we've identified that prolactin, which is the hormone that makes milk, also makes new myelin, the coating on the nerve cells. Pregnant mice actually make more myelin and can repair an MS lesion spontaneously better than an age-matched mouse that's not pregnant. But if you take a mouse that's not pregnant and give it an MS-like lesion and then squirt prolactin into it, it repairs the lesion quite effectively.

"I'm the expert on making new brain cells and new proteins and Wee Yong is the expert in models of MS to bring the two together. We think we're several steps away to testing it in people. So this is an example of translating knowledge into practice."

It's an impressive, convincing pitch. The institute has been building on a quarter-century of outstanding neurological health-care delivery and neuroscience research. Now it has reformatted to focus the hundred-plus specialists into specific areas such as stroke, MS, spinal-cord injury, and Parkinson's disease, where a critical mass of excellence aims to bring the programs to international prominence. The institute spans four inter-connected buildings on the U of C campus and is affiliated with the Canadian Centre for Behavioural Neuroscience at the University of Lethbridge.

It's Sam who brought our family into this fabulous adventure. We've found it thrilling to witness the institute expanding and seeing the ongoing success of its founding director. In 2008, Dr. Samuel Weiss, the fifty-three-year-old hockey fan, received a Gairdner International Award from a Canadian foundation that recognizes and rewards the work of the world's leading scientists. It's one of the most prestigious honours in medical science—more than a quarter of the recipients have gone on to earn a Nobel Prize.

Despite his accolades, Sam remains at heart a salt-of-the-earth family guy. "Oh, it's my life," he'll tell you about his wife, Dorothy Kemp, and their teenaged daughter, Shoshana. "Her name means 'rose' in Hebrew. We wanted children forever and it just wasn't happening and then Shoshana came along and she's my shining light. And all I want is for her to be happy and healthy and my life will be complete.

"Not only do I consider my family important, I also consider other people's families important. When all else is said and done, the only thing left at the end of the day is your family. I mean, friends are great, but the truth is, the only place where you can let your hair down is with your family. And just say, 'We're sure lucky to be a family.'"

Becky and I know exactly what he means.

CHAPTER 11

FAMILY MATTERS

What's Most Important

W ELL, THE HOTCHKISSES HAVE SURE BEEN lucky to be our family. And on this particular warm June Friday in 2006, there was our only daughter, Brenda Mackie, looking a cool, comfortable, and important part in a ceremony on the campus of the University of Calgary. Becky and I watched happily as our second-born of five kids was speaking as a co-chair of the $300-million fundraising campaign Reach! This was the partnership between the university and what was then called the Calgary Health Region (since folded into a province-wide health-system superboard).

This time, the contribution to the campaign was coming from an old family friend, none other than Boone Pickens, seventy-eight and thriving. Up specially from his ranch in Texas, he was looking sunny and smiling in his yellow tie and summer suit. It was another example of the largesse that had recently earned him a reputation as one of the top five philanthropists in the U.S. "We are thrilled to have the support of Mr. Pickens for our initiative," Brenda was saying. "This is our first gift to the American Friends of the U of C for the Hotchkiss Brain Institute and we are honoured that Mr. Pickens chose to support the Calgary community in this way."

What made his generosity so personal for our family was that he was donating $2.25 million to the Hotchkiss Brain Institute. "I lived in Canada in the Sixties," he told two hundred people in his engaging drawl, "and before that, I met Harley in a business setting and we became friends from 1957 till

Our family aboard the fabulous *Phocea* on a 2006 Mediterranean cruise: (from bottom) Tracy, Paul, Becky, me, Brenda, Jamie, John, Jeff, Sheryl, Richard, and Patricia.

now, real close to fifty years. When he told me what he was doing with HBI, I told him I was interested. So we talked, and from there came the gift."

Boone later mentioned to me, with the audience listening hard, "You know, you won't be surprised if there's another gift."

When I chuckled and said, "Oh, okay," he replied, "As it progresses, all I'm saying is you keep me up to date and I'm going to get interested and I very well could make another gift to you."

The gift he'd already given was funding for the new Boone Pickens Centre for Neurological Science and Advanced Technologies at the campus Health Research Innovation Centre. A dedicated floor of the Brain Institute would bring together researchers in three areas, Sam Weiss announced. "The three are the neuroArm program, which is surgical neuro-robotics; the second is the movement-disorders and therapeutic brain-stimulation program, which uses brain pacemakers to treat Parkinson's disease; and the third is the neuro-connections program, which is aimed at developing new strategies for epilepsy and seizure disorders."

Two years later, in June 2008, the centre named for Boone was officially opened and he showed up again. This time, as we were eating dessert during a celebration luncheon, he asked me to read aloud a letter he'd written:

> It is my intention to make a testamentary gift of Twenty-Five Million Dollars ($25,000,000) to the American Friends of the University of Calgary (the "Foundation"). It is my expectation that the Foundation's Board of Trustees would consider the use of this gift to support the Hotchkiss Brain Institute, including the Boone Pickens Centre for Neurological Science and Advanced Technologies at the University of Calgary's Health Research Innovation Centre.
>
> I anticipate establishing this gift within my testamentary planning as soon as possible. I will confirm with you when the gift has been finalized in my testamentary instruments.

I was almost overcome at this bequest that was more than ten times his earlier donation. As Brenda said, it was "jaw-dropping." And since then, our family is finalizing details for a significant endowment to provide long-term stability and to help continue to attract world-calibre leaders to the institute for its various programs. Proud of what it has accomplished under Sam's leadership in four years, we're planning to commit an additional $35 million through a combination of cash, securities, insurance, and estate planning. This and $10 million from our previous donations will culminate in an ultimate endowment of $70 million before any matching or support

Our daughter Brenda Mackie is co-chair of the Reach! campaign as Boone Pickens donates one of his two major gifts to the Hotchkiss Brain Institute.

from others. This is the area where Becky and I and our children believe we can make the most difference.

At the time of Boone's first gift, our daughter had been outspoken in telling an interviewer: "There's been this core group of philanthropists in Calgary that have been really involved for quite a number of years and they're getting tired of doing it—and it is time for a new generation to step forward. We have so many successful people in this city that we're lucky to be here right now. And it's time that they took an active role in giving back to the community. It makes the city much more vibrant and more forward-thinking if we get the younger people involved."

THIS WAS A HAPPY COMBINATION OF CIRCUMSTANCES for Becky and me—to be with a beloved child and a long-time pal when both were contributing in such a meaningful way. Measuring life, I realize again and again the immense importance of nurturing family and friends. Especially how you've raised your offspring with the hope of creating a loving environment from their very first days.

In our nine-hundred-square-foot Altadore home, we started having children early, and Becky always treasured the little ones. It's a confession that I preferred to have them housebroken and when they could talk—so I was the one who had to mature during that time. Essentially, all the care and handling fell to her, the changing and washing of diapers, the nursing, the superb cooking, and making our dinnertime the focus of the embracing co-coon she shaped for our family. She's not only a wonderful but an intelligent mother and, now, a grandmother who takes our children's children out for birthday lunches and goes on exciting vacation trips with them when they turn sixteen. As our children still say, "Mom never slacks off." She has always been our glue.

Some of the kids say they can't recall Becky and me ever raising our voices with one another. She was the peacemaker in the family, the parent who did all the enthusiastic hugging—while as first-born Paul says, I was "the most even-handed person with respect to portioning out affections." With Becky in charge as the gentle, day-to-day disciplinarian, our boys remember me as the one who gave spanks on the bum. "There was always the threat of the Belt," Richard says, "and he executed it a few times, and that was enough." They remember my warning any miscreants that I'd have them shipped off to tough St. John's-Ravenscourt School in Winnipeg: "You're going to be running six miles in bare feet in the snow," they claim I said. Above all, I wanted them to be the decent, caring people they became.

Our house was always a home, particularly when the kids in their early and teenage years knew they could bring their friends to our place, to play ball hockey in the basement and stay on for supper. There were pets to play with, including the hamster that went down the drain, a rabbit that a neighbour's dog killed, and our own dog and a cat. Our Lakeview home (where we lived for eleven years before moving to Eagle Ridge in 1976) had five bedrooms upstairs and the roomy basement, which Brenda says was "a good place to go with my boyfriends." She tells the story of being down there in the dark with one boy watching the Alfred Hitchcock movie *The Birds*—when I, the family practical joker, started making weird bird noises that scared the heck out of them.

We had help later on from Lottie Hingley, who'd been born in 1900 and despite her age could cook and care for the children when we were away. Plump, with short, dark hair, and spectacles, she babysat most of the time when we lived in Glendale and then in Lakeview. Our youngest, Jeff, says, "Our endearing Lottie was an institution in our lives. She'd stay with us and I remember she took me to my first day of kindergarten. We had contact with her all through her life. She'd come by all the time for family dinners. She was part of our family until her death, when we hosted her many friends at a farewell reception.

"And mainly the older kids played tricks on her," he insists. "She'd

Our beloved Lottie Hingley, part of the extended family as caregiver to our kids—who were not above playing practical jokes on her.

be washing dishes and looking out the window when Paul—from his room above—would lower a chair down on a rope in front of the window." John says, "She went ballistic. Lottie was just a really kind, gracious, hard-working lady." Paul—admitting "we'd harass her; it was like guerilla warfare all the time"—describes her as "as nice old gal."

In our Glendale years, when money was still tight, I gave the kids haircuts with my Acme Home Haircut Kit, which I wasn't very good with. "We were just the regular mooks on the street, just like everyone else," Rich says now. "We'd know it was Haircut Day, usually on a Sunday, and would stay out and away as far as we could, but sooner or later had to get something to eat." When they'd complain, I might say, "Well, you've got a lumpy head; I can't work with that." Or so they say I did.

All of our sons played the usual sports, from football to baseball, from skiing to soccer, and sometimes specialized in golf, fishing, and flying. But, not surprisingly, there was always hockey. The only two I coached for a single season were John and Richard, who played for a team in Glendale Meadows. As Rich recalls for me now, "I was down in that community shack and for some reason I wanted to play goalie. I lay on the floor and you put my pads on." I wasn't his coach for the next couple of years when he kept playing goaltender: "I thought I was good and we were in the playoffs and I got shelled for thirteen goals. And that was the end of my goalie career."

Brenda had fun on her figure skates on the community rink and took swimming lessons, but unlike her brothers never competed as a teenager: "It's hard in a family with highly competitive, athletic people."

Today, Paul is married to Tracy and it's interesting to hear her describe our grown-up children from her vantage point. She believes "their personalities are so extremely diverse. But fundamentally, they're all very similar with respect to things like their morals." Paul himself says, "We've evolved on our own—different—but we're all the same in the fact that we're independent." All of them have confronted unsettling challenges through their lives so far, yet they've handled even the most serious of them with fortitude and the spirit to keep thriving whatever their situation.

IS IT ANY SURPRISE, WHEN BECKY AND I THINK OF OUR kids now, that their interests and attitudes seem so strikingly like ours? Two of them, Paul and John, now work with the land, living on farms as their mom and I did in our youth. Paul tried teaching, executive-placement, and had his own natural-gas trading firm before dreaming up a herb and produce operation outside Calgary, where I still unwind with my own small vegetable patch of peas, carrots, beets, and lettuce. John first started a company with two fellow forestry grads doing landscaping and reforestation in Alberta and later took over a tree nursery I had started in 1980 on a farm purchased three years earlier near my Ontario homestead. Whenever possible, I love visiting him there. Richard, an ardent pilot and owner of a corporate charter airline, is as analytical and focused as he says I am, and also dislikes managing people. Though Becky sees all our sons as affectionate, the outgoing Jeff may be the most similar to her in his gentleness and caring, more fixed on family than business yet involved in real estate with me and managing our Hotchkiss family real-estate holdings, appropriately called Haven. And Brenda had her own successful bookstore before she took on co-running the Reach! Campaign. As brother John says, "She's probably the second-classiest woman I know, and the first is my mom."

Brenda and Paul were the two biggest readers in our home and their brothers sometimes claim they were the smartest. "Paul is brilliant," Becky says. "He can talk to anybody." Brenda confirms that, while adding, "My older brother is like a lot of first-borns—used to being by themselves." As Paul admits, "I've never felt the necessity of close friends. I've just been busy within myself."

Brenda says Paul tolerated his younger sister; he admits never being close to the next two boys during those early years. As a little kid, he liked to roam on his own near the city limits of Altadore: "I would get up early in the morning before anybody else was up. I just played outside behind the Glenmore Dam a lot in the summertime. Mom had three other little monsters to look after by then and Dad was busy working. I would wander around and explore; it was fun." At thirteen, he spent a summer away from home on Becky's farmstead where her brother Don grew tobacco and Paul picked it as I did as a kid, with horses to haul the leaves on a tobacco boat.

Winters, he played hockey every day, shooting puck after puck the way I had on the farm, and worked his way up to AA, the second-highest level in the minors. Though short and stocky, he carried himself with assurance as a centre and didn't back down from fights in a game. "The one thing I don't like is that in order to fight properly, you have to get mad. And getting mad, you lose control. You always end up feeling worse regardless of who wins. I got so many stitches that it became less a game of skill and more a game of mayhem and bloodshed. And once we got playing reasonably serious hockey, you got let down by teammates who wouldn't go that extra bit, just be lazy, and it would frustrate me.

"So I started skiing. The nice thing about it is you do it on your own time. You're the drummer and the marching band." Rich recalls, "Maybe I was eleven and he was sixteen, I love to ski and so did he. He'd go up to the mountains with his buddies and I'd tag along with him. Those are great memories for me being with all these older guys. Paul was probably one of the best skiers I've ever seen: he was a flamboyant skier and had these wild hats. After a while, he got tired of the crowd and he just stopped skiing."

Paul went to the University of Calgary to focus on history, a subject he enjoyed reading. But after considering courses that would lead to becoming a lawyer, he realized "it was absolutely at right angles to any talent I have. It was just a bloody disaster." He took a year off to ski and then attended the University of Alberta, putting himself through with summer work in Fort McMurray, helping install the underground power system for the oil-sands town and some months making $10,000. In Edmonton, he lived in residence with brother John and then together in a condo that Becky and I had got for them, where Richard later stayed. "I never saw much of Paul," John says. "He was a pretty popular guy with the girls."

Paul took an honours BSc in zoology, "which was a wonderful experience; I loved it." Once on a trip when Becky was pregnant with Jeff, the family tented across Idaho, Washington, and Vancouver Island, where nine-year-old Paul would drive his mom crazy collecting all the crawly critters, the snakes and sea slugs. As it would turn out, his interest in science continues in his fascination for experimenting on herbs and produce.

There'd be some side trips first. After zoology, he worked briefly for John's small reforestation company before deciding to become a teacher. He returned to the U of C for a year and a half to get an education diploma and do a practicum (while winding up in hospital for a couple of months with viral pneumonia). In his late twenties, he taught science at a high school, where he liked the students but was shocked at their level of learning. After failing 158 of 168 in his second semester, which caused a certain concern among the parents, he found many more kids working hard to pass the next time. It was there he met a young teacher's aide who became his girlfriend. The principal asked him to transfer to another school. Paul didn't and stopped teaching, being particularly unhappy with the mere $15,000 a year he was earning.

In 1980, he joined a friend's headhunting firm and began hiring executive talent in Calgary. His first month, he earned more than he had in a year's teaching. But then the National Energy Program froze the Oil Patch. Half a year later, when he'd bought out his friend's partner, Paul faced "an unbelievably brutal three years."

In 1985, a bright spot in his life was meeting Tracy, an investor-relations manager in a public company. They married in '86. He calls her "a very forthright, take-the-bull-by-the-horns sort of person—she brings organization to this relationship and is task-oriented and much more realistic than me."

Meanwhile, he became interested with another friend in the buying and selling of natural gas while the continent was moving to a deregulated industry. Brenda's husband, Jamie Mackie, was with Canadian Hunter Exploration and asked him to study deregulation for that Calgary petroleum company on a month-to-month basis. The contract was enough to convince Paul to do similar work for a half-dozen other companies. Within a few months, Jamie called to suggest teaming up with a self-assured fellow who'd been working in the gas sector for Noranda (Canadian Hunter's parent). Paul hired John Klarer to help create Tarpon Gas Marketing in 1987.

After a slow start, Tarpon managed to buy gas in Texas from Mesa Petroleum, Boone Pickens' company (with no input from me), and sold it to Wisconsin Power. "We never looked back," Paul says of those prosperous years. They'd take the risk of committing for a source of gas over here at, say, $1.50 a thousand cubic feet and arranging all the transportation to sell it successfully over there for $1.80. When John Klarer left, Jeff stepped in and the oldest and youngest brothers became close to one another. Over the next several years, Jeff handled the nuts and bolts of business: to keep track of the records, doing spreadsheets, monitoring the prices. At one happy point, rather than just operating on an immediate buy/sell basis, Tarpon ended up locating some firm space in Michigan to store gas, which it could parcel out at opportune times in the market. That's when I primarily came in financially, providing the equivalent of what Paul describes as "deep collateral."

They'd pushed the company up to almost $100 million a year in sales. As Jeff says, "It's fair to say that Paul had more of a stomach for risk. It felt like a crapshoot to me." But near the end of its nine years in business, Tarpon faced the bitter reality of increasingly nervous gas markets in late 1996. Its accountants had given them a clean bill of health, with a net of about $2 million after paying everything. Yet suddenly Tarpon couldn't make deals with anybody to buy gas to fulfill contracts. "The clouds of doom were over us. There was something strange going on behind the scenes," Paul remembers. What happened was that large corporations with substantial worth could afford to take massive risks and, in that world, Tarpon's only hope would have been aligning itself with access to much higher credit to keep operating.

It all came tumbling down as three other local gas-marketing companies failed at the same time as Tarpon. In fact, though protected from creditors, I left $500,000 of my priority position in the company as it was forced into receivership. Paul says, "It really helped us save face, but we both took a huge whack." It was a mighty blow for him and for us. But I know he'd worked hard and had been pretty good at the marketing before the crash.

He had some stock investments to carry him while he and Tracy recovered. Fortunately, they had a nice little ace in their sleeve. Back in '86, Paul had been hungry for the nice tomatoes in a BLT sandwich he ate on holiday in Florida. So he started raising them in his own backyard to replace the tasteless supermarket products. I sold them 10 of 160 acres we owned southeast of Calgary where they built a house and, with the same love of growing as I have, set up a modest greenhouse. (I started raising tomatoes, sweet corn, and cucumbers in there, a real treat to visit on cold winter days, and today continue gardening at Paul's place indoors and out.) With a couple of employees, it grew into a small business that supplied vegetables to specialty grocery stores. They had decided not to take me up on my offer to have them move to my family's original stamping grounds in southwest Ontario and oversee a tree nursery on land I'd bought in 1977. After Tarpon folded, the intrepid couple decided to get seriously into organic gardening in the Rocky View area. This was the birth of Hotchkiss Herbs and Produce with several greenhouses, heated with hot water, on a little more than an acre. Together we farm on the remaining 150 acres, where we share costs while Paul does all the work.

He was specially intrigued with the science of raising fussy heirloom

Paul in a greenhouse at Hotchkiss Herbs and Produce, which focuses on upscale restaurants and niche-type grocery stores.

tomatoes, the kind once valued for their flavours before large-scale industrialization arrived in agriculture. From scratch—with no previous study of horticulture—he learned how to deal with all the tricky testing of more than a hundred different varieties, now a core of about twenty that can be susceptible to diseases such as corky root rot, leaf moulds, powdery mildew, and tobacco mosaic. Over a season, that last condition has wiped out a crop in a greenhouse that can produce a peak of nearly five thousand pounds of tomatoes a week.

Working in the real world, rather than experimenting in petri dishes, Paul has since been developing the grafting of a resistant bottom of a hybrid plant with a non-resistant top. Essentially, he was crossbreeding the stabilized hybrids to produce his own discoveries in heirloom tomatoes. "I had a scientist come from the research institute in Brooks, where the government maintains a significant facility, and he was just amazed because they've been working on this for years without any success." With other vegetables grown in outdoor fields and within greenhouses spreading across an acre, Paul and Tracy have confronted more challenges. Among them, they've had to recoup after big hailstones that flatten spinach plants and tiny flea beetles that ruin the appearance of arugula.

Despite all these setbacks, their operation has grown and become renowned in Alberta and elsewhere. The *Brantford Expositor* in southern Ontario has raved: "Hotchkiss' tomatoes burst with real tomato flavour—mild lemon-coloured fruit, citrusy green tomatoes, deep purple and sweet red varieties that take you back to the summer garden." They bear names such as Prudence Purple, Green Zebra, and Dad's Sunset. The Hotchkiss Tomato is mentioned routinely in the media, served in fine restaurants, sold by carriage-trade grocers, and prized by the select flock of customers who get home delivery of their vegetables in the Calgary area. With greenhouse manager Lindsay Boothman and a seasonal group of Mexican workers, they grow a smorgasbord including basil and other micro-greens, broccoli, carrots, celery, Mediterranean cucumbers, and pole beans. ("A restaurant chef

Paul with Tracy—who handles everything from sales to marketing, picking to packing—and their vivacious eight-year-old daughter, Olivia.

called us to say his customers think these are the best beans they've ever had," Paul brags.)

Tracy handles the marketing and sales, deals with the paperwork, even helps out with picking and packing. All this while she's caring for the home they had designed—5,500 square feet on the main floor, with an enormous rundle-stone fireplace—and, most of all, being mother of their beloved daughter, our granddaughter, Olivia. Brought home in an open adoption when she was two days old, she's now (her mom says) "an eight-going-on-eighteen-year-old." She has her own horse, Angelina Ballerina, and takes riding lessons, is thrilled to do hip-hop dancing, and wants to be a movie or rock star—but she also loves reading and even spelling in school.

OUR DAUGHTER, BRENDA, WAS BORN PREMATURE AND only a slight handful, but—as it turned out—she had her big brother's braininess in that little head. It was a good quality to have in what would be a home of four boys to one girl. "A very clever girl," Becky points out.

Brenda reminisces: "I was very close with my brother John. Moving into our house in Glendale Meadows, I was four or five and we'd ride our trikes around the cement basement and were always outside playing on a street with a hundred kids. I remember Jeff being born and I was disappointed that he was a boy. But also taking on quite a bit of responsibility for him too, walking him around the street in his buggy. . . . In the house, there was a real division, I felt. We had this little motto that boys did the outside work and girls did the inside work. So I did the dishes and babysat while they'd cut the grass and shovel the walk.

"In elementary school, they had the acceleration program and you could do your first three years in two years. So I ended up in grade three being in the same grade as my older brother, but we never were in the same class. When I was at the end of grade seven, we moved into Lakeview and I went into an honours program at Viscount Bennett, a different school than my brothers."

As Becky says, "Going into junior high school, they put her into an advanced program and she was with girls who might be a couple of years older. She didn't study up to her capacity."

Brenda agrees: "I had a bit of a rocky grade eleven; it didn't go very well. I didn't go to school much and I was with a lot of friends, some of them a little sketchy. I was easily influenced. You look back and you think how much of that was just seeking attention that I didn't feel I was getting. I mean, who knows? You're a teenager as well and the only girl in the house and 'Maybe this will get someone to notice me or nobody will care if I do this anyway'—and all that sort of thing that teenagers think."

Richard says that, like her brothers, "Brenda used to push some of the envelope too. She and Mom used to get at it. Probably the same as every other girl, but she was Mom's only girl. We were cut quite a bit of slack because we were boys—and there's a double standard there."

Becky and I decided that it might be the appropriate time for our daughter to take her final year, grade twelve, at Balmoral Hall, a private girls' school in Winnipeg with high educational standards. Nestled on a bend of the Assiniboine River, it has had a distinguished history dating to the original school in 1901. Now, in the Sixties, most of the teachers were female and the students wore a standard green uniform of matching blazers, skirts, and socks. They didn't have to put on makeup at school for any boys giving them the eye. The expectation was that they got to class on time, had their homework assignments done, and talked to the other girls with respect.

"It was good for me," Brenda says. "First of all, I got away from that bad influence. Second, I had never lived with girls before. And all of a sudden it was like going to camp—it was so much fun. I don't remember before ever really talking with my brothers and then I get to this school where there's girl talk all the time. It gave lots of positive things to me."

"And," Becky says, "her marks were university level." She came home to take her first year of social sciences at the University of Calgary and then took a year off to work at my second employer in town, the Commerce. She enjoyed being a teller—"that sort of making sense of things, at the end of the day everything has to to add up, and I like that kind of order."

She decided to attend the University of Western Ontario to finish her degree. From past summers, she had warm memories of her visits to our traditional turf in the province, where she spent time with grandmas Hotchkiss and Boyd, her uncles Ralph and Blake, and plenty of cousins about. She took English, history, sociology, and even did a geology course—"and thought this isn't really me." One of the surprises for me now is that this personable woman admits: "I never ever took a class where I would have to speak. If I found out I had to do a presentation, I just dropped the class." A strange thing, seeing how well she handles herself today.

With a boyfriend in London, she stayed there and worked for Canada Trust, where she did some document writing. The job was "very boring, but it paid my rent. And then our relationship broke up in a very bad way, so I came back home. And then I met Jamie and we got married immediately."

Well, not right away, Becky insisted. "They waltzed into my kitchen one day, her eyes were just luminous and the size of saucers—I knew something was brewing. When they wanted to just go and get married, I said, 'You're my only girl. I want you to have a nice wedding.' They condescended to wait."

Brenda had met Jamie Mackie working at the Commerce—for one week, before he went off to do some better-paid labouring work. His girlfriend's father was a banker I knew and had got him a position, the way the dad had also found a job for Brenda. After that brief encounter, they didn't see each other while she studied in Ontario. When she returned in 1975, the banker mentioned to us that Jamie was home before doing his master's of science in resource management at Yale and had broken up with a girlfriend. Jamie came from an old Calgary family, his grandfather a mayor in 1901 and the developer of the Mackie Block (since torn down on 8th Street West) and the Lancaster building (still standing downtown).

"And so he called me," Brenda says. "His parents had a cabin out at Bragg Creek. I drove out there for the annual parade day and barn dance with a mutual friend. We just parked by the lake and here's this guy with curly hair and this tan and this big smile. He comes up and hugs me and it just felt like we'd been together forever. Which sounds so hokey."

After marrying, they both returned to New Haven to continue his master's while Brenda clerked in Yale's graduate office. Jamie went on to do environmental work for Dome Petroleum up north, then served on both the

Brenda and Jamie's family on a mountain holiday: (from left) a guide, Brenda, daughters-in-law Vanessa Mackie and Riva Mackie (standing), son Jeffrey, daughter Emily Radtke, Jamie, son Andrew, and son-in-law Patrick Radtke.

technical and commercial sides for Suncor, Hudson's Bay Oil and Gas, and finally Canadian Hunter. Moving on to the financial industry, he became an investment banker and founder of Wilson Mackie & Company with a friend, a founding partner and finance director of First Energy Capital, an investment advisor with National Bank Financial, and then chairman of his own J.F. Mackie & Company, an independent equity investment venture.

Coming home from Yale, Brenda had been pregnant with the first of their three, Andrew, Jeffrey, and Emily. A classic mom, she cared for them through their teenage years as they developed into the accomplished young people they are. The oldest, their free spirit, is Andrew, with two master's degrees—in architecture from Yale and fine arts from Cranbrook Academy of Art in Michigan. He and his wife, Riva, who has a degree in marketing, have opened an eco-oriented store in Calgary called Riva's, which sells everything from baby clothes to building supplies. Jeffrey was focused on definite goals, working for Suncor in the summer after getting his mechanical-engineering degree from Queen's University and then his master's from the University of Toronto. He now works for Jamie's firm as a broker. He married Vanessa and they have Dora and baby son Peter.

Emily studied engineering at Queen's University, where she met

Patrick Radtke. After three years, she moved to New York to pursue her dream of going to cooking school. Patrick followed her there and completed a master's degree in computer engineering at Columbia University while she worked in various restaurants and helped open a vegetarian café with a friend. In 2007, they moved back to Calgary. Patrick works in the oil industry and Emily enjoyed providing wonderful desserts for numerous clients until the birth of their son, Owen James, in August 2008.

As the kids were blossoming, Brenda—with her lifelong love of books—decided to bloom too and study library science at the Southern Alberta Institute of Technology. "And it was a remarkable experience in many ways," as she'll tell you. "My kids were all older and we were in this social circle, my husband with this investment firm, and we had all these entrepreneurial, successful, dynamic people around us. But at SAIT, nobody knew who I was. Nobody knew my father was an owner of the Flames. And I could be whoever I wanted to be. I never really thought of myself as being a smart person before.

"I met this fellow Mike Hare, who'd thought of being a librarian. I quickly realized I didn't want to ever sit and catalogue, but there was a whole section on children's literature, for instance, and I loved that. Mike and I would have coffee and say wouldn't it be fun to own a bookstore sometime? And he started working at a library and then at the Owl's Nest, the bookstore run by Evelyn de Mille. It was tiny and she had no computer or cash register." Now it was up for sale. "Everybody thought Mike and I were crazy to buy it in January 1996." Brenda quit her library course to become an entrepreneur.

The former owner had always stressed "good service, pleasant service" in a community setting, an atmosphere the equal partners maintained in the 450-square-foot bookshop on Bow Trail. Brenda and Mike, a former Eaton's retail manager, quickly realized they'd get more foot traffic at the relaxed mix of retail at Britannia Plaza, just off busy Elbow Drive. The clientele in the new location were mostly upscale women in the surrounding neighbourhoods. As the *Calgary Herald* has written of the transplanted shop, "its personal approach to selling books has been a hugely successful venture in an age of the proliferation of big bookstores." As Becky notes (and I agree), "Brenda came into her own with the Owl's Nest."

They computerized the store while Brenda preferred to work in the back on the business side. "I liked the ordering, opening up the boxes with all the new books and their smell—and when I was so excited about a book, I loved telling someone about it too. We had literary fiction, science fiction, romance, everything. Local book clubs bought from us. We hosted a mystery book club and stocked a big mystery section. We had authors doing signings then. After about six years, the space beside us became empty and we opened the wall to the Owl's Nest and it's now a children's store called Owlets. We never made a zillion dollars, but we more than broke even, which was a big deal in a little independent bookstore."

By 2004, after eight years there, Brenda had reached fifty—"a good time for something else, which I had no idea what that was. I was not working, I'd taken a year and travelled a lot and went to the gym and cooked and did a renovation on our house, all those things that I hadn't really had time to do. Still thought, *Okay, something's missing here.*"

Then in early 2005, she had a phone call from Bill Sembo, vice-chairman of RBC Capital Markets in Calgary. He said they were looking for a third person, a woman involved in the community, to help head the Reach! campaign being launched in the fall. He was a co-chair with Ken King of our Flames. In her meeting with them, she said, "I can't do this. This is not me, I'm not my dad." She felt they were looking for someone with more public profile than she had and more comfortable with public speaking. In followup meetings, Jack Davis, president and CEO of the health region, and his colleague Deborah Apps urged her to think of the greater good of the goal.

She and I talked about her decision. "It's a really big job," she remembers me saying, "and I don't know if that's what you should be doing." But, as she considered the possibility seriously and expressed her fears of fundraising, I said, "If you think you have to do cold calls, that won't happen. You will have lots of support."

Reflecting now, she says, "There was just something that kept saying 'You know, maybe this is me. Maybe there's a reason that I'm not totally saying no, why I keep talking to people about it. Maybe I kind of believe that things come to you when you're open to them. It's a huge, huge challenge for me and I can probably learn a lot doing it. And I'm interested in the medical side.'"

Brenda is doing all that now, as she did while speaking at the ceremony for the Boone Pickens Centre for Neurological Science and Advanced Technologies. "It was kind of scary, but I didn't feel nervous at all. It just felt really comfortable and natural for me." A very clever woman.

BECKY AND I HAVE THOUGHT OF OUR SON JOHN AS A Steady Eddie, a conservative family guy, as we thought he'd always be. He came from a long line of relatives who bore his plain-spoken name. It was handed down from a great-grandfather, a grandfather, and my brother Jack.

Our third-born had a sweet temper in his childhood. "I don't remember giving my parents too many hard times," he says. "Brenda and I were pretty close for a long time and then Richard and I were when he started catching up and playing sports." That's only when John's temper could flare. They played Kick the Can, road hockey with a tennis ball, occasionally even with me and other dads, and the two of them battling with friends in basement hockey—"till we were sweating and tired in some pretty mean games down there, never coming to blows, but pretty close."

"As a hockey player," Rich says of John's time on community teams, "he was very tough, had a great shot, and was a good scrapper. We ended up on the same team a couple of times and he was a force out there." Becky harks back to John in the midgets league: "He came home with a broken nose and a black eye, and I said, 'That's it, no more hockey.'" After a rival had slashed him in the face, he was off skates (for only a while) because there was no bone left in the bridge and then had to have another operation to open the nasal passages and get eight stitches in his eyebrow.

John was the only one of the boys who played much baseball, as a good catcher, into his mid-teens. In high-school football, he considered himself an average halfback: "I was only 150 pounds, but I was pretty quick, and on the track team. One time I was covering a punt return and there was the leading running back of the league when the coach said, 'Hotchkiss, your job is to make sure he doesn't get around you on the end.' He's coming my way, then cuts back the other way around the outside of me, so I just dove in front of his legs—and I'm telling you it was like being hit by a locomotive. My helmet went into the ground, my face mask busted right off. The whole thing was just full of mud, but I got up and remember hearing the coach saying, 'Good job, Hotchkiss, good job.'"

As well as playing soccer, he pursued the more gentle game of golf with Jeff and also with Becky, sometimes after school for a couple of hours. With her classy textbook swing, "she was a good athlete," he says. But hockey loomed as the important sport with him and the other boys, including the ritual of Hockey Night in Canada. "Every Saturday night in front of that TV in the living-room in Glendale with a big yellow bowl of popcorn (I think Mom still has that bowl). Because of Bobby Hull, I was a huge Chicago Blackhawks fan." He and I went every weekend to see the Calgary Centennials junior team in the Corral.

Graduating from high school, he spent a year, deep in the mid-winter, surveying wellsites in northern Alberta "and actually had a heck of a lot of fun." He enrolled in science at the U of A, specializing briefly in pre-dentistry until he met friends taking forestry and joined them in the program.

Other buddies in residence, where he shared a room with Paul, hailed from Sudbury and John can still sing the tobacco-picking lyrics in Stompin' Tom's "Tillsonburg." Surviving eighteen months there—"it was Party Central, and there's no way you could study"—he rented a house until moving into the family condo with Paul. And inspired by Richard, who had his private pilot's licence, John got his too.

During the summers, he'd worked only in heavy construction in Calgary. Now, with forestry degree in hand, he launched a venture with a couple of fellow grads and one of their brothers. Borrowing some money from us to buy a truck, they did reforestation for the Alberta government and timber companies and landscaping for the Lesser Slave Provincial Park. But the future in the business seemed unpromising. In 1978, two major events happened: he married Joan Medhurst from Medicine Hat, whom he'd met on holiday in Hawaii. When they moved to Red Deer, she became a kindergarten teacher and he began training for his commercial pilot's licence, as Rich had done.

The evening he rethought his future, I called him and asked, "What are you doing with your life?"

"Well, I'm going to be a pilot."

"A pilot is just a glorified bus driver," I replied—well before Rich set up his own charter aircraft company, of course.

As John explains today, "I wasn't very happy that night, but sort of changed my mind then." He agreed to go to Edmonton for an interview with my old company, Canadian Superior, and found a job on the drilling engineering side in 1980.

"The young guys who were engineers taught me a lot," he says about his six years there, "but then Mobil bought the company and moved the office to this stupid high-rise building in Calgary and I went from wearing a golf shirt and khakis to a suit and tie every day. They'd just moved us down, we bought a house, and I wasn't there for probably more than two months when big rumours were flying around Mobil that there's three thousand people about to get cut here. I get the knock on the door and the guy says, 'We don't need you.' But that wasn't that bad a thing. I was in the tiniest lime-green office and you had security cards to get into the bathroom so they knew where you were every second. You know, I don't even know if I had a position there."

With few roots holding him down in 1986, it took only two months for John to transplant himself, Joan, and their son Steve and daughter Katie—a twenty-minute drive from my old family fields in Ontario. That move was my doing, if anybody's. Originally, I had asked Paul to consider taking over the nursery that had grown out of the derelict tobacco farm I acquired in 1977 on the opposite side of Bayham Township, west of the Hotchkiss homestead. There were 287 acres of fields, wood lots, and several small streams flowing down to the Big Otter Creek. A year later, I bought an adjoining 100 acres to fill out a large bend in the Otter with more than two miles of continuous river frontage. The land was running with raccoons, rabbits, skunks, white-tail deer, and later wild turkeys. It turned out some of the property had been in the historic Talbot Settlement land grant once held by Colonel Thomas Talbot. My amateur historian's antennae went up when I read about this autocratic old bugger. An Irish soldier, he became private secretary in the 1790s to Upper Canada's lieutenant-governor, John Graves Simcoe.

Our improved acreage was now being run by a superb propagator named Murray Alward on what became Riverbend Farms, named for the Big Otter wrapping around the place. But, enticing as it might be, Paul decided to stay in Alberta. John, however, saw the operation and responded well when I asked if he'd like to be part of it. I would offer him just half the salary he'd been earning at Mobil.

"It clicked," he says now. "It made a lot of sense. I love the outdoors and I love plants and I love to garden." It was usually John who in his youth got the urge in spring to get things growing in the rear corner of my backyard garden in our Lakeview house and help me with the weeding and hoeing.

When he, Joan, and the kids arrived at Riverbend, there was only the first farm with two dozen greenhouses and a home built for Murray and his wife, Karen (who can whip up a fine mess of Lake Erie perch when we visit). Murray had been working for the McConnell family's big nursery locally when it ran into financial trouble and he was laid off. I talked him into working for me. As John says, "He'd started propagating a line of basic bread-and-butter varieties like junipers, little globe cedars, a few giant cedars, fruit trees, and Murray had customers who'd once bought from McConnell's."

We soon bought a second 106 acres in Malahide Township and a nearly new home next to this farm where John and his family lived, and a couple of years later we added another adjoining forty-six acres, which became the farm-business base with a new office, workshop, and equipment storage. "Murray was in charge, running the farm and I was on the digging gang: 'You go dig this, and this needs to be trimmed. . . .' And it was wonderful, to think back, just to do what you were told and at the end of the day, the time was yours. Then gradually this farm was growing and we started to be more business-like, planned and with budgets. I was keeping track of the inventory in the field, keeping track of the orders, all on a great big spreadsheet by hand when we didn't have computers here."

Eventually, with my further investments to finance more buildings and other capital expenditures, John and I struck a deal about eight years ago. Sitting on his veranda, I said, "It's time for me to move on. This is yours, do what you like with it. I'll still be supportive and interested. You build you own future here."

I kept holding preferred shares while John received all the common shares. He had some EnCana stock to invest and we have an agreement to have him repay the shareholder's loans as he can. As he says, "I got more serious a couple of years after I actually took over the farm. We've increased a lot of the production. You can see our sales going up, but our biggest problem has been our costs go right up too. We've got the nicest product; I honestly believe that because I see what other people are selling. There's just nothing better than what you see out here and it's a real challenge to get it this way." During John's tenure, the Aylmer Rotary Club in Elgin County has given Riverbend the annual award as Farmer of the Year.

Today, his nursery has three farms (an additional 186 acres acquired in 2003) and six houses, three barns, and 140 greenhouses on more than 780 acres. His right hand is Murray, who remains one of the best propagators in the business: "I just can't resist," he says. "I got everything going from soup to nuts." An interesting offshoot of his work is helping the Canadian Chestnut Council's research in restoring chestnut tree attacked by a virulent blight. Fond of the grand American chestnuts that used to grow on our family farm, I am a member of the Chestnut Foundation and donated some Riverbend land for the project. Murray, a member of the foundation's board, sprays and prunes the trees it's testing on the property.

Meanwhile, Murray and our son get along well: "John's a great guy and he works his butt off." Their main lines are flowering shrubs, such as spierias and hydrangeas, and ornamental evergreens, including cedars, junipers, yews—and much too much boxwood. "We went from growing 4,000 total units to over 30,000 a year," John points out, "and boxwood is a slow-growing plant so it's out in the field for six or seven years. That ties up a lot of land. Our biggest mistake has been maybe growing too much. We could actually keep things looking good, but we've got so much stuff out there.

"Even if it was all in perfect shape and nicely spaced—and even if it was all sold—we'd have a big problem. Because we just can't physically handle it; we can't get it out of the ground. We've got a constricted time zone here. In the fall, we have limited space. We don't store outside because it wouldn't survive. So we dig as much as we can in the fall, fill the green-

John at Riverbend Farms, growing flowering shrubs and ornamental evergreens on land not far from my boyhood farm in southwestern Ontario.

houses as tight as we can get them, and then in the springtime we've got just about five weeks of mass pandemonium to get everything done—digging, potting, and shipping."

Like Paul, he admits: "I know farmers are all the same—they all have their challenges with weather and stuff like that. And so do we, but we're a little bit different because we grow so many different things. Then there's the trimming, the fertilizing. You've got the insects and diseases and stock that all have to be sprayed and you're always depending on the weather. You can't spray if it's too dry, too wet and too windy, you can't spray if there's rain coming—all these day-to-day production things. And managing people is a real challenge."

Riverbend has about thirty-four men and women working the nursery, including Murray and Karen and three others full-time. In the past, John hired mostly the local German Mennonites, who'd moved to the area from Mexico, but (as his brother Paul does in Alberta) now brings in a dozen Mexican labourers between April and November.

Despite the problems, John believes Riverbend is at the point of becoming truly profitable. They use three salesmen agents who represent them with retail accounts in Ontario, Quebec, and Michigan, and John handles New York. "It wouldn't take much more in sales, 10 to 15 per cent to put us where we want to be. We're that close." The nursery has the potential to

John and Joan's daughter Katie weds Dave Shortreed in summery Victoria, with her brothers Steve and Matty and sister Allison—along with a couple of proud grandparents.

be a substantial business. It just needs to move up a notch. As Murray likes to remind me, with a chuckle, I once told him, "This is a good operation for patient capital."

John's own personal concern these days is that his family are no longer living in Ontario. After the first of their children was born, Joan quit teaching but later worked for a while in the nursery office and then did propagation with Murray and Karen. Becky and I were surprised and saddened when she and John separated three years ago and are now being divorced. "She's an incredibly wonderful woman and always has been," he says. "It's certainly wasn't her fault." He maintains a faithful, if long-distance, relationship with his four kids.

They were all together in Victoria in June 2008 for the wedding of Katie, a vivacious twenty-three-year-old (whose girls' hockey team won an Ontario championship), and Dave Shortreed. He's a teacher and she was heading into her final term in education at the University of Victoria. Brother Steve, three years older and quick-witted, was there showing off teeshirts he designed for Riverbend Farms, because of his interest in graphic design while studying communications and media culture at Woodbury University in Burbank, California. Allison—whip-smart like her sister and a teenage whiz in basketball and soccer—was now twenty-one and getting her bachelor of arts, majoring in psychology and the Bible, at North Central University, a Christian college in Minneapolis. And Matthew, who was born on the day our Flames won the Stanley Cup in 1989, was taking a bachelor of applied business and entrepreneurship, specializing in sport and recreation, at Calgary's Mount Royal College. Matty was on the team that won the juvenile Ontario hockey championship in 2007. I'm always happy to hear when John says his son "lives and dies with the Flames."

WHEN RICHARD WAS ABOUT SEVEN, HE SAW HIS FIRST four-engined DC-8 jet airliner sitting on the ramp at the old terminal of the

Calgary airport. That striking scene in a boy's mind set his compass for the future. He remembers that I didn't understand anyone's attraction to be a pilot, but (unlike my later advice to John) I told Rich if he did well at school, we'd help him to get his licence at sixteen.

Growing up, he had a lot of other interests As Becky says, "He was serious and smart and athletic." He skied with Paul, played soccer and hockey with John—and Jeff, who knows about golf, says he admired how his brother could really hit the ball. "Jeff and I played a fair bit of golf together," says Rich, five years older. "But he ended up beating me and then I said, 'Well, I've got to come up with another sport. I can't have the little bugger beating me all the time.'"

While having a passion for planes, he was also crazy about motorcycles. When big brother Paul had bought a Yamaha 175 just into his mid-teens, I warned him, "You can keep the bike or you can live here, but you can't do both." He soon sold it.

Rich, a determined personality, has his own confessional about that machine: "In the meantime, Paul left the keys in it. I would get up at 4:30 in the morning and push that bike out of the garage, down the street, and ride it for an hour all over the neighbourhood, and sneak it back in the garage. And I just loved motorcycles.

"So I got my first summer job when I was sixteen at a feed mill. It was the worst bloody job I ever had and only lasted a couple of weeks. My eyes would be all puffy and red; you'd have to get into a boxcar full of grain and shovel it out." Before quitting, he told Becky and me that he had to buy a motorcycle to get to work.

No, you're not, we said.

In fact, he then bought a 1973 Honda 350—"the most beautiful thing"— brought it home, and he and I had a big blow-out in the den.

"If I'm going to work, I have to be able to get there," he argued.

"You can take the bus."

"It would take me three hours to get the bus from Lakeview up to the northeast," he countered, padding his case like the lawyer he became. When I told him I'd drive him there and back, he said, "I bought the bike and I'm riding it."

Today, he'll point out, " I'll never forget the next morning. I got up and quietly pushed the bike down to the end of the driveway, started it and let it warm up, and just happened to glance up in my bedroom window." Becky and I were both gazing at him below, distraught—but he kept the bike. That wouldn't be the last of our concerns about him and his darned motorcycles.

At sixteen, as planned, he also started flying lessons and earned his licence. Finishing high school, he simply wanted to skip university and become a pilot. "You can go flying later," we insisted, "but you get an education first."

He did. His first year was science at the University of Alberta before he transferred to the U of C for business-related courses and in his third year decided he should go into law. He telegraphs the rest of his university years succinctly: "I wrote the law-school aptitude and did well on that, so beetled up to Edmonton and did three years of law school and then articled. And the day I got admitted to the bar, I said, 'All right, I got the piece of paper and I'm a lawyer and I'm quitting and I'm going flying.' Literally that day." As he knows, both Becky and I were scratching our heads about how Rich spent all that time to become a lawyer with great earning potential yet wanted to go fly airplanes. In the end, we told him, "You've got your education—something you can fall back on—do what you want to do."

He wanted to learn to become a professional pilot at the FlightSafety Academy in Vero Beach on the east coast of Florida. Since he was fourteen, his sweetheart had been Sharon Fitzgerald. Until three days before they both moved south together, she'd never ridden a motorcycle. He bought her a 400-cc bike and she learned how to handle it on a parking lot the day before they left. "She had guts," he says.

After he earned all his ratings there, they returned to Calgary and got married. He was hired to fly a Lear jet that two oil companies shared. One was Bow Valley Industries, owned by my former business partners, the Seaman brothers. The other was Sulpetro, which in its heyday was operating in Australia and the Sudan, as well as Labrador and middle America, under Gus Van Wielingen. He was an ex-U.S. fighter pilot in the Korean War and then a high-flying oilman with a wide reach (among others he entertained at his Calgary ranch was Prince Philip).

With three years full-time under his belt, he decided to do law on the side for the next couple of years. "Corporate flying has a lot of spare time, so I thought I could work out a deal to still fly but practise law." He and a friend, Dave Follett, started a small firm, Follett and Hotchkiss. "We were jack of all trades, master of none, Dave more of a corporate tax guy and I ended up doing real estate but wasn't keen on it. Fortunately, we had a good real-estate secretary who kept me out of trouble.

"But if I'm going to stick with this, I said, I'm going to specialize. So I had a lot of flying background and a law degree and looked around for a program of aviation law—at McGill. I moved to Montreal in 1986 with Sharon and rode a motorcycle there again."

But, as with John, two major events happened to Richard early in his career. In class at university, he met a Frenchwoman named Patricia Dukers, who had graduated from the University of Bordeaux. He left Sharon—luckily, they hadn't had children. "She's one of the few people that I honestly can't think of anything bad to say about," he says today. "She is just a sweetheart—but you make these decisions."

After McGill, he brought Patricia to Calgary. A month later, his wife-to-be (nicknamed "Duke") was on the back of his motorcycle on their way to Las Vegas when they passed through Jackpot, Nevada. A driver in a pickup truck didn't see them and crossed in front of the bike. Rich's body crashed into the truck's side and Patricia was sent flying about sixty feet. She suffered only a broken finger and a few scrapes. He had a compound fracture in one leg, a fractured hip, a large cut on his neck, and nerve damage in an arm. They were taken to a hospital in Twin Falls, Idaho. That turned out to be the same place Paul had landed a couple of years earlier when he crashed his BMW in the desert and, after several rolls, emerged from the disintegrated car badly bruised but with nothing broken.

We received the call about Richard from Dr. Michael Phillips at our Florida home. The orthopedic surgeon advised us that, while not life-threatening, his injuries were serious. We immediately flew to Twin Falls, having to overnight in Dallas, and saw our badly broken-up son the next morning.

He couldn't really walk for about five months. We flew Rich to Calgary for medical attention in familiar surroundings and took him and Patricia into our Eagle Ridge home, trying to make our invalid son and his new-to-us girlfriend as welcome as possible. "It was kind of the low point in my life," he says. "I needed to find some work and knew that aviation-insurance companies had claims attorneys who did litigation rising out of aircraft accidents, which was interesting to me."

He joined Canadian Aviation Insurance and went to its parent company in New York with Patricia for six months. Then Toronto for two and a half years, Chicago for six months to learn the underwriting side analyzing risk, back to Toronto for two more years, and finally to Vancouver as a western Canadian vice-president. Flying in his own small airplane, he made underwriting visits to aircraft operators—"and I'd come back and say, 'Duke, I think the guys that are running these business are having more fun than me.'" At this point, Patricia and Rich had the first of their three children, Tom, born in 1993.

Two years later, they came back to Calgary, where he applied for operating licences for a charter airline and found investors: Flames co-owner and financier Murray Edwards, Murray's business associate Larry Moeller,

Richard—owner of Sunwest Aviation and fervent pilot—in the cockpit of a Lear 55 somewhere over South America in 2001.

and me. Before Rich had to start a new company, the flight department of Home Oil was taken over by Anderson Exploration and sold him a King Air 200 and a Citation 2 while he added a Lear 35. The business got off to a flying start under Home's name with existing customers and his first own contract to manage Alberta Energy's two planes.

In 1988, the owner of Sunwest International Aviation Services died in a plane crash. Earlier, Rich had initiated talks with Gordon Laing about merging with Sunwest, Calgary's largest fleet of private aircraft. Six months after the accident, he rekindled the negotiations with Mark Eberl, then president, and the companies merged in '99. The two of them became dual managing directors.

As the *Calgary Herald* said in 2003, "most companies in the industry are small operators that concentrate on one sector of the business. Sunwest has a different approach . . . It does the traditional charter work, ferrying executives and celebrities around Canada and the world. Its planes fly many oil and gas executives and employees to the oilsands in Fort McMurray and back. But Sunwest has intentionally diversified its work in an attempt to weather the economic turmoils that have put some of its competitors out of business. The company does air medical work, flying patients around the world in planes equipped with advanced life-support equipment. Sunwest assists customers with airplane sales and acquisitions; the company also performs 'aircraft management' where Sunwest provides maintenance and crews for Calgarians who own planes. Several of the company's aircraft are also engaged in full-time freight work."

Cooling their toes in British Columbia's Kootenay Lake a few years ago are Patricia and Rich with their three kids: (from left) Claire, the youngest, Amy, and Tom.

In '06, Mark stepped down as a managing director but remained flying as a captain. Among Sunwest's seven current investors is Al Libin, yet another Flames shareholder, who sits on the management committee. "It's a different, difficult business," he says, "but Richard's doing a terrific job managing it." With bases in Calgary, Edmonton, and Vancouver, the company describes itself as Western Canada's largest and most diverse business aircraft operator. The Calgary operation has its own three hangars, including one housing the flight lounge and corporate offices, and leases three more. Half of its people include about a hundred pilots, while there are seventy more in maintenance and seven flight co-ordinators who schedule trips and order the wine and other niceties for clients.

Its thirty-eight aircraft number twenty different types of jets and turbo-props, from a Piper Navajo twin-engine piston to intercontinental jets such as a Falcon 900 and Challengers 300 and 604. Sunwest has management contracts for major Canadian energy companies. Its six aircraft capable of air-ambulance service—equipped for advanced life support and some holding multiple patients—do more than 150 medical patient flights a year. Its medi-vac charters have flown to every continent and done hundreds of medical repatriation trips from the U.S., Mexico, and the Caribbean. And it also buys and sells new and resale aircraft for management customers, third parties, and its own requirements. The cargo business ranges from freight for UPS to documents such as cancelled cheques for banks.

As Sunwest has expanded, so has Richard and Patricia's family. Tom is fifteen, a daredevil in sports who has suffered five concussions in the past ten years. He had his first ski-racing experience at a year old while riding down the slopes in Rich's backpack, but now is more of a free-riding snowboarder and a downhill mountain biker. He's gentle with his two younger sisters. Amy, now eleven, arrived seven weeks early in the world as her parents were holidaying in Naples. For someone as tiny as her mother and soft and like-able in manner, she's a competitive ski-racer. Claire, at seven, likes ski-racing but also figure skating, ballet, and singing. Very independent, Rich says, and she's not intimidated by her dad. All three kids, fluently bilingual, speak only French at home with their mom.

I SOMETIMES WONDER IF I WAS A LITTLE BETTER PARENT with Jeff, our last-born, than with the other children. In those early years, I was busier building a career while not spending enough time with the first four kids. In fact, Becky says fondly, "Jeff was the over-protected baby of the family, and never did anything wrong." Whatever the reality of that, he is a real people person today, who loves mixing with others, has solid friendships, and positions his own family as the priority in his life.

As the youngest, he was the butt of teasing from his siblings in a good-natured way. And sometimes got back at them: being ignored as a toddler once, he put an empty coffee can on one of John's fingers and stepped on it, opening a cut that needed stitches. While Rich admits he was sometimes mean to little Jeff, he adds, "I wasn't any meaner than Paul was to me." As for Paul, he'd shoot pucks at the drum set five-year-old Jeff got for Christmas, and the other boys might pull their kid brother's pants down or make him kiss a girl at a party. But by his early teens, Jeff would be invited to double with grown-up Rich on his motorcycle to fetch a Hawaiian pizza—"I felt this was fantastic. *I'm a person now.* It was so important to me."

At Central Memorial High, which his brothers attended, "I was scared to death to get in trouble. I was by the book and had good marks; I did bet-ter in math and science." As well as playing soccer and volleyball, Jeff was a capable, gentlemanly hockey player, though too nervous to want Becky and me at his games. He continued through Juvenile B till nineteen and later played on the Arizona State University team. But his true sport was golf, which he started at age seven, and within a couple of years was playing regu-larly with a buddy at the nine-hole Lakeview course for fifty cents a round. With no lessons, he became so accomplished with the clubs that his brothers could no longer tease him.

The summer he was fourteen, Jeff cleaned golf clubs and collected range balls for $2.80 an hour, loving his time among golfers. In the months after finishing high school, he focused on honing his game rather than working. That year he won the city junior golf championship and vowed to become a professional player.

I encouraged him to meet with golf coach Mike Holder at Oklahoma State (where Boone Pickens was such a supporter of the college), who might consider him for a golf scholarship there. Jeff didn't follow up. Instead, he went to the University of Calgary and, probably influenced by my career, took first-year geology courses. "But I just wasn't prepared for the load and the nature of the work. I switched into business to get a commerce degree."

Summers, he worked at a golf pro shop in Kelowna and then for Cana Construction as a laborer on the Petro-Canada building in Calgary—"with these tough, rough Italian guys telling me to pound those spikes into the ground"—but the following year was more comfortable in the company's project-accounting department. He'd also do two off-term stints in the insurance department of NOVA, where I was on the board.

"It's not that I had a great love for business then," he says, "but thought commerce might be a bit more generally applicable, given that I didn't know what I wanted to do. Because of my fits and starts in undergrad, I was basically on the five-year program. After my fourth year, a good buddy had transferred to Arizona State University and I went there to finish my commerce degree. That's when I tried out for ASU's golf team and made it to the third round out of six; I didn't get on."

He took his MBA there, specializing in finance, which proved a solid base for what he'd one day be doing. Meanwhile, as a Scotsman once wrote, "Golf is an ideal diversion, but a ruinous disease"—and Jeff couldn't cure himself of the game. At first, coming back home, he became another Hotchkiss offspring to work in banking, as Brenda had briefly, but in corporate lending for the Bank of Nova Scotia. Three and a half years later, golf reared up again, to no great enthusiasm on my part.

At twenty-six, he'd married Karen Bill, whom he met in Calgary. Now, two years later, he decided to quit his job and compete in the mini-tour golf circuit in the U.S. and the Canadian Tour. He and Karen first moved to Florida to stay at our place in Naples.

"It was fun and I'm glad I did it, but I cringe a little bit when I think back on it. Because it was such a long shot and putting on hold where I was really going to go. I did it for about a year and a half." His finale was trying out for the Canadian Tour for a second time in Kelowna at Gallagher's Canyon, one of the country's best courses, where he'd worked one summer. "It's a do-or-die kind of thing. I wanted to tell everyone"—including me, his dad—"that I was this good. Then on the eleventh hole, thinking I'm going to do this, I hit a ball and it was way left three feet in bounds right up against the fence. To try to whack it out, I had to hit it left-handed and got a triple bogey. I was just absolutely crushed. The next hole I birdied and kind of recovered. In the end, if not for that triple, I would've made that Canadian Tour."

Yet golf remained on his plate. At eighteen, he'd dreamed of launching a golf resort. But now he was working at no salary for two partners who'd pay him if a real-estate project materialized to develop land at Canmore, just east of Banff, for a hotel and a golf course. After little more than a year, he couldn't wait any longer for the development to happen. That's when Paul suggested he come to work with him in Tarpon Gas Marketing—a story already told.

Even before the company folded, Jeff had dipped his toe more serious-ly into development. In 1997, I was a partner with him in a four-lot project he identified in the Pump Hill neighbourhood in the southwest of the city. We bought the land, sold the lots to people for building high-end houses, and both Jeff and I made a profit. While at Tarpon, he took a stockbroking course as a backup and earned an award of excellence from the Canadian Securities Institute. Over three years, he managed a successful portfolio of stocks for Becky and me.

Meanwhile, he and I got involved in a long-time project developing land southeast of Calgary on a farm Becky and I had owned for a quarter-century. A farmer named Bob Busslinger and his wife, Tib, grew wheat, bar-ley, and canola in our fields—while I borrowed a spot near their home with deep black prairie soil to raise great vegetables (one season I planted two dozen varieties of my favourite, potatoes) and shared them with family and friends. The setting was beautiful, up high where you can see the city and the mountains. Earlier, I'd sold about fifty acres of this larger piece that the province wanted for a highway. Those proceeds paid for the farm we bought in Ontario, where John now runs the nursery.

Jeff set up a company named Augusta Developments, a name inspired by the Augusta Masters Golf Tournament. He'd found acreage in the Tus-cany area in the city's northwest and eventually went into a profitable hous-ing venture called Tanglewood with three partners—one of them whom looked with interest on our agricultural land. He was Sanders Lee, chairman of the Hopewell Group of Companies, which develops very innovative com-munities and has been Calgary's Developer of the Year five times. He's from Hong Kong, multilingual, a real gentleman in his forties—"whose brain works at a really high level financially," Jeff says. Sanders had thought the Tuscany project, with 150 lots, might be too small on its own for him as an

Jeff tapping the forehead of the statue of his daughter Annie at Calgary's Copperfield community, an investment he oversees for the family company, Haven.

investment. But he said he'd become a partner if we collaborated with him on 137 acres of our farmland next to property Hopewell owned.

We sold it to them and then bought back half at the same price in Haven, our children's company, with Spartan Holdings (owned by Becky and me) providing the necessary financing. Jeff oversees this investment. It was a way for Becky and me to transfer the future to our kids.

The first decision—supported by all his siblings—was to invest as a 17½-per-cent partner, with majority owner Hopewell and a neighbouring farming family, in a new community called Copperfield. Jeff drew on funds for Haven from Spartan loans while keeping track of the project through monthly meetings with the developers. Almost all of the loan has since been repaid. Starting in 2002, just east of the Deerfoot Trail, "it was a magical transformation of a raw piece of land at a faster rate than we all predicted," he says. In the end, Copperfield will have about four thousand quality homes, a shopping centre, and extensive recreational facilities on 575 acres of rolling hills with parks, pathways, and a wetland environmental reserve. It has been unbelievably successful. Jeff's Augusta and Spartan Holdings also each have five-per-cent interests with Hopewell in the regional Creekside Shopping Centre going up in the company's Creekside community developing in the West Nose Creek area of northwest Calgary.

Haven has already teamed with the other two partners on the same terms to invest next door to Copperfield within a transportation utility corridor in excess property owned by the province. The three of them have already invested in property across the corridor called Blue Sky, which may be a decade away from development.

Meanwhile, Jeff has partnered in a 138-acre parcel at Sylvan Lake, in central Alberta, with brother-in-law Jamie, Murray Edwards, Murray's lawyer colleague Bill DeJong of Fraser Milner Casgrain, and Bill's brother-in-law, Jack Corcione. The well-treed land, which Jamie bought from his father, has eighty-three lots to be developed as Lake Forest at the far end of the pretty lake away from the resort town. And in the ranching and wheat-growing area of High River, a forty-five-minute commute south of Calgary, he acquired land downtown for six retail, office, and residential buildings. His general contractor is Mayor Les Rempel, a builder who put up Jeff's own home in Calgary. The two of them are collaborating to develop forty-five housing lots on the east side of High River. Spartan has a small interest in these projects with Augusta.

Early on, when Jeff was monitoring the creation of the Copperfield community, he routinely drove through the development. He'd report to me on the numbers of houses rising: "Eighteen homes went up. . . . Wow, there's thirty-four now. . . . Can you believe this? There's now sixty." He stopped counting at about seven hundred. But whenever visiting there, he likes to stop at a bronze statue of a little girl. There's an inscription on a plaque that says, "The land is our heritage. The children are our future" and the statue is called "Annie at Play." He always gives Annie a little tap on the forehead.

It was a rendering based on photographs the sculptor took of a five-year-old version of Annie, one of the three girls Jeff had with his first wife, Karen. Rebecca (for Becky) is fourteen, sports-minded—badminton, track, horse-jumping—and plays guitar. Not only did she win a phys ed award in grade eight but also received the citizenship award as the student who best exemplified the school's values. (Rebecca once sent a posting to a California website called "My Hero," writing, "My grandpa is my hero because of the calm way he handles all of his problems.") Annie, now an all-around eleven-year-old, is respectful, helpful, and well liked—her dad's ongoing joke is his repeated, "Have I ever told you you're such a good kid today?" And Grace, nine, is an exuberant character, artistic and enthusiastic, who'll say, "I have to get to sleep so the morning will come early."

Jeff had wed Karen nine months after breaking off an engagement with another girl. A dozen years later, they separated and then divorced,

Jeff's combined families at our retreat in the Pelican Bay area of Naples, Florida: (front row, left to right) Grace, Annie, Sophie; (back row) Jeff, Rebecca, Carling, Sheryl, Shelby. Our villa has a small pool amid palms, bougainvillea, and hibiscus.

with dual custody of the three daughters who were living with their mom. He has since married a girl he fancied from high-school days, Sheryl, who taught elementary classes for nineteen years. Divorced, she brought her two daughters into the relationship—Carling and Shelby—and they've since had Sophie. Carling, an effervescent eighteen, has just entered on scholarship at the University of Calgary's Haskayne School of Business (named for Dick). Extremely conscientious—"She worked harder in high school than I ever did," says Jeff—she's another equestrienne and has lots of friends. Shelby is a horse-jumper too, a quiet sixteen-year-old with a keen sense of fairness and honesty, loyal to family, who nurtures her little sister, born to Sheryl and Jeff. Sophie, endearing and wonderfully emotional, has started kindergarten at five, is proud of her skating, and likes going on playground hunts for rocks and flowers with her dad.

"We have a really nice group of kids who all get along with each other," he says. In Becky's words, "Jeff has to be one of the best fathers I've ever seen."

MARRIED NEARLY SIX DECADES, BECKY AND I FOUND IT
tough, heartbreaking, to see three of our kids having to end their relationships. In the best of unions, as novelist Robertson Davies once said, "Marriage is a framework to preserve friendship." Becky and I are devoted friends
as well as partners with one another—as we are with all our children. Sure, in
life things arise with them that we don't agree with, but I feel proudest of
the fact that we have such a solid bond with these very different, special human beings.

And together we have fun with them. In 1990, we took the kids and
their spouses to Kenya on a safari organized by brothers Mike and Roy Carr-
Hartley—a once-in-a-lifetime trip that took us to Samburu tribal territory,
the Mount Kenya Aberdare forests, the Masai Mara park reserve where the
Great Migration of zebra and wildebeest flows from the Serengeti, and the
Swahili town of Malindi on the Indian ocean. For some time, we've tried to
take a trip with each of the kids and their spouses every year in rotation. For
instance, we've been to France with Richard and Patricia, to Italy with Jeff
and Sheryl, and to Africa twice with Brenda and Jamie.

One of those African holidays proved harrowing when Becky and I
were camped with Brenda and Jamie at a lodge and four tent cabins in the
middle of the delta of the Okavango River flowing into the northwest corner of Botswana. Out watching a pride of lions one afternoon, we heard of
a booming noise and a column of smoke in the direction of the camp. The
manager's wife came on the radio crying that the camp was on fire. Our
driver raced back, where we found the lodge in flames and two cabins starting to burn. All our money, airline tickets, and passports were in our cabin.
Yelling at me to stay outside, the driver ran in and rescued all our valuables
except for a bottle of Scotch. The energetic Jamie, meanwhile, organized a
bucket brigade with the camp workers pulling water out of a swamp. He
and the crew saved the remaining two cabins.

Our final trip in Africa was with John and Joan. We were part of a
group in a 757 flying to Ethiopia, Tanzania, Zanzibar, and South Africa, and
travelling from Pretoria on the legendary Blue Train to Capetown, and then
by plane to Victoria Falls, Zimbabwe, the Chobe game lodge in Botswana,
Namibia, Mali, and Morocco.

Our first cruise together was a very special private one in 2006.
Rich, who doesn't like big crowds, said, "Well, Dad, if you're going to spend
that kind of money, let's get our own boat." And I said, "All right. You organize it."

Seeking something larger than a 150-foot power vessel being offered,
he heard about the opulent *Phocea*, a 246-foot, steel-hulled, four-masted sail-

ing yacht—until recently the largest in the world. In September, the end of the season, it would cost the same as the smaller one to charter. We boarded in Nice, France, and sailed for a week in the Mediterranean down along the coast of Corsica. While we put ashore in a few places—golfing hiking hills, walking the beaches, driving jet boats—Tracy was among those who says, "The sights were very nice, but we quite enjoyed our trip on the boat." The captain was German, the mess steward French, and the crew of fifteen looking after the eleven of us mostly Filipino. We had a hairdressing salon, gymnasium, and a sauna. "We were together as a family," Tracy says, "and spent the seven days reacquainting ourselves with each other."

As Brenda recalls, "We just couldn't believe that we were having that experience. We all kept looking at each other and thinking, *Can this be real, can this be us from Calgary, Alberta, on this amazing boat?*" And more than once she reminded me, "Dad, this is a long way from Straffordville."

The *Phocea*, a splendid vessel taking our family to pleasurable ports at twelve to eighteen knots under sail through the Mediterranean.

THIRD-PERIOD THOUGHTS

I HADN'T THOUGHT MUCH ABOUT MARKING MY eightieth birthday on July 10, 2007. But the family did, with Becky and Brenda organizing a dinner at the Post Hotel at Lake Louise one day and then celebrating back at our country home in Bragg Creek the next. It was a gathering of the whole clan, including all the grandkids and Doreen and Don Warren. For the octogenarian hailing from the Straffordville area, I got a heck of a lot of attention.

At the hotel, our brood got up and said some nice and witty words while offering me joke awards. Jeff made a full speech and mentioned two important people in my life. "Mom, you're getting shortchanged in all this, but, as Dad has always emphasized, we know you've been such a big part of his business successes. More so, you and Dad led our family together, and in lots of ways you've been the leader and shown Dad the way.

"In many ways, Dad doesn't match up with the stereotypical image of a leader. He's not loud, bombastic, or flamboyant and has never had a staff bigger than one—of course, Doreen, who we appreciate for her unsung role in our lives, not to mention her indispensable role in Dad's business life."

Naturally, Jeff didn't miss making a crack that, while I now had softened up, he recalled an earlier incident when I lit into a car-rental employee "where 'bombastic' was an accurate reflection of Dad's behaviour. Although it takes the edge off the story, I distinctly remember Dad apolo-

Snapshots of joy: Celebrating my eightieth birthday in front of the teepee at our Bragg Creek country home with our family, Richard, Brenda, Jeff, John, Paul—and Becky beside me, as in all of our adventures in the five and a half decades of our marriage. And then sharing the fun this day with Doreen Warren, who has been my executive assistant since 1967.

gizing to the guy at the counter—and that may be the ultimate lesson."

He then gave me the Royal and Honourary Order of Hotchkiss Doctorate Award Excellence for Lifetime Achievement in Family Leadership and Car-rental Relations.

At this end of my game, hoping for overtime, I had a flurry of thoughts to ponder. Surrounded by kin, I was grateful for so much love radiating towards Becky and me. We have been able to witness so many of our kids' remarkable adventures and they've let us remain a real part of their lives.

Even in their adulthood, she and I have been lucky to lend them a hand on the way. Turning over the Ontario nursery to John was one lesson I'd already learned when my dad didn't get ownership of his farm until after his long-retired father had died. A good motto: pass important things on when you can to your loved ones while you're still alive—don't wait. Aside from setting up the ongoing Haven fund, we have helped our children in their various businesses and their personal involvements. Seeing them in their success is a gift to us.

I've also been wealthy with my friends. Locals including George McLeod, from my Canadian Superior years. The Seamans as trusted business colleagues and Doc and B.J. my partners in hockey. Dick Haskayne, who'd been with me on the board of the long-ago NOVA, Alberta Energy, and TransCanada Pipelines, yet the two of us still as tight as bark on a tree. Among other things, we share political views and for decades have each annually supported the Leaders Circle of the federal Conservative Party. Jim Palmer, lawyer and confidant for over forty years. Al Libin, who invested in the Flames and with whom I worked for Peter Lougheed, the Medical Research Foundation, and Foothills. The Mannix brothers, Fred and Ron, carrying on the family tradition. JR Shaw, founder of the Shaw cable empire, with whom I share a special friendship that even involves exchanging favourite garden produce. Sam Weiss, with our solid relationship at our Hotchkiss Brain Institute. Stan Grad, a petroleum engineer who now owns and farms the land that Carlo von Maffei had north of the city. And Doreen Warren, with more than forty-one years looking after me.

While many of my buddies live far away, we keep close through regular contact and occasional visits with one another: John Lamacraft from my Conwest years; Carlo von Maffei of our Sabre Petroleums; Boone Pickens, as ongoing business partners and special friends for more than fifty years.

There are Gary Bettman, with our fifteen-year hockey connections; Ed Koetsier, whom I partnered with in many oil and gas ventures; Jack Porter, from our Canadian Superior days; my Michigan State buddies Bill Calvert, Bill McCormick, Tim Monaghan, Jim Caird, Don King; Shirley

McClellan, from our political contacts. And of course all the hockey friends such as Jean Beliveau and past and current Flames players.

But so many others have passed away, among them Lloyd Bebensee, Harry Van Rensselaer, Bud McCaig, Harry Dernick, and too many others. Among them most recently, my dear friend Doc, who died in January 2009.

As a boy, I read Wordsworth's counsel: "Life is real! Life is earnest!/ And the grave is not its goal." From the standpoint of health, I used to feel kind of invincible, strong enough to shake off physical infirmities that arrive with age. Compared to Becky, who takes such good care of her body with exercise and diet, I've made excuses for myself. Not feeling perfectly well? Just plough on earnestly anyway. But in recent years, there have been warnings that must be heeded. For instance, I've known about the aneurysm lurking in my brain and have that annual MRI to monitor it. Now, a newer reality has emerged.

I'd been getting prostate specific antigen (PSA) tests annually for ten years to check for the prospect of prostate cancer. Then one day during my annual physical, my doctor Bill Hall was doing the usual rectal exam and said, "Harley, I think you're okay, but there's something there that doesn't feel just right." He sent me to Dr. Ted Elliott, a urologist I knew from my Foothills days, who found that my PSA level was normal but wanted another test in six months. This time, he suggested a biopsy: one of the samples taken was malignant.

That really grabs your attention. "It's early on and you can watch and wait," he said. "That's clearly one of your alternatives."

Or not. I knew that Doc Seaman and others had a freezing treatment called cryotherapy. I opted for brachytherapy, using radioactive seeds planted into the prostate. In October 2001, the procedure was performed by Dr. John Pedersen at the Cross Cancer Institute in Edmonton. It went well, except that five of the seeds migrated through my veins and lodged in my lungs, where they appear on X-rays but cause no difficulty. Afterwards, the level of my PSA seemed safely lower at 0.2.

Learning about the cancer in 2001 and news that it was returning in late '04 came at trying stages for me. The first time, my partners and I in the Flames were in the difficult process of buying out Ron Joyce and Grant Bartlett, who'd decided that the team had no future in Calgary. The next time, I was in the middle of the NHL's one-year lockout with the Players' Association, a tough period to deal with the most serious medical challenge I faced.

Meanwhile, through our former Flames coach Bob Johnson, I'd got to know Ken Johannson, originally from Edmonton, who played hockey at the University of North Dakota and later in Europe, and was now an administrator at the Mayo Clinic in Rochester, Minnesota. I started going to the Mayo for checkups every year and both Becky and I have had effective treatments there. (We've since donated $500,000 to the Mayo, directed to research in neurology and the brain, in recognition of our good friends Ken and his wife, Marietta).

My PSA began creeping up to the 3 level by mid-'05 and the clinic was suggesting hormone therapy for the cancer. I wanted a second opinion. Gary Bettman and Jerry Jacobs, the Boston Bruins owner, led me to Dr. Howard Scher, a world-class oncologist at the Sloan-Kettering Cancer Institute in New York. I liked this trim, fiftyish hockey fan who relaxed me as he explained his concern that the problem had extended beyond the prostate. His recommendation: start the hormone treatment immediately. I arranged to have it done in Calgary. At first, the PSA went down again as I returned to see Dr. Scher every three months for a whole battery of tests, including PET, CAT, and bone scans. At one visit, he decided to take me off the hormones because the body gets accustomed to them. However, half a year later, I had to restart them as my PSA level leapt, and I have since continued with the therapy.

I do worry about where this process is taking me. Becky and I talk about the condition; neither of us likes to consider its unpredictability. But prostate cancer is what it is and I don't dwell on it.

Over the past ten years I have suffered from lower back pain, but in the last two it has become more persistent and severe. Though I've lost some weight and have a more disciplined exercise and stretching program, a recent MRI shows major deterioration in my lumbar area. In the meantime, I've had an epidural in hope of relieving the pain. Eventually, the back might demand surgery.

The hard thing is to realize that into your eighties you can't handle these physical challenges the way you could at half that age. But it was John Diefenbaker, the former prime minister, who said the day before he became an octogenarian, "While there's snow on the roof, it doesn't mean the fire has gone out in the furnace."

WHICH IS PROBABLY WHY I'M STILL IN THE PETROLEUM game even now—in a small way, back on our Riverbend Farm on my original stomping grounds in Ontario. Mineral rights generally go with the land in the south of the province, as I was aware when I bought the first Bayham Township farm in 1977. Neither it nor the adjoining one hundred acres acquired the next year had been drilled. But immediately to the west was the old Richmond gas pool discovered around 1915 that produced for many years. (Just northeast of our farm, an abandoned well drilled in '36 reported a show of thirty thousand cubic feet a day from what's called the Thorold Grimsby sand sequence at a depth of fourteen hundred feet.)

I studied the old drillers' logs and had a geologist do a study, including a look at available drill cuttings. This zone is productive under the eastern end of Lake Erie, with hundreds of low-productivity gas wells, but in the area of our farm the geology suggested we were close to the edge of the promising sand. I was specially intrigued by the abrupt change in the direction of the Big Otter River that forms the boundary of our farm for more than two miles. All my antennae went up: this might indicate an encouraging deeper structure. I thought many times of drilling but knew the risk was high.

About 2003, I rejected a company's offer to lease the land for drilling. Instead, I decided to have my own Spartan Holdings lease three neighbours' blocks in case I ever decided to drill myself. Early the following year, a company drilled three successful gas wells from the same zone just east of our land. Heartened, I hired local petroleum engineer Mike Hunter while an experienced Calgary petroleum geologist, my friend Rick Rathier, volunteered to help.

And the Spartan well—Riverbend #1—spudded August 2008. We encountered the top of the clean, porous Thorold sand zone at 407 metres and after penetrating about a metre deeper, the well tested 1,408 thousand cubic feet per day. It's a good one for this area, though its thickness and extent are still unknown. Our lands give us room for several more locations and we'll drill more, subject to getting further production and pressure data from using the gas in our greenhouses over the winter.

Drilling on our own farm and doing it by going back to basic wellsite geology was a special adventure—nearly sixty years after I first got into the oil and gas business.

MY EIGHTIETH BIRTHDAY PARTY, WITH A BAND AND A barbecue, was vibrant with life in our beloved Bragg Creek retreat. The country home is traditional and tasteful with Becky's touches, yet there's a surprising authentic native teepee (decorated with a Flames logo) in the yard. With a golf course across the way, a forest behind, and the foothills in full view, this is a place for all of us to congregate, where the kids can gambol around the grounds. It's a contrast to the elegant city home Becky has created, a three-level penthouse near the banks of the Bow River in the central downtown, a walk away from my office (I should walk there more often). And in the very southeastern corner of the continent, we also have our nest in Naples, a mile from the beach, a Spanish-style villa with a private feel to it and wonderfully kid-proofed for family holidays in Florida.

The homes are all—as Brenda had said about that Mediterranean yacht—a long way from Straffordville.

As you measure out your years, each drop of beauty and happiness becomes more cherished. And, after all these decades, Becky and I treasure what we still think of as back home, in southwestern Ontario. On one recent springtime visit, we drove around Bayham Township with the sun out and a warm, soft breeze. In Straffordville, we went down Talbot Street, a main drag named for that eighteenth-century landowner, Colonel Thomas Talbot. There was the red-brick house where my brother Jack lived at Four Corners. It was near the general stores called McQuiggan's and Walsh's— the one owned by the granddad of my friend Gene Walsh, who was hanging on in that wagon I'd towed as a teenager hell-bent along the road with Jack's car. Just east along Talbot was my parents' retirement home, still with white vinyl siding and a lovely wrap-around veranda. "I always thought we should buy it as a place to stay when we were down here," Becky remarked.

Leaving Straffordville, we passed the old Luce barn where in 1950— with Becky at nursing school and me at university—a crook hid here in a tree after robbing a bank in Langton, near her farm, where her sister Thelma was a bank teller. Two local farmers chased the robber down the dusty road where he ambushed and shot them. He was eventually found and hanged.

We were soon at Guysborough Cemetery, dotted with cedars and climbing a low hill within a chainlink fence, which a plaque says was a bequest from my brother Ralph. He's buried here, along with brother Blake, my dad and mom, my grandpa John and his wife, Mary, whom I never knew. A worn tombstone shows that my great-grandfather John died in 1893. My lineage on one side of the family lies in this graveyard.

On we drove through woods where I once skated on sheets of ice around the trees. Turning left onto Gore Line, we approached the farm of my boyhood, but only one of our buildings has survived and the laneway is no longer lined with maples. A stream through the land had been my playground for sailing boats and fishing for a few little trout. A photograph of me in my Maple Leafs uniform was taken on a pond, an instant rink in the middle of a field. In my teens, I picked millions of tobacco leaves there. Now up another road, Becky and I came to the pasture for the Ayrshire cattle I had herded here and back morning and evening. I reminded her that after I'd won two dollars for a third prize in a cattle-judging contest, I treated all my pals to pop.

Crossing the township line from Elgin to Norfolk counties, we were on the sand road I walked more than a mile and a half with friends to elementary school. As Becky noted, "Easier on bare feet." We came to a house where she said, "Look at the beautiful flowers all around this perennial gar-

I'm poolside in Naples, with Jeffrey (Brenda and Jamie's son, at left) and Tom (Richard and Patricia's eldest) when the boys were much younger.

den." That's where our school had stood, where the teacher grew a garden to educate us kids about plants that interested me even then.

It was time to drive on to Becky's hometown. Not long after, we arrived in Langton, two concessions north of her family's farm, now run by her brother Don and his grandson, Gregory. I recalled the road that led to her two-room school up Horse Creek Hill where later, on the way to court her, I got stuck in the mud more than once. In the village, a little white building still standing at a crossroads had been a restaurant I took her to.

Now we were at the Langton fairgrounds. "My brothers used to bring their horses and have them judged at the fair," she recalled.

A large arena had risen on the site. But there was still a baseball diamond. "Home plate faced another way," she pointed out. "There were bleachers all around here."

We were remembering again. This was where it had all begun for us. That Labour Day in 1945, the grounds were teeming with people for the fair, showing off their livestock, produce, and pies to be judged, riding the Ferris wheel—and watching the ball game.

I was on the Straffordville Red Caps, playing against the hometown team coached by Becky's dad and with her brother as pitcher. I was pitching too, from afar, trying to win over this girl with red-blonde hair and hazel eyes. And at the end of the game, I bravely asked permission to come visit her the next afternoon.

Our nostalgic tour today had brought Becky and me to the very ball diamond where our lifelong love, with lasting bonds we built with family and friends, had been born.

APPENDIX

My mother, Carrie Edith (Todd) Hotchkiss

SHAKING THE FAMILY TREE

Our family's bloodline in North America on the Hotchkiss side goes back at least to the War of 1812, when British, Canadian, and native troops repulsed invading Americans trying to conquer Canada. As a history buff with illustrated maps of Canada's historic battles on my office walls, I find it fascinating that one of my direct ancestors fought in the indecisive hostilities that marked the last war on Canadian soil.

Our forebear was David Hotchkiss, my great-great grandfather, who was born in the Mohawk Valley in New York state around 1787 and as a young adult moved to the Niagara region of Upper Canada before 1810. There he married Temperance Johnson from Stamford, the village north of Niagara Falls. Her father, John, was among the 46,000 United Empire Loyalists—loyal to England's King George III—who came to Canada from the thirteen American colonies in 1783 after the British defeat in the American Revolutionary War.

David served briefly in the Canadian 2nd Regiment of the Lincoln Militia during the summer of 1812. He was apparently one of eight hundred on both sides wounded July 5 in the Battle of Chippawa, named for a river near Fort Erie, when British soldiers, militiamen, and Mohawks were forced to retreat.

We believe we're descended through David from Samuel Hotchkiss, born about 1622 at Dodington Parish, Whitechurch, County of Shropshire in England. Samuel's father, John Hotchkiss (born about 1580) was a draper and his wife, Samuel's mother, was Margaret Nevett.

Samuel was the ninth in a family of ten and the only one to emigrate to North America. In 1638, he was likely on the *Hector*, the first sailing ship from England to New Haven, Connecticut. He married Elizabeth Cleverly in 1642 and they had seven children. We think our line goes from their oldest son, John, born about a year later (although recent DNA work throws some doubt on his paternity). If we are correct, the line goes from the John *circa* 1580 through Samuel, three Johns, a Jason, and two Davids—the latter my great-great-grandfather *circa* 1787.

This David was granted land for his War of 1812 service. One of his sons, Miles Hotchkiss, wrote in an Elgin County Historical Atlas of 1885 that "at the conclusion of the conflict [David] took up a hundred acres of free grant land in the Township of Bayham, County of Elgin. Two years after coming to Bayham, David Hotchkiss lost his wife [Temperance] by whom he had a family of seven children, three of them John, Jane, and Miles now being alive."

We believe David, with his older sons, started clearing the Bayham Township land around 1820 and constructed log buildings and fences. Two years later, he and fifty of his neighbours signed a petition to improve the road north of Straffordville. In the 1828 Thorold Township census, the David Hotchkiss family lived at Allanburg near the digging of the Welland Canal from Lake Ontario to Lake Erie, but only Temperance and the three youngest children were at home. David and the other offspring were probably at the Bayham farm. By 1840, the whole family might have moved to the farm.

In 1838, the original Crown patent on Lot 27, Concession 5 (220 acres) was granted by the Crown to the Canada Company (incorporated by the British Parliament to obtain land in Canada and to promote its sale to prospective settlers). David probably lost the lot because he had not registered it based on the work he and his family had done.

The company sold Lot 27 to Martin Hubbard in 1850 and six years later Maria Hubbard sold the north half of the lot to Lorrance Stansell. In 1859, David's youngest son—my great-grandfather John (born 1818)—bought the 110 acres from Stansell. In 1845, John had married Hannah Eichenberg, a neighbour's daughter, who died in 1847 after the birth of son William.

In the 1851 census, John Hotchkiss was leasing the family farm, where he lived with his second wife, Catherine Losee, and their first son, Jesse. John's father, David, was now a widower and by the 1862 census was living in Walpole Township, Haldimand County, near his son Miles. Records show John's crops were wheat, buckwheat, oats, peas, and Indian corn.

John and Catherine had seven children, including John, my paternal grandfather (born 1858), who stayed on the farm and married Mary Smith. The second of their five children was my father, Morley—the fourth generation to till the same land.

These stories are among the many dug up by my brother Jack's son Ross, who has become the tenacious family historian, researching ancestries on both the male *and* female sides. My mother, Carrie Todd, compiled several versions of our family tree and stories that were a big help to Ross. In one, she recalled, "When we lived on this farm, there were still signs of the old garden where David Hotchkiss first had his home, likely in a log cabin, and lilac trees and a fall pippin apple tree which still has those lovely fall apples."

Mom was the third generation of James and Janet Todd, born in Scotland at the start of the nineteenth century and parenting four children. The eldest, David, wed Susan Sharpe and they sailed to Canada, making their way to West Oxford township, west of Woodstock—where, a generation later, my mother would go to high school by streetcar. Her sister Georgia, who became a strong conservative Republican living in Indiana, once noted about her grandfather, "David probably joined nostalgic clansmen who gathered on a Saturday night and liked to drink and inflict violence on one another. He is listed in the census as an engineer and stonemason."

The third of David and Susan's six boys and one girl was William, my maternal grandfather. He and his wife, Mary Jane (Carr), also had seven kids: Annie, Alice, Carrie (my mother), Ernest, Georgia, Archie, and Helena. William rented a couple of farms before buying his own spread in North Oxford, where he lived until his death in 1945—when I was sadly far away from home, serving with the Norwegian Merchant Marine.

The University of Lethbridge presents me with an honorary Doctor of Laws in 2007. Lethbridge is one of the universities doing research with the Hotchkiss Brain Institute.

RECEIVING IN RETURN

Being involved in philanthropic ventures such as the Brain Institute and the Calgary Flames' Project 75 has been rewarding on its own. And often, when you least expect it, the community recognizes your efforts in various voluntary activities. While I'm the front man for the Hotchkiss partnership, it's the unbelievably supportive Becky behind the scenes, who is the strongest thread that holds the fabric of my life together. So whenever there is public acknowledgement, she's always there sharing in whatever thanks come our way.

Over the years, I've been vice-chair of the Olympic Trust of Canada and chair of the Alberta governors when the successful 1988 Winter Games came to Calgary; head of the selection committee of the intriguing Manning Innovation Awards, recognized by Alberta's Ernest C. Manning Awards Foundation to present substantial cash incentives to Canadians with innovative talent in developing and successfully marketing a new concept, process, or procedure; governor and vice-chair of the Banff Centre, the globally respected arts, cultural, and educational institution and conference facility, while Becky and I have supported the Leighton Artists' Colony at Banff to provide space and time to professional artists creating a new work.

I sat on the council of the Alberta Order of Excellence, the highest honour the province can bestow on a citizen; was a member of the dean's advisory council of the U of C's faculty of medicine; acted as a director and on the executive committee of the Independent Petroleum Association of Canada; was a director of the Calgary Family Services Bureau and the Alberta Paraplegic Association and played several roles with the United Way of Canada on the campaign and fund allocations; served eight years on the foundation board of my alma mater, Michigan State University, and more recently on the President's Cabinet for a successful $1.4-billion five-year fundraising campaign.

The open recognition for this decidedly mixed bag of worthwhile experiences has come as some surprise. In my long life, I would have to put induction into the Hockey Hall of Fame as near the top of honours to come my way. Of course, being with Becky as I was invested as an Officer of the Order of Canada in 1998 represented a grand gift from my fellow Canadians in the formality of Rideau Hall with Governor General Romeo LeBlanc. The same year, being honoured with an Alberta Order of Excellence at Government House in Edmonton was more like a family affair with lots of kin and friends on hand. It was a particularly moving ceremony for this eastern-bred fellow who had adopted Calgary and the province as his home for most of his years.

Three universities have noted my community involvements by conferring honorary degrees. The U of C granted me a Doctor of Laws in 1996, as did the University of Lethbridge in 2007, in part for our family support of the Brain Institute. And Michigan State University conferred on me a Doctor of Science degree in 2000. That was after its College of Natural Science had given me an Outstanding Alumni Award; Mich State's Varsity Alumni "S" Club presented me with the Jack Breslin Lifetime Achievement Award; and the Frank S. Kedzie Society made me a member for major university support. Oh, and I also accepted a Distinguished Hockey Alumnus Award—though obviously not for my long-ago activities on the Spartans team. From the time I could afford to, I've supported the university and in later years with significant gifts. Becky and I donated $1 million to its $1.2-billion President's campaign and $500,000 for a Hotchkiss Endowment in the Department of Geology. An area in a new College of Natural Science building is named after us.

A special community project for Becky and me, with our many grandchildren, was the Children's Hospital in Calgary. During a major capital campaign headed by our friends Ann McCaig and Charlie Fischer, we dedicated a donation to a garden near the hospital's acute-care area with a plaque reading: "May those that stop here find strength and comfort in this peaceful place." Thinking of other kids with challenges, we were delighted to give $100,000 to the city's Foothills Academy, the first school in Alberta offering a full-time program for students with learning disabilities and providing a community-services component for professionals and parents. We were also recognizing Doreen Warren: her nephew, Gordon Bullivant, was the Academy's co-founder.

On the career side, I was pleased to be welcomed into the Canadian Petroleum Hall of Fame and the Calgary Business Hall of Fame and to receive the Calgary Chamber of Commerce/University of Calgary's Haskayne School of Business Distinguished Business Leader Award in 2006. That year, as my friend Dick Haskayne had been a couple of years earlier, I was honoured with the Woodrow Wilson Award for Corporate Citizenship from the Woodrow Wilson International Center for Scholars in Washington, D.C. Prime Minister Stephen Harper was honoured on the same program with the Award for Political Leadership. And Rotary International later recognized me as a Paul Harris Fellow.

And in '06, there was a nice tribute from my hometown of more than half a century with the City of Calgary Grant MacEwan Lifetime Achievement Award. It was named for a local mayor, a member of the Alberta legislature, and the province's lieutenant governor—as well as a prolific author of western history. One of his well-known quotes is a description of his boyhood in Manitoba before moving to Alberta: "Our farm neighbours were still without cars, tractors, trucks, telephones, electric lights and radios. Plumbing-wise they had three rooms and a path."

For the Ontario farm boy I was during the Depression, it's a fitting reminder of my luck in travelling so far through life and being so warmly received by the people surrounding me.

Photography credits:
Scan Dennie, Calgary (cover); Bob Hewitt, Victoria (colour section: 11); Toronto Maple Leafs (page 10); Milwaukee-Great Lakes Marine Collection of the Milwaukee Public Library/ Wisconsin Marine Historical Society (42); Michigan State University Archives and Historical Collection (50, 59, 60); Glenbow Archives PA-3527-3 (78); courtesy Boone Pickens (94, 119); courtesy Doc Seaman (96); courtesy Roseanne Doenz (top, 98); courtesy John Lamacraft (144); Getty Images (166); Calgary Flames (171, 174, 175, 178, 179, 184, 185, 188, 193, 194, 195, 196, 199, 201, 203, 208, 220, 224, 228, 230, 265, 268, colour section: 1, 2-3, 4); Hockey Hall of Fame (238); NHL Images (242, 251, 253, 259); courtesy Trevor Linden (256); Hotchkiss Brain Institute (270, 288, 295); Alberta Heritage Foundation for Medical Research/courtesy John Bell (284).

Unless otherwise noted, all images are courtesy of Harley Hotchkiss's personal collection.

Copyright credit:
"Tillsonburg" (page 32), copyright 1971, Crown-Vetch Music, written by T.C. Connors, authorized through www.StompinTom.com.

INDEX